T0328889

More praise for *Leading an Accounting Firm:*

"A great hands-on book for current and future professional services firm leaders. Troy Waugh shares with his readers a wealth of information and knowledge about authentic leadership through interviews with more than 40 professional service firm leaders."
—August Aquila, CEO, *AQUILA Global Advisors, LLC*

"Finally, there is a book on leadership that can apply to an accounting firm. We will include this great book in our leadership curriculum."
—William R. Hagaman, Jr., CPA, *Managing Partner and CEO, WithumSmith+ Brown, PC*

"It is no longer enough to be just a producer in a CPA firm. In order to be effective, you must also learn to lead. Troy has put together some excellent insights into what that means, beginning with self-leadership and continuing with staff, strategy, systems, and synergy. We all need to be thinking about the future and making ourselves better every day. This book provides a roadmap to do exactly that. Great job, Troy!"
—Lewis O. Hall, CPA/ABV, CBA, *Managing Principal, Keiter Stephens*

"Our firm has consulted with Troy and The Rainmaker Consulting Group ever since I became managing partner of our firm over ten years ago. Troy's knowledge has resulted in the development of many of our leaders and future leaders throughout the firm. This book captures many of those same concepts and will be a resource for all of us who are involved in firm leadership."
—Domenic E. Pellillo, CPA, *Managing Partner, Brown, Edwards & Company, LLP*

"Being able to inspire, influence, and create a thriving firm culture is a true leader's role. Troy's book touches on all aspects of becoming such a leader. It's a great read!"
—Ned F. Sheffield, CPA, *Managing Partner, Jackson Thornton*

"Troy's obvious knowledge of the accounting profession, combined with the input from seasoned leaders, makes this book a must read for anyone looking to enhance performance. It really drives home the vast difference between leadership and management. I have long been a believer that running an accounting firm is like coaching a team and the 'Pyramid of Success' is right on point."
—James A. Sikich, CPA, *CEO, Sikich, LLP*

"The perspective and insight brought to light through Troy's skillful interpretation of invaluable case studies from some great leaders makes *Leading an Accounting Firm* a seminal work that will serve as a guiding light to firm leaders for years to come. Thank you Troy, for this great contribution to our profession."
—Rick Solomon, CPA, *CEO, RAN ONE Americas*

THE
PYRAMID
OF SUCCESS

LEADING
AN ACCOUNTING FIRM

AICPA® PCPS
Private Companies Practice Section

Troy Waugh, CPA, MBA

Notice to Readers

Leading an Accounting Firm: The Pyramid of Success does not represent an official position of the American Institute of Certified Public Accountants, and it is distributed with the understanding that the author and publisher are not rendering legal, accounting, or other professional services in the publication. If legal advice or other expert assistance is required, the services of a competent professional should be sought.

Publisher: Amy M. Plent
Acquisitions Editor: Erin Valentine
Associate Developmental Editor: Whitney Woody
Project Manager: Amy Sykes
Cover Design Direction: Greg Duell
Compositor: Jason Reese

Contents

Foreword

Great leadership is an essential ingredient to the success of any CPA firm. The best leaders know that embracing change and taking calculated risks are what move a firm forward. Moreover, although the course for the firm is set at the top, it takes a talented staff to take the firm on that path. I truly believe that these are the essential ingredients for progress. Throughout my tenure as president and CEO of the AICPA, the AICPA has focused on building leaders in our profession. We launched several programs that develop young CPAs, current AICPA committee members and seasoned professionals, and our staff. No thriving business just lets change happen to it; you have to shape your future, and you need strong leaders to do that.

This book is part of our ongoing effort to support your leadership development. It is intended to provide you with an intelligent framework for developing your own leadership style, as well as the leadership skills of those around you. After all, many clients look to you—their most trusted business adviser—for direction and expertise.

Author Troy Waugh has made the secret to strong leadership understandable and achievable. Using the model of the pyramid to illustrate his concept, he builds a case for ongoing leadership development, guiding you through the essential ideas and practices that are at the core of great leadership and great firms—each idea building upon the next. Using this powerful framework, you can improve your personal leadership and build solid leaders around you.

I encourage you to explore Troy's own leadership experiences acquired throughout an impressive career as a CPA in public practice and at several companies. You'll learn about his specific development, as well as other approaches to leadership discovered by some of the profession's top leaders in public accounting. Not surprisingly, most well-led firms share the same crucial leadership tenants.

For readers who are starting their accounting careers, my advice is for you to apply the elements of this book throughout your professional life. Readers who are advancing in the ranks of a public accounting firm will find that this book will guide you beyond the mastery of technical skills to become a leader in your firm and community.

Our profession has been on the leading edge of American business for 125 years. Today and the decades that follow will challenge all organizations and professions. The quality of America's CPAs, their professional commitment, their ethics, their passion, and their dedication to leadership at all levels will ensure our profession's success for decades to come.

Sincerely—

Barry C. Melancon, CPA
President and CEO
American Institute of Certified Public Accountants

Preface

During my 20 years consulting with accounting firms, there is a key ingredient among those firms that seem to rise above the rest: great leadership. The same was true in the other businesses in which I served prior to founding FiveStar³, LLC. Although there are many books on the subject of managing an accounting firm, no titles are related to the power of leadership and its impact on an accounting business.

Over 30 years ago, I was privileged to be in an audience in which the famous UCLA basketball coach John Wooden was the keynote speaker. That day, he spoke on the pyramid of success that he used in coaching his teams to unparalleled success. I was particularly intrigued by the strength and durability of the pyramid structure. In Wooden's remarks, he said something like, "I don't have a copyright on the pyramid, so if you find it useful in your business or your writings, please use it with my blessings."

This book has 17 chapters segmented into 5 critical sections utilizing the pyramid's structure as a visual. In the base of the pyramid are 5 foundation chapters related to leading self. The next tier contains 4 chapters related to leading staff (others), and tier 3 holds 3 chapters related to strategy. Common management subjects are covered in 2 chapters related to systems, and the pinnacle section relates to creating synergy among the various tiers of building blocks of leadership.

In writing this book, I have interviewed nearly 100 leaders in the accounting profession, including over 40 interviews with CEOs of well-led firms of all sizes and types. In addition, leaders from the AICPA and various accounting alliances and several industry consultants add their points of view. In order to identify some great leaders, I interviewed many of my fellow consultants in the industry, accounting association leaders, industry publications publishers, and many others. Many of the leaders that I interviewed have led their businesses from start-up to being in the top 100 largest accounting firms in the United States within their lifetime. That is an amazing feat, considering there are nearly 50,000 accounting firms in the United States alone. Many of the leaders are present or former CEOs of notable firms who've been named as best of the best by the *INSIDE Public Accounting* newsletter, or their firms have been named as the best place to work by *Fortune* magazine.

Although these are great leaders, I've missed interviewing other great leaders of accounting firms. My selection process was exhaustive but not scientific. I simply asked people who I respected who they thought were great leaders, and I cataloged their names over a several year period. Those names that came up several times or the ones that had a compelling story were the ones that I ultimately selected.

In order to save on detailed introductions throughout the book, I would like to introduce you to the leaders in our industry, in alphabetical order, whom I interviewed for this book:

Chris Allegretti, **Hill, Barth & King LLC (HBK), a regional firm in Boardman, OH**

Richard Anderson, **Moss Adams LLP, a megaregional firm in Seattle, WA**

Anthony "Tony" Argiz, **Morrison, Brown, Argiz & Farra, LLC, a megaregional firm in Miami, FL**

Larry Autry, **Whitley Penn LLP, a top-100 firm in Ft. Worth, TX**

Kenneth Baggett, **CohnReznick LLP, a national firm in Atlanta, GA**

Robert L. Bunting, **Moss Adams LLP, a megaregional firm in Seattle, WA**

Michael Cain, **Lattimore Black Morgan & Cain, PC (LBMC), a top-50 firm in Nashville, TN**

Richard Caturano, **McGladrey & Pullen, LLP, a national firm in Boston, MA**

Lisa Cines, **Dixon Hughes Goodman, a megaregional firm in Rockville, Maryland**

Sam Coulter, **Coulter & Justus, P.C., a local firm in Knoxville, TN**

David Deeter, **Frazier & Deeter, LLC, a top-100 firm in Atlanta, GA**

Scott Dietzen, **CliftonLarsonAllen LLP, a national firm in Spokane, WA**

James DeMartini (James G.B. DeMartini, III), **Seiler LLP, a top-100 firm in Redwood City, CA**

Richard Dreher, **Wipfli LLP, a megaregional firm in Green Bay, WI**

Marc Elman, **PSB Boisjoli, a local firm in Montreal, Canada**

Keith Farlinger, **BDO Canada LLP, a national firm in Toronto, Canada**

Carl George, **Clifton Gunderson LLP (now CliftonLarsonAllen LLP), a national firm in Peoria, IL**

William Haller, **CapinCrouse LLP, a national firm in Indianapolis, IN**

William Hermann, **Plante & Moran, PLLC, a megaregional firm in Southfield, MI**

Philip Holthouse, **Holthouse, Carlin & Van Trigt LLP, a top-100 multioffice firm in Los Angeles, CA**

Robert Hottman, **Ehrhardt Keefe Steiner & Hottman PC (EKS&H), a top-100 firm in Denver, CO**

William Hubly, **Corbett, Duncan & Hubly, P.C., a local firm in Itasca, IL**

Gordon Krater, **Plante & Moran, PLLC, a megaregional firm in Southfield, MI**

Deborah Lambert, **Johnson Lambert & Co. LLP, a top-100 multioffice firm in Raleigh, NC**

Thomas Luken, **Kolb+Co., a local firm in Milwaukee, WI**

Ted Mason, **LaPorte Sehrt Romig Hand, a top-100 firm in New Orleans, LA**

Steve Mayer, **Burr, Pilger & Mayer LLP (BPM), a regional firm in San Francisco, CA**

Kristine McMasters, **CliftonLarsonAllen LLP, a national firm in Milwaukee, WI**

Tony Morgan, **Gollob Morgan Peddy & Co., P.C., a local firm in Tyler, TX**

James Metler, **vice president of Small Firm Interests, AICPA**

Hugh Parker, **Horne LLP, a regional firm in Jackson, MS**

Frank Ross, **Howard University in Washington, D.C.**

Daniel Schreiber, **JGD & Associates LLP, a local firm in San Diego, CA**

Gary Shamis, **SS&G Financial Services, Inc., a top-100 multioffice firm in Cleveland, OH**

David Sibits, **CBIZ Financial Services, a national firm in Cleveland, OH**

Terry Snyder, **president, PKF North America, an accounting firm alliance in Lawrence, GA**

Neal Spencer, **BKD, LLP, a megaregional firm in Springfield, MO**

Ray Strothman, **Strothman & Company, PSC, a local firm in Louisville, KY**

Charly Weinstein, **EisnerAmper LLP, a megaregional firm in New York City, NY**

John Wright, **Padgett Stratemann & Co., a top-100 firm in San Antonio, TX**

Leading an Accounting Firm: The Pyramid of Success

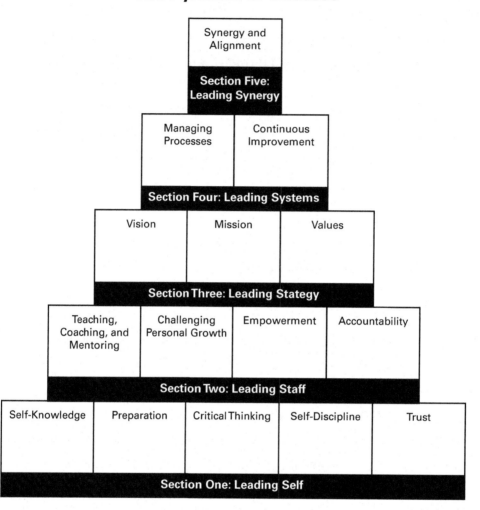

Acknowledgments

Although for the last three years, my life has been consumed with researching, interviewing, and writing this book, it would not be possible without the many contributions of other people. First, I'd like to thank my wife, Sheryl, for her patience with my travel and writing schedule. She learned to read and understand that absent look in my face, and she would say, "Go write, and come back when you can be present. It's okay."

This work would have been impossible without the contributions of approximately 100 leaders of our profession, over 40 of whom gave me extensive interviews and are listed in the preface to this book. These leaders shared their education, experience, and wisdom with me freely during several hours of interviews. They also read and corrected drafts of chapters as I would complete them. I owe a special debt of gratitude to several leaders who, because of their overall knowledge of our business, directed me to these terrific interviewees. Mike and Kelly Platt who publish the *INSIDE Public Accounting* newsletter and make an annual selection of the best accounting firms in the United States were particularly helpful. Bill Carlino, managing editor of *Accounting Today* magazine is a keen observer in our profession, and he directed me to several people.

Several leaders in associations gave me insights and were particularly helpful because they had worked with these leaders. Jim Metzler, vice president of Small Firm Interests at the AICPA; Terry Snyder, president of PKF North America; Deb Lockwood, former CEO of the RSM McGladrey Alliance; Jim Flynn, president of CPA Associates; and Kevin Meade, president of IGAF Worldwide all shared insights and wisdom with me and directed me to some of the great leaders in our industry, most of whom agreed to be interviewed for this book. Karen Kehl-Rose, president of Leading Edge Alliance directed me to several of her leaders who have been instrumental in conceiving and growing this amazing alliance of accounting firms.

I owe a special "shout out" to the leadership of my clients and the leaders on my team. For 20 years, I have been working as a consultant in the accounting profession after my public accounting, real estate investment, and magazine publishing experiences. Many of the clients that I've worked with have had excellent leaders. A consultant can have a significant impact with an accounting firm only if that firm has great leadership. Although a consultant can bring perspective, fresh eyes, and other experiences to the table, the quality of the implementation lies directly under the role of the leaders of the firms. I have learned a great deal from these leaders and have featured several of them in this book. Sometimes, I'm almost ashamed to say that I've learned more from them than they have from me.

My teammates at The Rainmaker Companies, LLC have provided me the space to write this book while they have been carrying forward the day-to-day consulting, training, and alliance services that we provide our clients. Patrick Pruett, president of the Alliance of Professional Associations and Angie Grissom, executive vice president of FiveStar[3], LLC gave me their full blessings and support while I was writing this book. In particular, I'd like to thank Cindy Luna, relationship manager with The Rainmaker Academy, who carefully read every word I wrote and gave me many substantive changes and improvements. Bob Fitts, controller, and Alice Waugh (my sister and our director of lasting impressions) proofread every word and provided me with many corrections and improvements to the text. Bryan Shelton, senior consultant, was very helpful in assisting me with the writing of chapter 8, "Accountability: Trust but Verify." His deep knowledge and work with our clients on this topic proved valuable.

Finally, I'd like to thank my editorial team. Whitney Woody and Erin Valentine at the AICPA have scoured every word and made many improvements in the text and really brought to life the meaning that I wanted to convey. Dr. Richard Crandall and Laura Creekmore assisted me with research and the early drafting of each chapter. The hardest part of writing a book is the first draft. Often, I'd sit for one hour and couldn't get anything written, and either Rick or Laura would help me through the writer's block, and I can't thank them enough.

Although this book is the first that has been written on the subject of leading an accounting firm, I hope that others will come along to add to the discourse for our profession. Many firms are very well managed but underled. I believe that principled leadership will keep the CPA as the most respected business professional for decades to come.

Troy A. Waugh

About the Author

Troy Waugh, CPA, MBA

Troy Waugh is the author of 3 books and has been selected as one of the 100 most influential people in the accounting profession for 9 years in a row by *Accounting Today* magazine. He is one of the leading leadership and business development consultants to the accounting industry. Troy and his experienced consultants have helped firms add more than $800 million in new business through their consulting, training, and alliance services.

As CEO of The Rainmaker Companies, LLC, Troy is the founder of The Rainmaker Academy, The Leadership Academy, The Rainmaker Consulting Group, The Alliance of Professional Associations (APA), and Enterprise Worldwide. APA now represents over 250 firms in 35 countries.

Troy's highly acclaimed books, *Power Up Your Profits: 31 Days to Better Selling* and *101 Marketing Strategies for Accounting, Law, Consulting, and Professional Services Firms*, have received praise throughout the world and have been translated into German and Spanish. Troy's articles have been published in *Accounting Today* magazine, *Practical Accountant* magazine, and numerous state society monthly newsletters. He has been publishing a "Marketing Moment" since 1992.

Troy holds an MBA from the University of Southern California and a BS from the University of Tennessee and is a CPA. He is a member of the National Speakers Association, the AICPA, and the Tennessee Society of CPAs.

Troy served several of the largest clients of Price Waterhouse as an audit manager. He became CEO of Advantage Companies, Inc., a Securities and Exchange Commission-registered company. During his years with Advantage Companies, Inc., Troy guided a complete repositioning of the company's focus from the hotel business to magazine publishing. During this period, he negotiated over 40 acquisitions or divestitures of businesses. Later, Troy became a senior vice president with Jacques-Miller, Inc., a real estate investment firm.

Why Leadership Matters

"One does not 'manage' people. The task is to lead people. And the goal is to make productive the specific strengths and knowledge of each individual."

~ PETER DRUCKER

Leading the Brightest of the Bright

CPAs and chartered accountants are some of the brightest professionals in the world. Accountants regularly rank in the top 10 percent on college entrance exams, and most people would argue that their intelligence quotients rank at the very top, as well.

This book is about leading a small (or large) group of very bright, somewhat introverted, and skeptical accountants toward a common goal. It's about

- ▲ leading a small team of auditors, tax accountants, or consultants.
- ▲ the new manager leading a group of accountants on an engagement.
- ▲ leading niches, divisions, and service lines.
- ▲ leading large organizations with many offices and hundreds of partners, owners, or shareholders.

When I became an audit senior and later a manager at Price Waterhouse, I mistakenly thought that the title on my business card gave me the right to tell people what to do. Looking back in horror, I know now that people didn't want to follow my leadership because they felt dominated and manipulated. It was a painful lesson for me to learn that I could manage projects and processes but not people. It took me many years and experiences to grasp the lesson embodied in Drucker's opening quote, and I am still working hard on it today. To be effective, you can't *manage* people; you must *lead* them.

This chapter makes the case for leadership. I have found that if people first understand the why of something, then the how, what, when, and where come easier. In the following pages, I will describe why leadership matters in CPA firms and what aspects of leadership matter most to those who are running those firms—often in their own words. The payoff (benefits) of great leadership will be discussed, along with some of the challenges of leading a highly skilled and intelligent workforce. We will also cover the leader's role in growing the firm and leadership compared with management. An interesting topic that we'll cover in this chapter is how leading an accounting firm has some similarities and differences to other business types. My hope is that you grasp the why of leadership and that it will encourage you to devour the other chapters that will take you through the how, what, when, and where of leadership.

Tony Morgan, founder and managing partner of the local firm Gollob Morgan Peddy & Co., P.C., in Tyler, TX, says, "Whenever we meet with college students, we see the gregarious ones in other fields of study and the more introverted in accounting, … but for a person to advance, he or she must be willing to take some risk and be willing to lead other people."

To bring these leadership lessons to you, I've interviewed nearly 100 leaders from accounting firms all over North America, like Tony Argiz, founder, CEO, and managing partner of the megaregional firm Morrison, Brown, Argiz & Farra, LLP, in Miami, FL, in the following section. Many of the interviewees' firms have been named best-of-the-best or all-star firms by various publications. A large number of my interviewees are leaders of firms that have progressed from start-up to becoming a member of the top 100 accounting firms in the

United States. At the end of 2010, there were approximately 25 accounting firms in the top 100 that are still in the first generation of their leadership. A few, like Reznick Group, are in transition from the first generation of leadership to the second generation. That is an amazing statistic when we realize that the United States has nearly 50,000 firms. So, I wanted to know what it was about the leadership of these firms that powered them into the best-of-the-best category or the top 100 in the first generation. What did their partners say about them? And what can we all learn from their insights, wisdom, and experiences?

Leader Profile: **Tony Argiz, founder, CEO, and managing partner of the megaregional firm Morrison, Brown, Argiz & Farra, LLP, in Miami, FL**

The leadership development story of Tony Argiz is one of the most fascinating in the accounting industry today. Born in Cuba, Tony was sent to the United States by his parents, who desperately wanted to keep him safe from the burgeoning Communist regime. Only 8 years old when he left, he became part of Operation Pedro Pan. He sadly remembers his mom working for days to make him a suit and an overcoat for the journey to the United States, but the regime's militiamen wouldn't allow him to take anything but the clothes he was wearing.

Raised in a Catholic boarding school funded by the Archdiocese of Miami, FL, Tony cried himself to sleep many nights because of loneliness and feelings of abandonment. Although he somewhat understood the dangerous political climate in Cuba at the time (the Cuban government had nationalized all businesses, including his father's wholesale meat business), he nonetheless spent many days sad and bewildered.

Today, Tony has become a recognized business and civic leader in south Florida. As the CEO and managing partner of Morrison, Brown, Argiz & Farra, LLP (MBAF) since 1997, he has led the growth of the firm to become one of the top 40 accounting firms in the nation. MBAF is also a 15-time honoree on the *INSIDE Public Accounting* (IPA) annual list of the nation's 25 best-managed accounting firms. Tony was also selected as one of the "Top Five Most Admired Peers" by the IPA 100.

Adam Spiegel, MBAF partner, says

> The best thing Tony has created within our firm is a culture of people who always seek to grow and improve. He is constantly encouraging each and every person to think, "What can we do next for our client, our firm, and our community?" The culture we have at MBAF requires us to work smarter and improve efficiency and effectiveness in the work we do on a daily basis. Many people who are no longer with the firm now miss this special culture.
>
> Tony is a strong believer that if you do not write down your goals, your chances of achieving them will be much diminished. Tony creates an environment of opportunity and sets the framework for unlimited growth and satisfaction in all our people. I truly believe that "the sky is the limit" is each person's opportunity at MBAF. It does not matter if you start in our file room or as the receptionist; what matters is your initiative, effort, and desire to improve, grow, and utilize the firm's resources to achieve collective and individual goals.
>
> Tony has led our organization through this economic crisis by teaching each of us to provide exceptional value-added service, to be consistent and diligent about

(continued)

3

(continued)

the communications with our clients, and to use our skills of professional skepticism to protect our number one asset: the firm. I believe that this brand of leadership is the reason that we have continued to grow as an organization through the economic crisis. Tony's ability to anticipate problems and, most of all, to provide solutions ahead of time has helped us and our clients survive and thrive. Tony has an impressive ability to get people to focus on the "solutions" and not the problems. This ability is imperative to the optimistic culture within our firm.

Tony encouraged me to get involved in Leadership Miami, where I met future leaders of our community and built relationships that have lasted 14 years. This program led to several important developments within our firm, such as our mentoring program. Tony then encouraged me to attend The Rainmaker Academy, and as a result of this experience, I have implemented several new principles into my day-to-day activities and into the culture of our firm.

We have just announced a combination with the firm ERE in NYC, and Tony's leadership through the year-long process has been unwavering. He has always been positive and optimistic that this combination will provide additional opportunities for each individual within the firm. Tony has been very concerned that both firms have a synergistic culture and that each member of the combined firm feels that this is a once-in-a-lifetime opportunity to be a part of a firm that is going to grow beyond its wildest dreams.

Well-known for his community and industry leadership, Tony has served on many boards and as chairman of many, including the Orange Bowl Committee and the United Way of Miami-Dade. Tony has actively served on leading industry associations, chairing key committees in furtherance of the accounting industry. He has served on the AICPA's Nominations Committee, the governing body of the AICPA's Council and the Private Companies Practice Section Executive Committee and its Technical Issues Committee. In 1986, Tony was appointed to Florida's Board of Accountancy and was then elected to chair the board. He chaired its Probable Cause Panel, as well.

Rosamarie Bravo, MBAF partner, says

Tony has a keen sense in identifying an individual's strengths. By doing this, he creates an environment in which everyone can succeed. I started to work at MBAF right out of college with no professional experience. After a couple of years, Tony would invite me to attend client meetings with him. At first I spent most of the time listening. Little by little he would give me more responsibility until it got to the point that he expected me to run the meetings. This experience allowed me to learn from Tony and gave me the confidence to believe in my abilities.

Tony is the epitome of a person that leads by example. Everything he expects us to do, he is always doing himself first. He is the first one working in the morning and the last one to leave the office. He tackles every challenge that comes his way and is always thinking about how we can improve and serve our clients better. Seeing his dedication and attention to detail inspires me to work harder to become a good leader of my team.

In high school, he found that sports provided him with many opportunities to learn to lead a team. Later, he pitched for Florida International University, which brought him back to Miami.

Leading the Organization

Tony Argiz found that his high-school sports experience gave him some of his first leadership training because

> In a sports team and an accounting firm, there's really no difference in leading. If you're on a baseball, football, or basketball team, you can't win by yourself. It's a team effort, and it's a team sport. My role is not only the management and making sure that we make the money, but it is to continually bring in business, whether it's litigation, for me to testify, or audit work or tax work.

Terry Snyder, president of the accounting firm alliance PKF North America in Lawrence, GA, agrees that leadership lessons are transferable across industries. "Some years ago, I would have told you there was a big difference between leading an accounting firm and other types of organizations," Terry says. "But that's because accounting firms pictured themselves as partnerships and, for some reason, thought they were void of good business principles. Partnership is a tax concept, not a business concept.

Terry continues

> I had a large church that was a client of mine. And I said, "You know what, when we walk out of these doors, you're running a church. But behind these doors, you're running a business. And if you're not successful at running your business, you won't be able to walk through the front door to the church."
>
> "No money, no mission, and no mission, no money," is a concept that applies to any organization. If you fail to keep the business side healthy, your profession or your organization will falter. And that takes leadership.

Of course, there are some differences in leading an accounting firm. First, you may have a larger percentage of really smart people than in other organizations. Second, the partnership model does not promote rapid decision making, so leaders must exercise patience. Other than those two, most leadership lessons will transfer very well.

Here's what several accounting leaders say about leadership across industries:

▲ Bob Bunting, former CEO of the megaregional firm Moss Adams LLP in Seattle, WA: "I think there are more similarities than there are differences between leading an accounting firm and any other organization. I think leadership skill sets transfer very well."

▲ Neal Spencer, former CEO of the megaregional firm BKD, LLP, in Springfield, MO: I'm not sure leadership is much different in an accounting firm from any other business. Leadership principles are leadership principles. Having come from the restaurant business, I look at running an accounting firm in somewhat a similar fashion. Like the restaurant business, the accounting business has certain peaks and valleys. You staff up accordingly for your peak season and right size accordingly as things slow down. If you're fortunate to get your staffing model just right, which is what restaurants try to do as they anticipate the timing of their lunch and dinner volume, you end up with a very profitable firm. What's different in the accounting business is you must balance your immediate staffing needs with making the appropriate investments in people and services to support your long-term vision.

▲ Jim Metzler, vice president of the AICPA: "The only thing that's different about leading an accounting firm, a regular business, or a trade association is the business model. The characteristics of leadership are probably similar throughout just about any organization."

▲ Bob Hottman, CEO of the top-100 firm Ehrhardt Keefe Steiner & Hottman PC (EKS&H) in Denver, CO:

> Some people understand what being a leader is and some people don't. I think everybody in an organization can and should be a leader. I believe one of the best leaders we have in our firm is our receptionist. She's a real can-do-attitude type of person, and people go to her for all sorts of things, even things way outside of her normal responsibility. If people come to you, they'll follow you. That's what being a leader is all about. It's not about some title.

The Leader's Role—Influencing Mission, Vision, and Values

The primary role of a leader is to live and breathe the mission of the organization that he or she is leading. The leader sets the priorities, influences the followers, and maintains values or standards that will ensure that the organization meets its purpose (or mission). Steve Mayer, founder, chairman, and CEO of the regional firm Burr, Pilger & Mayer LLP in San Francisco, CA, believes, "Once you are inspired, it's easy to be a leader because you're passionate about what you're doing. That's what it takes to influence others: passion for your mission. It becomes infectious, and people will follow your zeal."

Accounting Leaders Have to Shape a Vision for Their Firms
Larry Autrey, managing partner of the top-100 firm Whitley Penn LLP in Ft. Worth, TX, says

> It may not be obvious to people that the firm must define itself. If you are an oil and gas exploration company, then you explore looking for oil and gas. If you are a not-for-profit that takes care of kids, and you've got an emergency shelter and an orphanage, then you know easily what you do. But if you are an accounting firm, I think it leaves you the ability to be a lot of different things. I think both the positives and the difficulties of running an accounting firm are that the culture could shift based on who's at various levels if you are not careful.

Rick Anderson, CEO of the megaregional firm Moss Adams LLP in Seattle, WA, says, "I believe leading is influencing people to agree to follow you. In the end, everyone is a volunteer, and they will follow you because they want to, not because they have to. In most of my leadership roles, I didn't have authority to hire or fire or adjust the pay of anyone; I had to earn the right to lead."

An accounting firm is part business and part profession. The purpose of a business is to create and serve customers. A profession is an occupation, a vocation, or a career in which specialized knowledge of a subject, field, or science is applied. Accounting firms are full of people who want to apply their special knowledge or skill but could care less about creating and serving clients. How then do we develop a common mission for a firm, so that everyone is committed to carrying it out? This is the fundamental job of the leader.

Tom Luken, president of the local firm Kolb+Co in Milwaukee, WS, says, "Bob Kolb, the founder of our firm, worked closely with me because he knew I was a good business developer. I have always been inspired by trying to influence people to do things my way, rather than to tell them or boss them to do it my way. While I think my way might be the right way, I am not forcing them to do things my way."

Author of over 20 books on leadership and the foremost leadership expert in the world, John Maxwell said, "Leadership is influence, getting things done with other people." It's interesting that he has invested most of his life's work on the subject of leadership, yet he can boil it down to one word: influence.

Effective leadership is not about charisma or cleverness. Effective leadership is about having and communicating a compelling vision, having the dedication to work hard to achieve the vision, and taking responsibility and being trustworthy.

Hugh Parker, executive partner of the regional firm Horne LLP in Jackson, MS, adds

> Abraham Lincoln was not a universally loved person by any means, but look at his lasting influence. Leadership is about influencing direction; management is staying on top of details. Management actually has more to do with the routines. Leadership is symbolized in a Wayne Gretzky quote for me. He says, "Most people will think about where the puck *is*; I'm thinking about where the puck's *going to be*."

An effective leader creates vision and influences human action toward achieving the vision. Jim DeMartini, managing partner of Seiler LLP in Redwood City, CA, says, "The purpose of the business is to create a client and grow the client. The role of a leader of a business is to lead and teach our professionals how to create and serve clients."

Losing Focus

Accountants often get too caught up in doing the work itself and getting paid. Although one of the most highly attended and repeated sessions at Management of an Accounting Practice meetings deals with partner compensation, sessions on creating a client are often ignored. Ask many accounting firm partners, and they will tell you that the purpose of their business is to make a profit or to maximize partner income.

Although an accounting professional may only have one function—production—an accounting business has three basic functions: marketing, production, and innovation. One of the roles of the CEO is to ensure that a healthy mix of these functions takes place. Because of the profession's influence, many firms are production-oriented only. I contend that in such firms, the owners have created good jobs for themselves, but they have not created businesses. Only in firms with a healthy mix of marketing and innovation can there be a dynamic business.

When many people talk about marketing, they often mean the organization of the selling functions (that is, moving more of our tax, audit, and other services to the consumer). All marketing is communication, and all communication is marketing. Marketing begins with the client and the client's needs, wants, demographics, and values. Marketing does not ask, "What do we want to sell our clients?" Good marketing understands the client so well that you shape your service to fit the client's needs, and it sells itself.

A Sad Tale (Tail!)

With the growing importance of technology, many have toyed with the notion that a day will come when computers will make decisions and run the business. In fact, some have predicted the day when an accounting firm could be run by a computer, a man, and a dog: the computer would run the firm, the man would turn the computer on and off and feed the dog, and the dog would be there to keep the man from touching anything else!

But about the only real advantage that technology has afforded us has been to generate reams and gigabytes of information. Many firms are overloaded with information about every hour of service, yet they find it difficult to make good decisions because the information is not condensed and organized in meaningful ways.

Leading Versus Managing

Both leadership and management are crucial to the success of a business. However, leadership is different than management in many profound ways, and it is very easy to get confused about the subject. In this section, I'll cover some of the differences. In my experience, rarely can you find both extraordinary leadership and management qualities in one individual.

Management is more about efficiency, whereas leadership is more about effectiveness. Nothing will increase your effectiveness as much as raising your leadership ability. When you focus on your leadership ability, you encourage others in your organization to do the same. The result is that the effectiveness of your entire firm improves.

Leadership is not management, technical ability, or a title. Colin Powell, former U.S. secretary of defense said, "Leadership is the art of accomplishing more than the science of management says is possible. Leadership is both art and science. Some people have natural leadership characteristics. Others have learned to lead."

According to Mike Cain, founder and comanaging partner of the top-50 firm Lattimore Black Morgan & Cain, PC (LBMC), in Nashville, TN, "Leading and managing a business are clearly different. They're different skill sets, and they're both incredibly important. I think leadership has you looking down the road, trying to anticipate where things are going, what the trends are, where you ought to be positioned in the future."

You Need Both

David Deeter, founder of the top-100 firm Frazier & Deeter, LLC, in Atlanta, GA, says

> We have a chief operating officer and I would see this person as the leading manager. In addition, we have a controller and other positions that do a lot of management. But a firm needs a leading partner to help set the direction and tone of the firm. A leading partner keeps us focused on our future, our vision. He helps us maintain a sense of mission and values. Managing is more systems; it's organization charts. A great leader surrounds himself with great managers. Because, often, some of the best leaders aren't necessarily great managers themselves, just like a great pitcher may not be a great hitter.

Sometimes, a solid manager will become the managing partner, president, or CEO of an accounting firm. This person may have solid management credentials, skills, education, and experience, but somehow, the competition grows much faster, and the well-managed firm remains somewhat status quo. Such a firm may be well-managed but underled.

Growth is often a solid indicator of the skill set of the leader. If you are assigned responsibility for five clients, and five years later, the business from those clients is diminished, you might be a good manager but a poor leader. A good leader will grow the client relationships and replace the ones that go away.

On the other hand, you may see a high-growth firm led by a visionary leader that is crumbling from within. Such a firm may have strong leadership but poor management. Great leaders will make room for solid managers who can build and maintain infrastructure; otherwise, their dreams will be dashed.

Keith Farlinger, CEO of the national firm BDO Canada LLP in Toronto, Canada, distinguishes between leadership and management. "What we've done over the last two or three years is to start to lead from national office. You need to work on developing that vision from a national point of view, and we've been very aggressive in bringing in resources to help us reach that vision."

Leadership is more about doing the right things, whereas management is about doing things right. The leader must select the right goals from competing priorities and say no to others. Leaders are always looking at the relative importance of doing certain things, whereas the manager's primary job is to accomplish the high-priority goals efficiently.

New Skills

For accountants, leadership is very different than their craft. The accounting profession attracts a thoughtful, deliberate sort of person. Most accounting problems take thought, study, contemplation, and a deliberate approach to solutions; however, this is not so for leadership. Leadership requires in-the-moment decision making and action. As Carlos Ghosn, CEO of Nissan, says, "You learn to be a leader by acting, by doing." Steven Covey, author of *The 7 Habits of Highly Effective People*, said, "Gandhi demonstrated great leadership time and again, simply by going and doing what had to be done. His methods were simple and uncomplicated."

Are Leaders Born or Are They Built?

People come up to me all the time and say things like, "Leaders are natural" or "Leaders are just born that way" or "She is just a natural leader because she makes it look so easy." I have found that although some people are born with gifted intelligence, it can be frittered away without nurturing. I've also found that people of average intelligence can accomplish greatness with their lives because of dedication, learning, and hard work. In this section, we'll talk about nature versus nurture.

Ken Baggett, co-managing partner of the national firm CohnReznick LLP, says

> I believe people have some personality traits they are born with that help them become leaders, but I believe most people can develop leadership skills at some level if they are exposed and want to work at it. I had a wonderful experience as a young leader when I met Bob Bunting, the former CEO of Moss Adams. I had just become the managing partner of Reznick Group. He was speaking at a conference, and I approached him about spending a little time with him to learn how Moss Adams operated and provided leadership training. He immediately agreed, and I flew to Seattle the following week. To my surprise we started at 9:00 AM and ended our time together around 5:00 PM that day. Not only did I feel I had spent the day with "greatness," but I was amazed at how open Bob was. At the end, I asked him why he had allowed me so much time, and he said that when he became managing partner of Moss Adams, he was sent to another firm's managing partner for a similar full day of discussion. At the end, the managing partner said that Bob must offer the same assistance in the future when others came calling. That day taught me that you always share, you always make time, and you can always learn from teaching.

Both teaching and learning have a role to play as you work to develop your leadership skills. "A good part of leadership is having a pretty high IQ, some of it you are born with. But the molding of the behavior is what creates the leaders," says Bill Haller, managing partner of the national firm CapinCrouse LLP in Indianapolis, IN, "It's sitting under masters who have the ability to turn knowledge into skill."

Leader Profile: Bob Bunting, former CEO of the megaregional firm Moss Adams LLP in Seattle, WA

Robert L. Bunting was very shy and quite humble as a youngster. He was elected president of his high school student body but never viewed himself a leader. Bob taught accounting labs and majored in accounting at the University of Idaho, so he wouldn't have to go into sales or marketing. He wanted to be the best he could be from a knowledge application point of view. When he joined Price Waterhouse in 1968, he began to learn that leadership comes in many styles. His first mentor was a "techno-geek" and a leader in that people sought him out for his knowledge base—an instant connection for young Bob Bunting trying to find his way.

Bob says, "Hunter Jones, a PW partner, taught me that I could be a very substantial professional, that I could be technically very smart, and I could distinguish myself by having a grasp of a unique knowledge base," he says. "And basically be the only game in town or the best game in town in a particular area of knowledge."

When Bob began his public accounting career, he viewed each of his superiors as someone who could teach him valuable skills. It was this thirst for knowledge, his honesty, and his humility that helped him rise to the status of CEO of Moss Adams LLP.

From 1982–2004, Bob was president and chairman and still is an active partner of Moss Adams LLP. He is a past president of the Washington Society of CPAs and has served on the boards of the Catherine Holmes Wilkins Foundation, United Way, and Historic Seattle.

Over a long and successful career in the accounting profession, Bob is no stranger to awards and accolades. He's been tapped for numerous prestigious positions, including chairman of the AICPA, and president of the International Federation of Accountants. He was named to the Steering Committee of the International Integrated Reporting Committee, established to help drive forward the creation of a globally accepted framework for accounting for sustainability. In addition, several times, he's been named one of *Accounting Today* magazine's 100 Most Influential People.

INSIDE Public Accounting has three times named Bob as one of the five peers who accounting professionals most admire. Bob was one of the recipients of the AICPA's Gold Medal Award for Distinguished Service, the highest award granted by the AICPA. Bob served as chair of the AICPA Board of Directors in 2004–05 and is presently president of the International Federation of Accountants.

After all the other accomplishments, what makes the peer selection stand out? No suggested list of people is presented to the voters beforehand. They're simply asked to write down names of whoever comes to mind. Three hundred eighty-five firms participated in the survey.

Chris Allegretti, CEO of the regional firm Hill, Barth & King, LLC (HBK), in Boardman, OH, says

> I owe a great debt to Bob Bunting. When I became CEO of our firm, I reached out to talk with Bob, and he invited me to come to Seattle and meet with him. He invested an entire day with me and listened intently to my biggest perceived problems. He has met with me frequently as he has traveled to the east coast, and he always returns my calls. He really challenged me to develop a compelling vision of where I wanted to take the firm. He carefully explained how to create a powerful set of core values and beliefs under which we operate. When I asked Bob how I could pay for his service and advice, he simple told me, "Pay it forward. Help another new managing partner, and you will repay me." His humility and wonderful advice really encouraged me.

Types of Leaders

Great leaders must be adaptive to change. If we rely only on our experience, the ability to handle the new challenges that today and tomorrow bring is very limited. Some leaders operate well in a rapid-growth environment, and others operate better in slower growth. Some leaders operate best in crisis, and others lead better when things are more stable. Sometimes, the rapid growth leader cannot lead very well in a stable situation.

"There can be different types of leaders for different roles. A business that is growing steadily in a stable market environment will benefit from a leader who is also steady and stable. Whereas a business in crises may need a different type of leader for a period of time," says Bill Haller.

Bill goes on

> My partner, C.E. Crouse, is a great client leader. His skills fall into two areas: trust and competence. It amazes me at how much someone can foul up in a particular client situation, and C.E., with his calm style and his caring attitude, can make that client feel, "Not to worry; I am on the case. I will solve your problem and do it all gently without leaving any scarred bodies behind." He is a very Godly man. The way he deals with people, they feel better about themselves.

Dave Sibits, president of the national firm CBIZ Financial Services in Cleveland, OH, observes, "There are leaders who can grow firms to a certain size, and then, the business will plateau. My five and half years as part of the senior team of American Express helped position me to do the job that I am doing today: leading part of a public company."

Leaders have to understand the technical and human aspects of their firms. Gordon Krater, managing partner of the megaregional firm Plante & Moran, PLLC, in Southfield, MI, says

> I think we are technical by nature, and so we often look for what's wrong. I think engineers, accountants, and lawyers are generally those kinds of people. Professionals are doing intellectual work, and they want to make sure that the person who's leading understands that.
>
> We are all about people, not things. If I describe my leadership style, I'd say servant leadership. I don't really feel that I'm the boss; I feel like I'm here to create an environment where people can excel.

Bob Hottman agrees with Krater,

> I view leadership in a serving role as opposed to a commanding role. I think in a service business, a servant leader is going to be much more successful than a commanding leader will be.
>
> We use a tree to symbolize our firm and the roots being the core values, the trunk being the partners, and the limbs and the branches and the leaves being our clients and our people. And we know that tree will grow as long as we can develop partners. But the partners are on the bottom to support the organization. They're not on top coming down.

Effective Leaders Must Be Humble

Bob Bunting describes one of his firm's now retired office managing partners and her humble leadership style's dramatic impact:

> Out of her office, we've produced five managing partners, and we've produced four industry leaders and two specialty leaders.
>
> She is self-effacing. She defers credit to others. I think she systematically avoids being charismatic. She has very high empathy with people, but she is demanding. You tell her a sob story, she says, "Let's go to work on that; let's get that fixed; I'm going to help you, and

you're going to perform." And it's really masterful to combine the empathetic style of leadership with a very demanding set of expectations.

Because of her leadership, our firm is growing.

Now, in other situations, you have the guy who is the absolute boss; he is the smartest guy in the room, he makes great decisions, people always go to him for answers, and he gives them answers because he doesn't have time to bring them to the answers. How many leaders has he produced? Zero. People don't quit, but he is not enabling people or bringing people along.

Gordon Krater notes that humility has made successful leaders in his firm, as well. "Our former managing partner, Bill Herman, has a lot of fine leadership traits," Gordon says. "One of the best is he really doesn't care about the credit. But he'll take the blame. Even when somebody is trying to give him credit, he'd say, 'Well that's not me; that's the team.'"

On the topic of humble leaders, Bob Hottman says, "In Jim Collins's book *Good to Great*, humility was a common characteristic of the very best leaders. None of those people were rock stars. You would hardly know their names unless you'd really read the book and remember it, and so, that was an extraordinary characteristic that they shared."

Challenges of Leadership

Often, effective leadership goes unrecognized. Leaders who come to the rescue and solve problems appear like gallant cavalry officers on white horses. Books are written. Songs are sung. Speeches are made extolling the leadership of the "rock star" leader. But what about the leader who guides his or her organization to avoid calamities? Few people recognize the lack of calamity as worthy of speeches or accolades!

Leader Profile: John Wooden, Renowned Basketball Player and Coach

Often, we are inspired by the leadership that builds a sports team with extraordinary results over a long period of time. Hundreds of leaders produce a winning season or two, but very few successfully lead their teams over the years. Probably the most enduring record in sports is held by basketball coach John Wooden and his UCLA Bruins. Coach Wooden's teams achieved 10 national championships (including 7 in a row), 88 consecutive wins, 38 tournament playoff wins, 4 perfect seasons, and only 1 losing season in his 41 years of coaching. If the product of great leadership is results, these results make Coach Wooden a leader in a class of his own.

Coach Wooden says in the prologue to his book *Wooden on Leadership*, "Helping others to achieve their own greatness by helping the organization to succeed is what leadership is all about."

Coach Wooden lived by a simple leadership formula: C+F+U—conditioning plus fundamentals plus unity. In a professional firm, conditioning includes the mental, technical, emotional, and business training that enable you to sustain great results during high performance times of "busy season" or client deadlines.

(continued)

(continued)

> Coach Wooden was famous for his training and focus on fundamentals. In your firm, the fundamentals are great work and great client service.
>
> In Coach Wooden's mind, unity or team spirit meant a willingness to sacrifice personal interest or glory for the welfare of all. That is why he was willing to kick All-American Bill Walton off the team bus before a crucial game when Walton did not comply with Coach Wooden's rules on dress and hygiene.

Part of the accounting leadership challenge comes from the nature of a professional firm. According to Dave Sibits

> The little book *Herding Cats* by Patrick McKenna sums it up very well. The real challenge is that the professional service firm is made up of a lot of entrepreneurs. Trying to get entrepreneurs, who take pride in their individualism, to pull in the same direction is one of the major challenges. Getting them to work together, while really pushing them to exercise their own professional capabilities really makes it more challenging. It's way different than making paint or running a retail outlet. The closest thing to running a professional service firm is a football or a baseball team. These sports teams have professionals with highly elite skills, and to be successful, they must play as a team.

Working with lots of egos can be challenging for a driven leader, and sharing or giving away the credit isn't always easy, says Scott Dietzen, managing partner, Northwest Region, of the national accounting firm CliftonLarsonAllen LLP in Spokane, WA.

> I'm sure there are times when all leaders want to say, "Wait a minute, that was my idea." I have had to bite my tongue and say, "Yes, that person was fantastic, and they've really seized the opportunity," because in the end, what should be important to me is the firm moving in the direction towards its vision. As soon as I begin to wave my flag, the attention gets directed to the wrong people.

"When you're surrounded by a talented team, you also have to expect pushback," says Rick Anderson. "On any given day, any one of our 250 partners can question my decisions or motives on any subject. On the one hand, this serves as a bit of an irritant, but truly, I think it makes me a much better leader because I'm always growing in my knowledge, and my decisions are better because they are challenged."

I have found that leadership is very hard work and that most leaders get very little credit. Noted author and management expert Peter Drucker said that leadership "is mundane unromantic, and boring." If a leader has done a great job preparing his or her team for the downturns in business, rarely will others give him or her accolades.

The Measure of a Leader

I hope that I've convinced you of the need for great leadership in accounting firms and even described some of the qualities of great leaders. Whatever you want to accomplish in life or business is influenced by your leadership ability and the abilities of those around you. Noted leadership guru John Maxwell says, "The leadership abilities of those around you will never be greater than your ability as a leader. If their leadership abilities are stronger than yours, they will leave." But we're numbers people; we like things in black and white. So how do you measure a great leader for an accounting firm?

One criteria is growth of your firm and people. A manager can sustain things, but a leader should direct growth. This growth may not show quickly. For instance, you may lead your firm to new, more profitable areas as you divest older, stagnant ones.

According to Rick Anderson

> Leading the growth of the firm is my highest priority. Business development and sales are the measure of a good leader. If you don't grow, you won't retain your best people. If you don't grow the business, you won't attract the best new clients. Retaining the best people and attracting the best clients gives a firm energy at new challenges and continuously raises the bar on performance.
>
> There are three ways that you grow: you acquire firms, you bring in talent from the outside, or you grow your talent from inside. At Moss Adams, we would say that the most important long-term strategy is growing talent from within.

Growth isn't just about profit. Scott Dietzen reminds us that growth is also related to the vitality of an organization. "There is a very direct correlation in growing an accounting firm and leadership," he says. "Good leaders are so passionate about growth because they realize that growth brings energy, it brings opportunity and keeps morale high, and it forces people to think of new ways of doing things, and that makes it a very dynamic organization. And so I think great leadership demands growth."

BDO Canada finds growth so important that it doesn't just leave that job up to top management—everyone is responsible. "Business development is our whole organization; it's not just that partner who's beating the bushes," says Keith Farlinger. "It's all of us who have responsibility for business development."

Bob Hottman makes sales both a personal and firmwide goal. "I have a daily reminder that shows up every morning on my calendar at 5:00 AM that says sell, sell, sell, and every Monday morning at 7:45 AM, we have a business development meeting."

A second but related criteria is long-term results for the firm. In *Good to Great*, Jim Collins found clear distinctions between the top leaders he profiled and those who led similar companies. Other leaders often were more concerned with their own wealth and success, but the top leaders who Collins described were fanatically driven to produce sustainable long-term results.

John Wright, managing partner of the top-100 firm Padgett Stratemann & Co. of San Antonio, TX, says, "The same elements that make a good leader are the same elements of a good rainmaker. The core skills, which really revolve around being a good relationship builder, being a good service provider, being a good role model, all can be learned."

The word *rainmaker* comes up a lot when you talk about firm leadership. "Our firm's best leaders are my best rainmakers, and my best rainmakers are my best leaders. The rainmakers carry more credibility because they can attract clients," says Tony Morgan. "That same skill seems to attract good staff members. The ability to attract and influence a client to come with you has some of the same characteristics of the person who can attract, retain and lead staff."

Charly Weinstein, CEO of the megaregional firm EisnerAmper LLP in New York City, NY, takes business growth to an entirely new level.

> In business, the real test of leadership is how well you grow the business. We've had experience in many other businesses, as well as the accounting business. The first business we built was a health-care consulting practice. We sold it to Kurt Salmon Associates and distributed the proceeds to the partners. Next thing we built was an Internet company. We worked with one individual who had an idea. We fleshed out the idea together; built an Internet company; took it public at the height of the dot-com boom; distributed the shares to the partners; and in the IPO, we raised $40 million. Then, we built a hedge fund administration outsourcing business. We built the revenues of that business to about $5.5 million, and we sold it to a public company for $25 million and distributed that money to the partners.
>
> Next business we built was a company called Velocity Technology Solutions. We raised some venture capital, some private equity money, bought a division of Siemens, and spun it out into a separate entity. We distributed the stock to our partners just a couple of years ago. It's just a matter of time till that's another liquidity event for our partners.
>
> As other firms began to have slowdowns in their growth in 2008, we found that there was less competition out there for bringing talented partners into the firm. The cost of acquiring really top talent became a little more reasonable. So, we have been able to capitalize on a very strong balance sheet, a very strong capital position, excellent cash flow, and our existing base of talent and reputation to opportunistically acquire more people.
>
> An example of this is Michael Bright. He joined us, and we now have a thriving sports media and entertainment practice. We audit the New York Jets. We do significant projects for the NBA, for the NHL, for Major League Baseball. We have some high-profile clients, but we didn't get there without the right people in the firm, and we can't do the work without the right resources.

Third, you must *work* on your leadership skills. You will tend to use the skills that you have, but unless your situation and clients never change, you'll need new leadership skills as you go along. In one study of people who managed billion dollar companies or divisions, those who were successful when put in a new situation were those whose existing skills fit the new situations. As a leader, you'll make an effort to put your people in situations that fit their skills, but you'll really value those who can handle *different* situations. You should strive for the same thing with your own leadership skills. Different people need different things from a leader in order to perform optimally. As circumstances change over time, you'll need to be flexible, as well.

Whether you're just beginning to develop your leadership potential, or you're decades into leadership, you *can* improve your skills.

When I asked the accounting leaders who I interviewed for this book, "Are you a better leader today than you were five years ago?" every single leader gave me a resounding, "Yes." Top leaders are always working to be better.

Many of the leaders who I interviewed for this book attributed the development of their leadership skills to their progression on committees and boards of other organizations. Not-for-profit (NFP) organizations have become great development programs for leaders. Many of them set an excellent example for leaders in accounting firms and other businesses. (And you meet a nice variety of potential contacts who are willing to give back.)

Dave Sibits is a believer in the power of nonprofit work to develop leadership skills. "You develop leadership skill through participation in as many developmental activities as possible. Not-for-profit boards, the AICPA, industry associations, and your state society of CPAs are all great places to learn to lead," Dave says. "One of the early things that helped me understand leadership was serving on the AICPA's Tax Executive Committee. The people on the committee were real movers and shakers in our industry. Being a part of that committee really allowed me, as a young person, to hone skills to make myself a better leader."

Successful NFPs have learned that leadership and management matter even more for them than in business. Although they lack the profit motive, they must get results and be accountable to their donors if they are going to carry out their missions. Without leadership and management, nothing much gets accomplished.

The very best NFPs invest deep thought to their missions. They focus on objectives that have clear-cut implications for the work that their members, staff, and volunteers perform. The NFPs start with the customer (the community they serve), unlike many accounting firms that start with the profit of the partners and their organization.

Whether you're the CEO, a manager, a senior, or the receptionist, you can and should be a leader. And the opportunity to be a leader shows much earlier in your career in our kind of profession because you are leading something almost from the day you start.

"I was given an opportunity to lead an office in Bowling Green, KY, when I was a first-year partner," says Neal Spencer. "Thank God it was in a small office because I can look back on mistakes that I made that I would never do today. So, as I've gone from that small leadership opportunity to leading four offices in a region to leading the entire firm, I learned a lot along the way about what it takes to lead partners and an organization."

Hugh Parker believes, "Real leadership is the constraining resource in any firm's success or in any firm going to the next stage of development. We see an office plateau, and it's all due to the leadership."

With the challenges that leaders face, many accountants may turn away from the responsibility that leadership brings. But Carl George, former CEO of the national firm Clifton Gunderson LLP in Peoria, IL, has found that leaders also benefit from their roles. "Peter Drucker may have said that leadership was mundane, unromantic, and boring work. I know he's an icon, but I've got to tell you, I'm in total disagreement with that statement," Carl says. "To me, I had the best job in the firm, being CEO. It was exciting every day. Any time I had the chance to lead 2,000 people in CG, and I had the chance to help lead our revenue growth five times during my tenure as CEO, it was exhilarating. That's pretty good for a Hoosier boy from Indianapolis."

Conclusion

Your ability to raise your leadership ability is the most important factor in growing your team and business. Once you have mastered a certain amount of technical competence, it will be your leadership that will help you grow into the next level of business acumen. This book is designed to give you a road map for building a competent team of professionals to continue serving your clients in more sophisticated ways.

Section 1

Leading Self

"Don't wish it was easier; wish that you were better. Don't wish for less problems; wish for more skills. Don't wish for less challenges; wish for more wisdom."

~ JIM ROHN

In our pyramid model, the foundational stones are all related to self-leadership. Before anyone will follow you, you must prove yourself to be a person worthy of followers. If your personal habits are poor, your accomplishments are few, and your direction is aimless, then people will not be attracted to your leadership. In accounting firms, men and women are promoted to senior, supervisor, or manager primarily based on their technical skills. This position of leadership based on a title is the lowest form of leadership. The technical ability and title will only carry a person so far in leading others. John Maxwell defines leadership as influence—nothing more, nothing less. People with the least amount of influence lead from their title or position, whereas those with the most influence lead from who they are and how they interact with others. As we progress through this book, we'll focus on how you can make this progression.

Marc Elman, CEO of the local firm PSB Boisjoli in Montreal, Canada, who built himself up to run marathons in spite of his life-long battle with asthma, believes that leadership is a matter of showing the way, not just telling. "You abuse your position of leadership by telling someone what to do, as opposed to leading by positive actions. You can learn as much from someone's poor actions as you can from someone's positive actions," he says.

People move beyond title to become leaders, and others willingly follow for a variety of reasons. When you build relationships with other people, they may be more willing to follow you. If your followers believe that you are in it for them, they will volunteer to join you. When you demonstrate integrity, people trust you and will follow more easily. Leadership and accounting are very different, and although people might believe you can give the right tax answer, they may not have confidence in your leadership.

In the following chart, you will see both ends of the leadership spectrum: position power and personal power. Throughout this book, I will challenge you to move beyond the position power that emanates from a title, and instead, I will give you skills to help you develop your personal power to lead and influence people.

Position Power	Personal Power
Uses title to influence	Uses trust to influence
Directs	Leads
Influences others with titles	Influences the team
Speaks quickly	Speaks slowly
People follow because it is required	People follow because they want to
Titles intimidate followers	Results attract volunteers
Title will get you hours	Personal power will get you hearts

Some of the greatest examples of leadership are people who never held office. People like Gandhi; Mother Teresa; and Martin Luther King, Jr., had no title or position, but they used their personal power to change the world.

Bill Herman, of Plante & Moran, PLLC, in Southfield, MI, says

You never have enough information to make a perfect decision. It's oftentimes that the leader's ego got in the way of making a good decision. And so I think it's something that all leaders should guard against. When I look at athletes, I think of Tiger Woods as a recent example; I look at politicians or political figures; I look at entertainers. I look at leaders that you read about in the *Wall Street Journal* every day. Somewhere along the line, people told them how good they were, and they've told them that for so long that they started to believe it. I don't think many of them intentionally crossed the line.

Referring to Wood's 2009 personal scandals, Bill says

Tiger Woods said, "After a while, I felt I was entitled because I gave my whole to golf and am entitled to do what I want." He didn't set out to wreck his family and his reputation, but somehow, the lines got blurred. His ego drove his decisions.

I am a firm believer that you lead by example. For starters, I also think that any leader better take time for themselves, whether it's time off, taking care of yourself with exercise, eating right, the spiritual dimension of what you do. We have a saying: "the whole person comes to work." In our environment, that means if you have problems or you are imperfect, the whole person is coming.

The five foundational stones in our model are found in chapters 2–6, and the corner stones are self-knowledge and trustworthiness:

Self-Knowl-edge: The Inner Accelerator	Preparation: Ready for Seizing Opportunity	Critical Thinking: Creating Your Future	Self-Disci-pline: Be the Master, Not the Victim	Trust: The Leadership Imperative
Chapter 2	Chapter 5	Chapter 4	Chapter 6	Chapter 3
Section One: Leading Self				

Self-knowledge. The greatest leaders understand themselves first and foremost. Rather than operating from their emotions, the best leaders seek to understand their own motivations. Understanding your strengths and weaknesses can provide you a road map for improving your leadership skills. The men and women who have the most self-knowledge will usually be the most effective leaders.

Bill Haller, managing partner of the national firm CapinCrouse LLP in Indianapolis, IN, says, "People look at all aspects of you as a leader, so you have to be a pretty complete person. If you try to hide it, the only person you are hiding it from is yourself because what you learn is everybody pretty much sees who you are."

Trustworthiness. When you are trusted, people are more likely to follow you. We will explore the idea of trust from three perspectives: intent, integrity, and results. People will trust you more if they know that your intent is in their best interest. When you do what you say you will do, when your words and actions are aligned, and when you keep your promises, followers see. Sounds so simple, doesn't it? Lastly, you must be a person with results to gain the trust of people who are also advancing in their lives.

Preparation. One of the disciplines that the great leaders practice is investing the time to prepare. People who fly by the seat of their pants rarely make great things happen. People can't follow them because there seems to be no rhyme or reason for their actions. The best leaders prepare with their teams, so the followers know what to expect and how to proceed.

Critical thinking. Leaders invest time in thinking critically about their plans, people and organization. The ability to think critically, understand as many of the facts as possible, and yet be able to make a timely decision using their intuition is a key discipline of good leaders.

Self-discipline. The discipline to study one's self, to follow through on promises, to prepare for each initiative, and to think critically about your firm is required for a leader to succeed. In this world of distractions, it is easy to get sidetracked on meaningless activity. Leaders are more disciplined in saying "No" to many things and saying "Yes" to the few things that matter to their vision and team.

Ray Strothman, managing partner of the local firm Strothman & Company, PSC, in Louisville, KY, believes that in order to be sharp mentally, you have to be sharp physically. "I believe in keeping myself in excellent physical condition through a regular workout program. I am careful about my diet," he says. "When I am with a client, I have disciplined myself to look them in the eye and to be focused entirely on them. In fact, I try to position myself to avoid distractions when I am in a meeting with a client. We have a conference room that has a glass wall where people can see in, so I always position myself with my back to the glass wall, so that I don't see what's going on behind me."

Keith Farlinger, CEO of the national firm BDO Canada LLP in Toronto, Canada, also believes in leading by example. "I'm a big believer that you must lead yourself. You need to look after your health, being vital, maintaining your energy, eating all the right stuff," he says.

> You do need things that you do outside of the business because if you're just totally focused on business all the time, I'm just not sure you're as effective as when you have a life balance, and you have other things to get your mind off work from time to time, so that you could come back and look at it from a fresh point of view. And then the other piece is the whole learning piece. You need to have an ability to learn from others, to learn what your strengths and weaknesses are, and how to apply those strength and weaknesses.

Periodically, great leaders will reevaluate themselves and recommit themselves to leading themselves before leading others. There was the story of Gandhi meeting with a mother and her son. The mother asked Gandhi, "Will you tell my son to quit eating sugar?" Gandhi said, "Bring him back in a week." The mother traveled many miles home, then returned a week later with the same request. Gandhi then said to the boy, "Stop eating sugar; it will rot your teeth and make you sick." The mother asked, "Why didn't you tell my son that last week? I've traveled many miles to go home and return here." Gandhi said, "Last week, I was eating sugar. Before telling your son to quit, I had to quit eating sugar." Clearly, in leadership, actions speak louder than words.

Leader Profile: Rick Dreher, CEO of the megaregional firm Wipfli LLP in Green Bay, WS

Rick Dreher is the managing partner of Wipfli LLP, a top 25 accounting firm. He oversees the vision and strategy, leadership, growth, and overall performance of the entire firm. Rick was born in Alaska, where his father was stationed in the Air Force. He grew up working in his father's service station and was fascinated with counting the money and making change. That led him to major in accounting at the University of Wisconsin at Milwaukee, then to 10 years at Ernst & Young before moving to Wipfli in 1990.

Wipfli partner Jeff Greenway says

> Rick does a great job of meeting his commitment to others and really helps us think critically. For instance, if you ask him to review something, if Rick agrees to it, he will always meet his commitment. Many leaders just give cursory review and skim materials, but, rather, Rick will take the time to fully review and provide feedback. It makes you feel that he truly is interested in your ideas. Many leaders do not take the time, or they say they do but really only give it a half-hearted effort.

Claudio Diaz says

> When I joined Wipfli, I was one of seven leaders reporting directly to the previous managing partner. Rick sold us on the firm's need for a director of tax position because he knew that we were growing and would need that role. This clearly was an example of self-leadership. He stepped up and created his own plan, presented it to us, and was able to think through all the details.
>
> Rick raised the bar of excellence and visionary thinking so much that the decision for a new managing partner several months later was actually pretty easy. At that time, we had about 80 or so partners, and getting that band of leaders aligned

was no easy task. Even before he was selected, he met with different groups of partners and not only heard their voice but convinced them that he could take us innovatively into the next decade of growth and not lose our Wipfli Way. Well, the partner vote proved he had the ability to lead others. In fact, he lived out his commitment to meet live with each partner individually in his first 100 days in office.

Since assuming his role as managing partner, Rick has transformed the existing Wipfli leadership structure to include a chief operating officer and chief growth officer. This team collaboratively executes the firm's five-year strategic plan, enhancing client value and stronger relationships, while managing and improving the overall performance for the firm.

"That triumvirate has taken us from about $80 million in revenue to $134 million in a short 4 years," Claudio says.

This, to me, is a perfect example of leading management and how he organized the firm and delegated those pretty critical responsibilities to the right people to get the right results.

We designed our culture a few years ago and now call it The Wipfli Way, which helps us understand what's expected of us when we interact with clients and each other. And the beautiful thing is that neither Rick nor any of us on the senior leadership team built that; it was created by our associate workforce. We're so serious about this that we have a recognition program around those Wipfli Way qualities, with just shy of $1,000 in rewards every month. We also put it into our performance appraisals to ensure accountability. So, he's serious about leading strategy.

Rick is also an accomplished speaker and has delivered presentations to the Institute of Management Accountants, Inc.; Wipfli client groups; and various civic and charitable organizations. In Rick's free time, he enjoys the outdoors and traveling with his family. He is a member of the American and Wisconsin Institutes of Certified Public Accountants. He is very active in community endeavors, serving in leadership roles for a number of associations. Rick is the past president and treasurer of the Green Bay West Rotary Club; president and past treasurer of St. Mark Evangelical Lutheran Church; and past treasurer and chairman of the Budget/Audit Committee while serving on the board of directors for Cerebral Palsy, Inc.

Self-Knowledge: The Inner Accelerator

*"Knowing others is intelligence; knowing yourself is true wisdom.
Mastering others is strength; mastering yourself is true power."*

~ UNKNOWN

In this chapter, I will deal with a subject that many budding leaders fail to master: under-standing themselves. When you understand what makes you tick, what drives you, and how you come across to others, you will better be able to lead others. A man or woman who can't lead himself or herself will never achieve a level of personal power to attract others to his or her team. I'll share with you some personal stories of leadership, understanding, and growth and challenge you to begin the journey to understand yourself better.

I first took a personality assessment when I was 35 years old. The DISC profile scored me as a high "D," or driver (the other choices were "I" for influencer, "S" for steady, and "C" for conscientious). It was about 15 more years before I learned that I was overusing my natural communication style. Although the high "D" is good for developing determination and willpower, I overused my dominant style, and it hurt me with people.

I took a 360 degree survey when I was about 50 years old, and it surprised me that I was coming across as overly assertive, aggressive, and authoritarian. Having developed some hor-rible habits, it was very difficult for me to learn new ways of leading people. Had I had this information much earlier in life, perhaps my effectiveness could have improved sooner. The high "D" style served me well in building a business, but great people are reluctant to follow a domineering leader.

Although the other chapters in this section are also important, I've learned that a leader cannot engender trust, which we'll cover in chapter 3, "Trust: The Leadership Imperative," until that leader understands his or her personal blind spots. The leader with the most self-knowledge will also be better equipped to critically think, prepare, and discipline himself or herself.

Your Leadership Style

Your natural communication style affects the choices that you make in life, and the choices that you make relative to other people will influence them to follow you or not follow you. The more self-insight that you can develop, the more likely you will be to make effective choices in life. Without self-knowledge, we make choices based on habit or emotion rather than thought. The very best leaders have a great deal of self-understanding, and I want this for you.

Why is it that some leaders succeed and others don't? Some leaders live life to the fullest and develop their personal potential to its maximum. Some grow themselves to lead large groups of people, but others' growth becomes stunted at some level in their development.

Growth can stall for several reasons. Sometimes, you don't even realize that you're in a rut, or immediate demands of work distract you. Some people have no interest in improving themselves, others remain bogged down by the demands of basic survival, and some focus mainly on status or materialism. Others' personal growth is limited by obstacles, such as fam-ily dynamics, childhood coping mechanisms, physical or emotional illness, or through being beaten down by circumstances or other people.

Most people—even good leaders—have blind spots: areas of their personalities, commu-nication styles, or personal habits that sabotage their leadership influence. When your blind spot negatively affects others' willingness to follow you, your leadership influence will be diminished. The most effective leaders have studied their blind spots and have been able to alter their behaviors to become more effective. These effective leaders will also be able to adjust to the needs of the team, as we'll discuss more in the chapters on leading staff (chapters 7–10).

Most of the time, we cannot discover our blind spots without the help of others. It's often very difficult for leaders to gain self-knowledge because their followers may tell them what they *want* to hear, rather than what they *need* to hear. If the leader doesn't probe, then the leader may think that he or she knows when he or she doesn't.

Phil Holthouse, founder and managing partner of the top-100 multioffice firm Holthouse, Carlin & Van Trigt LLP in Los Angeles, CA, agrees. "It's particularly tough for somebody leading a firm or a team to get real, honest, constructive feedback. I think no matter how open you try to make yourself, because you're the boss, people are reluctant to critique you, and I think you can end up in a little bit of a bubble."

Gordon Krater, managing partner of the megaregional firm Plante & Moran, PLLC, in Southfield, MI, says

> I think knowing yourself is really important because there is a tendency for people to tell you what you want to hear. I saw it with others, and I experienced it myself. I think some of this is unintentional. I think it's just people trying to curry favor. It's just how human interaction can be. I insisted our management team go through the psychological testing we offer our clients because I wanted to understand myself and understand what we might be missing as a team.
>
> I think you can be deluded into believing your "press clippings." If you really don't know yourself, you are going to lose credibility with the people you are trying to lead. You really have to know yourself because they know you. If your perception is markedly different from others' perception of reality, then you have a problem.

In most cases, we are born with similar brainpower and the ability to grow into higher beings. As we mature, our self-esteem gets damaged, mainly due to misinformation from those around us, resulting in a lack of self-knowledge. The damage is subtle and keeps piling up, but it can destroy our motivation for self-development.

Keith Farlinger, CEO of the national firm BDO Canada LLP in Toronto, Canada, shares, "Self-awareness is critical to developing as a leader. We have a psychologist who works with our senior managers to help them develop skills to be a partner. So he suggested that we put partners through that same 360-degree process. It's very, very enlightening. If you understand how other people see you, it's a very powerful tool to help you change and adapt."

He learned a great deal about how others perceive him, and it has made a difference in the way he leads his firm, Keith says.

> The biggest blind spot that I found is that a lot of the people see me as not all that open, which is kind of strange because I feel like I'm very open. Many times, the strategy is ongoing in my head, and I'm thinking about what I'm going to deal with next. I might walk down the hall thinking I want to have this strategic discussion with someone, and I kind of ignore other people. Along the way, I need to slow down a little bit and interact more with other people who I walk by on a daily basis.

It can be difficult to get staff members to give honest feedback, Keith says, but it is very valuable for individuals and the organization.

> We have partners who believe the staff love them, and they're doing a fantastic job. When we do staff surveys, we find out totally the opposite. Some staff members interpret what the partner is doing as very negative, and we lose good people. So we need to understand ourselves. It's very difficult because most people don't want to be honest with you. They don't want to tell you how they see you, so you just go on and on not knowing yourself and not knowing how people see you.

Tony Argiz, founder, CEO, and managing partner of the megaregional firm Morrison, Brown, Argiz & Farra, LLP, in Miami, FL, shares, "When I first took over the firm in 1997, I lost about 40 percent of my partners in a matter of 12 months. I was too driven and too demanding, so I had to change. Great people are not going to work very long for a dictator. I learned to be careful in the way that I communicated with people."

The Value of Self-Knowledge

I didn't start reaching my potential in life until I was nearly 50 years old and discovered the pursuit of self-knowledge. I learned that many of the coping mechanisms I learned as a child were not as effective in adulthood. Psychologist Bill Plotkin describes these coping strategies as loyal soldiers. The strategies were helpful to you when you were young. Much like a soldier is loyal to his brethren, you become loyal to these childish coping mechanisms. They helped us cope with big, scary people when we were children, and we've remained loyal to them for many years. In developing greater self-understanding, you must recognize your strengths and weaknesses. Most businesspeople love to talk about their strengths, but don't like to admit that they have weaknesses.

Jim Metzler, vice president of the AICPA, says

> I'm not going to give you any names, but many of us in public accounting are very analytical—some say anal—in which we see things like a spreadsheet. Oftentimes, our own analytical skills overtake our ability to really listen, hear, value, and respect the opinions of others. I have seen many leaders trapped in that typical analytic behavior, which is critically important for accounting and tax.
>
> Through knowledge of self, 360s, and leadership coaching, people get that painful yet important feedback from others. I've seen some great changes come from understanding oneself. I've seen those analytical skills couple together with listening and consideration skills really make 1+1=10.

Ted Mason, president and CEO of the top-100 firm Laporte Sehrt Romig Hand in New Orleans, LA, shares

> Trying to understand what makes myself tick actually started when I was working at a bank. When they were considering moving the internal audit function to the CFO position, I was part of that evaluation process. I was subjected to a psychological evaluation over a two-day period. The result of the evaluation did not surprise. I was aware of my tendency, but it was amazing to me how accurate that information was. To give you an example, I was hard

on people; I used to throw hand grenades at partner meetings just for the sake of sport! I was a high-performing line partner and sort of a renegade. I didn't want to follow policies; I didn't want to follow procedures; I just wanted to be evaluated on results. Having that attitude, it was easy for me to throw hand grenades, which given what I understand today, some 15 years later, was just an absolutely horrible trait.

One of the first things I recognized when I became managing partner was that my style as a line partner and the director of the audit practice was not going to serve me well. I will tell you I had to have some very serious discussions with some of the other partners. There was a huge concern as to how I would handle the role. Sure, I could demand things, but ultimately, people would never buy in, and so we would ultimately never end up being able to achieve the objectives.

So, I got started with the 360 process myself, then our partner group went through it, and then we implemented the 360 through our entire organization. I have monthly one-to-one coaching with my mentor, where we go through the critical strategic things that we are dealing with. This helps crystallize my thinking.

Jim Metzler says

The thing that I look for first in a high-potential young leader is an emotional maturity to be able to seek feedback from others and make changes to be more effective. They must have an ability to connect with others through relationship skills. The way they make themselves vulnerable, disclose even the weaknesses about themselves, is a connection. I think connection skills are gigantic, and leaders must understand themselves to succeed.

Characteristics of Good Leaders

The first step on the road to achievement is being honest with yourself about yourself. Each of us can achieve more than we have achieved to date by constantly examining our actions and beliefs. The world that we live in changes constantly, but many people are so inflexible in their thinking that they fail to change with the environment. These people get left behind in every aspect of life.

Debbie Lambert, managing partner of the top-100 multioffice firm Johnson Lambert & Co. LLP, in Raleigh, NC, says

As I have learned more about leadership, one of the things I've changed is that I'm less directive. When I first became a leader, I tended to tell people what they ought to do. And now, if I'm talking to somebody who's an office lead, I'm much more collaborative. I sit down, and I hear them describe what's going on. I go in with an agenda. But clearly listening to their perception of something is information I need first. And then I listen to where they think they're going with it. Often, things turn out differently than I would have come up with on my own. And it's usually better.

I know people in their 80s who are young, flexible, and enjoying a successful life. I also know people in their 20s who are so inflexible that they are almost brain dead. Self-knowledge will teach you how you are holding yourself back. When you feel negative, you must work to change your attitude. Negativity is a disease that blocks your progress in life.

When Christ expounded the theory of forgiveness, he was speaking about a model for life. If you cannot forgive, you become bitter; bitterness breeds negativity, and negativity is the language of failure.

Self-knowledge is the key to high achievement. Rich Caturano, managing director of RSM McGladrey, Inc., in Boston, MA, says

I have been through all the testing. I have had a personal coach for 7 years. He knows my personality, but he never tells me to do anything; he just gets me to tell myself what the answer is. When I was tested, one of the interesting things that I found out is that I am an introvert. And when I looked at what my goals were in life, I had to realize that introversion was not my path to success. Now, I am able to get up in front of 1,000 people and not be nervous. It doesn't bother me at all. Natural introversion is my blind spot, and I have to be aware of it all the time.

Even small habits can make a big impact, Rich says. "Through understanding myself better, I also learned I had the bad habit of saying, 'to tell you the truth' when I started a sentence. It was just a habit and a throwaway figure of speech. But then a client asked me, 'So, part of the time, you don't tell the truth?'"

The best leaders are lifelong learners about themselves: why they think the way they think, and why they act the way they act. Self-knowledge is the most powerful learning one can gain. When the leader is a lifelong learner, others in the organization will be inspired to learn and grow, as well. The most effective leaders are those who realize it's what you learn *after* you know it all—after you rise to the top of your profession—that counts most!

Leader Profile: Charles Weinstein, CEO of the megaregional firm EisnerAmper LLP in New York City, NY

From the age of 6, Charly Weinstein instinctively knew that he wanted to be an accountant. No one in his family had ever worn a suit to work, and he knew nothing about the world of accounting, but somehow, he selected accounting and stayed on that course throughout his young life. Charly had a metamorphosis during his freshman year. "Not having traveled, not having been exposed to the business world, and not having been exposed to people, going away to school was an eye opener for me," Charly says. "At first, I didn't accept the concept of responsibility. I had a lot of fun. That very first semester I took a look at the work product that I turned out and realized that if I was going to be successful at anything, I had to work a lot harder." The self-knowledge and discipline that followed were precursors for his amazing leadership career in public accounting.

At age 19, Charly was a young magna cum laude graduate of the State University of New York at Binghamton, where he received his B.S. degree in accounting, and he interviewed with all the major accounting firms. He had never been around the business world. His mother bought him a wide-lapel, brown, pinstriped suit with an orange shirt and a very bright tie for his interviews. He now calls the get-up his "gansta" suit. Needless to say, his interviewing was very frustrating, and he received no offers. So, he took matters into his own hands by sending out resumes to firms that were advertising in the *New York Times*, and he landed a job with Maxwell Shmerler & Company.

Founding partner Richard A. Eisner says

Charly saw us with greater potential as we began our discussions with Amper regarding a possible combination. There was a great deal of skepticism, but he convinced the whole Executive Committee that merging was a once-in-a-lifetime opportunity. Everyone voted for it with great enthusiasm. I think right away something as simple as instead of being rated number 9 or 10 or whatever we were in New York, we're now after the Big Four; we're the largest firm in the city, and I think that's Charly's vision. Charly felt that we would be a much stronger factor in the market if he positioned us that way. I think that was all Charly.

When Charly came to the firm, I knew right away that this was a person of great integrity, and to me, that's the most important attribute of any leader. Charly had been with a firm that was approximately our size at the time. He had just been elected a partner when one of the Big Four firms took them over. They told Charly that he would have to earn partnership at the new firm. Charly then came to us, and we told him we would take him on as a manager, with the understanding that he would be a partner very quickly if he performed. We shook hands with Charly, no written contract. When the Big Four firm heard that Charly was going to leave, they changed their mind and said, "We'll make you a partner right away." Charly, without having spoken to us or anything at all, told them, "I agreed. I gave my word to Eisner, and that's it. I'm going with them." We knew right away we had someone with tremendous integrity.

It looked like a chance of a lifetime to be a partner, but he'd given us his word, and that was it.

In the beginning, Charly rose rapidly with us and was elected to our executive committee. In the early years on the executive committee, I found Charly was looking at everything from a dollars and sense point of view, like an accountant. Then, I saw Charly grow and change. You could see Charly start to make decisions that were more reflective of everything that was going on, not just the numbers.

Perhaps the one that may be the most successful is one we spun off where the CEO insisted on having Charly on his board after he spun it off. That's just the respect he had for Charly, and he knew Charly very well, and Charly now works with him. He's probably his most important advisor, and that business has grown beautifully. Charly has been enormously successful in molding that business.

Charly has been a real leader in the nonaccounting-related businesses we've built. He is the most important advisor of Velocity, a business we built and spun off.

He's a great role model to everyone in the firm. There's nothing that Charly won't get involved with. He's not too proud or not too high up to do anything. Anyone needs help in the office, Charly is there, very compassionate with people, worries about people.

Today, Charles Weinstein, CPA, is the CEO and a member of the executive committee of EisnerAmper LLP. Prior to the formation of EisnerAmper LLP, he was managing partner of Eisner LLP.

Charly has more than 25 years of audit, merger and acquisition, public and private financing, and industry consolidation experience, with a particular focus on Securities

(continued)

(continued)

and Exchange Commission reporting and compliance issues. He has served companies in a variety of industry sectors, including technology, pharmaceuticals and health sciences, manufacturing and distribution, and travel.

EisnerAmper LLP partner Rob Levine shares

Charly's leading strategy is highly effective because his core values are so positive, and he is always true to them. Underlying his vision and mission is one principal; he expects everyone at the firm in every situation to always "do the right thing."

It is inspiring to follow a leader that sets such a tone at the top and regularly reinforces it through his actions. His leadership has been invaluable over the years in working through challenging client matters as an audit partner and in developing our talented professionals as the leader of EisnerAmper University.

Charly was named 2007 Accountant of the Year by the Association for Corporate Growth. He is also the author of *Establishing a Financial Framework For Your Company*, published by Aspatore Books. He is a frequent speaker before professional audiences and was a member of the faculty for The Learning Annex, where he taught a course on accounting. He is an active member of the AICPA, where he serves on the board of directors, and has served as the chair of the Professional and Personal Liability Insurance Program Committee and on the Nominating Committee. Charly is a member of the boards of the Andrea J. Will Memorial Foundation; the Legal Aid Society of New York; and Velocity Technology Solutions, Inc.

The Crisis of Success

When times are great, business leaders and owners are often lulled to sleep by a malady that I've termed "a crisis of success." That simply means that during good times, owners become complacent, arrogant, and greedy. I'm sure there are other results of the good times, but the great leaders focus to avoid being sucked in by the downside.

Another symptom of this crisis is arrogance. When profits are at all-time highs, and clients are standing at the door begging to be served, some accountants develop an extremely overblown sense of self-worth. These business leaders appear on podiums and talk about how "I" did this or that. But just as the best leaders give credit to others, here they tell everyone that the reason we are in this up cycle is not something we've done. They are saying things like, "It's the new legislation," or "We didn't do this, and we are planning for the next downturn."

Greed shows its ugly head in the compensation plans that partners use to distribute all the money that is being made. Another subtle way that greed manifests itself is through the endless 2,500-work-hour years posing as diligence. Partners' pay plans zoom out of control.

When the economy is in an up cycle, or Congress has passed one of those laws that puts millions of accountants to work (like the Sarbanes-Oxley Act of 2002), many partners forget about the inevitable busts that come along every so often. While some partners are celebrating the good results of their firm, the effective leader is in the background thinking about how to prepare for the next *down* business cycle.

It is during the good times that accounting firms have available funds to invest in planning, training, reserves, building infrastructure, upgrading the IT systems, building a brand, building strong relationships with clients, and preparing for the downturn that will come. Unfortunately, over the last 20 years of consulting with firms, I've not seen one business plan that anticipated a down cycle.

"You can do your best work as a leader in the good economic times because you lay a solid foundation. It doesn't get recognized until the bad times," says Steve Mayer, founder, chairman, and CEO of the regional firm Burr, Pilger & Mayer LLP in San Francisco, CA.

> In the bad times, you have to make the toughest decisions, and I think that's where you have to steady the course. I think that the true leaders did phenomenal things in the worst possible circumstances. In the difficult times, you have to focus people on the good times ahead. Some of the most accomplished people fell on their butts and did nothing in the worst times. They were so used to winning that they never knew what losing was about. You know, even though we've grown, the last two years at our firm have been terribly trying in the sense of trying to motivate people: getting partners to agree to invest in the future in what I call R&D. We've brought on, I think, six or seven partners—hired direct partners—over the last two years and explained to everybody that this is an investment; this is going to help us in the future. And I think our firm right now is poised to do great things.

It can be hard to focus on preparation for the worst when times seem good, Mayer says.

> One of the most difficult tasks is to keep your key partners from becoming complacent during the great times. One of the things I've learned is that the partners who attracted a lot of work during the good times gave it to other people and then went out and picked up some more work; they're doing great now because they're in shape to do that. But the partners who just held on to their clients, they're not refreshed, and they don't know how to attract work and delegate it.
>
> There's a lifecycle for a client. Let's say you keep clients for an average of five years—just as a theoretical concept. If you have your same clients for five years, and you do nothing, at the end of five years, you're going to have less business. But if you take those same clients, and every year, you give a couple to somebody else, so they get refreshed, and they get a five-year term going, and then you go out and get some new ones, you're always going to be fairly busy. But people who hoard work lose business during the down times.

Building Leadership Ability for Better Effectiveness

Leadership determines a firm's effectiveness, and leadership ability determines a person's level of effectiveness. John Maxwell refers to the leadership lid. He says that a leader whose leadership ability is a 4 (on a scale of 1–10) will not attract anyone to his firm higher than a 3. What is your level of leadership ability? If you want to raise your entire organization or team, raise your own ability, and the total effectiveness of your team will also rise.

Though many of us would like to think otherwise, Maxwell says you can only improve so much through dedication and hard work. Accountants are hard workers. Do you fall into that category? If you are a 9 in the hard work department, there isn't much improvement you can make in the effectiveness of your team by working harder. You must improve your leadership ability.

The higher you want to climb in your team and firm, the more leadership ability you will need. Becoming the best businessperson you can be is complicated. You probably have a busy life filled with work, family, social life, and other activities. It's difficult to find time to do everything. By understanding yourself, you'll know what you need to work on to be efficient and focused in your efforts.

Commit to the Process

In Malcolm Gladwell's book, *Outliers: The Story of Success*, Gladwell theorized that if you invest 10,000 hours in something, you will master it. When accountants complete approximately 7 years of audit, tax, or consulting experience, they have achieved approximately 10,000 hours of billable time. Why, then, do we think we can simply read a book, take a class, or watch someone else lead in order for us to learn to lead?

The question is, Do you want to *know* about leadership, or do you want to *learn to lead*? If you want to learn to really lead, you will set yourself on a path to invest 10,000 hours in learning and leading over the next 5–10 years. Perhaps you've already begun the process. If so, then keep at learning to lead and attracting clients to your firm. (Don't get me wrong, you can develop habits, such as listening, reinforcing people more, or getting 360 feedback, that can quickly help your leadership, as well.)

Rick Dreher, CEO of the megaregional firm Wipfli LLP in Green Bay, WS, pushes partners and their staff to find and nurture the area of the business where they are strongest.

> My first 100 days as managing partner, I went out and sat with every one of our partners. The most important question I asked them was "Where's your passion? Don't tell me what you have to do when you walk through the front door on a daily basis; tell me what you want to do. Where's your passion?"
>
> I explained to our partners, the goal was a mindset: if I can find your passion, you will work, and you will never tire; you will work relentlessly; you will work with blinders on. You're happy and fulfilled. And you think that's not contagious in our hallways?

Opening Up for Growth

Nobody likes to admit, much less focus on, their weaknesses. Yet, when you gain self-knowledge—both appreciating your strengths and confronting your weaknesses—you are opening up new possibilities for growth and advancement in your career. So, be receptive to self-knowledge. Rather than being uncomfortable with facing your weaknesses, be willing to consider the information in a positive and constructive way. When weaknesses are identified, it doesn't mean that you're incapable of performing well. It may be that you haven't had to use these skills in your current position, or you've been able to hide them with your strengths. Self-knowledge gives you the power to makes changes in those weaknesses. It will enable you to understand your strengths and weaknesses and plot a course to maximally leverage both to achieve your goals.

If you want to know your strengths and weaknesses in material areas of your work (for example, preparing corporate financials), they are usually quite evident on paper (or monitor). However, the psychological, leadership, and social aspects of the business world are neither tangible nor easily measured. Self-knowledge is required to discern our needs in this realm.

Ray Strothman, managing partner of the local firm Strothman & Company, PSC, in Louisville, KY, says, "When we did a 360-degree employee survey, I learned some things about myself that I didn't know. I had a tendency to put off the things that were difficult to do. I would delay calling back a client until I had the full answer. It's easy to put it off."

Ken Baggett, co-managing partner of the national firm CohnReznick LLP, says that he has learned a great deal about himself through his firm's formal self-development program, including both personal strengths and weaknesses in his work habits and communication style. "Not everyone has my drive. Not everyone has my initiative," he says. "I love people. I have always been a people person. And when you enjoy others, it's sometimes hard to deliver that direct, straight, tough message.

I tend to forget I spend a lot of time and energy thinking on a subject before bringing it up to my partners. For others, when I bring up an item, this may be the first moment they've ever been introduced to the idea. In my impatience, I want them to catch up quickly, and I have to sometimes take that deep breath and say, "Okay guys, what don't you know?" I'll review things thoroughly and give people time to process.

They're required to go through a pretty extensive psychological evaluation and self-awareness and a structure. It is a very detailed 360 assessment where you pick a boss, 3 peers, and 4 subordinates. Everyone answers 70–80 different questions on you to really kind of assess your strengths, your weaknesses, your style, your personality—things of that nature. You also then do a self-assessment.

You then spend a full day in Ann Arbor in Dr. Joe's office. You usually get there the evening before; you start about 8:30 AM, and you go on till about 5:00 PM. And at the end of that day, you have covered your life. He doesn't start out with reviewing the report with you. He starts out like if you are in any other psychologist's office. He starts out with a blank piece of paper and says, "So, tell me about how it was growing up."

You walk out of there with probably four or five action plans. You're required to go back to your entire 360 group, collectively, and say to them, "Here is what I have learned; here is what I'm going to work on, and I'd like you to help me be held accountable to those changes."

Sometimes, how you act around your peers or your boss is much different than how you react to the people who work for you. There is a natural instinct to that, obviously. So, I think there is a lot more insight that comes out of the people below you than there is above you.

Build on Strengths or Improve Your Weaknesses?

Terry Harris, managing partner of McKonly & Asbury LLP in Harrisburg, PA, says

> I am a big fan of a strength-based organization and strength-based leadership. One of the most influential books that I have read was Marcus Buckingham's book *First, Break All The Rules*. To this day, it is required reading for our team. From that book and successor books from the Gallup organization on strengths, we developed a culture that focused on individual self-awareness, with each person discovering their strengths. Each member of our team takes the StrengthFinder 2.0 assessment, and that is shared among all team members. It is part of how each team member approaches their individual goals in the performance evaluation process. We fundamentally agree with Buckingham's premise that greater growth will be achieved by focusing on strengths rather than on weaknesses. Having said that, we also believe that it is a mistake to ignore any work on weaknesses.
>
> As part of my own journey of self-awareness, several tools have been helpful. First, the StrengthFinder assessment has given me insight into my natural talents, which for me are primarily relational. Some other tools that have helped me understand my leadership style, communication style, and decision-making process are the Myers-Briggs, FIRO-B assessment tools, and the Team Dimensions Profile.

I believe more in dealing with both. I believe that the "focus on your strengths" model will actually limit your climb up the leadership ladder. Buckingham himself worked hard to improve a weakness. When he was young, he had a serious speech impediment. He worked hard at overcoming this serious weakness and has turned this weakness into a great strength because he is a very effective public speaker.

Most businesspeople think that they're as good as their greatest strengths. For example, an audit manager may believe that her financial and analytic capabilities will enable her to one day become an audit partner. The truth is, however, that you are only as good as your biggest weakness. If the audit manager lacks leadership and communication skills, her specialized abilities will only take her so far.

Improving your strengths has a ceiling effect. If you work really hard to improve yourself, you can only get so much better. But you will get more bang for your buck when you focus on improving your weaknesses.

Think of business strengths and weaknesses as a mathematical equation. If you are an 8 at tax planning, but you are below average at communicating with clients (say a 4), then your overall performance would be moderate (12 out of a possible 20). If you focus on and improve your tax planning capabilities (say, from 8 to 9), you wouldn't improve significantly overall because you were already a capable tax planner (9+4=13). But if you improve your client communication abilities (say, from 4 to 7), then your overall performance would rise significantly (8+7=15). The more you improve your weaknesses, the better you'll be able to function as a leader, and the more prepared you'll be for advancement toward ownership in your firm.

Phil Holthouse agrees that improving a weakness can make a big difference in your effectiveness.

> I think most of the people of my generation are not terrifically current on technology and not as facile with it as the 23-year-olds that are coming out of college. I think it's a mistake if people in our positions within the firm don't force themselves to try to get decent at that stuff, even if we're never going to be as good at it as somebody who really grew up with a cell phone in their hand.

Internal performance reviews, like 360-reviews, are critical as well, Holthouse says.

> If you had a client that wasn't thrilled with your services, would you want to know? Absolutely you'd want to know, so you could try to fix it. And if your management style isn't going over real well, wouldn't you want to know? You can use 360 reviews as a launching pad for a constructive conversation about specific things you could do to improve in those areas. So, shift the dialog from, "My score was low," to, "How could we collectively do better in this area?"

Experience Matters

Do people ever know enough about themselves to determine the direction of their career journey? Historical self-knowledge—understanding the past experiences and influences that led to one's current level of development—is a key to shaping the future. Ask any first-time job seekers the main reason why employers rejected them, and they will tell you, "Lack of experience." Though this may seem unfair to the student who has worked hard in school, it should not be a surprise that employers value experienced workers. Experience is integral to knowing and understanding oneself and how one relates to different situations, circumstances, and roles.

Leader Profile: Gordon Krater, managing partner of the megaregional firm Plante & Moran, PLLC, in Southfield, MI

Growing up in Taylor, MI, where only about 10 percent of his classmates attended college, Gordon Krater benefitted greatly from a healthy family life. His dad was an accountant and his mom a nurse in an era when the professions were all about helping and serving. Gordon gravitated toward accounting, but his dreams were to be a coach and teacher. Gordon's father encouraged him to interview with Plante & Moran, by saying, "If there was a firm like Plante Moran when I was in public accounting, I'd probably still be there."

After being courted by all the large international firms, Gordon joined Plante & Moran, in 1980 after graduating from the University of Michigan. Gordon fell in love with the culture at Plante & Moran. He intended to only stay for a few years to gain some experience then move on to something where he could have a leadership role and some equity. His love deepened for the Plante & Moran culture, and he learned that he could have leadership and equity there, so he stayed.

(continued)

(continued)

Plante & Moran, partner Jim Proppe says of Gordon

Gordon is good at setting strategic direction by inviting different, even oppos- ing, points of view to make sure that we are thinking. He does that to make sure we're on top of our game, staying humble, and not drinking our own Kool-Aid all the time. In meetings, if he knows somebody has a different point of view, and if he knows the person is not speaking up, he'll call 'em out and say, "Hey, Charlie, you're being kind of quiet over there. Tell me what you're thinking." You always feel good leaving meetings, and you think, "Okay. My point was heard," or "I was chal- lenged, and I thought about something differently, and here's the decision." And when we all walk out of the room, we're going in the same direction.

Many of us were not supporting a particular candidate for partner, and Gordon brought in some different points of view, and it actually ended up swaying the group the other way. Gordon is always bringing us back to our principles and with the firm's core values.

Tom Doescher says of Gordon

Years ago, Gordon and I were both in the governmental practice. I'm a rookie part- ner in the hottest area of the firm. He's an up-and-comer nonpartner. There were a group of probably five or six guys at the same level as Gordon that were coming up. We were selling like crazy and bringing in clients faster than we could handle them. Someone came up with the idea that I should meet with this group. So, we'd get an agenda together. I would be the only partner in the room, and there'd be half a dozen of them.

We'd have this meeting, and I'd think everything went great. Later, Gordon would come to me and say, "You know, in the meeting we just had, I had some feedback for you. Did you want feedback?" And I said, "Sure." And he said, "You know, I don't think the group agrees with you in this particular initiative, and here's why." Then, he'd explain why and say, "You probably have another point of view, but I wanted you to have all the information. They're just a little afraid of express- ing their points of view. But I just thought you would want to know that."

That scene was a defining moment for our relationship and for the 35 years after that. I can always count on Gordon for giving it to me straight. As life went on, we kind of kid about who's mentoring who now because in his job before managing partner, he was actually my direct supervisor. I lead the manufacturing and distribution practice, and he was the partner in charge of industry groups. So, for about eight years he was my direct supervisor. It's his ability to deliver tough messages in an effective way that I think builds huge trust and has made me a bet- ter partner because of his feedback.

As managing partner, Gordon leads Plante & Moran, in the continued develop- ment of capabilities and processes that anticipate and satisfy client needs.

Gordon has given presentations to public accounting and consulting firms around the country on topics such as "Building a World Class Culture," "Partner Participation Systems," and "Matrix Management in a Professional Services Firm." Gordon says he was blessed with great mentors—Frank Moran, Ken Kunkel, and Bill Hermann—all of whom took a personal interest in seeing him develop not only as an accountant but as a human being.

Building Self-Knowledge

Self-knowledge is simply a matter of understanding yourself and knowing what makes you tick. Each of us is a unique individual, and not one of us is perfect. The first step to achieving what you are capable of is to know yourself and to be aware of all your strengths and weaknesses. The more you understand yourself, the more powerful your self-development.

Self-awareness may in itself be a necessary condition for self-knowledge to be sought after and developed in the first place. It requires a greater level of awareness for a person to become truly self-aware. It is the knowledge of one's self and properties and the *desire* to seek such knowledge that guide the development of the self concept. Self-knowledge informs us of our mental representations of ourselves, which contain attributes that we uniquely pair with ourselves and theories on whether these attributes are stable or dynamic.

True self-knowledge requires a lifelong journey. Sometimes, some extreme events or emotions can reveal new corners of our minds. I believe that it's possible to acquire such knowledge from different sources: from thinking in solitude or from communicating with other people. All the paths to self-knowledge are important to understand ourselves thoroughly.

Self-Knowledge Through Interaction With Others

Leadership requires on-the-spot interaction with people. Communication with other people is a very powerful tool to learn about new emotions, such as love or hate; therefore, it helps to investigate our own characters more completely.

Scott Dietzen, managing partner, Northwest Region, of the national accounting firm CliftonLarsonAllen LLP in Spokane, WA, says his wife pointed out a bad communication habit of his: he would continue to mentally process a disagreement he'd had earlier while he was speaking with someone else.

> In a meeting, it would be so obvious on my face. Sometimes, I would even start to mouth the words [rethinking the earlier conversation], and she would realize what was happening. She would say, "Who are you arguing with?" and I would realize that I had carried over a prior discussion. I was trying to defend my position, and it had so taken over my being that I was letting it influence other relationships. And so I have to be very aware of continuing to process something from a body language standpoint or my facial expressions.

Larry Autrey, managing partner of the top-100 firm Whitley Penn LLP in Ft. Worth, TX, also feels that self-evaluation is critical here, and he is aware of some of his characteristics that his own partners would regard as weaknesses. "I would acknowledge the fact that I may not have all of the details that some other person may when I needed to make a decision. But I went ahead and made a decision without all the facts, and you know, I have some partners who that really bothers," Larry says.

> I think about it, but I've not changed it. I'm okay with making quicker decisions, and a leader must be willing to do that; otherwise, the firm will be gridlocked. I have been more

careful around them and saying it openly as I had done in the past. But I'm not sure I actually changed that trait of mine. I have heard it referred to as making a "Marine decision." My tendency is don't spend three weeks gathering facts. Make a decision with whatever facts you have got in front of you.

The Undeniable Link: Lifelong Self-Learning and Leadership

Gary Confessore, Ed.D, is an adult learning expert, professor emeritus of higher education at George Washington University, and principal and owner at the consulting firm Human Resources Development Enterprises in suburban Washington. The opportunity to apply new self-knowledge on the job is one of the most underrecognized, yet most influential, motivators among adult learners, but Gary says that employers often underestimate its power. "Because the opportunity to use new knowledge on the job is so motivating, unexpected leaders often emerge from the shadows when given practical training opportunities that build their self-awareness," says Gary.

> We usually say, "It's important for you to learn these skills because …." The employer provides the motivation to learn. That approach encourages dependent learners; I provide the motivation for you to learn, and you depend upon a teacher or system to organize learning events.
>
> But that approach doesn't account for the person's motivation in the natural state. Natural motivation is really important. After a lifetime of going through K–12, college, and corporate education, we almost lose the habits and skills of being active learners in which we look at our situation and say, "The world is changing rapidly, but I need to not only stay abreast of the latest skills but ahead of the curve." Instead, people reach a point when they say, "I need to catch up." But if they want to stay ahead of the curve, that support system doesn't exist. Conventional systems take too long to get ahead of the curve.

Firms often mistakenly assume that the professional's motive to learn is job security, advancement, and professional compliance, when, in fact, the opportunity to attain new heights of leadership effectiveness is usually the more powerful motivator.

Because it's practically impossible to identify lifelong self-learners in the hiring process, it's almost impossible to identify who will be a future leader during the hiring process, Gary adds. "There's a disjunction between the behavioral intentions you'd seek and the likelihood that you'll discover them before hiring," he says.

> Don't try to find out if they're leaders beforehand. Hire them and see their strengths. Accounting firm executives understand that you have to provide CPE, that you can't just get an accounting degree and say, "You're trained forever." But the parallel they have to ask is, "Is this individual likely to be a lifelong learner who takes advantage of the opportunities we present them?" It's not just a matter of training but the intentions of the participants.

Other research shows that leaders of successful professional services firms perceive themselves as lifelong learners. For example, a 2004 study of CEOs at large American real estate companies found that self-identification as a lifelong learner was the number one common theme to which they attributed their success. The CEOs recognized that their job success requires a dedication to being a lifelong learner because continuous learning enables them to deal with the ongoing challenges in business. They also collectively believed that taking advantage of opportunities for continuous learning was one of the most important reasons that they were successful in business. They used phrases such as "learning faster than competitors" and "being a quick study" to express concepts that made them love their profession. Participants in the study agreed that with the development of new technologies, new laws, and constant restructuring of companies, they must continue to adapt and learn in order to remain successful. They actively sought robust training programs to obtain and develop new skills.

Another common characteristic was their shared appreciation for expertise, both in themselves and others. Participants in the study agreed that the accumulation of knowledge through experience and practice enabled them to become experts in the real estate business. They actively sought opportunities to continue learning from professionals in other fields.

Self-Knowledge for a Fulfilled Life

Bob Hottman, CEO of the top-100 firm Ehrhardt Keefe Steiner & Hottman PC (EKS&H) in Denver, CO, believes

> Self-renewal is about recognizing you need a good work-life success. You need to be successful at home, as well as at work. If it's all about work and never about your home life, you're not going be a balanced individual, and you're not going to do your family any good.
>
> Any time somebody has any kind of family issues that are significant, the first thing we do is we step in and let them know that the most important thing to them right now is the family. We'll take care of all their other needs with the clients and everything else, but it's important that they get that figured out, and we'll work with them to do that. When they see our support, their commitment back to the firm is exponential.

Hugh Parker, executive partner of the regional firm Horne LLP in Jackson, MS, says

> When I was about 18 years old, I was engaged in some bad behavior, not unlike any teenager. My granddad said, "You know son, when you make a decision, you need to be sure that that's a decision you can sleep with when you go to bed tonight." In other words, he was telling me that my actions should integrate with my sense of what is right or wrong.
>
> I've recently experienced an "aha" moment, where one of my direct report team members came in during a normal meeting and moved into a discussion about how he was looking at life and his direction. He said that one of the things he might consider was leaving the firm. For me that was an "aha" moment about our culture and the level of trust that person had in me. He was able to tell me that it was just something he was exploring. For me, it was a huge moment in that it really demonstrated the value of respecting people.
>
> One of the major difficulties in leading an accounting firm is we have trouble in separating our roles. The owners of an accounting firm have trouble in separating the roles from that of the owner and that of one who provides services to clients.

Do you have your share of leadership awareness? If the answer is no, then you may not be achieving your potential and have given somebody else your share. Start looking at your own self-development and asking some pertinent questions. You must take responsibility for your own path in life.

The only thing stopping you from reaching your full potential is self-knowledge: knowing what makes you tick and divining the direction you will go.

Ted Mason shares

> One of things that I discovered in my self-assessment was that I have a tendency to not be in the moment and not be focused on the issue at hand. So now, I work very hard to discipline myself to do be in the moment in every meeting. I put a couch, chair, and coffee table in my office. Whenever there is an issue somebody comes in they want to talk about, I make it a point to get out from behind my desk, and we discuss the issue in more of a living-room-type setting. That's one of those self-triggering mechanisms that forces me to be disciplined and stay in the moment and truly focus on the conversation at hand.

Conclusion

Studies show that people who lead happy and successful lives make full use of their talents and strengths. Most of us are so preoccupied with our busy routines that we operate on autopilot. We often don't know why we do what we do because we are driven by unrecognized impulses, preoccupations, and emotions.

Human beings are complex creatures, often wonderful, but sometimes perverse and sometimes destructive. Along with all our good qualities, there is a dark side to the human make-up. Though each of us is unique, we all share certain basic characteristics that have evolved with us and become hardwired (such as egotism, aggression, competitiveness, and tribalism). Knowing what these are can help us control them in ourselves and predict or forgive them in others.

It is not possible for individuals to meet all of their own needs. To develop our individual potential, we need close, supportive relationships. The greatest pleasure comes from our association with other people. We need each other, but we also can confuse, disappoint, and hurt each other.

To reach our potential, we need to develop such things as maturity, motivation, serenity, self-esteem, healthy boundaries, clear thinking, creativity, autonomy, and much more. As a leader, you have a great opportunity to help yourself and those around you develop fuller lives as more complete people.

Trust: The Leadership Imperative

"To thine ownself be true; … thou canst not then be false to any man."

~ POLONIUS ADVISES HIS SON IN *HAMLET* BY SHAKESPEARE

What makes a great leader? In most cases, people say trustworthiness.

The CPA has long been the United States's most trusted business adviser, but inside many of the best accounting firms, there is rampant mistrust of each other. We can attribute the mistrust to the backgrounds of the staff members who've lived or worked in low-trust environments, the skepticism that we teach and encourage, or the actions of people in leader roles. Trust can be selective. For example, you can trust me to accurately prepare your tax return, but you may not trust me to compensate you fairly. Trust can permeate our relationship. Mutual trust is a shared belief that you can depend on each other to achieve a common purpose. Businesses, teams, and accounting firms operate more effectively when there is a high-level of trust among all the staff members. Yet, we see a severe lack of trust across departments, generations, genders, and various levels of staff. It is the leader's primary role to model the development of trust.

In this chapter, we will explore the hard economics, as well as the social desirability, of building trust. I'll cover the elements of being a trustworthy person, such as integrity, intent, competence, and results. We'll delve into building organizational trust and how to rebuild lost trust.

A culture of trust in your firm can become a major competitive advantage. Trust allows your firm to both function and serve your clients better. Trust is rare; few companies truly have a trusting relationship between leaders and employees. Trust is a capability that is difficult for your competitors to observe and imitate.

In his book, *The SPEED of Trust: The One Thing That Changes Everything*, Stephen M.R. Covey explains that low-trust companies pay a trust tax, and high-trust organizations reap a trust dividend. Covey explains that trust is not just a socially desirable element to one's business. Covey says, "Once you understand the hard, measurable economics of trust, it's like putting on a new pair of glasses. Everywhere you look you can see the impact."

Neal Spencer, former CEO of the megaregional firm BKD, LLP, in Springfield, MO, says

> The first and foremost quality to be a leader in any situation is trust. If people don't trust
> you, they will not follow. Second, you've got to be there for them. Early in my career, I
> witnessed what I would call some pathetic leadership where a senior or a supervisor would
> make his people work on Saturday but *he* wouldn't come in! Third is just brutal honesty in
> all situations. Here at BKD, we call it "putting the moose on the table."

Stephen Covey's concept of the emotional bank account draws a word picture of trust. He urges people to make deposits of their own trustworthy actions. This series of deposits typically keeps our accounts in the black, so that if a withdrawal occurs (some breach of trust we commit), an apology and a solution to the problem ensures the continued success of the relationship. But one act of withdrawal may require 100 acts of deposit in order to balance the account.

Terry Harris, managing partner of McKonly & Asbury LLP in Harrisburg, PA, believes

> Trust is the core component of a successful organization. With trust comes alignment, and
> with alignment comes a team that all rows in the same direction, resulting in enthusiasm as
> the team succeeds. Trust is something that is earned over time, with decisions that are con-
> sistently focused on what is best for the organization and not for any one individual. Trust is

also built by having a culture of mutual respect for individuals within the organization at all levels. It is aided by transparency of the firm leadership. Open communication and dialogue on issues within the team enhances trust.

If I were to describe a person of integrity, it would be a person that keeps his word. When leaders fail to keep their word, trust is eroded. Trust, much like a good reputation, takes a long time to develop but only a very short time to lose. Honesty over time is the only way to repair trust when it is lost. When mistakes happen or errors in judgment are made that erode trust, an apology from a leader goes a long way toward the reestablishment of trust.

Trust Is a Competitive Advantage Inside and Out

Building relationships requires building trust. Trust is the expectancy of people that they can rely on your word. It is built through intent, integrity, competency, and consistency modeled by the leader. If a leader loves people but has no vision, then everyone will be lost without direction. If a leader is a great systems organizer but isn't honest, people will be hesitant to support any changes.

Lots of research evidence exists about the value of trust. Tony Simons's study, "The High Cost of Lost Trust," published in the September 2002 issue of the *Harvard Business Review*, focused on pinpointing the real cost associated with low-trust environments. The study surveyed 6,500 Holiday Inn employees in 76 international hotel sites to examine the alignment between managers' words and actual performance. The responses demonstrated that the hotels where managers followed through on promises and had behavioral integrity were more profitable. In fact, on a 5-point scale, a ⅛-point improvement should result in a 2.5 percent increase in hotel revenues.

Dr. Simons attributes hotel managers' lack of behavioral integrity to various blind spots, such as their failure to identify integrity problems within themselves. Simons discovered in his research that it takes evidence of only one lie for a manager to be branded a liar. In contrast, a person has to tell a whole lot of truth to qualify as a "straight shooter."

According to Stephen M.R. Covey in his book *The SPEED of Trust: The One Thing That Changes Everything*

> [i]n a Watson Wyatt 2002 study, high trust organizations outperformed low trust organizations in total return to shareholders (stock price plus dividends) by 286%. Additionally, according to a 2005 study by Russell Investment Group, *Fortune* magazine's "100 Best Companies to Work for in America" (in which trust comprises 60 percent of the criteria), earned over four times the returns of the broader market over the prior seven years.

Trust can be an important source of your competitive advantage because trust is valuable and rare. The level of trust that a firm's leader is able to garner from his or her staff is contingent upon the employees' perceptions of the leader's ability, intent, and integrity.

Bob Hottman, CEO of the top-100 firm Ehrhardt Keefe Steiner & Hottman PC (EKS&H) in Denver, CO, believes,

The purpose of business is to build trust and serve others. There's no question in my mind that if we can build trust within our organization, we can build trust with our clients. If we serve them the way we should serve them, we will continue to grow as an organization. We have a fairly large nonprofit practice. Our people get a lot of pleasure out of serving with those organizations because they can see the tangible results of what they're doing in the community. At the end of the day, we can sit there and say we helped that company be successful, we helped that business owner, we helped that CEO, and we helped that CFO be successful.

If you think about the four pillars of trust—integrity, intent, capabilities, and results—a lot of people will question the intent of the person who is a great talker: that interesting extrovert. Capabilities and results go hand in hand, and integrity and intent go hand in hand. Integrity and intent are at the core of trust, but in our business, you must also have the capabilities to get results.

You need to sleep at night with a sense of integrity, and you need to look at yourself in the mirror every morning. What you stand for is important, and that's what people look to you for in the long run. People can make mistakes, and people *will* make mistakes. We're human beings. But if you do what you think is right, and you do it for the right reasons, people will always respect you.

Trust is one of the most significant competitive advantages for an accounting firm. You recruit great people. They trust. They retain. They attract clients. You'll have huge turnover in your team members and clients if you don't have trust.

As Bob explained, trust is persuasive and inspirational to others. When employees work in a high-trust accounting firm, they bring the trust home to their families and encourage trust building. When an accounting firm team exudes trust, clients and other accounting firms want to emulate the culture. The friction that gets pushed out of the organizational system is palpable.

Leader Profile: **Scott Dietzen, Managing Partner, Northwest Region, of the national accounting firm Clifton-LarsonAllen LLP in Spokane, WA**

Scott Dietzen learned leadership from coaching basketball and baseball and teaching Sunday school. Scott learned to temper his hard-driving approach into a more inspiring and personalized approach when coaching and leading his teams. He uses these skills today in leading his 28 partners and 300 staff members in 12 offices.

Scott believes that coaching sports or teaching classes is great training for future leaders in his firm, and he encourages his developing staff members to do the same as they progress through the leadership ranks in his firm. Scott's first college degree is in agricultural economics. Having grown up in an agricultural community, he applies many of the principles of farming to growing and leading an accounting firm.

Rick Honsowetz tells about Scott Dietzen's early years

Scott had only been with LeMaster Daniels a few years and was progressing nicely. Scott had actually tried other careers (banking, insurance, and landscaping) before he decided on public accounting. Scott had a growing family and was feeling some of the financial pinch that we all feel early in our careers when we are trying to establish ourselves in our profession and, at the same time, devote ourselves to our families.

Scott received a job offer from a local medical clinic, which included a substantial raise from the salary he was making with us, and it would not have required those long tax-season hours. His wife was encouraging him to consider the offer, and he came to me to discuss his options. Scott was very transparent in sharing with me the details of his job offer and his thoughts and feelings as he considered his options.

Scott never demanded that we match or beat the offer—he was honestly seeking counsel as he approached his decision. I told Scott then that I saw real promise in him for success in public accounting. He had technical skills, but more importantly, his relational skills, integrity, work ethic, confidence, and wisdom were attributes that I told him would serve him well in our profession. I told him that I believed he had what it takes to become a partner with LeMaster Daniels and that if he did, he would soon be paying more in income tax than the total salary offer from that clinic. I cautioned that there were no guarantees and that much depended on him and his performance, but I cautioned him to not be too short-term in making this decision.

He decided to forego the offer and the immediate benefit that he would have derived. He was invited into the partnership within a few years of that conversation and was elected CEO of the entire firm after just 3 years as a partner—unprecedented in the 100-year history of LD.

I tell this story to young, talented accountants who work for us or to others who are making important decisions because I think it is an example of how to approach important decisions: gather all relevant information, and seek wise counsel. Don't let short-term issues get in the way of the important long-term consequences of the decision. Be willing to "suffer" in the short term for big payoff later—the principal of delayed gratification. Don't use ultimatums or draw lines in the sand to get your way. When you are given an opportunity, take inventory of your skills and talents, develop and implement a plan of self-development, and pursue the goal with passion.

Human resources director Alice Hardin adds

When I started with LeMaster Daniels 13 years ago, I made a point to find Scott's office, so I could introduce myself, learn more about him, and gain insight as to what he wanted to see happen in the human resources area for the firm. It became clear that Scott was the owner in the firm who was always assigned oversight for the projects and initiatives requiring strong leadership (i.e. LeMaster & Daniels University; the coaching program, which involved assisting new supervisors in coaching and guiding their new accountants; and the leadership program designed for managers who had the desire to move into an ownership position).

One skill that I really admire about Scott is his ability to show humility. Whenever someone on his team makes a mistake, Scott will take responsibility for that mistake by using words such as, "I must not have communicated very well," or "I didn't follow up like I should have, so we didn't get the results we expected." He always took the high road and never made anyone on his team look bad in an area where he felt the ultimate accountability rested with him. In working with Scott, his actions indicate he cares for you as an individual; takes an interest in learning

(continued)

(continued)

about you and your family; and he also shares about his family, so you are able to get to know him as a person, as well as a boss or leader.

Currently, Scott serves as an executive principal with Larson Allen LLP and is responsible for leading their offices in the Pacific Northwest region of the United States.

Trust has an important link with your organizational success. Trust elevates levels of commitment and sustains effort and performance without the need for management controls and close monitoring. Trust between a leader and an employee is based on the trustor's perception of the trustee's ability, intent, and integrity.

Dimensions of Trustworthiness

Want to build trust in your organization? I recommend that you begin with yourself by reviewing the ways that you intentionally build trust with others. Do you exhibit integrity—do what you say you're going to do—all the time or some of the time? If you find yourself always making excuses for why you didn't follow through with your promises, then trust will elude your mutual relationships. Next, examine your perceived intent. Do your direct reports believe that you are in business for them or only for yourself? If people mistrust your intent, you will have difficulty establishing mutual trust. Lastly, you must exhibit competence and results in what you do in order for people to trust you. I will examine these attributes more in the following paragraphs.

Trusting goes with competence, intent, and integrity. The more we observe these characteristics in another person, the higher our level of trust in that person. Competence is an assessment of the other's knowledge, skill, or abilities previously demonstrated to us.

Intent is our assessment that an individual we trust is concerned about our welfare. Your perceived intentions or motives are central. Honest and open communication, delegating decisions, and sharing control indicate evidence of one's intent.

Bob Bunting, former CEO of the megaregional firm Moss Adams LLP in Seattle, WA, says, "Some high-potential people don't trust some partners when they perceive that the partners' self-interest trumps everything else. They aren't going to share credit; they will pass blame and keep praise."

Integrity is the degree to which your actions integrate with your words. Integrity leads to trust based on consistency of previous actions, credibility of communication, and commitment to standards of fairness: the congruence of words and deeds.

Dave Sibits, president of the national firm CBIZ Financial Services in Cleveland, OH, believes

The most damaging thing in terms of developing trust is when leadership says one thing and does another. I had a partner who would say, "The fish stinks from the head." If the people at the top aren't living what they are asking the others to do, you have a lack of integrity that causes degradation of the success of the whole firm.

To me, integrity is doing the right thing. We had a situation a few years ago where we had to put two of our offices together as one. We believed that all the proper steps had been taken and that proper communication had been completed. But we were surprised because we had a jail break. By jail break, I mean we found out that a major part of one of the offices was leaving with their client records in the middle of the night. It was the result of that group lacking trust in the leadership that we were doing the right thing.

Oftentimes, the top leader lives in a bubble. Many people tell the top leader what they think he or she wants to hear, rather than what he or she should hear. Whether people are intentionally misleading the managing partner, simply being politically correct, or dropping hints, the effect is the same: the leader is not getting factual information on which to make decisions and take actions. When the leader is surprised by the consequences of one of his or her decisions, it is usually an indication that the leader hasn't been getting truthful information from those around him or her.

Tony Morgan, founder and managing partner of the local firm Gollob Morgan Peddy & Co., P.C., in Tyler, TX, says, "People are going to pay much more attention to what you *do* than what you *say*. We can't espouse a set of core values unless we partners live and model those values."

John Wright, managing partner of the top-100 firm Padgett Stratemann & Co. of San Antonio, TX, adds, "A leader's imperative is doing what you say you're going to do, giving team members the freedom to do what they're going to do, and let them do that in their own way."

Ray Strothman, managing partner of the local firm Strothman & Company, PSC, in Louisville, KY, believes, "Integrity is basically doing what you say you are going to do, just basically walking your talk."

Consulting Experiences

Over the last 20 years in my consulting practice, I have interviewed thousands of employees, team members, managers, and partners around the idea of firmwide trust. Because trust is an intuitive experience, I will provide several representative stories from various interviews to illustrate the fact that trust is a highly personal experience and in no way abstract.

When trust permeates an accounting firm, productivity and creativity will increase, and stress will be lowered. Here are some personal stories from in-depth interviews of employees in accounting firms, from all levels, genders, and generations:

Delegation

"When my managing partner gave me autonomy, he gave me the incentive to succeed, and so I always delivered for him. He is a quiet man, but he went out of his way to tell me he trusted me to handle a significant client situation and that he believed I would do an excellent job."—Senior manager

A Healthy Meeting Among Toxic Ones

"I attend several meetings every month. All but one has a passive-aggressive political climate, resulting in defensiveness, conflict, and stress. The one meeting that differs, despite its high operational impact,

features trust and support among those attending. Everyone brings his or her problems to the table and genuinely asks for help. There are never any undermining remarks. It is all due to the approach of our leader. She never takes us to task publicly, and she guides us in problem solving. She reinforces collegiality. This meeting gets things done inside an otherwise toxic culture."—Audit partner

Integrity

"The partner that I work for explains things to some of our clients and leaves out many of the facts and skews the situation to make him look really better than he is. Whenever he talks to me, I'm always wondering, 'What is the real truth in this circumstance?'"—Tax manager

Group Dynamics

"If the partners aren't interested in what I have to offer, why should I go out of my way to increase the profit of a firm I do not even feel part of? Trust appears to be related to group behavior. In order to build trust or improve it, it is important to listen and consider every employee's idea, ask questions, and involve everyone in the discussion."—Consulting partner

Intent

"One partner advises me to build my rainmaking skills, so I will have a strong future in this business. Another partner tells me that I'd better get my billed hours up to 1,800, so I'll look good. These partners don't seem to be on the same page, and I don't know who to trust."—Senior manager

Invested in Trust

"My managing partner is booked in 40 meetings a month with other partners. I don't see how he does it. When we meet, he is so focused on me and my success. We discuss the client challenges of the month. Occasionally, other things preempt our time, but he works hard to not let things interfere with our time. I knew it was a high priority for him to invest this time in me, so I trusted him and was more open. I worked extra hard to show my loyalty to him."—Construction industry leader

Rebuilding Trust Takes Time

"My senior tax partner broke her promise to me. I have tried hard to understand trustworthiness, so I planned to reach out and rebuild my trust in her. I am not going to give it back right away, as I needed time to set new boundaries. It is still not where it was, but I have started."—Tax senior manager

Lessons From Consulting Experiences

These interviews reveal that trust is a vital concept that is both highly appreciated and evokes strong feelings. Trust takes time and patience to establish. It must be done with repetition, interactions, and degrees of openness or delegation. Spending non-work time with coworkers nurtures trust and speeds up its effects.

The need for trust arises from our interdependence with others. We often depend on other people (and they on us) to help us obtain, or at least not to block, the outcomes that we value. Because our interests with others are intertwined, there is also an element of risk because we cannot compel the cooperation we seek. Therefore, establishing trust can be very valuable in all business interactions.

Dave Deeter, founder of the top-100 firm Frazier & Deeter, LLC, in Atlanta, GA, believes that integrity is simple, "It's doing what you say you're going to do."

Scott Dietzen, managing partner, Northwest Region, of the national firm CliftonLarsonAllen LLP, in Spokane, WA, clarifies, "Actions are always louder than words, to use the cliché; does our living match what we say we are doing?"

Gordon Krater, managing partner of the megaregional firm Plante & Moran, PLLC, in Southfield, MI, believes in the inner voice, "I think integrity is trying to do the right thing always, not if it's convenient, not if it's easy, but always. I say try because we are human. I think where people get in trouble is they hear that inner alarm going off, and they do something anyway."

In the accounting profession, integrity is a foundation stone. Integrity is one of those words that is easy to say but difficult to achieve. Although leaders agree that integrity means that your actions integrate with your words, what happens when you are prevented from fulfilling your promises? The key here is to communicate, communicate, and communicate. Align your actions with your words, so that they integrate in ways that clients and team members can clearly witness. If you simply don't perform according to your words without explanation, trust will be lost.

Ken Baggett, co-managing partner of the national firm CohnReznick LLP, says that one only has to follow two rules in order to achieve success.

> Recently, one of my partners repeated what I had told him years ago, "All I had to do is follow two rules. You always told me to tell you the truth and to never let you get blindsided." Anything else we could deal with, as long as our client isn't the first one to call me to tell me that there is a problem. Absent those two things, you can pretty much deal with anything else. You don't lie to me, and don't let me get blindsided.

Ken believes that in order to convince potential clients to utilize your business's services and to convince your employees to trust you, you have to follow through with what you say. "At the end of the day, I think there is a correlation between being able to convince someone that you can do what you say you're going to do," he says. "If you cannot convince others (i.e., potential clients to utilize your services), I don't believe you can convince others to follow you as employees."

Levels of Trust Development

Personality theorists suggest that some people are more likely to trust than others. Viewed as a fairly stable trait over time, trust is regarded as a generalized expectancy that other people can be relied upon. This expectancy rises or falls to the degree that trust has been experienced in that person's history. Our perceptions of others' trustworthiness are shaped by first impressions, but we can continue to build trusting relationships, even with those who do not trust easily.

Leaders are responsible to different groups, such as clients of the firm, other partners, and all staff members. Because each of these groups have different expectations and different ways of communicating, it is often easy to send mixed messages. For example, sometimes, partners want more billable hours from the staff, but leaders want to keep staff members from cracking under the pressure of work.

I believe that trust builds along a continuum, such that as trust grows to higher levels, it becomes stronger, more resilient, and changes in character. At early stages of a relationship, an individual will carefully calculate how the other party is likely to behave in a given situation, depending on the rewards for being trustworthy and the deterrents against untrustworthy behavior. In this manner, rewards and punishments form the basis of control that a trustor has in ensuring the trustee's behavioral consistency.

Individuals mentally calculate the benefits of staying in the relationship with the trustee versus the benefits of "cheating" on the relationship and the costs of staying in the relationship versus the costs of breaking the relationship. Trust will only be extended to the extent that this cost-benefit calculation indicates that continued trust will yield a net positive benefit. Over time, trust can be built as individuals manage their reputations and behave consistently, meeting agreed-to deadlines and fulfilling promises.

When people come to a deeper understanding of each other through repeated interactions, they may become aware of shared values and goals. This allows trust to grow to a deeper level. Both parties understand what the other party cares about. Trust at this advanced stage is also enhanced by a strong emotional bond between the parties, based on a sense of shared goals and values. So, in contrast to calculated trust, deep trust is more emotionally driven and is grounded in care, concern, and mutual satisfaction.

Leader Profile: Bob Hottman, founder and CEO of the top-100 firm Ehrhardt Keefe Steiner & Hottman PC (EKS&H) in Denver, CO

Bob Hottman quarterbacked his high school football team and believes that sports leadership can be a great metaphor for leadership in business. In high school, Bob started a lawn mowing business. First, he mowed yards by himself in his hometown of Denver, CO, and later, he hired a team to help him. Leading this small team taught Bob many of the leadership lessons he uses today. He committed to serving his team members because he learned that the way he treated his followers determined the way they treated his customers. He learned that customer service is the lifeblood of any business. Bob sees his leadership style as "servant leadership."

Today he is the CEO of Ehrhardt Keefe Steiner & Hottman PC (EKS&H) and has been providing accounting and advisory services for individuals, closely-held businesses, and public companies in the manufacturing, distribution, real estate, hospitality, club, and service industries since 1977.

EKS&H Partner Kreg Brown says

> Bob Hottman is a great leader of others because he conducts himself in a trustworthy manner and has tremendous vision. When I first interviewed with him over 10 years ago, I was looking for a firm with integrity and defined values. I asked

Bob, "Does EKS&H sell tax shelters or relationships?" Bob's answer was what I was looking for. He said, "We hold our integrity above everything else, and if we endorsed tax shelters or anyone else's financial management for a fee, we may find ourselves being tempted to compromise our own independence and trust. Selling access meetings or being a value-added reseller to a specific product would place us in situations where our objectivity from our client's standpoint goes away."

I am currently on our firm's board of directors and, as a result, have input to our partners' compensation. Bob insists on transparency in our partner compensation, so that everyone knows the compensation of each partner. This transparency builds trust and promotes open communication in our partner group. I also often witness firsthand Bob's willingness to help others before he helps himself. Bob always puts his partners' interests before himself, and whenever decisions come up that are close, Bob will always give his partner the benefit of the doubt. He is truly a servant leader.

Bob's leadership of himself has truly made him a leader of leaders. Through his trustworthiness, vision, and leadership, our firm has grown from relative obscurity to a top-50 accounting firm in America in our first generation.

Partner in charge of sales and marketing, Phil Doty, adds

Bob Hottman impressed me since our initial meeting over 8 years ago when I interviewed for a partner position at EKS&H. I had spent over 35 years with Andersen. I had not known Bob previously, and frankly, knew little about the firm, but from the first time I met him, I was impressed with his demeanor, including his sincerity and passion for EKS&H and its people. He talked about work-life balance in our early meetings, but I'll admit I was somewhat skeptical because I had heard that all before; it was often preached by public accounting firms but seldom practiced! He also spoke of the importance of the firm's core values, including "having fun," as well as the firm's vision and mission statements. He really emphasized the importance of the culture of the firm, and the more we talked, the more I came to trust him, as well as the other partners, and I accepted the firm's offer.

After over eight years, it has been very apparent that he spoke the truth. Bob, as well as the other partners in the firm, are driven by a passion for the firm's culture, people, and clients. I have seen Bob repeatedly make the right decisions, including making investments in people, training, office expansion, and difficult client situations. We all trust him to do the right thing for the long-term future of the firm, rather than short-term profits.

I could site a number of examples, but two come to mind. A number of years ago, Bob suggested we embark on 5-star training, where we would literally train everyone in the firm, from partners through administrative assistants, on the importance of delivering 5-star service. I was one of the more skeptical partners when he suggested this but, over time, realized that his vision of training everyone in the firm paid enormous benefits. Currently, we are engaged in a similar effort to train all our folks on building trust. We are making a considerable investment in this area because the partners, under Bob's leadership, believe it is the right thing to do.

Bob is one of the most exceptional partners and leaders that I have worked with, and I trust him to the fullest. He is a role model we all should emulate.

(continued)

(continued)

> **Lori Nelson, partner in charge of human resources, says of Bob**
>
> Bob does things that inspire others, as well as firm strategy. He meets with every new hire who joins the firm in a "welcome to the firm" session. This meeting occurs after someone has been with the firm for about a month, so they have been able to start to integrate and see and be part of our culture in action. This has always impressed me, and I know our new people really enjoy and appreciate this: the fact that the CEO of the firm makes time to share with them the meaning of our firm's core values, mission, vision, and strategy. New employees have commented to me that this session really helps give them a sense of belonging, connectedness, and being respected and appreciated.
>
> He also lets them know that his door is always opens and if they ever feel there is a violation of a firm core value to come and talk with him about it.
>
> Bob is past president of multiple industry associations and is active in a variety of community organizations, including Children's Hospital Colorado and the Denver Chamber of Commerce. Bob graduated from Colorado State University.

Building Trust

Trust building requires mutual commitment and effort, especially when attempting to de-escalate conflict. Nonetheless, there are several ways individuals can act on their own to initiate or encourage the trust-building process. This is accomplished by either taking steps to minimize the risk that the other party will act in untrustworthy ways or by policing one's own actions to ensure they are perceived as evidence of trustworthiness.

At the calculated trust level, individuals can take several steps to strengthen another's trust in them, particularly when these steps are performed repeatedly and within several different contexts of the relationship:

- ▲ *Establish consistency and predictability.* We can enhance the degree to which others will regard us as trustworthy when we behave in consistent and predictable ways. Every effort should be made to ensure that our words are congruent with our subsequent actions and that we honor pledged commitments. Our integrity is reinforced to the extent that we do what we say we will do.
- ▲ *Communicate accurately, openly, and transparently.* In addition, one should act openly (that is, be clear about the intentions and motives for one's actions). This helps the other party accurately calculate our trustworthiness because we are willing to act transparently and be monitored for compliance.
- ▲ *Perform competently.* One should perform one's duties and obligations competently. Individuals should continuously strive to demonstrate proficiency in carrying out their obligations. In some cases, this may entail updating skills and abilities as technology advances. As others contemplate how much to trust you, they will assess your qualifications and ability to perform.
- ▲ *Share and delegate control.* Trust often needs to be given before it will be returned. There is symbolic value in soliciting input and sharing decision control with oth-

ers. To the contrary, when such control is hoarded, and others feel that they are not trusted, they may be more likely to act out against this with behaviors that reinforce a distrusted image.

 A Leader's Perspective

"When it comes to leading, you have to do what you say you're going to do," says Keith Farlinger, CEO of the national firm BDO Canada LLP in Toronto, Canada.

"Integrity is all about doing what you say you're going to do. That helps people get to know you better and helps to build that trust with your partners, as well. Even in long-term relationships, trust and continued communication are critical. I had a long-term client. I got to know the family very well, and I spent a lot of time with this client. We had lots of philosophical discussions about life in his family and my family. We did a lot of really good things for his business. When I became the Toronto managing partner, I kept very few clients because the job was mostly full time. He was one of the clients that I kept. So when I became the CEO, a year ago, I had to tell this client, 'I can't look after this. I have to do a lot of travelling and so on, unlike another partner who's been working with you for a few years. Are you okay to deal with her?' He said, 'Absolutely. I know her, and she knows the business.' Six months later I got a call from the client's CEO. He said, 'Look, I'm having a hard time with the new partner because I phone her, and she doesn't return the call, and I don't know what's up with my work.' I said, 'I'll talk to her about it, and we'll try and rectify that.' And so I did talk to her about it, and she said it was a misunderstanding. Unfortunately, it happened again, and he decided to leave the firm. We spent 20 years building up a relationship, building up that trust, and there are certain values that the client has, and I agree the value should be returning calls. Subsequently, I found that the partner had too many things on her plate. However, with that loss of trust, we lost a 20-year-old relationship."

Communication is a vital part of building trust, Keith says. "Probably the most important thing is the rapport you build up with people. I was concerned that I was giving them too much information and insulting their intelligence. But what I found is that happens very, very rarely. They really do want the whole story and the complete presentation of what you are thinking and why."

Building Organizational Trust

Trust can be a touchy subject in an accounting firm. Many partners bristle at the suggestion of building trust. They say, "Why do we need to do that? Don't you trust me?" Consequently, rather than addressing trust alone, it is often better to incorporate measures of trust into already existing practices. Based on years of experience in the field of building trust and teamwork in an organization, the following ways to weave trust into an organization may be helpful:

▲ *Prepare a definition of trust for the firm.* The Oxford dictionary defines *trust* as confidence (an emotional word); reliance (another emotional word); or "a resting of the mind on the integrity, veracity, justice, friendship or other sound principle of another person or thing."

> Neal Spencer says
>
> Whenever we make a mistake, I like to use an autopsy without blame. When we screw things up, let the dust settle, autopsy the sucker, and see what we did wrong so we can learn and not repeat the mistake. Not to blame somebody because I think that's a low-level way of looking at mistakes. We encourage people to put the moose on the table, meaning that if they make a mistake, don't fall on your sword; put the problem on the table. We're all on the same team.

▲ *Include trust and ethical behavior items in surveys and focus groups.* Review surveys and other data collection tools, whether internal or external, for items that address trust. The challenge of involving senior partners on these sensitive topics is best accomplished using solid data for problem solving and action planning. It's one thing for *you* to say we need to focus on trust, but when peoples' clients or subordinates say it, they really listen!

▲ *Evaluate the organization's change management practices.* Nothing depletes trust more quickly, and sometimes irrevocably, than poorly implemented organizational changes. Knowing this, a leader will find ways to improve communications before, during, and after a change of any kind.

▲ *Conduct training for partners, management, and staff on improving trust.* Use your focus group or survey data to raise the issues. This means setting new expectations for a high level of trust for all supervisors, managers, and executives. No matter how talented the executive or manager, he or she must vigilantly and consciously guard trust quotients and frequently add to the "trust account." In order to build a successful firm, you have to start by building trust, says Mike Cain, founder and comanaging partner of the top-50 firm Lattimore Black Morgan & Cain, PC (LBMC), in Nashville, TN.

> I think you have to build trust by consistently doing the right thing in terms of looking at the firm first as opposed to yourself. You have to be able to put the firm first again and again. When you do, then people begin to trust you. They believe that you are going to think about things, you are going to listen to them, and then do the right thing for the firm. We have had partners from time to time in the past who didn't treat the staff with respect or who were indifferent to their clients. In those situations, we literally had to part ways with those individuals."

Consider conducting interviews to learn more about trust in your firm. Please see exhibit 3-1 for sample interview questions.

Exhibit 3-1: Sample Interview Questions for Gauging Level of Trust in a Firm

Sample questions could include the following:

1. Do you trust your supervisor? _____
   _____
   _____

2. Do you trust our CEO? _____
   _____
   _____

3. Give an example of high trust in our firm. _____
   _____
   _____

4. What does trust mean? _____
   _____
   _____

5. Give an example of low trust in our firm. _____
   _____
   _____

6. How do you know if you are being trusted? _____
   _____
   _____

7. What do you believe helps build trust in our firm? _____
   _____
   _____

8. Have you ever tried to rebuild trust with someone at the firm? _____
   _____
   _____

9. How did you go about that, and was it successful? _____
   _____
   _____

In his book *Wooden on Leadership*, Coach John Wooden said, "It's like character and reputation. Reputation is what others perceive you as being, and their opinion may be right or wrong. Character, however, is what you really are, and nobody truly knows that but you. But you are what matters most."

When Trust Is Broken

When trust is broken, I think the first thing you have to do is identify where it happened. Then, I believe it's critical that you apologize. If I don't apologize, that sends what message? The message of an apology is that you've recognized where the trust was lost, and you take ownership of it. The next thing you need to do is go about giving trust back the other way because people aren't going to give you trust unless you give it to them first.

Jim DeMartini, managing partner of the top-100 firm Seiler LLP in Redwood City, CA, says

> Trustworthiness and integrity are particularly crucial when you're managing a knowledge transfer business. And it goes to how you handle errors or oversights with clients. We demand that our people immediately take responsibility and cure the error; you don't want people hiding errors or problems because that can really do damage to the organization.
>
> The bottom line is when trust is broken, it can never be regained. But there's never, never a reason why trust should be broken. Maintaining trust has to do with having an unwavering commitment to integrity. Where an error has been made, we immediately go to the client, we tell them it's been made, and we make it right.

Carl George, former managing partner of the national firm Clifton Gunderson LLP in Peoria, IL, believes

> Whenever I've *not* done something I promised, the first thing I do is apologize. I go to him and I say, "I screwed up; I told you I'd do this and I didn't." I think that's key. I'm just a human being, so I'm going to make a lot of mistakes, and you go to the person you've harmed. I've done it with the board; I've done my management team this way, I've gone to staff. If I screw up I, I admit it, and I apologize. I don't try to bury it!

As the severity of the trust issue increases, the victim is more likely to experience stronger negative reactions, including a sense of moral outrage. Serious offenses harm trust severely, often to the point of complete destruction. These serious offenses may also stimulate the rapid growth of distrust. Accordingly, the victim is more likely to engage in more severe reactions to the trust violation, including exacting retribution, escalating the conflict, or terminating the relationship.

Rebuilding Trust

In Tony Simons's article "The High Cost of Lost Trust," we learn that *rebuilding* trust is not as easy as *building* trust in the first place. After trust has been damaged, there are two key considerations for the victim: (1) dealing with the stress that the violation imposed on the relationship and (2) determining if future violations will occur. After a trust violation and the fallout that ensues, the first critical question is, Is the victim is willing to reconcile? If the victim believes that the violator will not make efforts at righting the wrongs and minimizing future violations, the victim has no incentive to attempt reconciliation and restore trust.

There is a clear distinction between reconciliation and forgiveness. Reconciliation occurs when both parties exert efforts to rebuild a damaged relationship and strive to settle the issues that led to the disruption. Reconciliation is a kind of forgiveness when feelings of resentment are appeased, and amnesty is granted to the offender. However, it is possible to forgive someone without the willingness to reconcile and vice versa.

If reconciliation is the goal, then it must be initiated by the offender. It may be that there were unclear expectations that can be quickly clarified. Or there may be some explanation that places the unexpected behavior in context, so that the event is no longer perceived by the victim as a violation. Finally, apologies indicate remorse. These are important forms of communication that help restore balance in the relationship and convince the victim that it will be safe to trust again in the future.

Such a repair may involve acts of restitution that compensate the victim for the specific consequences of a violation. Restitution also carries important symbolism in that the offender is actually trying to redeem his or her trustworthiness with concrete actions. In calculated relationships, actions may speak louder than words, so it is imperative for the offender to honor trust in subsequent interactions with tangible offerings designed to restore "fairness" in the relationship.

Take immediate action after any violation. Offenders should act quickly to engage in restorative efforts. This communicates sensitivity to the victim and relationship and avoids the double burden that the victim has to incur by both suffering the consequences of the violation and having to confront the offender with the consequences of his or her behavior.

Apologize and take responsibility for your actions if you are culpable, and express remorse for the harm that the victim endured because of the violation. Your remorse indicates to the victim that you have also suffered as a result of your actions, and the victim may be less likely to pursue vengeance and escalate the conflict. Terry Snyder, president of the accounting firm alliance PKF North America in Lawrence, GA, says

> When trust or loyalty is damaged, it's hard to repair. But what really is the quickest way to repair it is for somebody to walk in and say, "You know what, Terry, I didn't handle this very well. I'm not happy with the way I handled it, but you know, it was my best shot at the time, and I hope I can get your confidence back. I would understand if you've lost trust in me. It was a misstep on my part, and if we can work this out, good. If not, I understand completely, but I'm going to give it my best shot." A humble apology like this will get you miles down the road to repairing lost trust.

Tony Argiz, founder, CEO, and managing partner of the megaregional firm Morrison, Brown, Argiz & Farra, LLP, in Miami, FL, says

> I was born with a little bit of street smarts. Maybe I'm wrong the first time around that I evaluate people, but it's usually a pretty good batting average. First time around, I try to trust everybody.
>
> Integrity is really what we sell. One thing that I learned early in my career, the Reverend Tim Dolan, who ran Georgetown University, would always say, "Think for yourself what's right and what's wrong. It's not what the law is, it's what's right and what's wrong." Each human being should have the conscious to really determine, based on their life experiences, if something is right or it doesn't look right or it's wrong. That's always the best pulse out there for you to follow in life.

A client of mine, Orlando Gomez, would always tell me in his business, "You know, if you take that business over there, the owners have a car leased under their business or bought under their business, they're running the gasoline through there, they're running this expense and that expense through the business. That's not having integrity or leadership. If you do that, every one of your employees is going to do it. So, you try to lead with your actions." And if people want to work late, hey, where is the managing partner?

When someone breaks your trust, it is very difficult to repair. I always like to give people second and third chances, so it would have to be pretty sad for someone to do something that would really break that trust because people can make honest mistakes; people can make wrong decisions. The key is to continue to mentor that individual and see if you can turn them around because, in most cases, if you give it the amount of time it requires, you'll be able to succeed. But you think to yourself, "Hey, in the next battle that I have, can I really depend on this individual?"

Hugh Parker, executive partner of the regional firm Horne LLP in Jackson, MS, says

I define trust as confidence that the person I'm dealing with has my best interests at heart, will do what he says he is going to do, and get the results that we both have in our minds.

A partner put a hidden camera in one of our offices to watch the people. One of the employees picked it up and brought it to the attention of the responsible parties. There was a direct Internet hook up, so this guy could monitor people from his office in another location. That is not who we are. He is a command and control person and he couldn't move forward. Although he was financially a very contributing partner he would not live our values.

Notice that although communication and action are both central elements of reconciliation and trust recovery, the repair process for calculated trust is predominantly a material, transactional effort. To simply give someone a handshake after this type of violation is not likely to help and could, in fact, make things worse. Something substantive, more than a cursory apology, must happen to repair lost trust.

Rick Anderson, CEO of the megaregional firm Moss Adams LLP in Seattle, WA, says

One crucial step in beginning to repair broken trust from a mistake or otherwise is to simply acknowledge that mistake. If you don't, it becomes even harder, if not impossible, to repair. I think the repair process first of all it requires effort on the part of both people to seek out opportunities to once again be where they want do business together. You've got to make it a priority to find a way to rebuild the trust. If you are going to just let it happen, I am not sure it will happen at that time because you have to replace the bad experience with some new good experiences. And that's most likely to occur if both parties make it a priority to do so.

In deep trusting relationships, trust of the other party is based on the shared values of the parties and their emotional investments. Thus, violations may lead the victim to conclude that the parties are not as "together" as they once may have appeared. Deep trust relationships are more heavily grounded in intangible resources, such as perceptions of mutual attraction, support, and caring for each other.

For the offender to reestablish intent, he or she should quickly and voluntarily offer a thorough and sincere apology, which conveys remorse for harm inflicted, an explanation of the details surrounding the betrayal, and a promise of future cooperation. The offender should explicitly recommit to the relationship and discuss strategies to avoid similar problems in the future.

As before, both communication and action are essential to the trust-rebuilding process, but deep trust repair involves an emotional and a relational focus. For example, simply paying some form of material compensation may not be sufficient to reassert shared values and rebuild the common sense of identity that was the foundation of the trust.

When deep trust has been broken, prescriptions for trust building entail a number of additional steps, such as the following:

▲ *Promote shared values and emotional attraction*. Individuals should model a concern for other people by getting to know them, engaging in active listening, showing a focus on their interests, recognizing the contributions of others, and demonstrating confidence in abilities of others.

   Jim Metzler, vice president of the AICPA, says, "My experience has been that when trust is broken, few people can really repair it. There are some difficult steps necessary to rebuilding trust. One step is coming forth with an attitude of humility. It's a long and difficult road but not impossible."

▲ *Create mutual goals*. Working toward the collective achievement of common goals fosters a feeling of togetherness. Parties create activities that define their commonality and uniqueness.

▲ *Establish a common identity*. Nurturing a common identity creates a sense of unity that can further strengthen trust. Engage in talk and actions that build a sense of "we" rather than "me." A common shared identity reduces divisiveness and encourages individuals to work together.

▲ *Reaffirm commitment*. Reassert shared values. Reestablish the effective connection in the relationship by expressing your emotional attachment to the other party, and strive to demonstrate that the relationship is a top priority.

Steve Mayer, founder, chairman, and CEO of the regional firm Burr, Pilger & Mayer LLP in San Francisco, CA, believes

It's extremely difficult to repair broken trust because you always wonder if you can ever trust the person again. I'm a forgiving guy, and I want to give people the benefit of the doubt. I always believed that everybody deserves a second chance and that everybody screws up from time to time. I've had people lie to me, and it takes a while before I can believe them again.

The first thing you must do is to admit that you're wrong. You have to talk it through, so everyone understands the extent of the collateral damage. It's going to take me a while to completely trust you again, but as far as I'm concerned, we have a clean sheet of paper.

So, I may think about things a little bit, but as far as I'm concerned, you're good to go. I got to be a little bit careful, but I'm not going to hold this against you the rest of your life.

There is also an important psychological role for taking responsibility for one's actions, communicating remorse, and going to special lengths to compensate victims for harm inflicted. These types of restorative actions may threaten one's ego or self-esteem, and the expected benefits derived from such actions may not be deemed to be worth the expected costs.

Another aspect to consider is the legal implications of our guidance. Although apologies convey remorse and responsibility that aids in the trust-rebuilding process, they also admit potential liability. If trust rebuilding is the priority, the offender will have critical decisions to make regarding whether and how to apologize. Once again, there may be instances when the costs associated with trust rebuilding are unfortunately outweighed by other considerations, such as minimizing legal liability.

Trust exists both in one-on-one relationships and in the firm at large. The confidence it provides permeates an organization through its people, departments, policies, products, and future outlook. Unfortunately, it often does not receive the overt focus and attention that it deserves, considering the vast impact that it has on an organization's performance.

Conclusion

In this chapter, you've learned how trust can be a competitive advantage for a team or firm. We've discussed trust as not only a socially acceptable characteristic but one that has a profit motive attached to it. I've challenged you to build trust on your team and in your firm, given you methods to repair trust when it is broken, and demonstrated that the leader must be trustworthy in order to build an effective, growing team.

Critical Thinking: Creating Your Future

"Begin challenging your own assumptions. Your assumptions are your windows on the world. Scrub them off every once in awhile, or the light won't come in."

~ ALAN ALDA

Most people take thinking for granted; they give it no thought or time. But without training in thinking and logic, you can't be thinking at your best. For the best leaders, making time to think is crucial to success. Microsoft founder Bill Gates says in his book *Business @ the Speed of Thought*, "Twice a year, I set aside all other issues to concentrate on the most difficult technical and business problems."

In John Maxwell's book, *Thinking for a Change: 11 Ways Highly Successful People Approach Life and Work*, he makes a convincing case that the ability to think sets man apart from other living things. The power of thinking lets you create your own destiny. You can choose to succeed through good, skilled thinking or be a failure by leaving this potent power untapped. Maxwell cites his "thinking chair," where he regularly invests time in deep thought, with orders to everyone to not disturb him while he is in this chair.

Maxwell reasons that great thinking has to be cultivated and refined. He argues that you can become a great thinker only if you are willing to learn how to do it. His book reveals a number of ways of thinking that you can employ to change your life for the better.

For some busy leaders who get caught up in the daily urgency of partner, staff member, client, and prospect matters, it takes real personal discipline to set aside time to think. Although some leaders like Lisa Cines, Chris Allegretti, and Hugh Parker set aside specific times weekly or monthly for critical thinking, there are other ways to fit critical thinking into your schedule.

For leaders like Rick Anderson, CEO of the megaregional firm Moss Adams LLP in Seattle, WA, critical thinking takes place on long plane trips from the West Coast to the East Coast and back. Scott Dietzen, former CEO of LeMaster Daniels, now executive principal of the megaregional firm Larson Allen LLP in Spokane, WA, says, "My critical thinking has tended to be in shorter bits, but the ritual for me right now is—and I'm embarrassed to tell you this because of the amount of time—but it's on airplanes."

Breaking out of the regular routine during travel inspires other leaders in their critical thinking, as well. "Some of the best ideas we've gotten in the vision of our firm have come on my backpack trips. So, I go on two or three backpack trips a year," says Steve Mayer, founder, chairman, and CEO of the regional firm Burr, Pilger & Mayer LLP in San Francisco, CA. "The thought of the ESOP was on a backpack trip, the thought of ringing the Bay was on a backpack trip, a lot of the way that we have done our systems and procedures were things that I've thought through while hiking."

> Taking time to think and put one's role in context on every initiative, client engagement, or firm project is a sign of a good leader. Terry Snyder, president of the accounting firm alliance PKF North America in Lawrence, GA
>
> > My very first major job at Andersen was working for Kenneth Anderson (no relation to Arthur). Kenneth seemed very intimidating. I was doing procedures and tests on cash and accounts receivables on this very large account. Kenneth was coming to the first review of preliminary work. I had stayed up at night reviewing my section of the files. I was prepared, or so I thought.

As I went down for breakfast to meet with Kenneth, I was prepared to answer any question on the work I had done. He had the work papers pulled up. He had those glasses that are kind of half glasses, you know. And he looked up and he said to me, "So what are sales? Were there any new products?"

I said, "If you had asked me anything about the areas I was responsible for, I was prepared to answer, but I don't know the answer to those questions."

He looked at me said, "When I come to a job, the first thing I do is I get the minutes. I talk to some of the people. I get a good idea of what I'm about to audit. You have to think critically about what you are doing, so you can put your detail work into context."

You have to be able to think, and I look for that quality in people. Thinking is a big leadership issue that many people forget. It was established very early in me by Kenneth Anderson, and I've never forgotten that.

In this chapter, we are going to explore the leader's effective use of critical thinking. We will share stories of failures and successes of several leaders. Also, in this chapter, we will give you some concrete standards by which you can align your thinking, so that it is deep and effective. Wrapping up the chapter, I'll share with you a glimpse into the Socratic method of thinking: that of asking deep probing questions of yourself and others.

What Is Critical Thinking?

Some of the early Greek philosophers became masters of critical thinking, a term derived from the Greek words *kriticos*, meaning discerning judgment, and *criterion*, meaning standard. So, critical thinking might be described as discerning judgment using standards. Socrates was an early adopter of deep critical thinking. He used probing questions to find truth, meaning, and judgment, developing the art of Socratic questioning to reach a more profound level of logic, understanding, and reflective thought. In essence, Socrates' method was an example of the search for higher meaning or true wisdom.

One definition of *critical thinking* might be the ability to consistently assess the quality of thinking to arrive at wise judgments. In essence, critical thinking is about learning how to think (by using certain elements) and how to judge (by using certain standards) and improve the quality of your thinking, as well as the thinking of those around you. Whenever you employ certain standards of thinking, like Kenneth Anderson, you will teach important leadership lessons to those around you.

Critical thinking is often used without understanding. Sociologist Dr. Richard Paul, co-author of *Critical Thinking: Tools for Taking Charge of Your Learning and Your Life*, describes the term *activated ignorance* as "taking into the mind and actively using information that is false though mistakenly thinking it is true." Critical thinking is not being cynical. Being cynical or having that healthy skepticism is common practice in the accounting profession, but it is a low form of critical thinking. Critical thinking does not mean having a critical attitude or being negative on every issue.

Being aware of one's own thought process is an important first step in critical thinking. The mark of a good critical thinker is the ability to continually monitor thought patterns for emotional, analytic, and psychological biases. An inquisitive mind and approach is another factor in critical thinking, not cynical but questioning. Socrates taught us to ask many questions to develop a greater understanding.

Critical thinkers invite contradictory information that does not match what is already accepted. Gary Shamis, founder and CEO of the top-100 multioffice firm SS&G Financial Services, Inc., in Cleveland, OH, provides an example of putting this into action. "Twelve years ago, we put together an outside advisory board made up of three counselors. We meet with these people, and we bare our souls. You don't want people who're going to stroke you; you want people who're going to challenge you."

Critical thinkers are comfortable mulling many ideas and studying things in different ways. Finally, they like to hold their thinking to high standards of objectivity. Taken together, these attributes give critical thinking its robust qualities.

It's hard to get challenging input. For example, Bob Bunting, former CEO of the megaregional firm Moss Adams LLP in Seattle, WA, says, "I changed from a guy who liked people to agree with me to a guy who realized that if people won't disagree with me, nothing was going to happen because they weren't engaged. If there is no real conflict, nobody is helping improve the decision; nobody is really buying into the decision; nobody is committed to the decision because there is nothing going on."

Critical thinking helps simplify complex situations, and it is required for success in larger, more complex accounting firms. Yet, it is not a common skill. In a recent study supported by the W.K. Kellogg Foundation, only 4 percent of the U.S. organizational population was considered highly competent in strategic thinking.

A major part of solid critical thinking is gathering the thoughts of your partners and others around you. Although this is sometimes very difficult to obtain and often confusing, it will add to your "pool of meaning," which can help guide you. One of the most difficult aspects of gathering ideas from your team is sorting through the fuzzy information. Information you may obtain from your team may be fuzzy because your people are telling you what you want to hear, rather than what you need to hear. Some people are timid around the leader, and some people want to polish the leader's apple, so to speak. Some of your partners may have their own agenda, and that agenda may not be team or firm oriented. As Bunting has been able to do, you might want to place more value in the information that you receive from those who vigorously debate you. Or as Shamis has done, you might wish to employ an outside board of advisors who are independent and will be less biased. Most of all, you'll want to use the standards of thinking in the next section and the Socratic method described at the end of the chapter.

Thinking Standards

Standards help measure the quality of one's thinking. In the book *Critical Thinking: Tools for Taking Charge of Your Professional and Personal Life*, coauthor Dr. Richard Paul lists nine intellectual standards that critical thinkers use to raise the quality of their thought. They are as follows:

Clarity	Relevance	Logic
Accuracy	Breadth	Significance
Precision	Depth	Fairness

Critical thinkers apply these standards to their reasoning to create a more valid pattern of thinking. As one might expect, some standards are more applicable to certain elements than others, with one exception. Paul maintains that clarity is a gateway standard. Each of the elements must be clearly understood for critical thinking to occur. Essentially, this is the "meeting of the minds" before serious thinking begins. Clarity does not provide comprehension, but it makes comprehension possible. "I like to make sure I have a clear understanding of the facts before I make a decision," says Mike Cain, founder and comanaging partner of the top-100 firm Lattimore Black Morgan & Cain, PC (LBMC), in Nashville, TN. "Sometimes, that might take a while."

Once an element is understood, one can apply the remaining standards to achieve a robust level of thinking. The best way to apply these standards to a particular element is by asking a question related to the standard. For instance, the critical thinker may ask of a particular element, Is this accurate? Is this truthful? How can one verify this? Using the precision standard helps critical thinkers refine information.

Applying these standards is very difficult to do on the fly. Although you may be very intelligent, it is very important to set aside some alone time to think deeply and apply each of these standards. Ken Baggett, co-managing partner of the national firm CohnReznick LLP, places emphasis on alone time and planning processes. "If leaders aren't spending quiet time somewhere alone, collecting their own thoughts and planning, then you're a last-minute Charlie and a gunslinger; you'd just shoot from the hip. You'd better be one hell of a good aim," he says.

Ken spends time at a house in the country and out on his boat to get away from the office and the daily distractions. He does take his BlackBerry, though, but not to take lots of calls. "If I find myself with something I really need to follow up on, I will just stop the boat and sit there and send myself an e-mail for follow up later," he says. Once, he returned to the office on a Monday morning and had 23 messages from himself.

While investing this critical thinking time, you might well employ the Socratic method of asking probing questions of yourself. One question should always be, Could the facts I have and the assumptions I am making be more exact, or are they close enough for decision making? Relevance helps distill the complexity of critical thinking by helping focus one's thinking on the parts of a scenario that relate to the question or decision at hand. Usually, leaders are overwhelmed by problems, information, conflicting situations, assumptions, personal paradigms, and implications. Asking "How is this relevant?" is a simplifying step toward better decision making.

Critical Thinking Applied: Phil Holthouse

Once per year, Phil Holthouse, founder and managing partner of the top-100 multioffice firm Holthouse, Carlin & Van Trigt LLP in Los Angeles, CA, attends an executive MBA program at Harvard University School of Business. During this week-long program, Phil is away from the firm and its clients. From 8:00 AM until midnight, Phil and his classmates (mostly nonaccountants) are doing cases with Harvard faculty and study groups. These programs outside public accounting give him a broader view of the business world.

Phil explains

> We studied a case on the Toyota manufacturing method. You might think, what does that have to do with public accounting, but if you read how Toyota analyzes, diagnoses, and addresses problems, there is no doubt in my mind you could apply it to any type of business. Their theory is if you find a problem, you have to upstream it, so that it's not just the person on the assembly line solving that particular problem right there. If 10 different assembly lines in Toyota are set up the same way, they can fix it in all 10 places. For a firm like ours with 7 offices, the analogy is terrific.

> [Another case study was on an Army procedure called an] after-action review. Any time there's a major incident, the Army does a very detailed breakdown of how did we plan for it, what happened, what happened differently than we expected, what happened similarly to what we expected, what are we going to change about our policies or procedures going forward, what can we learn from it? And we now do that in our firm.

> I would've never thought of applying an Army-based strategy to an accounting firm, but if we have a situation where something blows up, we use this military approach of going back and saying step-by-step, Exactly how did it fall apart? What was our fail-safe that didn't catch this? How do we change that process going forward and try to build in the mentality that problems are okay, but then, let's see what kind of a fix we could do to it? I don't think I would have focused on things like that.

Depth and Breadth

The breadth and depth standards seem complimentary: either something is too narrow or too shallow. Do I need the information to be a mile wide and an inch deep? Or, must I really probe deeply in a critical "high-risk" area. We are looking for harmony between this breadth and depth. For instance, you should be looking for breadth in point of view, concepts, and implications like Terry Harris, managing partner of McKonly & Asbury LLP in Harrisburg, PA, obtains from meeting with three other firm's leaders twice per year to critically think about best practices. These meetings are described later in this chapter. At the same time, one needs depth in information, facts, and assumptions like Phil Holthouse obtains from his after-action reviews. In essence, these standards lead to the question, Do I have a wide enough view with sufficient detail?

Logic

Applying the logic standard requires a basic answer to the question, Does this make sense? Another question could be, Does this opinion jive with the facts? Here, the accountant's inquisitive mind, full of healthy skepticism, is an asset to critical thought. Then, logic requires one to reflect and reconsider any conditional statement or information.

Significance

Usually in any undertaking, a small number of actions will yield a large portion of the results. In some cases, the Pareto rule that says that 20 percent of the actions will cause 80 percent of the results. The significance standard helps us determine the most relevant 20 percent that will contain 80 percent of the impact. Significance is usually a first step toward preparation and planning.

Chris Allegretti, CEO of the regional firm Hill, Barth & King, LLC (HBK) in Boardman, OH, learned that investing in critical thinking and preparation pays off in the long run. "If you looked at my calendars, you'll see something on there about every three months that just says planning day. Those planning days allow me to stay focused on, What are we working on in the business?"

He doesn't take phone calls or open his e-mails on planning days. "I may not even come into the office that day," he says. "I reconnect with the priorities. The ritual that day is to really go through those notes and say, 'What did I promise? What do I need to do? What do I need to do to get back on track and where I want to be?'"

Fairness

Although clarity is the beginning standard, fairness is the final standard for eliminating personal bias. A trusted leader will always ensure that his or her decisions are fair to the team before being fair to himself or herself. The leader must ask if the decision is fair to everyone concerned or if his or her personal interests distort thinking. As a leader's ego enters the thought process, critical thinking becomes poisoned with ulterior motives, resulting in poorer decisions. Ego may selectively choose information, using only comfortable, familiar concepts. It can leave unfamiliar assumptions unquestioned, leading to inaccurate conclusions. The fairness standard seeks to prevent thinking that benefits the leader above the team.

Leader Profile: **Tony Morgan, founder and managing partner of the local firm Gollob Morgan Peddy & Co., P.C., in Tyler, TX**

Tony Morgan rode the school bus one hour each way to school as a youngster. During these bus rides, he became an avid reader, a habit that he credits for helping him develop his interest in critical thinking. To earn money for college, Tony worked on weekends during the school year and full time during the summers in a steel mill and in the Texas oil fields. When they graduated from college, Tony and his wife moved to Tyler, TX (population 60,000 at the time), the largest city in which the two of them had ever lived.

(continued)

(continued)

"Tony is a great leader. He does not believe in mediocrity, and the bar is always high," says partner Lisa Robinson. "This pertains not just to those he leads; it applies to all aspects of Tony's life. He absolutely leads by example. It has been a pleasure to have been mentored by Tony for the last 28 years. I am honored to claim him as a partner, as well as a friend."

Tony is a founding partner of Gollob Morgan Peddy & Co., P.C. Prior to starting the firm in 1982, he worked 10 years at a local accounting firm, where he was also a partner. He has now been the managing partner of Gollob Morgan Peddy & Co, P.C. for one decade. Tony led the 60-person firm to be named one of the best of the best by *INSIDE Public Accounting* newsletter. He is responsible for a variety of clients and focuses a significant amount of his time on business valuations and litigation support.

Tony graduated cum laude from Stephen F. Austin State University in 1972, with a bachelor's degree in business administration. He serves on the boards of numerous professional and community organizations. He's also an avid outdoorsman, and when he is not in the office, he can be found at his cabin in Jefferson, TX.

Applying Critical Thinking

In his book *Critical Thinking: Tools for Taking Charge of Your Professional and Personal Life*, Dr. Paul describes a liberal education as thinking for yourself. What an appropriate way to describe a liberal education! In accounting firms led by dictators, even benevolent dictators, the culture of thinking for yourself is not universally tolerated. That is one reason why it can be very difficult to manage people who've had a liberal education.

In our consulting practice, we've run across several firms that are run by controlling managing partners. In one large firm, the managers are not allowed to talk with an existing client about a possible service without the permission of a partner. One of the great challenges in dealing with such a firm filled with "yes men" is that without the ability to think for themselves, these "think-less" accounting firms drift toward a commodity-only practice and fail to bring full value to their clients.

Additionally, noncritical-thinking accounting firms reject different points of view to the extent that they become obstinate. In the old days, these kinds of accounting firm's partners and staff members were exploited by a tyrannical managing partner. However, in today's modern firms, such exploitation rarely works. The best people leave, the average people remain, and the firm drifts into mediocrity.

In order to help you grow beyond mediocrity, we will discuss some common myths about critical thinking, give you some tools to think like a leader, and wrap up this chapter with a brief overview of the Socratic method of thinking.

Myths About Thinking

As we seek to improve our critical thinking, we must first confront some commonly held myths:

▲ I'm smart and know a lot of facts, so thinking is natural and I don't have to think about it to do it well—**you do!**

▲ Intelligence and critical thinking are synonymous—**they aren't!**

▲ The brightest of the bright, our partners, should just know how to think well together—**they don't!**

Leader Profile: Hugh Parker, executive partner of the regional firm Horne LLP in Jackson, MS

Growing up in Mississippi, Hugh Parker learned a great lesson from his first employer during his high-school years: make things a little better each time you do something. If you approach business or leadership opportunities with a continuous improvement mentality, it's like compound interest at the bank—you'll get better exponentially.

Hugh became a business major, earning his master's degree and a PhD in accounting at Oklahoma State University. He's the only PhD leader of an accounting firm in the top several hundred largest firms. While working for a small CPA firm and teaching university accounting classes, he became interested in the art of leading people. He believes that the key to leading others is gaining and maintaining their respect.

Hugh serves as executive partner and chairman of the board of Horne LLP, one of the 50 largest accounting firms in the United States. He has more than 25 years of business valuation and litigation support experience. He is a member of numerous professional organizations and serves as chairman of the board of the Mississippi Symphony Orchestra.

Critical thinking plays a large part in his leadership style. Hugh says "My personal written goals are that I devote at least four half days a month to working on and thinking about our business."

"Hugh has led us into projects and engagements that we would not have done without him being at the helm," Horne LLP partner Mike Roberts says.

> He has enough confidence in us as a group and as a team that he will lay us out there on the risk continuum (for lack of a better word) to get us to go different places. He has definitely tried to make us a larger, more successful, better structured organization through his example.
>
> We recently had a lot of uneasiness within our partners because we have been compensated well for many years, and last year was a tough year. We had a good, trusting environment, but when the money started getting tight, there started to be finger pointing. It was very difficult for the partners to feel that they were being fairly considered. We had a fairly good partner evaluation program, based upon a lot of accountability. But in some of the offices, they didn't feel that they were able to present their side because so much of it was numbers driven. In 2010, we completely revamped our partner compensation.

(continued)

(continued)

> We went to a partner evaluation team. Hugh led this effort, and it was very tenuous for all the partners, wondering "How will I be judged?" Hugh was open-minded. He took criticism, even if it wasn't warranted. He changed his opinion to align more with what the partner group wanted to do. He was very outspoken, very confident, but in this situation, he let the partners have their voice. He listened more than he spoke. He worked to get us to a new place, to bring back teamwork, to bring back profit and did an exemplary job in that. He believed in the perspective, the vision of the future end result. Now, he didn't come with a premade plan. He came with a general outline of what he thought and involved partners at every level.
>
> The process produced a great outcome. We have trust today that we didn't have, that's probably better than we've ever had.

Learning to Think Critically—Like a Leader

One of the best ways to learn to think critically, like a strong leader, is by understanding the elements of reasoning, using the standards previously discussed. To take this learning one step further, Dr. Paul developed a valuable model in the book *Critical Thinking: Tools for Taking Charge of Your Professional and Personal Life* for learning critical thinking: a checklist to make certain we've covered all the bases. The Paul model is an approach to critical thinking that allows for easier mastery of this essential leadership skill. I think this model makes critical thinking easier to understand, teach, and practice. As a leader and critical thinker, you will have to commit to each of the following steps to reach the level of what Dr. Paul terms the "Master Thinker."

The Paul model has the following eight elements of reasoning:

Purpose	Question
Information	Concept
Inference	Assumption
Point of view	Implications

These elements are explained in the following sections.

Purpose

Leaders must assess the purpose of their thinking and resulting actions. You may ask, Is my purpose in line with my desired outcomes? At times, the noncritical thinker will delude himself or herself about the true purpose of a thought. For example, a tax senior may say that he wants a difficult assignment because it is challenging. The true purpose may be gaining an advantage over other seniors for a promotion to manager. The CEO may delude himself that he is bringing an acquisition to his firm to build critical resources, but in reality, he is seeking the increased recognition and income that comes with running a larger firm. The leader who thinks critically looks deeper for the true purpose and will try to ensure that he or she is not unwittingly deceiving himself.

Question

Socratic questioning is crucial to critical thinking. The leader can look at Socratic questioning in three ways:

- ▲ The need to continually use questions
- ▲ The interrelationships of questions
- ▲ The need to get answers to critical questions at the right time

The critical thinker must identify the primary issue, problem, or question at stake. The savvy leader will continually ask whether he or she is trying to answer the right question. Dr. Paul categorizes questions into three types: fact, preference, and judgment.

Phil Holthouse says

> We debate things in our firm very aggressively. The model of our partnership decision-making is let's debate it. I know which partners may be at extreme sides of different issues, and so we'll call them out and say, "Okay, Greg, I got the impression you think this is a horrible idea. Why do you think it's a horrible idea?" Put them on the spot to defend their position, and then, I've got somebody in mind who I know is on the opposite side on a particular issue, and so we get that cross-argument. Once you can get the debate started, people will almost always jump in, at least at our firm.

For leaders, questions of judgment require the most focus. Although questions of fact have one right answer, and questions of preference have many answers, questions of judgment require more complex thinking skills.

Information

Many years ago in the accounting industry, the possession of information was a key to our power in the world. Some people still believe that information is power. If information were power, then librarians would be the most powerful people in the world. Nowadays, in the Google world we live in, there is no shortage of information. This phenomenon is a problem. The leader must determine what information is necessary and be able to judge the quality of that information. Dr. Paul writes about three ways the mind takes in information: inert information, activated ignorance, and activated knowledge. Inert information is noise and confusion. Activated ignorance is using false information as truth, and that can lead you into disaster. Activated knowledge is truthful information that may lead to wise decision making. Critical thinkers are generally skeptical of information, and they rely heavily on intellectual standards to help evaluate data. Effective accounting firms avoid getting bogged down in information. Their leaders make decisions with the information available at the time. In cases like this, critical thinking is even more important to ensure reasoned, sound judgments.

Ken Baggett realized that he'd invested many hours thinking about a new subject before bringing it up to his partners. He shares

> One of the things that was pointed out, and this came out through my day with our firm's psychologist, Dr. Joe, was I tend to forget I spend a lot of time and energy thinking on a subject before bringing it up to my partners. For others, when I bring up an item, this may be the first moment they've even been introduced to the idea. And my impatient piece is I want them to catch up quickly, and I have to sometimes take that deep breath and say, "Okay guys, what don't you know?" I'll review things thoroughly and give people time to process.

When leading knowledge workers, Baggett's experience is a good model. When we have invested hours thinking through something, we must give our partners and team time for processing.

Accountants tend to be trained to be very analytical and to make the right decision. Trying to make the perfect decision can lead to the famous paralysis by analysis. In fact, anyone can make the perfect decision if ALL information is known, but life isn't like that. For instance, you may know the accounting facts, but you can't know everything that the client is thinking. There is always uncertainty, and you need to fight perfectionist tendencies. Often, a good decision made promptly is better than an improved decision made slowly. In addition, perfectionists forget that decisions aren't always final. When you decide and take action, you gain new information. This input can allow you to adapt and improve your original decision before the slow deciders have made their first decisions. And, by the way, a faster decision-making style will please your entrepreneurial clients that grow significantly because that's how they make their decisions!

Concepts

A concept is an idea or object that makes some other idea or thing comprehensible. Some people call this a paradigm or a way of viewing things. It would be impossible to understand the world without using and understanding paradigms and concepts. Consider this simple example: the concept of time makes the idea of a watch or calendar possible. We have all read about people who were great conceptual thinkers, people like Albert Einstein. These people had the ability to think in different dimensions by using known ideas in a different way. Conceptual thinking is what many people refer to as outside-the-box thinking. Conceptual thinkers are able to change focus and see things differently. They remain open to new information and ideas.

Noncritical thinkers are unable to change their paradigms. Noncritical thinkers get stuck using the same or even incorrect concepts to interpret the world. Many times, the trap is constructed by a person's education, upbringing, and belief system. One way to counter this is to challenge yourself. "I get my best ideas from interactions with others," Charly Weinstein, CEO of the megaregional firm EisnerAmper LLP in New York City, NY, says. "So I find people to talk to, and I pick their brains. I glean ideas from other leaders, people in different market spaces, people in different businesses, successful people, and interesting people. I try to absorb those conversations and come out with a new idea that I think makes sense for our firm."

The master critical thinker forces the mind to think of different ways of integrating ideas. Strong critical thinkers are strong conceptual thinkers who exhibit the mental agility required to rapidly and comfortably change their thinking to analyze their situation.

Inference

An inference is the thought process that uses assumptions to make a decision. Inferences can be good or bad. The key to understanding inferences (conclusions) is evaluating the underlying assumptions and applying good judgment to arrive at the correct conclusion. Critical thinkers resist the urge to jump to conclusions. They carefully evaluate and interpret the available information, and then, they assess the validity of the underlying assumptions. This kind of deliberate analysis leads to a better conclusion.

Assumption

Great critical thinkers remain very aware of their nonfactual assumptions. Not that we need to question all the simple assumptions that help us make it through the day, but those assumptions tied to inferences (conclusions) with large implications need careful thought. The leader attempts to bring the assumptions into a conscious level of understanding, so these assumptions can be evaluated and validated, rejected, or updated.

Leaders must make assumptions about the future. For example, when will our country adopt International Financial Reporting Standards? The assumption on this will drive our preparation for serving our clients' needs in this area. Our assumptions can be either an explicit conscious statement of belief or, more likely, a subconscious belief taken for granted. For example, in leading my firm, am I operating under the assumption that our country's tax system will remain the same in coming years? Assumptions can be based on how one believes the world should be or can describe the world as it actually exists. Many times, this contrast in assumptions creates conflict for the critical thinker. We have all used conscious assumptions to help drive planning when there is a lack of good information. This is a perfectly logical and reasonable approach to thinking. However, the assumptions that we make with our subconscious mind are not always thought through.

Point of View

Looking at scenarios from several points of view aids the leader's critical thinking. For instance, critical thinkers may look at a business from the financial domain, the customer domain, the legal domain, or a combination of the three. You may think about your business or client's business from the point of view of the owners, the employees, or their families.

"To open myself to new thinking, I attend conferences," says Terry Harris. "One of the things that I've found really helpful is connecting with a few managing partners of other firms. In IGAF Worldwide, there are three other leaders that I meet with at least twice a year. [Within our firm], we try to do two retreats a year. One of those retreats always is a strategic planning retreat."

The ability to consider other points of view can be very insightful. Solid critical thinkers are first aware of their own points of view then acknowledge other points of view and note the contrast. Critical-thinking leaders operate without letting their point of view exclusively dominate the thought processes. One approach requires the critical thinker to deliberately enter another point of view, but it requires mental focus to eliminate one's biases against doing so. Critical thinkers do not see opposing points of view as a threat but, rather, as another belief to be understood and, perhaps, even adopted in some form.

Accepting various points of view does not lead to whimsical decision making. On the contrary, other points of view will constantly challenge your thinking. In all leadership instances, exploring different points of view will help a critical thinker better understand the situation and clarify uncertainty.

Implications

Implications are potential consequences of a decision. Considering implications and potential consequences of action or nonaction is a major activity of top leaders. Consequences happen after the decision. Critical thinkers must evaluate the implications of their actions. Leaders should think about three kinds of implications: possible, probable, and inevitable. First, consider all the reasonable possibilities, everything from best case to worst case. If this set is comprehensive, it will include the consequences of an action. Next, consider which implications are the most probable in a scenario. Finally, identify any implications that are inevitable. "Leaders have a great responsibility to be forward-thinking on behalf of the entire firm," Marc Elman, CEO of the local firm PSB Boisjoli in Montreal, Canada, says. "One of the jobs of a leader is to try to avoid catastrophes, so they're always looking around corners and looking to the future."

Relationship of the Elements

In this model, each element of reasoning is linked directly with the other elements. As new information becomes available to the leader, assumptions may change. Changes in information will generate new questions, impact a point of view, or require new concepts. If we change our assumptions, inferences and conclusions will be affected.

Deep questioning permeates the entire model; we must ask questions to understand each of the elements. For instance, the critical thinker must ask the following questions:

- ▲ What is my real purpose?
- ▲ What is the key issue?
- ▲ What is the most relevant information?
- ▲ What are the correct concepts in this case?
- ▲ Are my assumptions valid?
- ▲ Have I drawn the correct inferences?
- ▲ What points of view matter?
- ▲ What are my desired implications?

The interrelationships between the elements of critical thinking meld into a dynamic system of thought. This kind of thinking requires flexibility of the mind.

Conclusion

Let's put some of this knowledge into perspective and learn to use Socratic critical thinking. Critical thinking is useful for monitoring the quality of your and others' thinking. Using the following 20 questions, one can learn how to use both dimensions:

1. What questions do I have about this situation?
2. What facts do I know to be true?
3. What is the key issue?
4. What information do I have too much or too little of?
5. What questions should I be asking?
6. What questions are forbidden to ask? Why?
7. What conclusions have I already made?
8. What other conclusions could be made?
9. What assumptions underlie these conclusions?
10. What assumptions would radically change my conclusions?
11. Whose ideas are missing from the issue at hand?
12. What is my personal point of view?
13. What are other points of view?
14. What outcomes could result from various decisions?
15. Which outcomes are most probable?
16. What are the risks associated with each outcome?
17. What are the payoffs of each outcome?
18. Are there outcomes that are inevitable based on this thinking?
19. How do these outcomes relate to what I want?
20. Does all this seem fair and selfless?

Although you'll find these questions useful in your thinking process, you may also come up with a different approach that fits your style. The value is in having a structured process. Too many people wing it, so that their analyses and decisions have no consistency and don't reflect underlying values (think politicians!).

Leaders must learn to practice the skill of critical thinking, so that it becomes second nature. The more you practice thinking, the quicker your thinking will improve. Initially, this practice will be awkward, especially as you challenge your mind to think in new ways, remain flexible and open to change, and confront your ego. As you become more skilled, you will be able to help others improve their critical thinking skills, as well. The leader can challenge the thinking of others by explaining the concepts of critical thinking in a practical way. The master critical thinker teaches by demonstrating his or her skill, so that others can watch and learn.

Kris McMasters, CEO of the national firm Clifton Gunderson LLP in Peoria, IL, says

There's nothing more valuable than when you have time to just stop and think about the business. I find that I have to schedule time on my calendar and discipline myself to critical thinking; otherwise, the crises of the day will consume my time. My best time for working on strategy and vision is on weekends. I'm not under pressure, and I can really sit back and focus on what needs to happen going forward.

Preparation: Ready for Seizing Opportunity

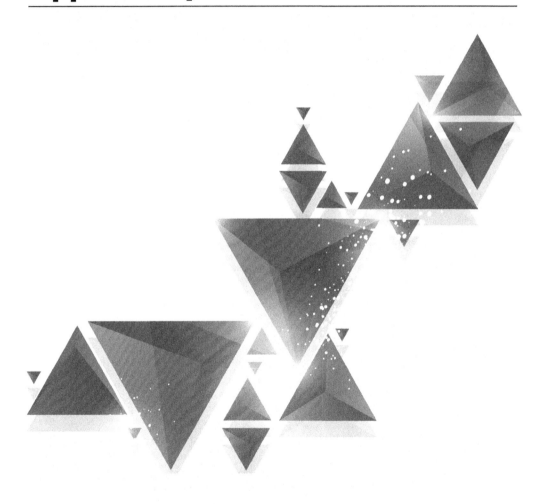

"Spectacular achievement is always preceded by unspectacular preparation."

~ ROBERT H. SCHULLER

Mother Teresa once said, "We can do no great things, only small things with great love." When you take pride in perfecting the minor details of serving a client or handling an employee, big things begin to happen in a positive manner. Championship basketball coach John Wooden would invest the first few minutes of the first two weeks of practice demonstrating to every player how to properly put on his socks, shoes, and shoelaces. He wanted no slippage and no blisters taking any attention away from the important elements of the game of basketball. What things in your firm are the equivalent of teaching your staff how to put on their socks and shoes?

Leadership consists of both science and art. Proper preparation and planning is the science, and adapting to unexpected changes and seizing unexpected opportunity is the art. Some people invest so much time preparing that the project never gets launched. Others just seem to wing it. So, what is the proper balance between preparation paralysis and winging it? This chapter will give you tools to improve both the science and art of your leadership and preparation skills.

Keith Farlinger, CEO of the national firm BDO Canada LLP in Toronto, Canada, says that preparation is essential to seizing opportunities that lead to your vision.

> You need to be aware of opportunities out there, but when there is an opportunity that allows you to take a quantum leap, seize it. You need to know where you're going, what your vision is. I say to our up-and-coming leaders, "If you get a chance to do something different or to progress, make sure you seize that opportunity; don't wait for it to come around again."
>
> If you're not prepared, you're probably better off postponing things until you get prepared rather than go in and try and wing it. I've had situations where I have gone in and tried to wing, it and it just doesn't work very well.

We are all blindsided by adversity from time to time. The best leaders understand this and are seldom thrown off stride when it occurs. They prepare for the opportunities that adversity presents; namely, they know that their response can separate them and their firm from firms whose leaders get stunned and disheartened when fate frowns. Expect to encounter rough patches and use them to become stronger.

Leading Through Disaster

Ted Mason, president and CEO of the top-100 firm Laporte Sehrt Romig Hand in New Orleans, LA, relates his experiences preparing for disaster

> On the Friday before Hurricane Katrina hit New Orleans, we held a staff meeting to discuss the potential impact. We reviewed and distributed our disaster recovery plans to the entire staff and basically said, "Let's just be prepared." Sunday morning, I woke up about 5:30 AM and caught the weather predictions and realized we were going to be in a mess, a world of trouble. So I called Deb Lockwood of our alliance to get an 800 number, so we could communicate with everyone. We sent an e-mail out to everyone.
>
> The hurricane hit on Monday, and none of us anticipated anything like what hit us. We learned very quickly that no matter how good your disaster recovery plan

is, it can't anticipate every situation. An example of that is we had cell phones. Everybody felt like we were covered. Well, nobody realized that the cell towers all ended up in a centralized office in an area that would flood. We lost all communications with everybody. We were fortunate there were a few of us who had stayed in the area. Tuesday morning, three of us met in our North Shore office. We didn't have power, but we started mapping out some possibilities we would try to get things back up and running.

The partner in charge of our North Shore office contacted building management, and we grabbed additional space. We didn't know if we were going to need it or not, but we didn't want to get squeezed. As the benevolent dictator, I made a decision without contacting any of my other partners. I realized everybody was spread throughout the country, and we had no communications. We had a blog set up, and I went on with a blog and made a commitment to everybody at the firm that their job was safe, their payroll was going to continue, that we were in good financial condition, and we would be able to survive. I told them that while this was going to be the greatest challenge we would face, it was also probably going to be the greatest opportunity we would ever have in our life: to be able to rebuild soon.

I would tell you in hindsight that it's probably the best thing that ever happened to us because there were a lot of firms that didn't make that commitment on the front end. Their partners kind of wiggled and were indecisive and wishy-washy. Our commitment went a long way.

This approach didn't sit well with some of the partners. But we were committed to our clients and our team members. We decided we were going to move on, we were going to keep everybody, and we made a commitment to them. We told our team members to take care of what you need to take care of with your family. Whenever you can get back to work, get back to work.

We were not able to get the office running for about three and a half weeks. But in the meantime, we got in touch with everybody. We were up and running quicker than most of our competitors. We pulled everybody together for a staff meeting about four weeks after the hurricane. I laid out the entire situation for the firm. We were at risk for about 25 percent of our client business.

I felt like it was my responsibility to put a good face on our situation. The last thing staff needed to worry about was the survivability of the firm. I never doubted we would survive, but I just didn't know what it would look like. I told them we could sit here and not do anything. Or we could be more aggressive. and we could ultimately make it our greatest opportunity.

From August to October, Mason and his partners lost $900,000, yet they kept all their employees at full salaries and paid team bonuses. Taking care of their employees through this crisis paid huge dividends for their firm. The Laporte Sehrt Romig Hand partners' commitment to their team filtered out through the community. As a consequence, some of the best available talent was attracted to the firm.

Ted continues, "It really catapulted us to a different level. When Katrina hit, we were a $7.5 million dollar firm with 54 people. Today, we are a $19 million firm with 150 people. We have been chosen one of the best firms to work for the last 3 years. The quality of the people that we have is as good a group of people as you can imagine."

Preparation, Preparation, Preparation

Just as realtors preach location, location, location, accountants should be the biggest advocates of preparation. It's our thoroughness and consideration of all the details that protects clients. Yet, in our own internal work, leaders do not always take time for proper preparation. As mentioned earlier, accountants are a smart bunch. They are very capable of winging it, but that won't produce the most effective results over the long run.

They say that luck is preparation meeting opportunity. Success comes to those who are ready to sail when their ship comes in. Those who learn the value of preparation too late can't always recover. It has been said that nobody plans to fail, but many have failed to plan. Preparation involves critical thinking, research, planning, training, and organization. Proper preparation provides a process to help you to persist through the difficulties of any initiative.

Leader Profile: Keith Farlinger, CEO of the national firm BDO Canada LLP in Toronto, Canada

Keith Farlinger, CEO of BDO Canada LLP, was motivated to succeed early in life by a failure. He wasn't selected for an advanced program when he was in seventh grade because he was not fully applying himself. He made a deal with the teacher that if he would work hard and get results, she would place him in the select program. Such motivation has lasted a lifetime for Keith, as he ascended the ranks at BDO Canada LLP to become its CEO in 2008.

Growing up in Cornwall, Ontario, Keith took his first accounting job with BDO Canada LLP in his home town as a co-op student. He transferred to Toronto later for more experience and a bigger challenge. Within two years, everyone above him, except the partners, had left the firm or been promoted to partner, so he was thrown into the deep end of running engagements and the audit team at a very young age. This experience helped him formulate a life-long philosophy of seizing opportunities because they may not reappear.

BDO Canada LLP chief operating officer Russ Weir says, "BDO completed a strategic plan in 2007 for the next five-year period. This strategic plan set stretch goals for the firm to take it to new heights."

Keith, who was part of the process, also felt that it was important to focus on the foundation of the firm and led a task force to revisit the firm's vision and values. This year-long process involved many meetings, and once the group was close, Keith led the firm in discussions on the topic, making over 20 different presentations and group sessions, including the firm's Policy Board (our board of directors) and the management team asking for feedback and comments. This process culminated in a firmwide vision-values celebration where all local offices celebrated the result with team building celebrations unique to each location.

The resulting vision and values is now a bedrock to the firm's future, and we will measure every future endeavor.

We could not have completed this project without Keith's vision, passion, and leadership. Many groups challenged us as to the real value of the process, but the firm's partners and, indeed, our staff embraced this vision—a true testament to Keith's leadership.

Not only has he risen to the top of his firm, he has served at the top of his profession. Keith recently served as chairman of the Canadian Institute of Chartered Accountants.

BDO Canada LLP's human capital officer, Emree Siaroff, says of Keith

> Keith communicates, inspires, and practices the art of patience as a key leadership tool in our firm. Unlike the CEO in a corporation who must answer to a board, Keith Farlinger also reports to the individuals he is leading. He has taught us that the key to effectively doing this is to show great patience in effectively communicating to, involving, and soliciting feedback from the owners.
>
> A year into his term, Keith began to look at how having an effective vision would align the partners and the firm towards achieving its desired state. In his mind, this vision would mean that all the partners would need to take part in the process. This had never been done so thoroughly before. In a firm with 350 partners located in almost 100 offices, Keith traveled across the country listening to the ideas and thoughts of the partners. Over the course of a year, starting at the management team and board level, he and his management team held face-to-face meetings with as many groups of partners as possible. When we finally launched the final vision, it was to a group that was aligned and focused on the desired future.

Keith believes that leadership consists of creating a clear vision for a group of partners then leading them to attain that vision. BDO Canada LLP had been a firm that was locally led and supported by a national office. In the old method, BDO Canada LLP had many directions, depending on the number of offices in the firm. Keith has changed that model, so that the firm has a strategic direction that will benefit all the stakeholders of the firm, with a firmwide vision and strategic plan: that of one firm. He sees his primary role as the development of the vision and then alignment of all the pieces of the firm, so that friction is reduced and better results occur.

"Prepare thy work without, and make it fit for thyself in the field; and afterwards build thine house." In Proverbs 24:27, Solomon is simply saying do first things first. A job such as arranging your office furniture must take second place for serving a client's needs. Preparing to work in the correct order can be as simple as learning to follow the directions in a preexisting process. However, many people would like to think that the old ways don't work. They disregard the wisdom of the past and elect to go through the school of hard knocks. Solid preparation can save years of frustration.

An effective leader develops the ability to correctly identify the key details in serving a client (such as building the relationship, managing expectations, cross-serving, and handling mistakes in a responsible manner); attacking a market; or working against a competitor to create advantages.

Just as a good accountant isn't sloppy with financial and tax matters, a good leader isn't careless about the details of leading a firm, especially in good times.

Bob Bunting, former CEO of megaregional firm Moss Adams LLP in Seattle, WA, argues, "Most accounting professionals would agree that true leaders do their best work in hard times. I think leaders, even the best leaders I have ever seen, are not at their best advantage in good times. I would admire somebody who could do brilliant things in wonderful times, but I am not sure I've seen a lot of that."

Scott Dietzen, managing partner, Northwest Region, of the national accounting firm CliftonLarsonAllen LLP in Spokane, WA, agrees

I think it's very difficult to lead in good times. As goofy as that sounds, leadership is tougher in good times because battling complacency is more difficult than helping people who are dealing with fear and anxiety. It's easier to get the attention of those in fear. It's no different than coaching a team that is playing an opponent who is much beneath them. Most teams always play down to the level of their competition, and I think organizations are very similar.

Developing Your Leadership Skills

The ability to lead is really a collection of skills, nearly all of which can be learned and improved, but leadership ability does not come overnight. Learning to lead is complex and requires preparation and learning. The most insidious danger is actually when you have developed a successful leadership style. Situations change, and different people respond best to different leadership styles. However, when you are successful with one style, you will tend to use it across all situations and people, which is less than optimum.

In a study of top leaders from a variety of fields, leadership experts Warren Bennis and Burt Nanus discovered that there is a strong link among personal growth, preparation, and leadership. "It is the capacity to develop and improve their skills that distinguishes leaders from their followers," say Bennis and Nanus. Good leaders are learners, and the learning process is continual—a result of persistence and preparation.

As long as a person does not know what he or she doesn't know, he or she will never grow. When you recognize areas where you can improve or adapt your leadership skills, and you begin the discipline of preparing to lead, terrific things begin to happen in your life. In this book, I've attempted to provide a pyramid for self and team improvement. Former British Prime Minister Benjamin Disraeli said, "The secret of success in life is for a man to be ready for his opportunity when it comes." When a person prepares daily for the challenges of leadership, his or her leadership skills begin to develop. An old proverb says that champions don't become champions in the ring—there they are merely recognized. Champions grow from intensive training before the fight. Even if you have natural talent, you will benefit from daily preparation to lead.

Laying the Groundwork by Seeking Input From Others

One important factor that leaders can forget is that it's not your job to come up with all the answers or even decisions. Often, the people on the front lines can provide valuable input. You need to gather it before you move ahead.

When I became CEO of Advantage Companies, the firm was in a serious financial condition because its former management team had misspent much of its capital. During my first meeting with the board of directors, I had prepared a long list of priorities for their consideration. I laid the list on the table and began to expound on the necessity for raising new capital and rebuilding some of the infrastructure. At the time I was 31 years old, and the average age of the directors was about 60 years old! I was planning to bowl them over with my creativity and drive, but, I was not fully prepared.

About one hour into my presentation, one of the directors spoke up and said, "I think we should sell one of our pieces of real estate and use the equity for our capital needs. No banker in his right mind would lend us money, and no investor would put money into this operation until it gets on its feet." The board quickly approved the idea, and I was instructed to sell the real estate in Bossier City, LA.

Although I had prepared for many hours thinking through various options, the one thing I had not done was ask the directors for their input. From that day forward, when I was preparing for a board meeting, I consulted several directors *before* the meeting, and they previewed my plans. That system worked much better. Together, we turned the company around and began to make profits.

Even when you actually know all the right answers, a smart leader seeks input from others. It will provide buy-in and more enthusiastic participation from those you consult, if nothing else.

Preparing to Lead Strategic Initiatives

The accounting and finance world is in constant motion. Our firms and people are challenged daily with conditions that change at the speed of light. To succeed in this rough business environment, firms frequently undertake strategic initiatives. Examples of such initiatives could include the acquisition of another accounting firm, the implementation of a new business model, the change of the firm's reporting structure, adopting a new practice management system, or going paperless.

Too often, there is little preparation for the introduction and implementation of major new initiatives. Missteps in preparing, planning, and executing initiatives waste time, money, and other resources. At times, the chaos resulting from poorly prepared and implemented initiatives lessens employees' respect for their owners and leaders. When major initiatives fail or fade, accountants become cynical and more resistant to the next big initiative.

A number of preparation processes are available. I want to propose a preparation process that clearly lays out the steps to achieve a prepared team and that will help you accomplish your vision and carry out your firm's mission.

Accomplishing the firm's initiatives requires the leaders to set a clear direction from the beginning. The leader's role is to create an environment that prepares and supports those who must carry out the many details that will determine the success of the endeavor. You must create and communicate a vision, set a strategy, and identify the right people to execute the strategy to achieve your goals. Leaders must ensure that those executing the strategy have enough time, money, and resources. In our consulting practice, we have developed and tested a process and set of tools to assist leaders in planning and preparing to implement various firm initiatives.

These eight preparation tools have been tested to help you prepare to lead any initiative or team. Although these tools are guides, they do not need to be implemented in the exact order given:

1. Prepare a vision for the initiative by creating a high-resolution picture of the future.
2. Clarify each person's role on the team-driving the initiative.
3. Assess the opportunities that the initiative will bring to the firm.
4. Understand the threats that are likely to impede success.
5. Outline any research for fact-finding that must be accomplished before launching.
6. Budget the resources that will be needed to carry out the initiative.
7. Develop the project game plan.
8. Launch the initiative with overwhelming power.

Step 1—Prepare a High-Resolution Picture of the End Game

Even under the best circumstances, a firm's initiatives still have the potential for going haywire. Busy season, competing priorities, and time and money constraints frequently sidetrack initiatives before the vision is achieved. A shared vision is the catalyst that will prepare your team to overcome these constraints and barriers. A leader's first challenge is to create and communicate a high-resolution picture: a vision for the undertaking that aligns with the vision for the firm. In chapter 11, "Vision: Reality in the Future," vision is discussed in depth, but here is a quick example of a high-resolution picture of the end game:

> To be a dominant accounting firm serving construction firms in our state, with at least 30 of the largest 100 contractors as clients by the year 20XX.

Too often, what is missing is a strong sense of purpose and direction to guide staff members through the rough patches. First, gather any of the firm's vision documents and prepare them for review by the leadership team. You may not have to recreate the vision for the firm if you already have a clear picture of the future. If you find more than one document that is pertinent, you might want to consolidate or summarize them.

For example, most good vision documents answer the following:

▲ What is the owner's vision of the initiative or the firm in one, three, or five years?
▲ How would the firm treat people, clients, employees, families, and the community?
▲ How would you like the firm to be characterized by outsiders and insiders?
▲ What is the end state of this project, and how does it fit the firm's vision?

▲ What are the values that the firm stands for?

▲ State what makes the initiative worth doing. For example, "Our costs aren't competitive, and we are losing market share."

▲ State the possible consequences to the firm of not succeeding with this initiative. For example, "Our level of client service may decline, and we won't be able to compete."

▲ Complete a step-by-step action plan for moving from the present state to the end state.

▲ What approach will you use?

▲ Set assignments of tasks and deadlines for their accomplishment.

Then, you can create the initiative vision by stating the specific reason why the firm is introducing this particular endeavor. How does it support the overall vision of the firm? For example, "A major goal of our firm right now is to reduce our costs. To do so, we must become more efficient in the delivery of our products and services."

 A Leader's Perspective

Bob Bunting gained his success by facing difficult issues within his firm, not by shying away from tough decisions. "I've really worked hard with leaders to recognize that anything that the partners will find difficult to accept should first be brought up as a trial balloon," he says. "Bring it up, get people to talk about it, and allow them to process the idea until they have mulled it over. You don't really bring it up to be voted up or down. You bring it up, so it can be discussed. Then, one day they accept this very difficult concept because you kept pressing on the issue, but you gave them time to be used to it."

Bob faced the same issue that many firms are facing today: early or founding partners established a retirement payout that was not sustainable over the long term.

"People who had worked into their 40s and helped pay off a bunch of other people were now being told they're not going to get what they paid out to others. So, we had to raise the issue, and then take everybody through the mourning process. We had to clarify the belief that the change was inevitable. What we had was simply not workable, and we had to get used to the idea that a realistic plan that you can count on is better than an unrealistic plan that will fail you when you need it most."

Include a description of the current state and a picture of the desired future state. Also, describe what it will take to close the gap between the current state and the desired future state. For example, "Our current culture supports complacency. Our future culture must focus on continuous improvement and constantly raise the bar for performance expectations. To get there, we will need to clarify performance goals for each department and person, develop systems that reward continuous improvement, and provide leadership to guide the culture change."

Step 2—Clarify Each Staff Member's Role

Do not confuse your individual roles and goals with the overall goals of the initiative. You must specify each person's responsibilities, goals, and actions. People on the leadership team may have activities that impede the group's goals. For example, you may have a leader assigned to a role to refine and challenge everyone else's ideas, action steps, and purpose. Or suppose that the mission of your firm's initiative is to implement a new tax-processing system. Your role as leader could be to set the budget, the general direction, and time lines for the project. You may have another leader oversee the entire design phase. Another person could lead the implementation of the new tax process. If the leadership team chooses to oversee and direct project management, the duties will be much more extensive than if the team chooses to set direction only.

If you adopt the role of setting direction only, then you must appoint a project leader or manager to carry out the more intensive management of the initiative. Each person on the leadership team must have a clear understanding of his or her role in the process of executing the initiative. The team should discuss the behaviors that will be consistent with its roles. Leaders are natural advocates for the team's or firm's initiative, so your words and actions will be watched by everyone to see if they have integrity. It is easy for misguided leaders to undermine their own projects by missing meetings, making cynical comments, and not carrying out the proper role. It is crucial that all people on the leadership team discuss and commit to integrated words and actions, so that followers are not misled or confused.

Step 3—Assessing Potential Opportunities

You must quantify the potential payoffs that are expected from the initiative. Projecting the benefits will give your team motivation to move forward and overcome the obstacles that will pop up from time to time.

To complete this step

▲ clarify the expected outcomes of the initiative in financial and other meaningful terms.
▲ list any factors working for you, such as a good economy, loyal clients, industry expertise, a trusted reputation, or a skilled group of professionals.
▲ critically think through ways to capitalize on these factors, such as having several important clients endorse the initiative as being very important to them.

Step 4—Understanding Possible Threats

Although opportunities give us hope and motivation, we must also assess the external threats to the firm's initiative. List any external factors that may slow you down or cause you to fail. Things like a workforce that is adverse to change, software that has not been fully beta tested, or team members who haven't experienced this process before are threats to consider.

Gordon Krater, managing partner of megaregional firm Plante & Moran, PLLC, in Southfield, MI, was taught early to assess the threats.

My first day at Plante Moran, Frank Moran taught me my first leadership lesson. I was 22, and he was 62. He came by, and he said, "Hey, do you play racquetball?"

And I said, "Well, yes I do."

He said, "Do you have your stuff in the car?"

I responded, "Well, yes I do."

He said "Let's go play at lunch."

I said, "That would be great," thinking to myself, this should be an easy match; I'm a pretty good athlete.

We went to play, and he says, "I'm going to spot you 15 points, and we are going to play to 21."

He didn't even break a sweat, and I was running all over the court, and he hardly moved. I was pretty confident, and Frank proceeds to beat me 21 to 18. I found out later he was state squash champion. Later, he asked me, "So, what did you learn?"

And I said, "You mean about racquetball? Because I learned a lot about where to put the ball, so you don't have to move."

He says, "You learned not to underestimate people."

And I said, "I sure did," and I thought what a wonderful lesson right out of the gate.

Step 5—Gather and Review Relevant Research

Before initiating a project or setting a budget and action plan in place, leaders must gather as many facts as possible. Consider questions like these:

▲ Has another firm attempted this in the past?
▲ What experience do the partners, leaders, and managers have in this particular type of endeavor?
▲ What are our clients' attitudes on this?
▲ Do we have confidence in any outside consultant we may be using?
▲ What are the legal and ethical implications?
▲ Have others failed or succeeded?
▲ What does the trend in the economy tell us?
▲ Are we leading the competition, or are we following them?

Step 6—Budgeting Time, People, and Money

One of the many issues that I've found in strategic plans is that many firms lay out plans but fail to allocate budgets. A plan without a budget allocation is a nonplan. Usually, it says that everyone hasn't agreed to the plan, perhaps the managing partner who is holding the purse strings. This will cause enormous confusion and nonaction toward the initiative. You have made decisions that will set the stage for the initiative. Now, using the following key steps, work through the issues that will allow you to develop a budget for carrying out the project:

▲ Describe the initiative deliverables.
▲ Identify a person or team with responsibility for each deliverable.

▲ Describe the leader's roles pertaining to each deliverable. For example, perhaps one of the deliverables is training on a new service. It is the leader's responsibility to see that someone on the team will develop an in-depth training module for the launch of the new service.

▲ Estimate costs, both in people hours and dollars for this initiative.

▲ Estimate the return on your investment from the resources that you commit to the project.

Step 7—Develop the Initiative Game Plan

Because change-initiative projects tend to be complex, a detailed project game plan is essential for each initiative in the game plan. You use the big-picture game plans to record tasks, time lines, responsible people, and costs. Game plans make everyone aware of the deadlines, reduce uncertainty, and communicate steps in a logical order. You may need to adjust your game plans later based on responses from critical stakeholders, reports from your teams, and other factors.

Nevertheless, the leadership team should establish a preliminary game plan to guide the firm in its overall approach. Here are some steps that you could use to prepare this game plan:

▲ List the strategic objectives that will be accomplished in each period of the plan.

▲ List the main initiatives necessary to accomplish each objective.

▲ Give your best estimate of completion dates for each initiative.

▲ Define a measurement for each initiative, so you can determine the level of success.

▲ Designate who owns the responsibility for each deliverable.

A sample of a big picture, firmwide, or initiative game plan is provided in exhibit 5-1 found at the end of this chapter.

Step 8—Launch the Initiative With Overwhelming Power

If you've ever watched the space shuttle blast off toward outer space, you have witnessed the power necessary to launch any new initiative. Over 95 percent of the total power necessary to launch a space shuttle and return it safely to the earth is expended in the first 5 minutes of its blast off. Once the space shuttle has pierced the atmosphere and broken free of gravitational pull, the next 2 weeks of its mission use only 5 percent of its total power. This is how you must think about launching a new initiative.

Bob Bunting launched an initiative with the power from the top, hoping to increase his firm's expertise in certain areas.

> We have some people we've brought in, and they comfortably engage other people in their work because they were raised in big firms where you don't hoard the work. They so easily leverage themselves. As we looked at our specialty areas where we wanted to be breakout leaders professionally—in banking and telecommunications—in some places, our growth

required us to go out and get additional help; in other cases, we weren't really getting off the ground, and so we didn't have the right kind of leadership.

Bob asked his industry group leaders to name their competitors, and he identified 45 people who were "eating Moss Adams's lunch," so to speak. He called each one of the 45 personally.

I told them the truth. I said, "We are looking at you because you are a very effective competitor. We want to dominate our market space. We think that you can help us do that. We think that what we do is very important, and we may even think it's more important than your firm does; I don't know the answer to that question, but if you think that's a possibility, maybe you'd have lunch with me." Well, out of 45 people, no one turned me down for lunch!

But it was because the CEO called, and it was because they thought they were pretty good. But if they had a peer from Moss Adams calling them up, that doesn't quite get them the level of recognition that they think they've earned. And I have to agree that they've earned it because they are eating our lunch in the marketplace. We hired 23 people over a 30-month period as a result of that effort.

Preparation Is for Action

All advanced manager training courses will tell you that if you want to get something done, give it to a busy person. Busy people have momentum, and they have no time to make excuses. Conversely, the professional student is a common phenomenon on college campuses. This is the student who is always learning but never graduating or getting a job. The same is true with many accounting firm teams: they love to spend time planning, but they're not as good at the real work of implementation.

Rick Anderson, CEO of megaregional firm Moss Adams LLP in Seattle, WA, shares

Within the practice of accounting, there are people who believe you can take your time and evaluate, evaluate, evaluate, and never decide or act. Leadership is not like that. Leadership requires you to be prepared to make decisions quickly, in the moment. For instance, client service is only good when it's delivered on time and right, and sometimes, you don't have a lot of time. There are times when people are too deliberative, even within the practice of public accounting.

Your leadership team is responsible for the success or failure of your firm's initiatives. You must prepare carefully from the beginning, and you must prepare a game plan that will allow others to accomplish the initiative goals and realize successful outcomes. The more carefully you prepare up front, the easier it will be to achieve your objectives. Most firms' initiatives are expensive in both dollars and time. If it is worth it to invest these precious resources in the initiatives, it is certainly worth it to invest the time to prepare. Failure is the reward for those who disregard the need to be prepared.

Leader Profile: David Sibits, president of the national firm CBIZ Financial Services in Cleveland, OH

David Sibits grew up in the inner city of Cleveland, OH. Dave played both football and baseball as he was growing up, and he was captain of his teams. He learned teamwork and leadership playing sports and today relies on many of his sporting experiences to build teamwork, get people in the right roles, and challenge his teams to greatness.

Sibits joined the IRS right out of college. Before becoming a leader on a national stage, Dave became managing shareholder of Hausser & Taylor, a large local firm in Cleveland.

Today, Dave is president of CBIZ's Financial Services practice group. Prior to joining CBIZ, Dave was executive managing director of RSM McGladrey's Ohio region. Prior to RSM McGladrey's acquisition of American Express Tax and Business Services (TBS), he was the executive managing director of the TBS Eastern Region, which included 35 offices in 13 states.

Dave was an integral member of the TBS senior leadership team and worked with his colleagues at RSM McGladrey to ensure a smooth integration with TBS.

Deborah Wechsler Kelm says of Dave

> Dave Sibits has guts. The reason I say that is because there were several times when Dave recommended me as the person to take the lead on some very important and complex national projects. (This was during the period that we were part of American Express.) These projects, such as the national client survey and national business development incentive program, were very time consuming and required working with a variety of key people throughout the organization. Moreover, these projects were of considerable interest to our entire company, and their success or failure would be obvious to everyone.
>
> Once Dave recommended me, he stepped aside and just assumed that I would handle the assignments in a cost-effective, professional, and creative way. As a leader, Dave had confidence in me and let me take the ball and run with it. This is very noteworthy about Dave's leadership style. He has the courage to assign others tough tasks, but he also has the insight to know which people he can count on to make it happen. Dave has no interest in micromanaging a project. It is so important to someone like me to know that your leader has total confidence in your abilities. I never felt that Dave was looking over my shoulder to make sure I was on track. He knew that I would keep him informed, but he didn't want to be involved in the details. This quality enables Dave to achieve much by staying focused on the big picture and using his intelligence and business savvy to develop strategies and solve problems.

Getting Started

Depending upon your personal leadership ability, once you get underway, you will start to attract a following to your cause. Do not look for others with their own missions to jump on your bandwagon. You need to first find your own following, or rather, your own following will find you. As your leadership ability grows, you may "lead a pack" if you are able to attract other leaders to your mission. Remember that servant leadership is based upon a how many can I help mentality, rather than trying to acquire as many followers as possible.

As you work to prepare your own leadership and a committed group of followers, keep the following ideas in mind:

1. Small groups can prepare more efficiently. Smaller teams improve creativity, accountability, a sense of ownership, and execution.
2. Utilize staff members at appropriate levels of your firm to prepare their sections of any initiative. Although current leaders are typically selected to oversee major strategic objectives and initiatives, it may be helpful to assign up-and-coming leaders to smaller roles to test them and give them experience.
3. You learn a great deal about potential future leaders by how they think and act. The best leaders think about others and their mission more than they think about themselves.
4. You will begin to get more clarity on your life mission as you become prepared to lead. Leadership preparation is not learned solely in the classroom, just as you cannot learn to play golf simply by reading a book or watching a video. At some point, you need to get a club in your hands and play the game.

Conclusion

One of the greatest leaders of the United States was Theodore Roosevelt. He was also physically one of the toughest men ever to hold the office of president. He was a cowboy, a cavalry officer, an explorer, and a big-game hunter. He held regular boxing matches at the White House. After he left office, he was shot on his way to give a speech. With a bullet in his chest, he insisted on giving his hour-long speech before he allowed the doctors to attend to him.

But Roosevelt was not always so vigorous. As a child, he was physically weak, with horrible asthma and poor eyesight. His father told him, "You have the mind, but you have not the body, and without the help of the body, the mind cannot go as far as it should. You must make the body." Roosevelt began spending time every single day building his body for the rest of his life.

When he died, a book was removed from underneath his pillow. Even near death, he was preparing himself for a new challenge. That's the way it is with leadership; everyone has the potential to be a great leader if they will apply themselves daily to the challenge.

When you are well prepared, you instill confidence in your team members, and their trust in you grows. Poor preparation has the opposite effect.

Exhibit 5-1: Sample Firm Game Plan

Vision

10-10-50: 10 offices, 10 Years, $50 Million in Revenue

Rank in the top 100 accounting firms to work for in the United States in *Accounting Today* magazine.

Mission

We at Smith and Jones commit our resources, our intelligence and our strengths to helping clients make wise and long-lasting financial decisions.

Core Values

We commit to **integrity** above all else, so that our actions match our promises.

We commit to **five-star client service** that focuses on heart, mind, and a sense of urgency in the pursuit of results for you.

We commit to **results** by providing customized real value to our clients.

Strategic Objectives

1. Strengthen the culture of the firm by improving accountability.
2. Strengthen the loyalty of the largest clients of the firm.
3. Intentionally grow the firm revenue by 10 percent and net profits by 15 percent per year.
4. Improve the efficiency of services delivery.
5. Organize a more robust training effort throughout the firm.
6. Improve the compensation system of the firm, so that people have incentive to help the firm achieve its goals.
7. Focus on leadership development at all levels of the firm.

Exhibit 5-1 continued

Strategic Objective	Measure-ment	Initiatives First Year	Due Date	Assigned To
Strengthen the Culture of the Firm by improving account-ability	Firm, team and individ-ual scorecard averages	Implement a balanced scorecard system for the partners of the firm Meet with each partner once per quarter and set challenge goals Review Key Performance Indicators with each partner quarterly	1/10	John
Strengthen the loyalty of the largest clients of the firm				
Intentionally grow the firm revenue by 10% and net profits 15% per year				
Improve the efficiency of ser-vices delivery				
Organize a more robust train-ing effort throughout the firm				
Each strategic objective must have a measurement to know when it has been achieved and a selection of initiative to move from the present to the end vision.				

Self-Discipline: Be the Master, Not the Victim

"Talent without discipline is like an octopus on roller skates. There's plenty of movement, but you never know if it's going to be forward, backwards, or sideways."

~ H. JACKSON BROWN, JR.

Before you can lead others, you must have the self-discipline to lead yourself. However you define success in your firm, you must set the example. Your team must see you demonstrate your total commitment and effort toward your definition of success. When you model this approach, most of your team members will follow your example. You'll be able to identify those who are not committed, and you can determine whether you can develop this commitment in them.

There are a number of ways to define self-discipline. We all know what it is in a general way, but some ways of looking at it may provide more ideas on how to benefit from it. Standard definitions emphasize controlling yourself and your desires. When you control yourself, you have the ability to master your future rather than be the victim of circumstances, feelings, and emotions. I prefer the following definition: the ability to take action, *regardless* of your feelings.

Some would advise you to control your desires or emotions. I don't believe that you can control your emotions; you can only deal with them. In his landmark book, *The 7 Habits of Highly Effective People*, author Stephen Covey defines *proactive* as the ability to choose your response after you've had an emotional stimulus. His very first habit is be proactive. I think he means that when you live your life according to the principles of human interaction, you can master your response to any situation.

In this chapter, we will discuss the benefits that self-discipline can have on your leadership focus. Such focus is one of the keys to business success. I'll introduce two extraordinary leaders who've built their leadership style around different styles of self-discipline. Lastly, I'll share some practical tips on improving your focus and self-discipline.

> A leader has to do what needs doing, even when it is unpopular.

When you put off firing someone, giving critical feedback, or talking to a hostile client, you are not leading. Don't let your emotions, feelings, and preferences interfere with doing the jobs that need attention. That's self-discipline and leadership.

When you develop self-discipline, you will clear your life of distractions that stop you from achieving your potential. You will have a focus that is rewarding in itself and that keeps you functioning at a high level. Discipline grants you a freedom that isn't possible to attain any other way.

This isn't a popular view. Our society tells us that discipline or structure means constraints—that rules are bad. But in fact, accountants are ideally trained to deal with disciplined structures like the tax code, auditing standards, and financial reporting guides. Although external rules may chafe, internal rules (self-discipline) allow us to become our best selves.

Self-discipline is required to rule your thoughts and be in control of your mind. The stronger your self-discipline, the more control you have over your thoughts, and consequently, your powers of concentration get stronger. When you are the master of your mind, you enjoy inner peace and happiness. Outer events do not sway you, and circumstances have no power to unsettle your peace of mind. This might sound unbelievable if you have not focused on self-discipline before, but experience will prove to you that all the preceding is true.

Self-discipline does not mean following a restrictive lifestyle. It is a very useful inner power that enables you to persevere and not give up, in spite of setbacks. It grants you the ability to resist impulses and distractions that stand in the way of attaining your goals. In fact, it is one of the most important pillars of real and stable success as a leader. The possession of this power leads to self-confidence and self-esteem and, consequently, to happiness, satisfaction, and real strength.

So long as you are operating alone, such as playing golf or tennis, or as a sole practitioner, self-discipline alone will take you far. And if you want to go fast, you can choose to go alone. But if you wish to go a long way, you will build a team to go with you. As we'll discuss in later chapters, building a team requires a new level of team discipline—a willingness to be governed, as Neal Spencer, CEO of the megaregional firm BKD, LLP, in Springfield, MO, calls it. But first, we'll explore the power of self-discipline.

Rick Dreher, CEO of the megaregional firm Wipfli LLP in Green Bay, WS, believes that his firm offers much more than a commodity service because of the personal discipline of his partners. "The differentiation between the firms is going to be in the execution and behavior. I think those are critical—who can get there quicker, better, bigger, faster. To reinforce the firm's value to clients, Wipfli returns to its service theme: we create lifetime relationships." In a firm as large as Wipfli LLP, it takes many self-disciplined leaders to carry out their competitive advantage as expressed by Dreher: execution and behavior. When leaders of a firm begin exercising self-discipline, a corporate culture of discipline begins to form, and such a culture can last for decades.

Leadership Demands Sacrifice

Leading any organization is no easy task; it can be lonely at the top. Leaders are pulled in many different directions, yet they must keep a clear vision of where they are headed.

One of the most difficult challenges of self-discipline comes when the leader must sacrifice for the greater good of the firm. Sacrifice is constant in leadership. As you rise in leadership, you give up many rights (the right to go home at 5:00 PM, the right to the biggest paycheck, the right to blame someone else for failures, and so on), and you assume many responsibilities.

As an example, Bill Haller, managing partner of the national firm CapinCrouse LLP in Indianapolis, IN, emphasizes

> In our firm, to be a strategic, high-earning partner, you have to be able to grow the practice. Once you start focusing on and branding as a niche firm, your communications turn off as many people as you turn on. You want the whole brand to help market for you. Now, we are getting smarter and smarter on how to protect the brand. Our brand permeates everything we do, from how we recruit, to how we do an audit, to how we interview, to how we relate to our own people, so we are just branding what we have an interest in doing.

We have an empire strategy—some might call it a category killer. With the empire strategy, we do a few things really, really well, and we focus on one industry: Christian not-for-profit organizations. An empire strategy can be good news and bad news. We travel a lot; we operate out of over 30 states. A fortress strategy would be if we were in a particular town, and we wanted to grow and protect our clients, we would be developing a lot of product lines and serving many industries.

Leader Profile: Marc Elman, CEO of the local firm PSB Boisjoli in Montreal, Canada

Although Marc Elman was a severe asthmatic as a youngster, he challenged himself to do what he could to conquer the effects of the disease. He began jogging, then running, and later running marathons. Approximately four years ago Marc completed an Ironman Triathlon in 13 hours that consisted of a 2.4-mile swim, a 112-mile bike ride, and a 26.2-mile marathon. He believes that for a person to lead, that person must first lead himself or herself. Then, he or she can lead others through the life that he or she models.

"If you are going to lead others, you must be willing to be out front and often heading into the unknown. That is scary," Marc says.

Marc's father pushed him into the work world, and he learned quickly that manual labor was not his cup of tea; however, he enjoyed selling Amway and Filter Queen products and clothing in a retail store. He learned to meet people and provide customer service. He overcame his introverted instincts by moving out of his comfort zone into direct sales, where he was very uncomfortable and yet exhilarated. At age 17, he traveled to Israel and parts of Europe, expanding his mind to the global opportunities for interacting with other people.

Partner Steven Moses describes in detail how Marc has affected his life and career.

> I would not be who I am or what I am today without Marc Elman's leadership. I talk about it every day with my wife. Marc's a role model who rubs off on me professionally and personally. He exhibits a constant striving to be the best.
>
> Marc became the leader of the firm through a drive to lead the firm as a business and build up the people and partners to be their very best. Marc realizes you're only as good as your people.
>
> His strengths in leadership are several. Number one, he leads by example, which is very important. Number two, his business sense is crucial. He has this incredible focus and places our firm within the best strategic position of advantage, identifying opportunities, putting a strategy in place to profit from those opportunities.
>
> Marc is very good at identifying people's strengths, and he has the ability to draw out the best of those strengths from the various players to stretch their comfort zones. So, when you're able to get people to go outside their comfort zones, you get great results, and you make the people better professionals.

Marc has been leading PSB Boisjoli for over 10 years. Challenging both himself and others, his leadership has carried the firm into the major leagues of accounting, tax, and consulting services for local, national, and international companies. Marc joined his firm in 1982 upon completion of his studies in accounting. He obtained his CA designation in 1985 and became a partner in 1988 after successfully leading the tax services division for several years. He also acts as an executive and board member for community and charitable organizations, including schools and youth camps.

As they climb higher in the organization, successful leaders learn that their level of sacrifice grows. You will never be asked to sacrifice your life by leading your accounting firm, but sometimes, the pain of sacrifice may be very great.

Self-Discipline Makes You the Best You Can Be

Rather than taking a walk, you feel too physically lazy and prefer to work at your desk until you have mentally exhausted your mind and body. You might know that you need to improve your eating habits, stop smoking, contact your best client, or meet your lawyer or banker referral source for breakfast, but you put it off another day. You don't have the persistence to change your habits.

Does this sound familiar? We all have had experiences like these. It seems like we all have some habits that we wish we could change, such as procrastination, smoking, excessive eating, physical or mental laziness, or lack of willpower. Self-discipline makes a great difference in our lives and brings inner strength, self-mastery, and decisiveness. Rather than being the victims of our impulses or circumstances, we master our lives.

Self-discipline is the ability to reject and overcome procrastination, bad habits, and impulses. It is the ability to make a decision and follow through with it, the inner strength that overcomes resistance for taking action, and one of the cornerstones of spiritual and material success.

Everyone has inner impulses that can make us act or speak inappropriately or fail to act or speak as we should. Self-awareness enables us to become conscious of the impulses, and self-discipline enables us to reject those impulses when they do not align with our values and the principles of human interaction.

The first 22 years of my business life had been constant change and lack of focus, so that I could never establish any momentum. During 6 years with Price Waterhouse I moved twice and had to reestablish relationships. During 8 years at Advantage, I bought or sold more than 40 of our businesses trying to find the right mix. During 8 years at Jacques Miller, my role went from one thing to the next almost every year. Little did I realize that the frustration I was experiencing was the perfect preparation for building a new business devoted to helping accounting firms grow. The Price Waterhouse experience gave me the credibility to relate to accountants and consultants. The Advantage years gave me intense leadership lessons about leading a large organization and reporting to the Securities and Exchange Commission and shareholders. The Jacques Miller experience gave me experience in segmenting and targeting a market. All of these are skills that I have relied on as I have led FiveStar[3], LLC. At the beginning of FiveStar[3], LLC, thankfully, I had built a great deal of the self-discipline that it would take to build a new business from the ground up.

Self-discipline helps us choose our actions and reactions instead of being ruled by them. Possessing self-discipline won't make life dull or boring. On the contrary, you will feel more powerful, in charge of yourself and your surroundings, happy, and satisfied. Believe me, it is not difficult to develop these powers. If you are earnest and willing to become stronger, you will certainly succeed.

Your Inner Circle Values

Former Corning Incorporated CEO Amory Houghton shares the advice that his predecessor gave to him. "Think of your decisions being based on two concentric circles. In the outer circle are all their laws, regulations, and ethical standards. In the inner circle are your core values. Just be sure that your decisions as CEO stay within your inner circle."

We are all aware of leaders who pushed beyond the outer circle and got caught, either by the law or their financial failures. More worrisome are the leaders who moved outside their inner circles and engaged in marginal practices, albeit legal ones. Examples include cutting back your long-term investments to meet the short-term compensation goals, bending compensation rules to pay partners in spite of marginal performance, using accounting tricks to help clients meet the quarterly expectations of security analysts, and booking revenues before products are shipped or services are delivered in order to pump up earnings per share.

All leaders feel the pressure to perform. As CEO, I feel it every day when problems mount or sales lag. As a leader, you know that the livelihood of your employees rests on your shoulders. Little by little, the pressures to succeed can pull us away from our core values, just as we are reinforced by our success in the market. The irony is that the more successful we are, the more we are tempted to take shortcuts to keep it going. The external rewards, such as compensation increases and admiring peers, reinforce our actions and drive us to keep our actions going. In order to avoid these traps, a leader must remain vulnerable to the advice of others, stay humble, be willing to take all the blame and give away the credit, and continue to invest in the elements described in chapters 2–6: self-knowledge, trustworthiness, critical thinking, preparation, and self-discipline. No one is perfect in these areas, and we must resist the notion that when we achieve success, we have achieved perfection.

Delay of Gratification

There is a potential paradox in self-discipline. Some people exhibit self-discipline, and some don't. Even more complex, some people exhibit self-discipline in some situations but not in other similar situations. For example, I exhibit self-discipline in my work, but when I'm on vacation, I just allow my feelings and moods to guide my days. Recently, one of my clients shared that she was very structured and disciplined at work and in her personal life until a few years ago. She said, "I found the discipline, structure, list making, adherence to schedules was destructive with my family. So, I found that I needed to change at home to be less structured at home." I suggested that those same consequences may be occurring in her work relationships, and she agreed to work on them.

In a related vein, many people say, essentially, "I could have self-discipline if I wanted to, but I don't particularly want to." Shy accountants say that they could sell their services, but they don't like the sales image. People who avoid decisions say that they could make a decision, but they don't really need to now. Leaders say that they could forge a new vision for the firm, but they're doing just fine without it.

Considerable research has accumulated to suggest that many of these examples stem from a habit of not delaying gratification. Delaying gratification means waiting for a larger reward rather than taking a smaller, immediate reward. For instance, a young child who delays gratification will wait one hour for a full candy bar instead of taking the half candy bar offered to him or her now. Many studies have found that young children's tendencies to delay gratification can predict success years later as an adult.

Some of this delay of gratification effect may stem naturally from biological-based impulse control. However, people can be trained to delay gratification. In the final few pages of this chapter, I'll share with you some tips to help you build stronger self-discipline.

Self-discipline is the ability to reject instant gratification in favor of something better. It is the act of giving up instant pleasure and satisfaction to meet a higher goal. However you're inclined based on your childhood impulses or the way you've achieved past rewards, you can control and apply self-discipline now. It gives you the power to follow your values; stick to your decisions; and not change your mind too often, thereby enabling you to reach your goals.

Self-discipline enables you to follow thoughts and behaviors that lead to improvement and success. It also gives you the power and inner strength to overcome bad habits, procrastination, fear, and laziness and to persevere in whatever you do. Self-discipline is of vital importance for mastering any subject and developing any skill.

Five Qualities of Self-Discipline

I have struggled with self-discipline myself, so I have focused on changing several of my habits over the years. As I changed my habits, I thought of the practice of self-discipline as having the following five facets:

1. Self-knowledge
2. Strong relationships
3. Commitment
4. Living your values
5. Self-coaching

Self-Knowledge

We talked about self-knowledge in chapter 2, "Self-Knowledge: The Inner Accelerator." To achieve self-knowledge, you must develop an awareness of your purpose. Many people want to become leaders without giving any thought to their purpose. They are attracted to the power and prestige of leadership positions and the rewards that go with them. But without a sense of purpose, leaders are at the mercy of their egos and vulnerable to impulses. You can't adopt someone else's purpose and still be an authentic leader. The purpose for your leadership must be uniquely yours. When you have this self-knowledge, you can apply the principles of self-discipline to realize your goals.

Chris Allegretti, CEO of the regional firm Hill, Barth & King, LLC (HBK) in Boardman, OH, shares, "One of the things that I think separated me was my discipline to learn practice development. I always had very real goals around practice development and made sure that I pushed that."

A business can have very disciplined employees who daily punch the clock; sit at their desks for eight hours; produce their workpapers, returns, and reports; and give their firm a day's worth of production for a day's pay. Some firms have learned to engage the hearts of their team members and, by doing so, have harnessed additional energy to accomplish more. In recent decades, businesses have evolved from maximizing the physical output of their workers to engaging their minds. To excel, great companies go one step further by engaging the *hearts* of their employees through a sense of purpose. When employees believe that their work has a deeper purpose, their results will vastly exceed the results of those employees who use only their minds and bodies. This becomes the company's competitive advantage.

Most of the accounting firms of the leaders who I interviewed for this book have been selected, either nationally or locally, as one of the best places to work. This is symbolic of firms that are capturing the hearts and minds, as well as the billable hours, of their staff members. Many accountants do not see the need for capturing their team members' hearts, so they flounder along in mediocrity.

The discipline one needs to capture the work hours of employees is modest; however, the self-discipline that it takes to capture team members' hearts require a high level of thinking and doing by the leader.

Strong Relationships

The discipline to develop close relationships is another mark of a leader. In today's world, relationships take discipline to build and maintain because there are so many distractions. Unfortunately, many leaders of major accounting firms believe that their job is to create the strategy, structure, and processes. Then, they just delegate the work to be done, remaining aloof from those doing the work. This detached style will not work. Today's employees demand more personal relationships with their leaders before they will give themselves fully to their jobs. They insist on having access to their leaders, knowing that it is in the openness and depth of the relationship with the leader that trust and commitment are built.

Focusing on relationships in a successful firm is important to Rick Dreher. "There are a whole bunch of firms that are really more of a loosely associated group that comes together to share administrative resources—you know what I mean? Don't kid yourself. They call themselves partners, they come together in a very loose association, but they're all in it for themselves."

Commitment

When you begin to develop self-discipline, you will likely fail to meet your standards at first. Expect yourself to fall down several times, whatever habit you are working to change. Perhaps you'd like to check e-mail just three times per day and focus on a major project at other times. If you've been in the habit of checking your e-mail every time you get to a stopping point in your work, it's likely that you'll continue to do this unconsciously.

For all our rainmaker students, we advise them to invest the first hour every work day to their practice development activities. We have learned that for most of them, it requires enormous self-discipline to change the old habits of putting off the important work of practice development. One managing partner told me, "Our staff put off marketing and practice development activities until after their billable hours, their vacations, their holidays, their video games, and smoke breaks. When we allocated the first hour each day to business development, we started getting results."

When you fall down, don't berate yourself; instead, seek clues to strengthen your commitment to self-discipline. When you can hone in on the reasons you slip up, you can avoid those issues and improve your self-discipline. Commit to persistence, and keep going even when you feel like quitting.

Write down your goals and keep track of the times that you succeed in your new efforts at self-discipline. This commitment will improve your efforts.

Living Your Values

You may have a great deal of self-discipline, but to teach it, you must demonstrate it. Without self-discipline, you can't gain the respect of your followers. During the years 2008 and 2009, the economy in the United States declined. The major thing that I learned during these difficult years was that I had lost some of my self-discipline. Being a leader of my company, my lack of strong self-discipline became evident in others in my firm. Some of them watched me come in late, leave early, and take long lunch breaks. They saw me do this for years, and they didn't appreciate the fact that I worked early mornings and late nights at home on projects and traveled 150 nights per year to our clients. What they saw was my lack of self-discipline on office days. I had to change that because the tone that I set was the one that they would follow. Today, I am in the office before 8:00 AM and rarely leave until 6:00 PM. During my office hours, I set a pace that demonstrates a sense of urgency.

Sam Coulter, founder and president of the local firm Coulter & Justus, P.C., in Knoxville, TN, says, "Farming taught me determination as much as anything. We didn't have a lot of good equipment, so what we did have broke down a lot. My farm family taught me you had to get the job done no matter what. I believe this is also necessary in an accounting business; we must meet our client's deadlines and achieve their goals no matter what."

Sam is still learning to be a better leader, even though he is 62 years old and working 3 days per week. "One of the strange benefits of this 3-day week I am working is that there is a 4-day weekend every week. During those 4-day weekends, I have time to think about the opportunities and problems we are encountering. Those days are the days when I probably accomplish more for the business than I do the 3 days here in the office. I am able to clearly think about our business and then make an impact when I return the following week."

Leaders are defined by their values and character, which are shaped by personal beliefs developed through study, introspection, consultation with others, and a lifetime of experience. These values define the leader's moral compass. Ethical leaders know the true north of their compass, the difference between right and wrong, and have a deep sense of the right thing to do. Integrity is required in every leader. Integrity is not just the absence of lying but telling the whole truth, as painful as it may be. Without complete integrity in your interactions, no one can trust you. If they can't trust you, why would they ever follow you?

Self-Coaching

You will set the tone for developing your self-discipline. Even when you share your goals with others, you are your own most important coach. Self-discipline can be learned and developed, but it is often a significant challenge. Look for smaller challenges at first to practice your system and develop your confidence. In the last couple pages of this chapter, I'll share with you some self-coaching methods that will help you build a stronger commitment to discipline.

Scott Dietzen, managing partner, Northwest Region, of the national accounting firm CliftonLarsonAllen LLP in Spokane, WA, shares, "You've probably heard the story of John Wooden training people to put their socks on. I forced my players to iron their shoelaces. They could not have a twist in their shoelace. I wanted them to be disciplined to the small details. Part of it was just the discipline of making sure that their shoelaces looked really sharp; it's to send a message: you need to be disciplined in all areas."

Most of all, be an encouraging coach for yourself, not an overly critical taskmaster. Anticipate imperfection, but strive to eliminate it. Celebrate your victories. When you waver, think about this quote from motivational speaker Robin Sharma: "The price of discipline is always less than the pain of regret."

Leader Profile: Neal Spencer, former CEO of the megaregional firm BKD, LLP, in Springfield, MO

Neal Spencer grew up moving from city to city with his family, as his dad's job required. Although Neil felt the pain of the dislocations, he learned to adapt to new situations and the new relationships that invariably came with moving around the country. The same sense of dislocation seemed to challenge his early college and work years. Neil tried college but dropped out to go to work. In the restaurant business, he moved from Wendy's to Red Lobster, from Arkansas to Wisconsin, and from cook to manager before committing himself to the studies required at the college level. Finally, he committed to college and succeeded well.

BKD LLP partner Bob Brandenburg says of Neal Spencer

Neal is gifted in many ways, particularly when it comes to people. He takes the time to get to know people and gains a deep understanding of their individual personalities. Not only does Neal learn about their personal lives, but he learns how each individual thinks and how they react. I often believe that Neal knows people better than they know themselves. He understands how to assist people with challenging situations; he understands their limitations; he understands what drives them to excellence; he understands how to inspire them. He waits patiently for the right opportunity to challenge his people.

For example, I was a manager and serving our region's largest hospital client. The relationship was new, so we were in the early stages of building rapport with the client. They had a savvy board, with many successful business leaders who were actively involved in the hospital's governance. Enron had recently failed. We were presenting the annual audit report to the board of directors; Neal was the partner on the account. I was expecting a challenging board meeting.

The morning of the board meeting, a major event occurred, preventing Neal's attendance. Neal looked to me and said, "You have to lead the meeting. If you want to be a partner someday, you have to act like one. Good luck." Initially, I was angered and felt abandoned by Neal. I vividly recall standing at the head of the long boardroom table, alone, receiving questions from board members about Enron and how our audit protected their interests. These were very tough questions, particularly for a relatively young manager.

After the initial panic, I felt a sense of calm. I reflected on some advice Neal had provided me, "Clients pay for your point of view. Give it to them." And so I did. I simply told the board what I thought. I did my job and did it well. Neal knew I was ready for the challenge, even before I knew I was ready. I felt as much job satisfaction that day as any time of my career (other than being elected a partner). I could not wait for the next opportunity. It was this experience and a consistent pattern of similar experiences that inspired me to follow Neal anywhere he would take me.

BKD LLP partner Joe Meyer adds

Neal Spencer is one of the most interesting and effective leaders I have ever encountered. As is the case with most successful leaders, Neal enters meetings and strategic sessions with information and possible endgames. Based on his study of the particular issue, I believe he quite frequently knows what is right. However, how he uses the information and his initial sense of where he believes the strategic direction should end up is where he differentiates himself from other leaders and, in my opinion, is where the magic of his leadership really happens.

Neal listens intently to the conversation. This lets everyone know that he is open to their points of view. He sits back (with a bit of a smile on his face!) and allows the dialogue and back and forth to continue. He always has brief notes in front of him (handwritten). He will ask open-ended questions—not statements of fact—that generally cause half of the audience to rethink the previous positions they have espoused. He has a unique way of bringing out the opinions of everyone, even those who generally do not contribute significantly in group settings. He truly facilitates a process.

While I am quite confident that in most situations, the endgame is very close to what he envisioned before he entered the meeting, I also know that at times, he has allowed his mind to be changed based on the session. Just as importantly as this willingness to have his opinion changed based on the input of others is how the group feels when it is time to conclude and execute. Many leaders do not have

(continued)

(continued)

a process to bring the group along through the decision tree. In these cases, at the end of the process, many in the group feel that the leader simply dictated the answer to the group but used the meeting as cover. At the end of Neal's meetings, the group feels engaged and ready to act. They know that their opinions were heard and that Neal truly wants to hear positions and opinions from all parts of the compass of possibilities. I think we all know (and trust) that his instincts are generally spot on, but we appreciate the approach he brings to the decision-making process.

Neil is CEO of BKD LLP, the 10th largest CPA and advisory firm in the United States. Although BKD LLP operates from 29 offices in 12 states, the firm serves clients in all 50 U.S. states and in 40 other countries. Neil is responsible for the leadership and strategic direction of the firm's more than 2,000 personnel, including approximately 250 partners. He entered the public accounting profession in 1986, joining BKD LLP's Little Rock, AK, office as a staff accountant. There, he focused on health care for the next 10 years and became partner in 1995. He then transferred to Louisville to lead the firm's Kentucky offices. He was responsible for the offices in Bowling Green, Owensboro, and Louisville, KY, along with Evansville, IN, and their 150 personnel. Neal served as an active client-service partner and member of the BKD Health Care Group. He worked with hospitals, skilled nursing facilities, and community mental health organizations.

He is a board member of the AICPA Foundation; is president of the BKD Foundation; and was recently elected to serve a three-year term on the management board of Praxity, AISBL, the largest international association of accounting firms in the world. Neal is president-elect of the board of directors of the OTC Foundation, the fundraising arm of Ozarks Technical Community College. In 2003, he was recognized by the Sam M. Walton College of Business at the University of Arkansas as accountant of the year in public accounting.

Neil has been involved with numerous boards both professionally and in the community. He believes in giving back to the community and has taught junior achievement classes and continues to be an active supporter of the United Way. He graduated in 1985 from the University of Arkansas, Fayetteville, with a BSBA degree in accounting.

What Are We Leading *Toward*?

As this is written in 2011, the United States and other countries are still recovering from the financial shock waves caused by the collapse of several major corporations, prompting a massive government bailout. Looking back at the scandals, the disruption in the world economy, and the unsettled stock market, leaders of accounting firms are more uncertain than ever before. Rather than allowing this uncertainty to immobilize us, we must recognize the power that we have as the most trusted business advisers and use that power to be a force for good in the world.

What if all business leaders were committed to improving the lives of their customers, employees, and shareholders? Are we prepared to

▲ be inspired by our mission, not our money?

▲ live by our values, rather than our egos?

▲ build relationships through our hearts, rather than our status?

▲ model self-discipline, so that we would be happy for our families to read about our behavior on the Internet?

Money alone is insufficient to provide either security or happiness for our families and employees. Making a difference in the businesses and lives of others can bring unlimited joy, and leading a life of service can bring fulfillment.

In the movie *Coach Carter*, Samuel L. Jackson played the title role: a basketball coach asked to coach a team of losers. The main thing that he taught his players was self-discipline. Through self-discipline, conditioning, and some talent, the team became a championship team. It takes a leader to set the example of self-discipline. Other leaders follow it, and managers are able to continue it once it has begun. However, self-discipline must first be demonstrated by the leader.

At some point, a business will gain momentum. When I was moving from job to job in my early career, I was never able to gain momentum. Finally, after beginning my accounting consulting business in 1991, strong self-discipline enabled me to gain business momentum. Momentum is a leader's best friend. With momentum, you look better than you really are, and it will make a huge difference in your firm. Once you gain some momentum, it is much easier to continue and guide than it is to initiate.

Focused Growth Is a Priority

The best leaders always seem to have a clear set of priorities before them. It's something that good leaders do, whether they are leading a large firm or a small one. Using the Pareto rule, we know that 20 percent of our effort produces 80 percent of our results. It's easy to look back and see this play out in hindsight, but when looking forward, it is sometimes difficult to know what falls in the important 20-percent category. Start out setting priorities for small projects and build your priority muscle, so that when large assignments come along you can determine which actions will make the most of your time.

Tony Argiz, founder, CEO, and managing partner of the megaregional firm Morrison, Brown, Argiz & Farra, LLP, in Miami, FL, has learned that developing a greater understanding of his clients' businesses pays off.

> In the old days, you could go out on the golf course and sell yourself with just your title and a friendly face. Then, about 15 years ago, the world began to change; people also really valued your intellectual knowledge. What I tried to do in auto dealerships is to know that business like an auto dealer more than an accountant. I wanted to learn, How do they make money? How do you generate more profits in your repair shop, in your parts department? Why are some people successful in used car sales and others aren't?

To focus your priorities on the most valuable work, you have to consider the following three elements:

▲ Where will I get my best return?

▲ Where will my talents make the most impact?

▲ What is necessary?

Terry Harris, managing partner of McKonly & Asbury LLP in Harrisburg, PA, believes

> In the public accounting environment, it is important that your organization have a clear
> mission and that you have the ability to differentiate yourself from your competitors. In our
> organization, things that differentiate us are the service attitude of our team, our focus on
> technology tools for our team, promoting a culture that values individual team members,
> and niche practice areas where we excel in our markets. Creating a culture of "fun" is also
> at the core of who we are as an organization.

Terry's firm also sets its priorities by defining its niche.

> You gain efficiencies by having a niche because you're knowledgeable at it. You've got
> people who can perform at a higher level because of that niche. Secondly, you can develop
> tools that make it more efficient to implement the process. Third, you become known in
> a region or the state or whatever, depending on how large a market you're playing in. You
> can add value to your clients, and you have some pricing power when you have a niche, as
> well. All this helps to create a barrier to entry for competitors.

Using Self-Discipline to Focus

In many cases, the leader's best return will come from properly delegating action steps to
people and empowering them to accomplish their jobs. If you delegate a project when you
have the most expertise, it won't get done with the same quality that you would do it, and it
won't get done as quickly. But, you must also know that if you do the project yourself, then
you can't do something else that may have more impact, and your subordinate won't gain
valuable experience. Leaders must learn to get their best returns in working with people by
delegating and empowering them. This will help you obtain the best long-term return on
your time.

Veteran consultant Jay Nisberg says, "When you focus on expertise in industries rather
than service areas like audit and tax, you can develop a regional or national identity. A good
example is Gary Shamis in the food industry. His firm SS&G grew to a certain level in
Cleveland, expanded it to include Ohio and surrounding states, and now his firm is national
in scope in their service to food-service companies."

Next, consider where your talents will make the most impact. Are you better at accounting or communicating? Are you better at looking forward or looking back? When you focus
yourself in your area of your best talent, you will be happier, and your returns will be greater.

Lastly, we must understand what is necessary. We all have bosses. In some cases, our boss is
a team member, and in other cases, our boss is a client. We must ensure that we're meeting
the boss's needs with our actions, regardless of whether the boss is someone else at the firm
or the client.

One of the most notable business leaders of our time is Jack Welch, the former chairman of the General Electric Company. When he assumed leadership in 1981, the company was already a great success, but Jack believed that you could only coast one way. He set about to reprioritize GE's business on a worldwide basis. In his book *Jack Welch Speaks: Wisdom from the World's Greatest Business Leader*, Jack said

> To the hundreds of businesses and product lines that made up the company, we applied a single criterion: can they be number 1 or number 2 at whatever they do in the world marketplace? Of the 248 businesses or product lines that could not, we closed some and divested others. Their sale brought in almost $10 billion. We invested $18 billion in the ones that remained and further strengthened them with $17 billion worth of acquisitions.
>
> What remained, aside from a few relatively small supporting operations, are 14 world-class businesses … all well-positioned for the [coming years] … each one either first or second in the world market in which it participates.

You must develop the self-discipline needed to focus on a small scale before you can focus on a large scale. What about you and your firm? Are you first or second in your market in your service and product lines, or do you have a series of products and services that are just average? What can you be the best at in your market? Becoming the best takes strategy, self-discipline, and focus. Take some time to reassess your own priorities. Are you like GE was, spread all over the place with many services, or are you focused on a few things that will bring the highest return?

In the mind of effective leaders, time is a tangible commodity. It cannot be recovered once it is lost. However, time used correctly is among your most potent assets. Many ineffective leaders struggle with time. It is intangible in their minds, vanishing without any trace of results. A leader must not mistake activity for achievement.

Without self-discipline, you will fail as a leader. Nobody is *entitled* to leadership. In fact, most of the people who take over leadership roles because of their entitlement (longevity, family relationship, book of business) will fail miserably at leading others. They tend to lead by saying, "Do what I say, not what I do." You will not be able to identify a single great leader who has achieved success without diligent hard work and self-discipline.

Call it focus, persistence, or determination; they are all the same thing. Losing focus or quitting before the task is complete is a failure in leadership. Few things are more important than leaders who possess an unyielding relentlessness toward the vision and goals of the firm.

Building Habits of Self-Discipline

Self-discipline is critical to a successful life. As they say, "You make your habits, and your habits make you." Some people have natural leadership instincts, yet the ability to lead is actually a set of skills that can be learned. The following daily habits will help you, your staff, and your clients grow.

Invest Five Minutes Each Morning to Meditate on the Major Areas of Your Life

Particularly look for areas in your professional life, your marriage and family, your community, and your spiritual life where you may have not done what you said you would do. Think about any instances where you have been dishonest, cut corners, been inconsistent, or not kept your word. Then, commit to correct those instances by appropriately dealing with the consequences of your actions.

Bill Hubly, founder and managing principal of the local firm Corbett, Duncan & Hubly, PC, in Itasca, IL, believes, "For a leader, everything starts with discipline. I get up in the morning and exercise first thing. It's a discipline of setting good habits. It starts the day out right. That puts me in the proper mindset and frame of mind. When I come to the office, I must be in a positive mood, show positive energy, and give people the right example. Discipline, for me, sets the entire tone for what I do. I determine my attitude."

Make Self-Discipline a Part of Your Daily Ritual

When beginning any skill development, you should begin small and build up over time. Perhaps setting aside one hour per day in which you will exercise extreme self-discipline then adding a new hour each week would help you get started. You might consider engaging a coach to support you during the development of your routine of self-discipline. Most research proves that just thinking about developing self-discipline will be successful in less than 5 percent of professionals. Writing your self-discipline goals will have a dramatic effect by raising your probability to more than 25 percent (that's a whopping 500 percent increase). Sharing your plan to increase your self-discipline with someone else will increase your probability to more than 50 percent, and asking this person to hold you accountable increases your odds to more than 75 percent. When you and your coach have met regularly for 24 months, and you have been credible with your efforts, you can ensure success nearly 100 percent of the time.

No matter how busy he is, Ken Baggett, co-managing partner of the national firm CohnReznick LLP, always returns phone calls and e-mails.

> I'm a real big believer in returning phone calls and e-mails quickly. I'll give you an example of it. That is my call sheet today. Before I go home tonight, all five will have been called.
>
> I have one particular partner who struggles with that concept sometimes, and I was chatting with him one day, and I said, "So, why don't you like me?"
>
> He said, "What do you mean?"
>
> And I said, "You must not like me. You never return my phone calls; you never answer my e-mails."

Of course, Ken's partner assured him that this was not the case, but Ken's concern was not about his personal relationship with the partner.

> I said, "God only knows what you're telling your clients because I'm your partner, and I see you; I know you like me. If you are responding to your clients in that same manner, it's even worse. You're telling them not only you don't like them, but you don't care about them."

Bill Haller adds, "I don't think a leader could lead if they don't have great discipline and project management support. I return phone calls and e-mails in real time because when somebody is asking for my input or asking for a direction or decision, it's happening now."

Dedicate Yourself to Lifelong Learning

Leaders become great by dedicating themselves to a high level of learning, growth, and improvement. Use your self-discipline to invest at least four hours each week to learning something new. Do not settle for just knowing *how* to do something. Dig deeper by asking why, and then, go find the answer. Interview an expert, write an article, make a speech, or enroll in a class to find the answer to a question that is on your mind or the minds of those who follow you.

When I joined Price Waterhouse, the office managing partner, Fred Frick, advised me to invest at least an additional 10 percent of my work week in self-improvement, such as reading, taking classes, participating in Toastmasters International or other community activities, and listening to audio programs. Fred reasoned that if I invested an additional amount of time in self-improvement, then I would advance more quickly in my career. It took a great amount of self-discipline to follow Fred's advice, and I am eternally grateful to him for mentoring me in this manner.

"Competency is crucial in an accounting firm leader," Bill Haller says. "When I walk into firms that are struggling, I often encounter partners who have lost their CPA competency. They are not good tax guys or good auditors. People don't respect them. They have delegated technical competency to the people underneath them."

Accept Responsibility

Great leaders master their lives; they never play the role of a victim. They recognize that part of being a great leader is ultimately being responsible for all of your successes and failures. Analyze your current projects on a daily basis and ask yourself, "Have I done all that needs to be done? What have I not done that I should?" Once you have analyzed each project, if you find a weakness, go the extra mile by working extra hours, hiring an outside expert, or getting creative to repair the weakness—or to turn it into a success!

Phil Holthouse, founder and managing partner of the top-100 multioffice firm Holthouse, Carlin & Van Trigt LLP in Los Angeles, CA, says it's critical for leaders to facilitate effective communication as part of accepting responsibility. "I see e-mail as very dangerous. If people are upset about something, it's so much easier to take a hard shot in an e-mail than it is to say it to somebody to their face. So, if I'm copied on e-mail exchanges, and I see them start to escalate, I will jump in and just say, "You two need to get in the same office or get on the phone."

Face Your Fear to Develop Courage

Leaders inspire others when they face their fears and demonstrate courage. There can be no courage without fear. Invest at least two to four hours each week doing things simply for the sake of developing courage: make a difficult phone call, speak to an audience, hold a difficult conversation, learn a new skill, write an article or a top 10-list, or visit someone you have always wanted to meet.

The Truth About Self-Discipline

There is a misconception in the public mind regarding self-discipline or willpower. It is erroneously thought to be something strenuous and difficult and that one has to exert and tense the body and mind when expressing it. Because people believe it to be so difficult, they avoid using willpower, though they are conscious of its benefits. They acknowledge that the employment of willpower in their lives and affairs will greatly help them and that they need to strengthen it, yet they do nothing about it.

Your discipline gets stronger by not allowing the expression of unimportant, unnecessary, and unhealthy thoughts, feelings, actions, and reactions. If this negative energy is not expressed, it becomes positive and is stored inside you like a battery. It then becomes available at a time of need. By practicing appropriate exercises, you develop your powers the same way as a person who trains his or her muscles in order to strengthen them.

Conclusion

Self-discipline involves choosing your actions according to your *values* instead of how you *feel* in the moment. Often, it involves sacrificing the pleasure and thrill of the moment for what matters most in life. Therefore, it is self-discipline that drives you to

- ▲ continue your work on a project after the initial rush of enthusiasm has faded away.
- ▲ devote the first one to two hours each day to an important project without interruptions.
- ▲ go to the gym when all you want to do is relax.
- ▲ wake early to work on yourself by meditating, studying, or writing.
- ▲ say no when tempted to break your diet.
- ▲ check e-mail only at specific times of the day.
- ▲ limit text messaging to specific times.
- ▲ leave your phone behind when attending meetings.
- ▲ hire an accountability coach who will challenge you to grow

Section 2

Leading Staff

What kind of people are you currently attracting to your firm? When I visit an accounting firm, I can tell a lot about its leadership by the people on its staff. The quality of the people in your organization does not depend on your human resources department or hiring process; their quality depends on you the leader. In this section, we are going to discuss building other leaders and creating a multiplier effect of leadership development within your team and firm.

In his book, *The 21 Irrefutable Laws of Leadership: Follow Them and People Will Follow You*, John Maxwell explains the law of reproduction. He says that we have a choice of either addition or multiplication. We can lead people and help them be successful, or we can raise up leaders who, in turn, will lead other leaders. So, the real question is, Are you recruiting potential leaders, or are you settling for followers?

Leaders who train, coach, and mentor followers focus on improving their weaknesses, treat everyone the same to be fair, grow by addition, and affect only the people they personally touch. Leaders who train other leaders focus on strengths, treat every person individually, grow by multiplication, and affect people far beyond their own personal sphere of influence.

In his book *Wooden on Leadership*, Coach John Wooden said, "Ultimately, I believe that's what leadership is all about: helping others to achieve their own greatness by helping the organization to succeed."

One of the crucial understandings that everyone must have when leading other people is that everyone has a different perspective. Every person you lead has a different family experience, education, and communication style. Because of these and many other differences, you cannot take a one-size-fits-all approach to leading. Steve Mayer, managing partner of Burr,

Pilger & Mayer LLP in San Francisco, CA, says that you can't make assumptions about how other people will act based on your own experiences.

> I coached in a very poor area of San Francisco. About 70 of our 80 kids on the team were from the projects in the Bay Area. Many of those kids were from broken or single-parent homes. One of our kids suffered a concussion. I couldn't reach his parents, so I drove him to the hospital. The hospital workers wouldn't take care of him because we didn't have the right paperwork. Finally, I located his parents out fishing on a pier. I drove out there and said, "Your son is in the hospital," and they asked me if I would take care of him because they still wanted to fish for another hour or two. I was 17 or 18 years old and I thought, "God, not everybody grew up in the same family I did." So, I don't take for granted that people grew up or think like me. When I begin a relationship with a partner or client, this realization has helped me understand better where other people are coming from.

Mayer's experience working with youth has profoundly affected his understanding of the importance of mentoring, as well. Approximately 20 years after those coaching experiences, he ran into one of his former players at a black-tie dinner for a charity. "He said, 'Coach Mayer, I still talk about what you taught me on the football field. I played college ball and pro ball. Then, I blew out my knee, so I couldn't play anymore, and now, I spend all my time working with underprivileged kids. It's all because of Coach Mayer and the other coaches.'"

Many people believe that if the cause is good, then people will follow, but that is not the case. People follow good leaders first, and then, they will pursue the vision. When we have that understanding, we see how necessary it is to develop great leaders around us. When people don't buy the vision or leader, they seek another leader. When people don't like the leader, but they like the vision, they seek another leader. When people buy into the leader but not the vision, they keep the leader and seek a new vision. When people buy into the leader and vision, they create momentum.

The most stable and successful accounting firms have leaders who create a leadership culture. The best firms are willing to invest in their people today for a greater return tomorrow. Achievement is derived when someone is able to do for himself. Team success comes when the leaders and followers do great things together. Real significance in life and business comes when the leaders train up other leaders to carry on after they have gone.

Eventually, every leader leaves his firm. Some may step back gradually; others may do it abruptly. A huge part of a leader's role is to prepare the next generation of leaders to carry on after he or she has left. When all is said and done, your success as a leader will not be graded by what you have done. You will be graded by how well your firm or team did after you were gone. Your lasting legacy will be judged by your succession.

In this four-chapter section, I will address the four key elements in building a great team:

▲ Teaching, coaching, and mentoring
▲ Challenging personal growth
▲ Empowerment
▲ Accountability

Teaching, Coaching, and Mentoring: Multiplying Your Leadership	Challenging Personal Growth: Leading the Whole Person	Empowerment: The Secret to Exponential Growth	Accountability: Trust but Verify
Chapter 7	Chapter 9	Chapter 10	Chapter 8

Section Two: Leading Staff

As a leader, if you will concentrate your efforts in these 4 areas, you will be focused on the 20 percent of the things you can do that will get 80 percent of the results in developing great people and teams.

Everyone watches the leader. Remember when you were in high school, and you always knew the kids in the class ahead of you, but you didn't know many in the class behind you? It's the same concept. When you are the team or firm leader, everything you do provides a teaching moment. How seriously do you regard this role? A good leader will recognize his or her teaching power and can begin to coach others in specific skills related to running an accounting business. Great leaders select a few future leaders for personal mentoring. Mentoring is the highest form of teaching because it extends outside the confines of the everyday work life of an accountant.

The best leaders are great at building long-lasting relationships. They know that you must touch people emotionally before moving people into action. Bill Hubly, founder and managing principal of Corbett, Duncan & Hubly, PC, believes, "As a leader, you live in a glass house, and you need to set the right example as a leader every day. That's critical if you expect other people to develop leadership skills because they're watching you and learning from what you do."

Personal growth is the essential ingredient for young accountants to grow into maturity. *Personal growth is not professional growth.* It has nothing to do with becoming a better accountant. Personal growth has everything to do with the emotional intelligence, social intelligence, and relationship ability of people. When you truly care about your team members, you will be willing to risk the relationship with them to help them grow. If you don't care, then you can avoid the conflict by not challenging them, and they will not mature. Rather than reacting negatively to personal growth challenges, rising leaders will welcome it. As a leader, your role is to challenge your staff members to be the best they can be both professionally and personally.

Bill Haller, managing partner of the national firm CapinCrouse LLP in Indianapolis, IN, takes the personal growth of his team members seriously.

> I think loving your employees means that you are going to have the patience, the honesty, and the responsibility to make sure that you do what's right for them. Sometimes, that might be telling them no. Once a month, the partners have a prayer meeting where we pray for our staff and our clients. Our directors and managers get together on a phone call around the country to do the same thing. Our commitment to CapinCrouse staff is we pray for them, we care about their families, and we care a lot about their careers.

For a leader to grow others and build a strong team, he or she must delegate authority and risk to others. Empowerment combines all the pluses of the micromanager and abandonment leader with none of the negatives. Empowerment allows you to assess the risk in the assignment with the training and experience of the staff member and then select an empowering strategy that works best in each situation.

Finally, holding staff members accountable for great performance is a key ingredient in successful leadership. Without accountability, you can achieve only a 50/50 chance of success, even with the most dedicated and talented work force. In this challenging era of business, 50/50 is not enough and will not make you great. In chapter 8, I will build a case for accountability and then provide some power tools to help you succeed.

Leader Profile: Frank K. Ross, CPA, director of Howard University School of Business Center for Accounting Education in Washington, D.C.

When he first arrived in New York, Frank Ross was dazzled by the experience of immigrating from St. Kitts. Over the next 40 years, Frank developed great leadership skills in himself and thousands of others who worked alongside him. To get a real sense of this American leader, you must read his book *Quiet Guys Can Do Great Things, Too: A Black Accountant's Success Story*. As the first black partner at Peat Marwick (now KPMG LLP), he endured verbal abuse from some white partners, but Frank set an example for everyone by his personal leadership.

Frank points to the mentorship of several partners who challenged him to be the best he could be. Sy Bohrer and Jim Powers mentored him in both technical and client service skills and taught him many valuable leadership lessons that he passed on to thousands of up-and-coming KPMG LLP team members and partners.

Frank rose to become a member of KPMG LLP's board of directors and the chairman of the board of the KPMG Foundation. After a stint in the New York office, he was selected as the mid-Atlantic area managing partner for audit and risk advisory services and managing partner of the Washington, DC, office. In December 2003, he retired from KPMG LLP after more than 38 years of service. Today, Frank is the director of the Howard University School of Business Center for Accounting Education and a visiting professor of accounting, teaching auditing and ethics.

In 1968, Ross was one of the 9 cofounders and the first president of the National Association of Black Accountants (NABA). His personal leadership has been instrumental in the growth of NABA to more than 5,000 members today. Frank's business life exemplified mentoring, challenging personal growth, empowerment, and accountability.

Richard D. Parsons, chairman and CEO of Time Warner, Inc., says

> As a West Indian immigrant, Frank and his family took a giant leap of faith when they decided to make the journey to America. People of color have always had unique obstacles to overcome as they strove to make a way for themselves in this country. But, imagine a young Frank K. Ross, unfamiliar with either the white or black cultures of America in the 1950s, living in Yonkers, plunged into the thick of the civil rights movement, and trying to become one of the first African Americans to make it in the old boy world of corporate accounting.

Elaine Hart, Frank's former administrative assistant, recalled one such incident in particular

> There was one group of new hires that came in, including quite a few African Americans, one year. And I don't know what it was about this group, but whenever things didn't go their way, they would use the race card. They expected that because Frank Ross was black, he would support them, but he wouldn't. At first, I wondered why Frank didn't step up for them, too.
>
> After we talked, I fully understood his rationale. He told me they were not holding up their end of the bargain. He had had meetings with them, and their work was substandard. One young man came in and talked with him. Frank told him he couldn't use the race card every time things don't go the way he wants. "Before pulling the race card," he said, "make sure it's a race issue." In this case, the youngster simply wasn't performing up to the firm's expectations and then questioned why he wasn't getting the good clients. But when he was given the good clients, he wasn't performing.
>
> The advice Frank gave him was, "You will always be under the microscope in corporate America. The only way you'll make it in this environment is to consistently cross every T and dot every I, in spite of what everyone else does or gets away with not doing." He told him that he had been given an opportunity that few people got and that if he blew it, it would follow him.
>
> It is very impressive to say that you work at KPMG. It is so important coming into a place like this to have a mentor, and Frank served as a mentor for blacks and whites. He tried to work with that group of young people and impress upon them that theirs wouldn't be an easy job but that once they proved themselves it gets a lot easier. Even now, Frank serves as a mentor to a lot of people in this field, and he has helped a lot of people's careers.

Frank is a graduate of Long Island University, where he earned a bachelor's of science in accounting and an MBA. He received the Distinguished Alumni Award from Long Island University in 1998 and an honorary Doctor of Humane Letters degree in 2001. In October 2008, *Accounting Today* named Frank to its 2008 list of the 100 most influential people in accounting.

Frank is a board member of Pepco Holdings, Inc., and Cohen & Steers mutual funds group. In addition, he currently serves on the board of the following not-for-profit organizations: Hoop Dreams Scholarship Fund (chairman of the board), the Greater Washington Urban League (treasurer), and the Howard University Chartered Middle School of Mathematics and Science (treasurer).

Leading staff members depends on your own dedication to self-knowledge, trustworthiness, critical thinking, preparation, and self-discipline. You must first lead yourself, and then, you can successfully employ the challenges of teaching, coaching, and mentoring; personal growth; empowering; and holding staff members accountable.

What is the payoff for you? The benefits that you will receive from growing other leaders are immeasurable. Not only will your team members lighten your burden today, but they will also revere you tomorrow. Your influence will reverberate through the next generations of leaders, much like the impact that Herb Kelleher, the beloved former CEO of Southwest

Airlines, has had. Herb Kelleher was a man who could connect with people and build relationships. I cut this full-page ad out of *USA Today* more than 10 years ago:

Thanks Herb

For remembering every one of our names.

For supporting the Ronald McDonald House.

For helping load baggage on Thanksgiving.

For giving everyone a kiss (and we mean everyone).

For listening.

For running the only profitable major airline.

For singing at our holiday party.

For singing only once a year.

For letting us wear shorts and sneakers to work.

For golfing at the LUV Classic with only one club.

For outtalking Sam Donaldson.

For riding your Harley Davidson into Southwest Headquarters.

For being a friend, not just a boss.

Happy Boss's Day from Each One of Your 16,000 Employees.

When a leader has built a relationship with his or her people, you can see it in the way that the team performs. Although vision sets the direction of your firm, and relationships set the culture, the staff members and their talents determine the potential of the organization. Ultimately, the leadership of those staff members determines the success of the accounting firm.

Teaching, Coaching, and Mentoring: Multiplying Your Leadership

"If you want 1 year of prosperity, grow grain. If you want 10 years of prosperity, grow trees. If you want 100 years of prosperity, grow people."

~ CHINESE PROVERB

All leaders teach; good leaders coach; great leaders mentor.

Everyone in a leadership role, whether appointed or earned, teaches followers. Some teach unconsciously simply by their modeling of professional behavior and technical skill. They do not realize how others may be learning. Some leaders teach positive traits, and some leaders teach poor behavior. Some followers take refuge under the poor leader and may say

- ▲ "Well, he doesn't get his billing out on time, why should I?"
- ▲ "She doesn't always agree with the other partners and will let us know."
- ▲ "He treats staff members with disdain; why should I respect them?"

Good leaders are aware of their impact on others and actively teach and coach with purpose.

This is probably my favorite chapter in this book. When I was asked to teach a month-long new staff members' class when I worked at Price Waterhouse, I was bitten by the teaching bug. I enjoyed the rush of others learning and applying the skills that I was helping to teach. I especially loved seeing some of the students years later and hearing them tell me all the things they had gotten out of my class. Over the years, I have worked hard to develop my teaching skills. Nevertheless, over the years, I noticed that teaching wasn't quite fulfilling enough because I witnessed little or no change in my students, so I began working on coaching—nurturing, challenging, and even demanding that students act on the learning. By focusing on coaching, I have had a bigger impact on people around me. Over the last 10 years, I have worked deeply with a few people to help guide their lives beyond the work day, and I have found a new and exciting experience. I hope you will benefit from my experience, along with the others who have given me insights.

Good leaders take responsibility for using all the teaching moments available to improve the professional skills of their team members. Richard Brehler, former Plante Moran director of training, says that even casual encounters are great teaching moments. "Conversations in the hallway are remarkable and are often underrecognized as teaching opportunities."

Larry Autrey, managing partner of the top-100 firm Whitley Penn LLP in Ft. Worth, TX, feels the burden of setting the example for his firm, but sometimes, it crops up in unexpected ways.

> I used to believe that I had to personally work more hours than any person in the firm to be the example. Over the past few years, my partners told me that I was asking them to cut back on the hours they worked, and they indicated that I had to cut back in order for them to cut back. I have got to be willing, and they have to believe that I am willing, to do whatever I ask them to do.

Great leaders guide team members toward positive technical and personal conduct through one-on-one and group teaching programs, as well as individual and group coaching sessions. Both teaching and coaching are often done around a single skill set, such as practice development.

Sam Coulter, founder and president of the local firm Coulter & Justus, P.C., in Knoxville, TN, says, "I am involved in the more significant new client opportunities. I think a leader must lead in the marketplace, so the next generation witnesses it. So, when my partner, Ron

Justus, or I go with our team on a pursuit, that prospect knows he or she will be an important client for this firm, and our team members see us living the things we ask them to do."

It is important that protégés learn the art of decision making, both from learning how you and the partners make decisions now and in beginning to make their own decisions with your guidance. Once protégés understand an issue from you, they will be able to support partners' decisions and, when feasible, explain them to others. Regardless of whether people agree, once they understand the issues, they are less likely to gossip or cause dissension within the organization. Accurate information and communication always improves a firm's culture.

In this chapter, we will focus on effective teaching and training programs. I'll challenge you to think beyond check-the-box compliance continuing professional education (CPE) and seek training that provides a change in your skill and a return on your time and money investment. We will dig into the leadership aspects of coaching in groups, as well as one on one, and how to really make a difference in the skill level of your protégés. Lastly, I will touch on the life changing, career transforming nature of mentoring: what it is, the benefits to you and your protégé, along with some tips on how to be more effective as a mentor.

Developing Skills Over a Career

If a person is to grow professionally, he or she must continually be open to new skills. For example, when a person joins an accounting firm, that person must learn to apply his or her university education to the practical business of accounting. As one continues his or her professional growth, there will come a time when he or she must learn leadership and management skills. A few years later, the possibility of transition from employee to business owner presents itself, and this transition creates a huge growth opportunity for accountants and consultants. In each of these stages, a completely different set of skills will be required to continue growing.

Frank Ross, director of Howard University School of Business Center for Accounting Education in Washington, D.C., shares

> Beyond my family and community, there were others who touched my life in irrevocable ways—people like Emsar Bradford, the first black CPA I ever met. He was my first role model in the accounting field, and he taught me a number of life lessons that would stay with me. More than anything, he showed me what was possible, in spite of the odds.
>
> During the 38 years I worked at Peat Marwick, which merged with Klynveld Main Goerdeler in 1987 to form KPMG, I had the pleasure of working with some of the best accounting professionals in the world. Many of these men became friends after they were mentors, and each of them played critical roles in the support and counsel I needed during my journey.

Figure 7-1 illustrates the changing needs of accountants over a lifetime in public accounting. The left axis portrays the amount of training, coaching, and mentoring one receives, some of which can be informal. The left axis could mean only 40 hours, or it could mean as many as 600 or more hours. The bottom axis portrays a time line, from entry into the profession until retirement, and it could span 20, 30, or even 40 years. The general trends illustrate

Figure 7-1: Accountant's Professional Development Continuum

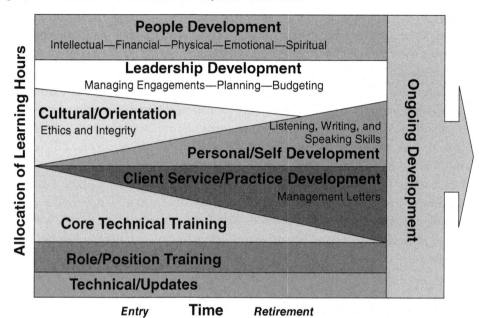

that a professional invests more in the technical track of public accounting early in his or her career and more in people development later in life.

Figure 7-1 illustrates the ideal progression of a person joining an accounting firm right out of the university and progressing through a lifetime career in public accounting. We have found that, left to their own designs, some accountants will repeat the heavy technical training throughout their careers. For some, it's almost as if they end up having one year of training 30 times. With a mentor or coach, an accountant can progress throughout his or her career, so that there is continual growth in the protégé.

If you're not careful or don't have a good mentor looking over your career, it's easy to become complacent, particularly once you become a partner in an accounting firm. It is easy to believe that you have all the answers. Clients and employees start telling you that you're the best and brightest. If you believe them, then it is difficult to stay at the top of a large organization. Once you become a partner, it is easy to stop listening and learning.

Terry Snyder, president of the accounting firm alliance PKF North America in Lawrence, GA, sees value in career-long training.

> One of the things that has always interested me is, Why did certain firms go to this high level of success? What characteristics did they have? The real answer was that these firms invested heavily in training and leadership. I think the big 8, the big 4 today, and some of the more successful firms like EisnerAmper and Wipfli have embraced the concept of not only having good top leadership but training the second and third tiers of leaders and having really good team members who are willing to let the leadership lead. And I think that component is huge.

Training Begins One on One

In his book *Outliers: The Story of Success*, best-selling author Malcolm Gladwell found that smart people can master most anything with approximately 10,000 hours of application. That explains why CPAs can master their profession after 5 years of college and 5–10 years of practice. With 10,000 hours devoted to the development of technical skill, one can master accounting. However, it takes more than technical skill to be a true leader in an accounting firm.

In a *Harvard Business Review* article titled "Teaching Smart People How to Learn," Professor Chris Argyris says that many smart professionals develop a God-like complex. People assume that a good doctor, lawyer, or accountant must be good at other things, as well. Because someone is quite good at the developed skill, he or she often loses the persistence to master another skill, such as taking on the leadership responsibility of a partner or running a business.

Although Ken Baggett, co-managing partner of the national firm CohnReznick LLP, deeply respects his employees, when one of them struggles with a bad attitude, he has no problem coaching very provocatively.

> I always look for those opportunities to teach. I can remember one of my very, very fine partners was struggling with some technical and attitudinal issues. After dinner, one night on a trip, he and I sat for a while longer. Well, that was a golden opportunity for me to coach and mentor, but it didn't go well, quite frankly. As a matter of fact, it went so badly that I suggested that if he could not change, he needed to go upstairs, pack his bags, and take the next flight home. I told him that when I got to the office two days from then, I could be signing off his resignation letter.
>
> He went upstairs; he called me back and said, 'Can we have breakfast?' We did the next morning.
>
> And the next morning, he said, "I get your message. Tell me what it is I really need to do."
>
> I said, "I'm not going to tell you. So, why don't you tell me what you think you need to do?" He listed out exactly the things he needed to change, and he has changed them all. He went from a young, immature partner to one of the strongest operating office managing partners I have today.

There are many times that a leader must challenge his protégé to perform at a higher level and get out of a rut. The example that Baggett shared with me is one of those situations when the leader must be willing the shake his protégé out of his comfort or complacency zone. The leaders who are unwilling to have this "straight-talk" type of coaching will end up with a team of mediocre partners.

It is crucial that such a tough-love conversation not get hostile. The leader must not allow his or her emotions to overflow into name calling or making indefensible charges. Calling a protégé a slacker, an idiot, lazy, or similar names will never produce a good result. Making indefensible charges like, "You never complete your work on time," or "No one likes you," will only work to create hurt feelings, resistance, and return hostility.

To be effective, the leader should give his or her tough message with love, with statements like, "You are very meaningful to me, and I think you can do better," or "I really care about you, and I'm going to give you some very tough information that may hurt your feelings. If you don't change what you are doing, I'll change what you are doing, and it may mean that you will have to leave." The key to giving tough messages is to be respectful while being clear.

Learning to lead or manage a business also requires investing many hours in the behavior changes necessary to learn these skills. Gladwell notes that it doesn't matter at what age the learner puts in the 10,000 required hours. Too many professionals think that they can take shortcuts. Some think that they can read a book and become good at client service. Others think that they can take a class and master selling skills. CPE and other training sponsors often cater to this misconception.

When you are responsible for training a person, write down the initiatives and actions that he or she needs to perform at peak level. Be as specific as possible in each of your direct reports. Don't make the mistake of overemphasizing results (for example, increase billable time by 200 hours). Instead, focus on activities that each person needs to accomplish for the results to occur (for example, visit each of your largest 10 clients twice between engagements for breakfast or lunch, meet with one referral source per week, and so on).

Bill Haller, managing partner of the national firm CapinCrouse LLP in Indianapolis, IN, shares

> We call it blueprinting. Every partner is blueprinted at the beginning of the year, and we use this to lead and manage our nonbillable time. Our nonbillable allocation comes first. We start out with 2,600 hours and decide together the most important thing a partner should accomplish and allocate time and resources to that. In our firm, available billable time for partners is what's left over after we get them blueprinted for other things.

I am a huge believer in the teaching method of explaining, demonstrating, imitating, correcting, and then repetition. The old adage that practice makes perfect is untrue. Practice only makes permanent, and practicing the wrong methods will deepen those wrong methods in the fabric of your organization. The things that you teach are best demonstrated. It's not what you say but what you do that speaks the loudest, whether it's the act of being on time, showing respect, listening, challenging wrong thinking, or constantly teaching people how to perform at their peak level.

Teaching

Training Programs Demonstrate Your Commitment to People

It was reported by some of its partners that Andersen invested nearly 7 percent of top line revenue in training. Andersen's spin-off, Accenture, invests a similar amount, and Deloitte is ramping up its training investment with a brand new physical university campus in Dallas. Although many firms have tried to shortcut the expense, the best firms are still making substantial investments in providing career-long training for their staff members. Tom Luken, president of the local firm Kolb+Co in Milwaukee, WS, says "At Kolb, your first few years of training are technically focused. Once you've been with us a few years, you become a leadership trainee. The business schools focus on technical courses and are not preparing the college students for critical thinking as much as they need to be successful in business." This is why the best people will view themselves as lifelong learners, which we will discuss more later in this chapter.

Such programs need not be set up and administered from within the firm. Although some firms are able to provide their own universities, others band together regionally or through their regional or international associations to provide this training. These firms are making strong statements to their team members, such as the following:

1. You are important to us.
2. Your growth and development are important to us.
3. It is a better idea to train you for the future and risk losing you than to not train you and risk keeping you.

Gary Shamis, founder and CEO of the top-100 multioffice firm SS&G Financial Services, Inc., Cleveland, OH, says

> I developed an internal leadership program that is made available to everybody in our firm. We created 6 courses over a 3-year period. Some of them are taught by outside people, and some of them are taught by inside people. We'll have anywhere from 35–60 people attend these classes. It's just trying to give them some of the skills that we've had to learn on our own. We teach things like practice development, the metrics of running a CPA firm, different management styles, and how to service clients.

Scott Dietzen, managing partner, Northwest Region, of the national accounting firm CliftonLarsonAllen LLP in Spokane, WA, shares that his firm is sold on the value of training.

> We have definitely taken an investment approach to training by building our own internal university. More importantly, in the area of leadership development, we spend approximately $8,000 to $10,000 per year on the individuals in that program and they are in it for 18 months. Our women's leadership program is probably $50,000 a year. We have invested in two series of 'The Rainmaker Academy' and have found that to be very beneficial for our up-and-coming senior managers and newer partners.

A Plan for Adult Learners

There is a big difference in knowing the rules of tax and accounting and knowing how to teach the application of those rules to your client service team. The best leaders take meaningful steps to develop a learning organization. Although e-mails and edicts have some impact, a great demonstration is often the most effective tool for change.

Hugh Parker, executive partner of the regional firm Horne LLP in Jackson, MS, says

> People learn by using their brains. Some teachers are like, "Come to the feet of the oracle."
> But the oracle method of teaching is only good for facts. It is a very efficient way to transfer

facts but a poor teaching method. We have many different delivery mechanisms for training. You don't have to go sit in the bricks and mortar to be at the feet of the oracle.

CPE is big business because accountants must log at least 40 hours annually to remain certified. Some professionals pursue far more than the minimum to develop or maintain leading-edge skills. Yet, many accountants and their managers are content to attend check-the-box programs that provide very little in positive behavioral change or return on investment (ROI).

Couple this low emphasis on training with the fact that hundreds of aging accountants will sell their firms at low prices because they have no one to succeed them. No one has been trained to run the business, so the aging owner finds buyers only willing to pay a pension for a few years and sells the business for cents on the dollar. In many cases, the seller retains the risk of client attrition, so the new owner has all the upside.

Ted Mason, president and CEO of the top-100 firm Laporte Sehrt Romig Hand in New Orleans, LA, adds, "I believe the so-called 'soft skills' are the hard stuff because we really haven't been trained in the process and also because they deal with difficult things. We just don't get enough of that type of training."

Successful organizations don't regard training for any team member as an act of compliance. At the FBI, for example, training can make a life-or-death impact and have profound consequences on national security. According to Ralph C. Kennedy in the article "Applying the principles of adult learning: the key to more effective training programs," which was included in the April 2003 edition of *The FBI Law Enforcement Bulletin*, FBI training officials are advised to "avoid placing officers in the position of being passive recipients of facts …. Adult learning activities should include action and involvement." The FBI further notes, "Unlike young people, adults enter learning activities with an image of themselves as self-directing, responsible, mature and independent learners. Adults generally resist situations where they are treated like anything other than responsible adults."

As the FBI correctly notes, "Explaining the desired information and behaviors will not improve performance. Effective training must include learning tactics that are proven to change behaviors."

Gary Confessore, EdD, is an adult learning expert, a professor emeritus of higher education at George Washington University, and principal and owner of the consulting firm Human Resources Development Enterprises in suburban Washington. He says

> Traditional professional education programs tend to follow a formula: we appraise what information we believe needs to be known, such as what skills or knowledge need to be learned to be a CPA—a sort of job task analysis. Then, we decide what a person needs to be taught and in what ways a person is most likely to gain those skills. In every case, there's a need to practice the skill. The notion of recency and repetition (how often we use the new information and practice it) is critical to effective adult learning. If we set up programs just to passively read or hear about a subject, it's not as effective as using the information. If you want to be sure people are learning skills to solve problems, you must give them the opportunity to actually *do*.

The effectiveness of such techniques was demonstrated when U.S. Airways Flight 1549 landed in the Hudson River in January 2009 without a single casualty, Gary says.

> Applying knowledge learned in training is often hard to do, but the pilot had been through similar scenarios in training simulations. Many responsibilities aren't life-or-death situations like landing a plane in the Hudson River, but the event highlights the effectiveness of having a training process that involves acquiring knowledge followed by the opportunity to practice, apply, and teach it.

Learning to lead is more like the emergency landing of an aircraft than it is providing accounting or tax services. Leading requires real-time decision making and action, whereas solving most accounting and tax problems allows one to make considered, often slow, decisions. Leading requires immediacy of communications and decisions.

Ray Strothman, managing partner of the local firm Strothman & Company, PSC, in Louisville, KY, takes training to a new level.

> We believe in sharing our education and training with our clients, referral sources, and our community. We sponsor an annual seminar series, and it is extremely successful. We are always right there in front talking about various topics that affect our clients and friends, so this has been a great business development tool. We can effectively accommodate an average of about 100 participants in these seminars. These are business owners, clients, chief financial officers or controllers, and maybe referral sources.

Leader Profile: William Hubly, founder and managing principal of the local firm Corbett, Duncan & Hubly, PC in Itasca, IL

Bill Hubly learned many leadership skills through his basketball prowess. As captain of the team at the University of North Dakota, Bill was chosen to lead by his peers. Although he wasn't a "rah-rah" type of vocal leader, he set the example for hard work and dedication. Today, Bill leads his firm with humility and an awareness that everyone is looking at him.

Partner Dan Duncan says

> When we formed our firm, Bill had visions and strategies on how he wanted to grow. He had lots of energy and enthusiasm for developing niches. We found our international partner, Koh Fujimoto, as we were building our niche infrastructure. Koh had worked at Andersen and was the CFO at a large Japanese company.

> We needed an audit manager, and Koh was reassessing his career. He joined us and, over time, captured a new vision for himself and us, with Bill's leadership. Although English wasn't his primary language, with Bill's tutelage, Koh built our international practice.

> And you know, as an organization, we supported the hits and misses. Koh, through Bill's leadership, has worked hard to make that a firm niche.

> I think a lot of our success has to do with the confidence that we have in Bill as our leader. Because if we didn't have that confidence, we wouldn't be growing like we are today. He has the respect of everyone, and he has a clear vision for the firm.

Under Bill's leadership, Corbett, Duncan & Hubly, PC, was named a best-of-the-best managed firm by *INSIDE Public Accounting*. In addition, Corbett, Duncan &

(continued)

(continued)

Hubly, PC, was recently named as one of 2010s best places to work in Illinois.

As a recognized leader, Bill has given presentations on business and financial topics at various seminars, including Enterprise Worldwide's annual conference, Boomer Consulting's Circle meetings and Lorman Education Services. He is also a sought-after speaker on strategic planning, organizational alignment, and leadership topics.

Bill credits his parents with instilling the values of honesty, integrity, individual responsibility, and commitment. He attributes his success and leadership skills to understanding the benefits of teamwork and goal setting, something he learned while playing college basketball. His personal vision is to make a positive impact on everyone he meets.

When not leading the firm and serving clients, Bill enjoys spending time with his wife, Jodi, and their four children; coaching youth sports; exercising; golfing; skiing; traveling; and reading.

Creating Purposeful Training

Leading accounting firm executives worry about how to develop their staff members into leaders. They express the desire to develop leaders who can play a role in the firm's long-term growth and profitability. They encourage their professionals to engage in philanthropic and civic activities, volunteer, network, serve on committees, and so on. They take younger team members on sales calls and to recruiting fairs. They create compensation systems and career ladders that reward activities believed to encourage leadership and practice growth. And yet they waste enormous resources on CPE activities that simply fulfill perfunctory regulatory requirements.

We wouldn't expect our teenagers to learn how to drive a car by watching us drive one for years, but is that basically what we're expecting of the staff members whom we hope will help lead our firms?

Richard Brehler, former Plante & Moran, PLLC, training director, points to the medical model and notes that young doctors don't spend nearly as much time in the classroom as they spend in clinics. "At Plante & Moran, we've tried to recognize that's how partners are grown," he says. "All partners are responsible for the long-term development of a small team. It's not an engagement team. It's not a job assignment. It takes gentle persuasion relentlessly applied, but the goal is to keep each person's career developing."

Plante & Moran, PLLC, also uses a preengagement checklist to ensure that the firm's leadership and human resources goals aren't overlooked on the job. It helps the leaders consider which team members need to learn particular new skills and which team members can teach them. The checklist forces the team to have a 15-minute preengagement conversation to reflect on what skills each team member can develop during the engagement. It also provides a mechanism for a 15-minute postengagement conversation about how to avoid or resolve any problems should they arise again. "We used to suggest the preengagement and postengagement conversations, and people would say that it sounds good, but it would never get done. This helps make sure it does," Brehler says.

The public accounting profession's traditional CPE model, which assumes information is available and can be repeated through testing, does not incorporate effective adult learning techniques. It also doesn't help firms seeking to advance the contemporary competitive competencies of their professionals by arming them with the new indispensable skills required to compete in the modern marketplace.

Cutting-edge professional training programs that routinely incorporate the principles of adult learning are more common in other professions endowed with critical public trust, such as law enforcement, aviation, and medicine. To help their professional staff members master skills, accounting firms should look for programs that are built upon established principles of adult learning and that approach training as a fortification of survival skills that generate ROI.

There is overwhelming evidence that effective adult learning has unique characteristics, such as the applicability to the job, the opportunity to perform with excellence, and the responsibility of teaching others. It's no secret that training can be a significant line item in any firm's budget. For those reasons, accounting firms should establish some nonnegotiable criteria for training programs built upon demonstrated principles of adult learning. These criteria ensure that its investments in training will provide the firm with enduring value that will play a key role in sustaining its long-term future.

The following are important questions to ask to ensure that training programs meet the firm's objectives and generate ROI:

▲ Is the curriculum based on principles of effective adult learning and education?
▲ Does it combine study with on-the-job experience and independent exercises?
▲ Does the training program provide ongoing follow-up and support?
▲ Are behavioral changes deliberate rather than incidental results of the training?
▲ Are learning activities transformational for the participants?
▲ Are expectations of participants clearly defined?
▲ Does the program incorporate accountability, follow-up, and reporting activities?
▲ Are participants expected to cascade teach the information to others?
▲ Can the program demonstrate ROI for the firm?
▲ Is the program specific to the business of public accounting?

Both tangible and intangible ROI should play a major role in your decision to select or develop a training program. Tangible ROI would be dollars of new revenue or profits, whereas intangible ROI would be more effective communication skills or better client service. Even the intangibles should be observable. Effective learning systems should be able to demonstrate not only the effective transfer of knowledge but also how that knowledge benefits the firm, both directly and indirectly.

ROI is an area where many training programs fall short; the overwhelming majority can demonstrate features and soft benefits, but the ability to demonstrate measurable results eludes most of them. Accountability-based programs document before-and-after results for leadership and business development training programs. By establishing ROI criteria for training, firms can substantially reduce the overwhelmingly vast field of available programs and select from among the few that can concretely demonstrate the benefits they provide and the return that the firm can anticipate. These types of reputable training programs build projected ROI into their systems and readily provide robust ROI calculations to clients based on the results generated in the past.

Look for training programs that use a recording structure as part of their accountability component. Such structures establish the validity of the results and reinforce designated goals. They measure dollars created as a result of the training, and they should show how much your firm is investing in the training and the estimated resulting increases in revenue that the training should yield. Intangible results, such as recurring business, increased participant abilities, improved staff retention, and the results of cascade training within the firm should also be considered because they make up a significant component of ROI.

For professional services firms, an additional factor inherent in the best training programs—one that is more subjective but a significant contributor to ROI—is the ability to impart practice economics to participants. The value of increasing revenue is lost if the new work isn't profitable; good programs teach participants how to focus on profitable business activities and how to avoid unprofitable new business. Programs that yield maximum ROI teaches students how to assess the costs associated with different types of engagements and helps them master metrics such as leverage, utilization, billing rates, realization, and margin. Participants in the most effective leadership programs learn how to assess an engagement's profitability, so that they can channel their energy into high-value activities.

Profession-specific training based upon proven principles of adult learning provides maximum benefit to participants and their sponsoring employers. Such training regimens tend to be transformational in terms of leading to significant and desirable behavioral change. They are cognizant of the challenges and goals facing employers' businesses and proactive at building mechanisms into their curricula that prepare participants to meet their industry-specific challenges and objectives. These programs embed strong components of accountability, practical experience, follow-up, and ongoing support in their training techniques, reinforcing desired behavioral change and contributing significantly to both tangible and intangible ROI. They can document ROI to ensure that the training investment is paying for itself and earning returns, but benefits also include intangible returns, as well.

Steve Mayer, founder, chairman, and CEO of the regional firm Burr, Pilger & Mayer LLP in San Francisco, CA, says

> One of my mentors told me to plant palm trees. He explained that you may sit underneath the palm tree, but you probably never planted it. The guy who planted it never got a chance to sit under it because it took a long time to grow.
>
> The idea is that you have to start the thing for other people. It's what my parents did for me and what I hope to do for my kids. It's what I want to do for our younger, bright professionals who will someday soon lead this firm. We've gone from zero to being in the top 100. Maybe they will take us into a new Big 8.

Coaching

Working One-on-One Raises Your Commitment and Retention

Another hallmark of effective adult learning programs is the expectation that participants will teach their new knowledge and skills to others. According to Confessore

> A system of acquiring knowledge, the opportunity to apply it, and the opportunity to teach it follows a well-established series of effective adult learning principles. That's where accountability comes from. If I'm responsible for helping you learn, I better know the material and how to organize it. This is an essential approach used in medical training; it's why residents are actively involved in teaching interns. Medical educators also spend a lot of time guiding fourth-year students to teach fundamentals to first- and second-year students. The idea is that you never learn as well as when you teach. This approach forces participants to take responsibility for what they learn and demonstrate.

Sam Coulter says that his firm has made teaching others a requirement of those who attend training.

> The challenge for us is to apply quality training where we are not just meeting requirements but are actually getting something out of it. Cascade training is very important. In the past, we sent people to expensive training programs, and they brought back nothing. Furthermore, much of the material they learned was not retained. I think if you send a person to a training school, then I think you bring it back to six others in the office.

The concept of cascade training is a powerful tool. Cascade training takes place when a person attends a class and returns to his or her firm and teaches the material to other people. We have found that the teacher always learns more than the student. When a person attends a class, his or her attention will be magnified when it is known that he or she will be expected to teach the material after class. We've found that the people who do this well follow a few simple rules:

1. Cascade teaching works best when it is done very soon after the initial class is attended; otherwise, the learning begins to fade from the mind, and the desire to cascade teach begins to wane.
2. Cascade teaching works best when the logistics are kept simple, so that only two or three people are retaught, and small rooms are used.
3. The teacher selects a small portion of the full material to cascade. For example, you might select to teach two people one hour of the material for every four hours you attended the course.

A number of years ago, we were implementing an in-house version of The Rainmaker Academy for a firm. This firm had a staff turnover rate of 28 percent and nearly 40 percent when the partners were removed from the equation. Within 2 years, that turnover had been reduced to less than 10 percent, and the firm credited one aspect of The Rainmaker Academy program: the cascade teaching requirement. Before this was installed, staff members felt like just another replaceable laptop. When senior managers began to cascade teach the material to the young people, two important things happened: the staff finally felt that someone cared about their career, and some of the teachers went beyond teaching to coaching.

Coaching gives a better ROI because it requires staying with your learner through the trial and error necessary for true growth. Plante & Moran, PLLC, has a buddy system, so less experienced staff members have a nonpartner to whom they can turn when they are confused or frustrated. "The buddy's responsibility is to make sure the new person feels welcome, to see that they have work to do, to close the door when somebody is confused," according to Gordon Krater, managing partner of the megaregional firm Plante & Moran, PLLC, in Southfield, MI. As a consequence of its emphasis on career development, Plante & Moran, PLLC, has one of the lowest turnover rates of any accounting firm in the country and is a 13-year regular on *Fortune* magazine's annual list of best places to work.

On-the-Job Training Helps Coaches and Mentors

Experts agree that adults who participate in job-related training learn very differently than younger students who are still studying the basic core subjects of academia. Adult learners have a different self-image, more life experience, a fear of failure, and a greater expectation to use learning. Adults also learn at a slower rate and may have a shorter retention of new knowledge unless the new information is used quickly and reinforced effectively. In addition, adults participating in professional education have different motivations, interests, values, and attitudes than younger students who are following an academic path. These differences form the basis for the principles of adult learning and effective instructional methodologies tailored to adults.

The younger professional generations are somewhat different than previous generations. The Baby Boomer generation thinks and perceives things differently than accountants from generations X and Y. Younger generations are more confident in their abilities, perceive loyalty differently, expect training that helps their development, want more balance between work and family, and are not intimidated by rank. In the past, communication between ranks was much less frequent due to traditional hierarchies, but with today's e-mail and Internet capabilities, staff members and junior partners are well informed of issues and able to interact frequently with senior partners.

Gordon Krater says, "Our team partner program helps you to be able to bounce those things off of people. One of the critical things is that you never feel alone in this big organization. We always make sure that we got you connected, and you can't slip through the cracks."

A 2004 study of CEOs of large American real estate companies showed that all participants had a common belief that their role as trainers and teachers was one of the most essential factors in their own success. The CEOs in the study all believed that in order to stay profitable amidst constant change and fierce competition, they had to build an environment where all employees learn from each other. They recognized the power of their own positions. They realized their responsibility to transcend power dynamics within their organizations, so that they could help employees learn from each other, collaborate, and work together.

Charly Weinstein, CEO of the megaregional firm EisnerAmper LLP in New York City, NY, says that his firm realized that its future depended on dramatically improving the provided training

> We had been studying the demographics of our partnership, and we saw how much older we were getting as a firm. We had so many partners who were going to be retiring in the next 3–10 years; we realized that we had to grow leaders who could take over. Rob Levine was one of our leading audit partners, but Robby wanted to mentor and teach and grow our young people. We took him off the line, which was an unbelievably significant investment, and he has done an amazing job over the last 4or 5 years. While we teach some technical skill, we have leadership skills and communications and people skills. We have a unique professional services college where we bring in our clients, referral sources, and CFOs. Rob has built an unbelievable program for our future leaders, our clients, and our community. Last year, we offered 28,000 credits internally to our staff.

Other research shows that leaders of successful professional services firms perceive themselves as lifelong learners. For example, the same 2004 study of CEOs of large American real estate companies previously referenced found that self-identification as a lifelong learner was the number one common theme to which they attributed their success. The CEOs recognized that their job success required a dedication to being a lifelong learner because continuous learning enabled them to deal with the ongoing challenges in business. They also collectively believed that taking advantage of opportunities for continuous learning was one of the most important reasons that they were successful in business. They used phrases such as "learning faster than competitors" and "being a quick study" to express concepts that made them love their profession.

Participants in the study agreed that with the development of new technologies, new laws, and constant restructuring of companies, they must continue to adapt and learn in order to remain successful. They actively sought robust training programs to develop new skills.

Coaching does not always require the coach to be a professional expert on the subject. Many professional golfers don't have the patience to teach. Teaching requires one to break down the steps of a skill into incremental lessons, so the student is progressively challenged. Scott Dietzen shares a leadership lesson that he learned as an inexperienced baseball coach.

> Here I was coaching baseball I had played only as a youth. I did not understand the technique because of extensive experience. I had learned by observing other coaches. I was much more open to the fundamental technique of playing baseball and the strategy of baseball because I didn't have any preconceived notions. In my current leadership, I think I am actually more open-minded in those areas where I am not the technical expert. I'm more willing to receive knowledge from others because I don't have my own history.

Leader Profile: **Steve Mayer, founder, chairman, and CEO of the regional firm Burr, Pilger & Mayer LLP in San Francisco, CA**

Steve Mayer, founder, chairman, and CEO of Burr, Pilger & Mayer LLP, grew up in San Francisco and graduated from the University of California at Berkeley. As captain of his baseball team and later when coaching football, Steve learned teamwork and leadership lessons for a lifetime. Steve, his founding partners Henry Pilger and Curtis Burr, and many others have built their firm from scratch into one of the top 100 firms in the United States, which is quite an accomplishment for a first-generation accounting firm among 50,000 other firms in the country.

Henry Pilger, a founding partner of Burr, Pilger & Mayer LLP, says

> Steve Mayer is a tireless worker and leads by example. I don't know of anyone who works harder or is more fully committed to driving their firm towards excellence. There's never time to relax and think we're finally there because just as the partner group is getting comfortable with its latest achievement, Steve is in front of us with a new goal, a new vision, and a new mountain to climb. His favorite expression is "Failure is not an option," and it resonates throughout our partner ranks. We have a very talented group of partners who all are capable of significant success, but the success we've had as a firm is larger than the sum of its parts. It is clearly due to Steve's leadership and vision, and there isn't one partner in our firm of more than 50 partners who would dispute that claim.

Steve leads his firm like he was coaching an elite sports team of professional athletes. He seeks the best talent that he can lure to his firm. He invests in their continuous training to become better at their technical and personal skills, and he continuously challenges his partners to be more excellent than last year. Steve also shares the wealth with his 350 employees through his firm's employee stock ownership plan.

Steve's 35 years of professional experience working with individuals, as well as private and public businesses, has touched almost all of the firm's practice areas. His own work has included audits and reviews of financial statements, implementation of computer and accounting systems, preparation of forecasts and budgets, litigation support, bankruptcy consultation, valuations, and business plan and loan package development. In addition, he has consulted with management concerning Securities and Exchange Commission requirements, mergers, reorganizations and acquisitions of businesses, and negotiations of venture capital financing.

Steve serves on the boards of the San Francisco Chamber of Commerce, as well as many other schools, banks, businesses, and organizations. He loves traditions and annual events, including 36 consecutive years backpacking with friends, 35 of the last 37 California versus Stanford games, and 39 consecutive San Francisco Giants openers. He missed the opener in 2010 for the first time in 40 years: the year that the San Francisco Giants won the World Series!

The Leap From Coaching to Mentoring

Mentorship is a buzzword these days. Yet, it seems to have different meanings for different people. Some consider it a form of counseling, communicating, or learning by example from someone usually senior to you, but others call it leadership. A simple definition of a mentor is someone who advises you, guides your career, and is an advocate for you to give you more opportunities. An individual can have mentors in different areas, and they can be from outside where he or she works. And, more subtly, mentorship can be partially mutual. For instance, in the book *Managing Generation Y: Global Citizens Born in the Late Seventies and Early Eighties*, the authors Bruce Tulgan, Carolyn Martin, Mary George, and Eileen Klockars point out that a young generation Y employee can mentor an older employee about technology or social media while being mentored, in turn, about how to perform a job. Whatever you want to call this kind of helping relationship, it is something that certainly can be beneficial to any organization. It is a proven approach and valuable tool for leaders.

Although I have had the benefit of many coaches in my lifetime, I've only had a few mentors. Often, I'll ask and audience, "How many of you have had a mentor in your business life?" I am stunned that less than half of the senior people in accounting firms have experienced the power of a true mentor.

Great Leaders Mentor

A mentor is a person of greater knowledge or wisdom who shares his or her experience to help develop the abilities of his or her protégés. Mentoring helps prepare team members for increased responsibilities by encouraging job competency, education, professional development, higher education, and serving the needs of the firm and your clients. Mentoring encourages people by promoting communication and personal and professional development. A mentor is an individual who advises and challenges you to do your best on both a personal and professional level. Everyone needs a mentor; mentoring is where serious personal leadership starts.

Great leaders not only take responsibility for teaching and coaching, great leaders will mentor selected protégés in their professional as well as personal lives. Debbie Lambert, managing partner of the top-100 multioffice firm Johnson Lambert & Co. LLP in Raleigh, NC, agrees: "The best leaders and practice developers will be people who can mentor others. Those same people have that skill of the pied piper; people want to be their clients, and team members want to work with them. Leaders influence other people. They lead them into something they want them to do and get them to understand why it's important."

Generally, mentors fill four roles: adviser, coach, facilitator, and advocate. As an adviser, the mentor should encourage two-way communication and feedback and assist the protégé with thinking through career and performance decisions. As a coach, the mentor helps clarify developmental needs, recommends training opportunities, and teaches skills and behaviors. In facilitating, the mentor should assist the protégé in establishing a network of professional contacts and help him or her identify resources for problem solving and career progression. As an advocate, the mentor could represent the protégé's concern to higher management levels concerning specific issues, arrange for the protégé to participate in high-visibility projects, and serve as a role model.

Bill Haller believes that the mentor-protégé relationship takes on different characteristics based on the skills of each person. "When I am mentoring somebody, I am his or her advocate. When I coach somebody I am trying to deliver a skill or a process that they didn't have before. So coaching is pretty directive."

Sports offers us many examples of great coaching and mentoring. If you look at a guy like [Los Angeles Lakers coach] Phil Jackson, he was a coach, but he seems to be a coach with very highly skilled players. So, he would probably be a mentor to them—their advocate—so he could deal with troubled people because they felt like they had a friend in Phil. Whereas a guy like Bobby Knight didn't mentor anybody; he coached kids with talent and gave them more talent than they had before. But no one would come to him with a problem; he has no patience.

Tony Argiz, founder, CEO, and managing partner of the megaregional firm Morrison, Brown, Argiz & Farra, LLP, in Miami, FL, likes the sports coaching metaphor, too. "I loved Johnny Wooden, the famed UCLA basketball coach," Argiz says. "Did you see how Kareem [Abdul-Jabbar] and [Bill] Walton spoke about him on television when he passed away? That guy had really touched peoples' lives."

Charly Weinstein says

> I have been very fortunate to have a lot of rabbis (meaning teachers or mentors) at every level, even today. A number of years ago, I was voted in as a third managing partner at Eisner LLP to Dick Eisner and Teddy Levine. The first 3+ years, all I really did was follow Dick and Teddy to meet their contacts. I learned how they ran the firm, how they made decisions. and how they treated clients and team members from a leadership perspective. I learned integrity, harmony, consistency, and fairness. In the 40-somewhat years that they ran the firm together and the 21 years I have been here, I have never seen them be in anything other than lock step. On every decision, every matter, they manage to have a harmony between them that permeates the culture of the entire firm.

Many firms grapple with what to do with former leading or managing partners, but they can make excellent mentors for up-and-coming leaders. Bill Hermann, former managing partner of Plante & Moran, PLLC, shares his role today. "I'm doing a lot of mentoring now that Gordon is managing partner. I'll work with an individual who's got a problem with a supervisor. A lot of times, it's helping somebody understand that the problem they've got isn't necessarily their supervisor; maybe it's where they're at and what they're doing." Some firms will ask retired partners to mentor selected protégés, and they can be very effective with this role.

Bob Bunting, former CEO of the megaregional firm Moss Adams LLP in Seattle, WA, believes that up-and-coming leaders must also take personal responsibility for developing a mentor relationship. "If you want a mentor, you'll find one. I realized early on that it was up to me to find a mentor," Bob says. "I began to see that almost anybody I came in contact with who was my superior could teach me a lot. And it was up to me to get that out of them because they weren't necessarily going to be skilled at teaching."

Mentoring appeals to the new generations' desire for relationships. Generations X and Y are loyal, but their loyalty is based on a bond of trust, and this trust can best be achieved through a mentorship program. Building trust will not only benefit both the mentor and protégé but the entire firm.

Neal Spencer, former CEO of the megaregional firm BKD, LLP, in Springfield, MO, joined BKD in Little Rock, AK, and was mentored by Dean Davenport, whose forte was a commitment to great client service. Moving from Little Rock to Bowling Green, KY, Neil became a huge business builder for the firm. BKD's management committee accepted his offer to open a Louisville, KY, office from scratch in 2002. He then helped lead the practice to being one of the largest in the region, and he credits Davenport's mentoring for his success.

> Working for and being mentored by Dean Davenport was a terrific experience. Typically, we either met with new prospects or presented audit reports at our clients. He threw me into some difficult situations. To this day, I don't know if he did it on purpose, or he just didn't want to go do it himself. At a very young age, I got thrown into some tough situations with some hospitals that were in financial trouble. The boards were in turmoil. Sometimes, the press would be there while you were presenting your audit report. And he'd sit on the sidelines and let me handle it.

Part of the joy in mentoring is helping rising leaders find their own answers to tough professional situations, says Gordon Krater.

> We had a young man who was going to leave the firm. He is an absolute star. He had this great opportunity where he'd be the CFO of a publicly traded company. We talked through it. In our talk, I said, "So, if you are successful, you are going to be the CFO of a publicly traded company? Maybe you will worry about the quarterly earnings, so that you may sacrifice long-term decisions for short term?"
>
> He said, "I really don't want to be a CFO of a publicly trading company."
>
> But he had to come to that conclusion, I couldn't say it for him.

Mentoring: Benefits for the Firm

Mentoring should be encouraged because everyone gains when there is a healthy exchange of information. Not only do the mentor and protégé benefit from this exchange of ideas and information, but your firm as an organization will benefit greatly.

Bob Hottman, CEO of the top-100 firm Ehrhardt Keefe Steiner & Hottman PC (EKS&H) in Denver, CO, says

> I actually made partner at the ripe old age of 29 with Panel, Kerr, Forrester, and I learned a lot there. My biggest mentor at PKF was Galen Drake, who did a phenomenal job with people. Galen taught me to be very up front with people, to be honest with people, to share exactly what's going on with people, not to lead people down a path that wasn't there. I also recognized that you better take care of your high performers because if you support mediocrity, that's what you're going to have.

Each time you have a discussion with another staff member, you have the opportunity for informal mentoring to take place as you provide insights based on your own experiences. Make the most of these informal interactions; their potential for future impact is significant.

Whether mentors set aside time on their schedules daily, weekly, or monthly is not as important as being accessible and prepared to listen and respond to their protégés when needed. The person being mentored needs to feel that you are on his or her side. Mentoring is not effortless, and time will be required. Both parties must be active participants and work out a schedule that is best for them.

It is important to understand that the development of protégés is an ongoing process for everyone. Mentors should relate personal and professional experiences to protégés. They should practice positive communication skills and ensure protégés do the same. Mentors should discuss and exemplify your firm's core values.

"Most CEOs and managing partners of firms really grew through the ranks of their firms. For the most part, they never really had any formal preparation for the roles that they assumed," Chris Allegretti, CEO of the regional Hill, Barth & King, LLC (HBK) in Boardman, OH, says. "I'm just very, very thankful that in my case that I had some phenomenal role models to learn from."

Chris credits his mentor Bob Bunting for providing good examples and a guiding hand early in his career. "He told me one of the expectations is that I pay it forward—that I give back to this industry. He made that very clear. He's very passionate about the profession that we share. He taught me a lot about leading. He also taught me a lot about accountability."

Chris recalls an incident that happened when he started working at HBK

We were doing some consulting work for the hospital here in town, and I remember back in those days, we had very clunky, old audit bags, very heavy things that we'd carry files in. After consulting with the board, Mark (the partner in charge of our group) got up. He grabbed these two heavy audit bags, and we were walking down the hall. I remember the chairman of the board of the hospital said, "Hey, Mark, isn't that what your flunky is for?"

Mark turned around and looked at him and said, "I don't hire flunkies. This is my next partner," and introduced me to him.

That was meaningful, that Mark could make me feel that special. I was a very, very young staff person, someone who had not contributed to that meeting. I was there listening, observing. But, frankly, what he showed in me is confidence. That to me was leadership. And that story has always stuck with me. I tell it probably more than people want to hear, but to me, it's how you make staff and team members feel.

It is important to remember that the senior leader of an audit or tax team is not the only leader. The CEO, senior partners, managers, supervisors, and other leaders are responsible for the development of those junior to them. This provides "ownership" for all the partners and also develops a network of contacts and information sources for everyone. By developing an atmosphere of interaction between all levels, a sense of belonging to something special should develop, and this can only result in a stronger and better accounting firm.

Bill Hubly, founder and managing principal of the local firm Corbett, Duncan & Hubly, PC, in Itasca, IL, says

> Larry Kendzior was a partner in the first firm that I joined. Larry had Big 4 experience and joined this smaller firm. He took me under his wing to teach me the ropes of the profession, not from the aspect of getting the job done, per se. He focused on how to work with your team and service the client. Later, Dan Corbett became my mentor. He really just grabbed me and said, "I'm going to try to develop you in every way that I possibly can. Come along with me on this sales call, or come along with me on this client meeting. You don't need to say anything, but I just want you to observe, so that you can develop your skill sets on how to service the client."

Bill also believes that it's important for all members of leadership to mentor others and for a firm to deliberately create relationships beyond supervisor-staff connections. "The mentor must offer his protégé an avenue to get it right that's outside of the direct reporting relationship," Bill says.

Whereas mentoring tends to be directed at teaching the junior staff members, it actually can and should extend to everyone within a firm. All partners, managers, and supervisors should be mentors and protégés at the same time because everyone who enters our profession needs helpful guidance and assistance in order to perform their duties to the best of their abilities. And all employees, whether new or old, have valuable experiences that should be passed on to others.

Although the common thinking is that the mature, experienced leaders are always the teachers, that is not always the case. One of the partners I worked for at Price Waterhouse always asked the opinions of his managers, seniors, and juniors. He said

> I could learn technology better from a younger person because he has had more recent training in it. I could learn how to relate to younger people by asking the young people that worked for me how to better relate. And I could learn to relate to people with different backgrounds and perspectives than mine when I called on my younger and, sometimes, more observant team members to give me a clue.

One of the problems of instituting a formal mentorship program in an accounting firm is that our leaders are already so overwhelmed with other important requirements that mentoring seems to be just one more thing to add to their already demanding schedules. How can one make time for mentoring?

I would argue that to some extent, mentoring is already taking place without credit being given to the mentor. For instance, there is a group of new partners and senior managers who are almost accidentally being mentored on a daily basis: the client service relationship managers. All these are vital positions, and due to the nature of their job, they have daily contact with partners more senior to them. These relationship managers observe leadership in action. They learn how decisions are made and what questions to ask. They see firsthand how lives are impacted, how politics play into situations, and many other issues. Each of these is being mentored to some extent, either formally or informally. The partners need to recognize this and take advantage of it by encouraging the protégés to ask questions and discuss issues when the opportunity presents itself.

It does not have to be just at the top levels that daily contact and one-on-one discussions occur. This can and should apply at the smallest team level. Managers and supervisors in all positions can and should mentor those junior to them.

Modern technology has actually made it easier. With e-mail, a protégé can seek advice or guidance any time, and if it is not an emergency, the mentor can answer the questions and provide thoughtful advice at his or her convenience. Thus, mentoring can take place at just about any time.

Mentors are not expected to have all the answers. Sometimes, just listening attentively is all people need. Mentoring is a fundamental responsibility of all leaders. It helps protégés reach their full potentials, thereby enhancing the overall professionalism of the accounting firm. Additionally, when an interest is shown in others, your firm is able to retain its most valuable asset: people.

Bill Haller says

> In orientation, we tell our new team members, "If you are high potential, we are going to get involved with you. We invest our time with people who can take what we do and leverage it." It sounds harsh, but it's really not. A lot of managers get into the trap of spending too much time with problem performance. But my attitude is invest in good performance. One of the things we do early on is when we are on-boarding newcomers, we create coaching and mentoring relationships. One of our internal values is that we care about the whole person, and we want them to be successful in their life's roles, whether it's being a great brother, a great sister, a great husband, a great father, and all those things.

▶ A Leader's Perspective

Haller describes a unique mentoring position at his firm:

> We just promoted a young man to being a firm chaplain. We have never had that role before, and people say, "What the heck do you need a chaplain for?" Well, if we are going to walk the talk about caring about the whole person, when somebody has a death in the family or health issues, then we want them to be touched. We don't do counseling and interventions; that's not his role. But his role will be to make sure that our struggling people would be prayed for. He might organize or conduct Bible studies or create support communities of people who are struggling with common things.

> We really get involved with the whole person, and we care about that. We want our people to feel like they are part of something bigger when they work with us. We want our team members to feel that working with CapinCrouse is more than just a job.

Debbie Lambert says that mentors can also help protégés discover talents they haven't yet acknowledged.

> I have one guy who's just superb technically, doing just a great job with his client. He has great people skills. I was trying to mentor him in marketing. I said, "You really need to step

up to the plate on rainmaking," but the younger accountant resisted, coming up with reasons he could not focus on building business. I just kept pushing and pushing him. It took us two years. I really had to push him in little steps. Once he started doing it, it looks like I unleashed mad man. He's a wonderful practice developer today.

I knew he had the right skill set; he just didn't know. He didn't have the confidence. And that was really where I had to really step in and cause something to happen. I broke it down into tasks, and he looked at those tasks and said, "Well, I can do this. This isn't that hard; you know, I can organize this."

Conclusion: The Impact of Training

Here's an undeniable fact: accounting firms that survive and thrive into the next decades will be those with strong leadership across the board, not just at the top. Too many unpredictable factors play a role in the survival of any business. As we move forward into the 21st century, business leaders will continue to grapple with the ever-changing pace of technology, economic ups and downs, contraction and expansion of the available talent pool, the aging of the Baby Boomers, revolutions in communication and energy, and so on. All businesses—both yours and your clients'—will be expected not only to adapt quickly but to innovate cutting-edge systems to meet challenges and opportunities that rush toward your firms. Leadership is no longer a wish-list qualification for partners and new hires; it's a non-negotiable competitive imperative and a key to survival.

The era when firms could approach training as a check-the-box ritual of regulatory compliance is over. Globalization and intensified competition have rendered that approach obsolete. Firms positioning themselves for a competitive future depend on professionals who have outstanding social, sales, communication, and leadership skills, and that trend will continue into the future.

Implicit in the idea of empowering team members and holding them accountable is their education and experience. We will discuss these concepts in chapters 8, "Accountability: Trust but Verify," and 9, "Challenging Personal Growth: Leading the Whole Person." In order to hold anyone accountable for a project, process, or result, that person must have had the relevant training to be able to do the job. The same is true with empowering. In order to delegate and empower people to take on larger and more risky assignments, it is crucial that the person be well trained for the job.

It is much better to invest in the training, coaching, and mentoring necessary for your protégés to progress in their careers and perform great work than it is to repair and recover from major mistakes. It is also much better to train people and risk losing them than to not train your team members and risk keeping them.

Accountability: Trust but Verify

This chapter was coauthored with Bryan Shelton, senior consultant at The Rainmaker Consulting Group.

"Great companies have high cultures of accountability...."

~ STEVE BALLMER, MICROSOFT

One definition of accountability is an obligation or willingness to accept responsibility or to account for one's actions. Accountants, of all people, should be able to *account* for their commitments and behavior. One of the worst things that a leader can do is avoid responsibility for his or her own mistakes. In fact, great leaders take responsibility for their subordinates' mistakes. The great Alabama football coach Paul "Bear" Bryant would say, "If it was successful, the team did it. If it failed, it was my fault." That's a way to build serious loyalty in your staff or team.

As Bill Hermann, former managing partner of Plante & Moran, PLLC, says, "I think a wonderful trait in a leader is to not worry about grabbing the credit. Give the credit out liberally. If something goes wrong, take the blame."

In this chapter, we'll discuss why accountability is so important in business, what accountability is and isn't, and how to move from a low- to high-accountability environment. At the end of the chapter, you will be introduced to some tools that will enable you to implement an accountability culture into your firm with a minimum of pushback from your team members and partners.

In some accounting firms, it is mainly the partners who resist accountability. Some partners' attitudes are as follows:

▲ I've made the partnership and am totally responsible for myself and don't want anyone else to hold me accountable.
▲ Let's implement an accountability system for everyone but the partners.
▲ The managing partner's role is to manage everything else except the partners.

My experience has been that the only method for creating a high-accountability culture is for the owners to lead it. If the partners opt out, so will others. The result will be a ragged and, most likely, failed accountability initiative. As you are reading this chapter, think about your own firm and how these elements apply first to your partners and then to your team members.

Why Is Accountability So Important in Business?

First, consider the economic impact. It's estimated that a lack of accountability costs corporate America tens of billions of dollars each year in terms of absenteeism, rework, missed deadlines, conflicts, and misunderstandings among staff. Accounting firms lose millions more when they lose loyal clients due to poor customer service. In our consulting practice, we've encountered firms with over 50 percent of their worked hours as nonbillable and unaccounted for. Most firms are challenged with managing the nonbillable time to the tune of 16 percent to 30 percent wasted. Without good accountability, an accounting firm with $5 million in annual revenue might be wasting as much as $800,000 per year in nonbillable time for which there is no accountability. A $50 million firm could be wasting up to $8 million per year.

While he served as CEO of the megaregional firm Moss Adams LLP in Seattle, WA, Bob Bunting learned that partner accountability is essential.

> The biggest problem that every managing partner has, in my opinion, is accountability from his own partners. Most new managing partners don't have the personal or organizational power to be an absolute autocrat.
>
> To get accountability, you need communication where you put the problem in front of somebody in a nonpejorative way, and you get them to agree to what they're going to do about that problem. Then, you have some kind of a follow-up mechanism that says, "We're going to discuss your progress on this change you've committed to in 90 days."

In many accounting firms over the last decade, it seems that the organizational pendulum has swung from authoritarian to permissive. I've been in dozens of firms in the last five years whose dominant founding partner has retired, and now, the firm is being led by a very permissive leader or, even worse, a committee. Firms have been caught by a double whammy of a shortage of qualified accountants and a mentality of entitlement in younger generations. These forces have caused some leaders of accounting firms to cater to the whims of the younger employees. Creating a great place to work takes good judgment from the leaders regarding the proper amount of flexibility, so that people are dedicated and engaged in their profession.

Although young employees bring vitality, technology savvy, and new perspectives to your firm, many of them will benefit from the structure that a high-accountability environment can bring to their lives. The transition from the relatively unstructured university life to the highly structured boardroom of many of your clients is difficult for many people.

In chapter 10, "Empowerment: The Secret to Exponential Growth," we will delve into empowerment. In that chapter, I will cover many of the judgments necessary to know the right amount of authoritarian leadership or the right measure of permissiveness. We'll discuss micro-managing, abandonment, the experience of your team members, and the risks involved in their assignments in order to create a good formula for leading.

Some owners have said to me, "We selected him as managing partner to manage everything except us partners." When I hear a statement like this, I interpret it to mean, "We will give lip service to accountability, but that is all. My personal preferences supersede the needs of a growing firm. If we wanted accountability, we would accept that leadership from our managing partner."

It is difficult to lead and manage accountability in professional firms. Professional firms must manage both the performance of their professional responsibilities and also the profitability of their businesses. Many partners or owners of firms resist attempts by their managing partner to instill accountability, but they will follow a great leader.

It has long been reported that a sign sat on President Harry Truman's desk in the White House that read, "The buck stops here." Over the last 70 years, this concept of personal accountability—especially in business—has lost its popularity.

Accountability in your firm means that partners and staff members can count on one another to keep performance commitments. Accountability can result in increased synergy, a safe climate for experimentation and change, and improved solutions because people feel supported and trusted. All of these positive results create higher employee morale and satisfaction. Those who believe that you can hold staff members accountable while partners do what they wish also probably believe in the tooth fairy.

Accountability and productivity are about getting things done—all the right things—accurately and on time. Employers invest heavily in their employees, from hiring costs to payrolls, but how many are getting all the results that they could? In accounting firms, accountability for billable hours is fairly easy compared with that portion titled nonbillable. Accountability in the nonbillable category is essential for the most successful firms. Blaming and finger-pointing are all too common in business today. How many times do employers hear excuses like these:

▲ It's not my fault the manager didn't review my work for two weeks.
▲ The marketing director just wasn't able to attract any business.
▲ My partner dropped the ball.

Accountability Is the Opposite of Permissiveness

The lack of accountability in accounting firms protects the worst partners and employees and hurts the best performers. If you don't believe me, tomorrow, ask five employees who the worst performers are in your firm. They know, and they're also likely to add, "Why doesn't someone do something about it? It's hurting our client service and profitability. He's just skating, and the rest of us are paying the price."

One of Chris Allegretti's, CEO of the regional firm Hill, Barth & King, LLC (HBK) in Boardman, OH, mottos for management is praise publicly; criticize privately. By taking every step with integrity, Chris continues to run a successful company and manage a productive staff. "Did you do what you said you were going to do? One of the core principles of being a leader is having that integrity. So, ultimately, what it gets down to is no one cares about the activity. They want results. You can't ask people to do the right things, and then, ultimately, allow people to do some wrong things and not deal with them."

Increasing Accountability

How do we go about changing this culture in our own firms? First, let's consider what accountability means and then define how to build a culture that encourages accountability. If you walk into a room and ask 10 people what accountability means, you'll likely get 10 different definitions. To some, it's something you make people do, as in holding people accountable. To others, accountability means accepting responsibility.

In my opinion, accountability is not something you make people do. It has to be chosen, accepted, or agreed upon by the people within your firm. People must buy into being accountable and responsible. For many, this is a new, unfamiliar, and sometimes uncomfortable way to work. Learning how to become accountable involves an element of discipline. Most importantly, individual purpose and personal meaning come from accepting responsibility and learning to be accountable.

Bob Hottman, CEO of the top-100 firm Ehrhardt Keefe Steiner & Hottman PC (EKS&H) in Denver, CO, believes, "Holding people accountable, having empathy, and listening are critical elements in a good leader. No matter how poor your innate leadership skills are, you can learn to do all those things better."

Accountability means being responsible for something. In most businesses, accountability opens the door to ownership, and employees acknowledge that they're responsible for some aspect of the business. Accountability can be understood better when you see your firm as a system of individuals linked by mutuality and trust, each taking personal responsibility for achieving something meaningful: the vision, mission, and values of your firm.

In order to establish accountability, you need to have clear and agreed-upon expectations for performance.

> ### John Wright, managing partner of the top-100 firm Padgett Stratemann & Co. of San Antonio, TX, says
>
> In its early stages, people used accountability as a club, and that's not what accountability is. Accountability, to me, is merely the honest communication of results achieved that were based on a set of expectations. Looking back, where we traditionally failed was clearly defining those expectations.
>
> We brought in a partner from a national firm to upgrade the scope of our tax practice. His role was to change the way we look at bigger consulting opportunities. After he had been here a year, he culturally wasn't that good of a fit. In his mind, he was doing what was expected of him and that was to make things better. In some partner's minds, he was doing the exact opposite and tearing us down. So, what ended up happening is he was being held accountable for not doing ABC and D, but ABC and D were never communicated to him. He was doing EF and G, which we were thinking he shouldn't be doing. Ultimately, it led to his termination after about two years. That was our fault for not setting clear expectations at the beginning.
>
> About that time, we were interviewing another potential partner who had come out of a national firm. Because of our bad experience, I got strong pushback from some of our partners.
>
> I drew up a set of expectations that were very clear. It was a very simple two-page bullet points listing: this is what we expect from you and what we believe to be all the important categories to be an equity partner. And I can tell you that today, he is one of the best partners we have. He is now an executive committee member and one of the key leaders of our firm.

Leader Profile: Richard Anderson, CEO of the megaregional firm Moss Adams LLP in Seattle, WA

Rick Anderson held many leadership roles in his youth, from president of his senior class and captain of most of the sports teams to leader at the manufacturing plant where he worked summers. Rick joined Moss Adams LLP in 1973 and worked his way up to become the head of the audit department, then chief operating officer working under the renowned Bob Bunting, and finally chief executive officer in 2004. In all phases of his life and career, Rick studied leadership. Although he probably had some natural leadership talent, Rick worked diligently to hone those skills.

Moss Adams LLP partner Bob Hinton worked with Rick as an office managing partner and industry group leader for many years. Hinton says

> I appreciate his adherence to our Moss Adams PILLAR values (passion for excellence, integrity, lifetime learning, accountability, and respect). These core values drive Rick's decision making and his overall relationship with his partners. That said, accountability to Rick is about challenging our firm leaders to aspire to higher results. This process is clearly a collaborative process but also is very challenging. From an accountability standpoint, Rick expects excellence and challenges us to achieve it. He often says he is delighted but not satisfied since he believes we never arrive at success. This passion for excellence is contagious and is based on his strong relationships with his team and is how Rick motivates us to want to be accountable to excellence.

Director of marketing Leslie Robertson adds

> Highly-driven people can quickly lose motivation if they're micromanaged. Rick doesn't do that. He holds the sales and marketing team accountable, but he does so by setting clear expectations then empowering us to chart the course. He rarely dictates a path. He certainly inspects what he expects (his accountability mantra) but accomplishes this respectfully through coaching and seeking to understand. His supportive nature builds loyalty and translates into our holding ourselves accountable for our growth.

Moss Adams LLP's director of sales, Scott Jensen, says

> In these challenging economic times, many leaders bellow from their office to get out and sell. But that is not Rick Anderson. At Moss Adams, Rick has been very clear on setting the expectation for selling. We have 240 partners, and while each one owns a part of the firm, they also own a part of our pipeline, which has grown from nothing 4 years ago to over 6,000 opportunities. No one person is exempted from our growth cornerstone, and we have developed a sales culture in large part due to Rick's committed, supportive, and accountable persistence. I say committed as in just about every venue: office meetings, industry group retreats, leadership calls, and so on. Rick speaks to the need to actively and successfully sell.
>
> I say supportive because Rick is always available for a new pursuit meeting or a client retention activity, such as a service interview. We just name the time and place, and he will adjust his schedule to meet the need. Finally, Rick is accountable. His goals include the firm's performance on sales, and he has not abdicated those goals to others. I believe his commitment to business development and his personal accountability makes him an effective leader for the firm.

In addition to his role at Moss Adams LLP, Rick has been a leader in the profession of public accounting for many years. He is currently chairman of the blue-ribbon panel established to address how U.S. accounting standards can best meet the needs of users of private company financial statements. Rick currently serves on the board of trustees of the Financial Accounting Foundation (FAF). FAF provides oversight for the Financial Accounting Standards Board and the Governmental Accounting Standards Board. He was a member of the AICPA Council for three years, is the immediate past chair of the AICPA Major Firms Group, and has been involved with other professional committees.

Measuring Accountability

Holding people accountable is really about empowerment and choice. When people have more choices, they learn to be more responsible. When they become more responsible, they can earn more freedom. By being accountable, they earn the trust of partners, managers, and other staff members. When they are more accountable, they understand their purpose and role within the firm and are more committed to making things happen.

Jim Metzler, vice president of Small Firm Interests at the AICPA, believes that a big issue in the accounting profession is individual measurements versus group measurements. "So many firms think it's about Bill's book of business, Jim's book of business, Jim's billing, Bill's billings versus the group," says Jim. Jim thinks it should be about the tax department, the accounting department, or the audit department.

Jim says

> I've been in many a firm where the whole firm can be down on the bottom line year to year, yet certain partners make more money than they did the prior year. This goes to the saying, "There can't be any winners on a losing team." So, moving oneself from individual to group and putting some risk in the group, that's what's needed to break through to the other side.
>
> I live in a highly-accountable organization: the American Institute of CPAs. I have observed some accounting firms switch from low accountability to high accountability. What happens is we see better results every single place we go where that has taken place. I've never seen the results decline from more accountability.

When partners struggle to reach business objectives and cannot identify why employee performance is not succeeding as planned, it may be time to consider more accountability. Partners of firms come to realize that their success in areas such as client service, employee retention, reliability, and overall goal achievement is directly associated with accountable employees.

Although Ken Baggett, co-managing partner of the national firm CohnReznick LLP, celebrates his employees and their hard work, he also expects a high level of performance from each of his staff members. "Most people make a mistake because either there is an emotion or a time line that drives them. Our workload can tempt people to be careless. The first time this happens, the conversation is stern, but it's a conversation. The second time, it's a warning. The third time, it's an action," he says.

Many large businesses use a ranking system to promote high-performing staff members and distinguish them from the poorly-performing employees. The goal is to replace the poor performers with more promising, motivated employees. For many years, General Electric has identified the top 20 percent, the middle 70 percent, and the bottom 10 percent of its 100,000-plus white-collar employees. The bottom 10 percent are given a short time to improve. Former GE Chairman Jack Welch said those workers would eventually be fired anyway, and delaying the inevitable until they are midcareer is "a form of cruelty." Rick Anderson, CEO of the megaregional firm Moss Adams LLP in Seattle, WA, shares, "Some people are able to scale with the business because they recognize the need to do things differently, seek input and training from people both inside and outside the organization." Others don't.

Gordon Krater, managing partner of the megaregional firm Plante & Moran, PLLC, in Southfield, MI, says

> We set goals, measure results toward our competencies. We will lay out a path for you to improve on your competencies, and we set result measures. You can always get better. We have to earn our fees every day. What does that mean? It means that when I am going to meet with a client, I am not just going to show up. I am going to be prepared with a point of view.

How Does Individual Responsibility Factor Into a Group Setting?

Not all owners are capable or willing to follow through with their commitments to their fellow owners. Some people mean well, but they take on more than they can hope to accomplish. They *intend* to honor their commitments but get distracted by other work and don't have a system to reinforce their commitments to themselves and others. Others simply have built a habit of agreeing to do something and then not following through because they do not know how to do it (and they are often afraid to ask for help). Most partners I've met are like the first two examples. Also, some will always be loners, no matter what kind of training you give them. Unfortunately, a few partners in our profession have a passive-aggressive approach to authority, leadership, and their teams.

More than 90 percent of accountants can work well with other people in a team or firm. The ability to function as a member of a team is a critical component of success in business today. As a team member, failure to follow through on commitments can cause the team to fail and that particular team member to become a weak link. A good performance system motivates employees and helps them understand that their personal accountability means success for the entire firm and that each employee's own personal accountability is required for the team to succeed.

Once you understand the kind of partner you are dealing with, then you can determine the best method for gaining true accountability. Partners who take on too much or those who haven't been taught well can be trained over time to become successful. Those who are, by nature, loners or passive-aggressive toward leadership must be isolated from the team because they will infect others.

David Sibits, president of the national firm CBIZ Financial Services in Cleveland, OH, shares

> When I became managing partner at Hausser back in 1991, we were pretty much a collegial society, which is code for low accountability. We had too many partners, and those partners really didn't make much of a living. Firm profitability was okay, but it was spread among so many people that it looked pretty weak. We had a system that was primarily driven by tenure versus anything else. Beginning in 1992, we began to use scorecards and set specific goals for individuals. We implemented a system with equal base compensation. Everything else was rewarded based on performance. In about 6 years, we went from a firm that was marginally profitable to one of the top 2 or 3 firms in the country. We were a bottom line prepartner comp in the 47 percent range. It was all the result of increased accountability. Now, that didn't happen overnight. We had many difficult conversations with partners who struggled with being governed, but we fought through all the temptations to revert to the low accountability of the past.

Both partners and employees benefit from an environment in which all staff members embrace individual accountability. Partners will see the increased productivity that comes with setting deadlines and being clear about expectations and responsibilities. Staff members will take more ownership, feel improved job satisfaction, and experience more success.

Tony Argiz, founder, CEO, and managing partner of the megaregional firm Morrison, Brown, Argiz & Farra, LLP, in Miami, FL, uses a unique accountability tool at the end of each year.

> June is a critical month for us because it's our year-end, so we try to convert our accrual earnings to cash. So, we really get a lot of team building and calling clients and picking up checks. I mean we do a clean house. Our receivables by the end of this month are the lowest that they'll be the rest of the year because we just clean house.
>
> Unless its cash it's not worth a damn.

What Should Partners Know About Performance Measurement?

Imagine a good performance measurement and accountability system as a road map to better client service, better compensation for the productive staff members, and bench strength when it comes to succession of leadership for your firm. Setting quantitative and qualitative expectations and behaviors for staff members can help them achieve greater levels of success. Employees want to know what road to travel, the tasks that they need to accomplish, and the milestones along the way. When expectations change or are unclear, it's like running a race without a finish line. The result could be burnout, lack of motivation and purposeless effort, or just mediocrity.

Initially, performance measurement is not welcomed by employees, partners, and staff members alike. But once partners and team members take more ownership of tasks, personal accountability emerges, stress lowers, productivity increases, and job satisfaction improves.

When partners are committed to accountability, change happens not because the leaders mandate it but because individuals are energized and motivated to approach their jobs more effectively.

Unfortunately, the word *accountability* often connotes punishment. When firms use accountability only as a big stick for punishing employees, fear and anxiety permeate the work environment. Staff members are afraid to try new methods or propose new ideas for fear of failure. On the other hand, if approached correctly, accountability can produce positive, valuable results.

Positive Results of Performance Measurement

A well-executed performance management program can lead to positive results, including the following:

- ▲ Higher morale and team member loyalty
- ▲ Improved performance
- ▲ Increased feelings of competency
- ▲ More staff member participation and involvement
- ▲ Increased team member commitment to the work
- ▲ More creativity

These results occur when staff members view performance measurement programs as progressive methods of completing work. Using a performance scorecard system, which we'll discuss later in this chapter, involves team members in setting goals and expectations. In this case, staff members find that they understand expectations better, are more confident that they can achieve those expectations, and perform at higher levels. Improved results also occur when team members don't associate accountability with negative consequences

Implementing Accountability for Positive Results

Initial employee reactions to performance measurement will be mixed. Some people will embrace accountability, and others will resist. Even those team members who are highly productive may resist because they may see it as adding administration and nonbillable work to their crowded agenda. For some of these reasons, we have found that the best way to implement an accountability or a performance measurement system is to approach it incrementally. Beginning with the owners of a firm enables you to change the tone at the top and models the responsible behaviors for others to witness.

Leaders can practice accountability for positive results by following good performance management principles. Leaders need to

▲ involve employees in setting objectives and give them the authority to accomplish those goals.

▲ coach team members when they need help and support them in all aspects of the job.

▲ monitor progress toward goals and provide feedback that includes credible, useful performance measures.

▲ provide the training and resources that employees need to do the work.

▲ recognize employees for good performance, both formally and informally.

The very best accountability systems are those that help hold people accountable to their own growth goals. In our Rainmaker Academy training course, we use a credibility index (CI), revenue action plan (RAP), and results report as our accountability tools. Participants set their own plans, submit their RAPs to us, review the RAP with their supervising partner, and have a check-in with a coach approximately two months later. During the coaching check-in, participants report their follow-through on the requirements of staying in The Rainmaker Academy program. The coach records their responses in a CI. Students know that if they fall below 90 percent credibility, they will be asked to leave the program. Then, two months after that, they report results against the RAP. This is the very best way to create accountability: help hold people accountable to their own goals.

These accountability tools were designed by us to measure the behavior change and results of our training programs. The CI is a tool that simply measures approximately 20 disciplines that participants commit to do. For example, read the preassigned book, turn in your RAP, follow through on your 21 face-to-face appointments, and so on. We have found that activity will always precede results. In order to ultimately get results from their Rainmaker Academy experience, participants must make appointments and use their learning.

The RAP is a more detailed tool that students use to plan, track, and communicate their sales call activity and results. We expect students to make 21 face-to-face sales calls between classes and have found that the ones who get big results are the same ones who make the calls. Students who do not make their planned calls are always the low performers in each class. During the first year of the 2-year Rainmaker program, we place more emphasis on the activity level than results because we know that the participants' follow-through on the activities will lead to results in year 2.

Accountability Through Measurement: Scorecards and Performance Pay

How do you get your employees to view the company in the same way as an owner? There is a large disconnect between how an employee views a company and how an owner views it. Owners worry about profitability, top and bottom lines, the company's short-term and long-term success, employees, and the list goes on. Employee views are typically much more self-motivated; they want to know when they get their next check and how they can receive a pay raise. In some examples, when owners do work, they are 50 percent more productive than employees. They have more invested, psychologically and financially, and simply care more. So, how do we bridge that gap in views? One way is to implement a performance pay system in which employee bonuses are tied to organizational success.

Here's a six-step framework to build accountability in individuals:

1. Decide what's important for each person.
2. Set objectives to grow.
3. Align systems.
4. Work the plan.
5. Innovate purposefully.
6. Step back and appraise performance results.

One of the keys to building a culture of accountability is to find a way to lead people without ruling them. Leaders have to hold followers accountable, especially other partners. Many followers fail to focus on their highest priorities and get lost in the minutia of their everyday work lives. They work by default; their training and experience prepared them to be an accountant. It is the leader's role to provide systems for accountability and demonstrate to his fellow owners that their accountability and credibility are in the best interests of the firm. If integrity is a core value of the firm, the leader must challenge his partners to live up to this core value.

Ways to Establish Staff Member Accountability

Anyone who has ever bought a house knows firsthand that homeowners have more reasons to maintain and improve their dwellings than renters. For a homeowner, there is no landlord to call when something goes wrong, and the homeowner is compelled to make improvements to maintain and boost property value. Can the benefits and responsibilities of ownership also apply to an individual's skills? The answer is yes. Many firms are now proving that individual skills ownership has its advantages.

The skills of employees may account for 85 percent of a company's assets. Employee skills determine the speed and success with which projects are completed, objectives are met, and services are delivered. However, as any partner knows, it is the individual employee, not the company, who has ultimate control over how well skills are maintained and developed. So, how can partners motivate employees to improve critical skills and take greater ownership of their career development? The answer is relatively simple: give employees the means to objectively measure their skills, identify areas of improvement, and provide access to learning resources to close skill gaps.

Progressive firms are implementing skills measurement systems that dramatically reduce the burden on partners to create individual career development plans. Instead, they are making employees more accountable for their own learning and development based on objective feedback from skills assessments. There are three strategic components to this approach:

1. Provide objective metrics for measuring skills.
2. Establish accountability.
3. Foster continuous improvement.

Simply telling the individual that he or she is responsible for critical skills provides little in the way of actionable information. Give the same employee a resource for assessing particular skill sets from an extended selection of subjects, however, and the equation changes. The employee can take stock of a particular skill, assess the value of that skill, and identify how and where that skill can be improved.

To make skills ownership possible, use objective metrics, and demonstrate how the metrics apply to a range of critical skills. An effective measurement system delivers assessments to employees on demand. The employee can access the system online, select a skills assessment, and complete the test for immediate results. The system calculates scores based on the employee's answers to test questions—questions that are selected dynamically to test the user at his or her skill level. Employees achieve a detailed view of their critical skills, with the ability to repeat assessments and track growth and improvement.

Scott Dietzen, managing partner, Northwest Region, of the national accounting firm CliftonLarsonAllen LLP in Spokane, WA, says

> A leader must be able to communicate clearly about what the nonnegotiables are and how we should respond and be respectful to others. We have found the balanced scorecard a valuable tool. The first step was just getting people to do a scorecard, and the next step was holding periodic scorecard meetings. We began by thinking that if we did 10 short meetings, giving more rapid feedback, it would work. I kept telling our HR department, "Don't get hung up with the fact that it isn't perfect. Adapt a little bit more." Over the last 6 years, we've refined it to the point that we have very clear goals, and 4 times a year, the person goes in, and they have very specific instructions to comment on the progress related to their goals.

Establish Accountability Through Communication—Set Expectations and Reinforce Success

Although providing employees with the tools to measure skills is beneficial, smart firms are communicating expectations to translate "nice-to-have" measurement tools into "must-have" skills improvement objectives. How can employee skills ownership be translated to skills accountability?

There are two answers: set skills requirements and a clear communications process. An individual employee, for example, may receive a selection of skills to track, based on that employee's job-role function, with assessment due dates and assessment score objectives. With an objective measurement system in place, the employee has the ability to take assessments, access learning resources as needed, and take repeat assessments over time to track improvement until baseline objectives are met. The result? The measurement system gives the employee the ability to prove skills ownership, as well as providing the responsibility for skills upkeep.

Accountability also requires a documented, repeatable communications process. Without a formal communications plan, skills initiatives run the risk of falling into disuse. From program introduction to the assignment of skills assessments, the delivery of organization-wide results, and the promise of employee incentives, communications play an essential role in an ongoing process for establishing and reinforcing skills accountability.

Accountability Through Measurement

An Introduction to Measuring Performance

It's no secret that accountants love hard numbers; our businesses thrive on keeping accurate records and reporting our findings to our clients. Why then, with all our love for numbers, do we not keep, maintain, report, and use them when it comes to our employees? This section will give you the tools necessary to implement a performance measurement system that helps you create a culture of accountability in your firm.

Several dimensions are relevant in measuring human performance, including quality, quantity, timeliness, and accuracy. A measurement system can be created by taking the organization's future goals and strategic initiatives and aligning them with each employee's performance. Once a performance measurement system is in place, any size firm can improve employee performance and increase the bottom line. But first, you must determine what needs to be measured.

Leader Profile: William K. Haller, managing partner of the national firm CapinCrouse LLP in Indianapolis, IN

Bill Haller is the managing partner of the national firm CapinCrouse LLP. CapinCrouse LLP is a multioffice firm that focuses its practice on not-for-profit entities, primarily Christian organizations.

The firm has a who's who client roster in some of the largest and most well-known Christian organizations in the world. With 16 partners and over 100 associates, the firm operates in over 30 states and serves more than 700 not-for-profit entities, including more than 300 churches and denominations; over 100 clients with international operations; 70 employee benefit plans; and 50 colleges, universities, and seminaries.

Although the firm has 10 offices spread across the United States, Bill works from his home office in Bonita Springs, FL, which is 500 miles from the nearest practice office.

CapinCrouse LLP partner Gregg Capin says

Bill has an intuitive sense of what is not being said, including impediments and blockages that can be distracting to focus and performance, as well as the ability to confront issues and behaviors in a very positive manner, followed by holding people accountable. But even better is his ability to identify and employ ways to maximize and build upon individual strengths and to minimize and take out of play weaknesses.

In the course of leading our partner meetings, Bill has demonstrated effort and ability to communicate with each person in advance of the meeting and, as a result, to take unnecessary surprise, drama, and controversy off of the table, resulting in more effective and productive meetings.

Bill's expertise includes more than 35 years of experience in public accounting, with the past 20 years focused on firm leadership, quality control, management, and technical training.

Having been involved in the early stages of development of the AICPA Peer Review Program, Bill has trained peer review professionals around the country and performed peer reviews of dozens of CPA firms. He specializes in audit and accounting, as well as strategic areas, such as organization development and planning, quality systems and process improvement, and financial management.

The following four critical guidelines will help you in the art and science of measuring performance:

1. *Tie measurement to a specific performance.* Defining exactly what you want tells the performer what you expect. A measurement system will fail if the performer is left guessing. For example, having a measure such as "wanting more business" from a partner leaves the partner with a lot of questions. Tightening up the statement a little by saying "$50,000 in business" is better because, now, at least the partner knows that a productivity goal has been set. When you say, "Cross-sell $50,000 of services to your top 10 existing clients," the partner knows exactly how to focus his or her efforts.

2. *Focus on relevant performances or results only.* Measures should consist of performances that produce business results. If the measure does not directly produce results related to the business, then you should reexamine the importance of the measure. Examples of relevant measure include billable hours, first-pass accuracy, productivity, realization, and skill development in a niche or new area. Although wearing proper attire might be important to the company image, it rarely affects the bottom line directly, so it should not be included in a performance measurement system.

3. *Focus on all relevant performances of a performer.* There is a saying in the study of measuring human performance: you get what you measure. This is especially true if an incentive or bonus system is tied to the measurement system. If the focus of a measurement system is a single behavior, then that behavior will be produced, but most employees are

responsible for multiple results. Measuring all relevant performances tells the employee that all aspects of the job are important to the organization's vision, not just one.

4. *The measure must be in the performer's control.* A measurement system must avoid measures that rely on someone else's behavior or results. For example, measuring charge hours and setting up a charge hour goal cannot be the only financial measure for staff accountants. Although it is important, this measure is not completely in the performer's direct control. Staff accountants are not responsible for a book of business; they work on what is handed down to them by partners. When staff accountants do not reach a charge hour goal, there are at least two possible reasons why:

   a. The person is slow, spending too much time on nonbillable work or spending too much time doing something else not related to the job.

   b. The partner is not providing enough work for the staff person.

   Making sure that the performer has as much control as possible over the measure will allow both the person and organization to have a clear view of the person's performance.

These are the critical guidelines for a measurement system, but keep the following items in mind, as well. The closer the line of sight the performer has to the result, the more likely it will affect the performer's behavior. This goes back to the fourth control guideline. The immediacy of the consequence is important in affecting human performance.

Rick Honsowetz, Scott Dietzen's long-time partner at CliftonLarsonAllen LLP, shares critical advice that he received from Scott

I was a young partner in charge of the office and was struggling with the performance of an experienced staff person. Formal evaluations of this person each year were painful for him and me because his performance, in terms of staff leadership and business development, did not measure up to his experience and technical knowledge.

Scott's advice to me was blunt but very helpful (here was this young staff accountant lecturing the PIC); he said, "Why are you beating this guy up every year for not achieving a level of performance that he obviously either is not capable of attaining or is choosing not to? If he was able or wanted to get to that level, he would have done it years ago. Why not sit down and work out a performance plan that suits his abilities and desires and design a compensation package that is appropriate for that performance?"

Looking back, that seems like basic advice, certainly not rocket science. But at the time, my frustration had gotten the better of me, and I couldn't see a solution. That staff person is still with us almost 20 years later and performs very well within the parameters we set all those years ago—his evaluations are now a pleasure, and he is fulfilled and challenged in his work.

Scott's boldness and confidence (as a young staff accountant) in giving that advice to the PIC told me much about his wisdom, confidence, and maturity. It also reminded me that in managing staff, care must be taken to understand the person's strengths and limitations.

When you are ready to begin using a measurement system, be sure to confirm that the focus of the system is correct. Remember, you get what you measure. When you are training new employees, focus on behaviors, but with an established performer, the measurement system should focus on results.

After Measuring, Now What?

Whenever a new measurement system is put into place, performance improves. However, this increase in performance is short-lived if management is only measuring performance. To maintain and continue to increase performance, you must ensure that your firm culture includes these three values:

▲ Goal setting
▲ Feedback
▲ Coaching

Setting Goals

Goal setting clarifies what's expected from a performer and provides a goal to strive for. A simple way to set performance goals is to have a regular meeting in which a partner and an employee develop an individual game plan. A game plan consists of three to five initiatives that the protégé will work on for a period of time. Examples include charge hours goals, average realization rates, niche or skill development, obtaining or maintaining a CPA, or the management or development of other lower-level employees. The number of initiatives should depend on the complexity of the tasks or time requirement needed to complete each one. If initiatives require more time than is available, then use milestones to gauge completion. Be sure to consider the firm's overall strategic vision and the employee's interests when you set the goals.

Frequent Feedback

Setting performance goals provides employees with information about the organizational needs, but providing employees with frequent information on how they are doing is key to improving performance. The frequency of feedback matters. The more frequent the better because it gives the employee time to adjust performance before negative consequences. Some good rules of thumb include the following:

▲ Start by giving feedback frequently, and then, fade it back to an easily manageable time frame. For example, start monthly; then bimonthly; and later, every four months.
▲ Give feedback on relative measures or initiatives only; this will keep the feedback objective.

▲ Concentrate on the measures that need constant feedback first. Charge hours, realization, and utilization rate feedback should be given every time.

▲ Deliver individual feedback individually and group feedback as a group.

▲ Develop a report; let the employee see his or her performance relative to the goal and the last time feedback was given.

Coaching

When your employees know how they should be performing and how they are performing, you should provide coaching or training if they are unable to perform at an appropriate level. The employee may lack a skill, use outdated techniques, or lack experience to know the tricks and tips for using your system. By looking at the data and reviewing it frequently with the employee, you will both see the areas that need attention. You can work together to take appropriate action and prevent either the need for you to fire someone or have the employee quit out of frustration.

Neal Spencer, former CEO of the megaregional firm BKD, LLP, in Springfield, MO, describes the partner coaching process at BKD, LLP

> Our accountability system is spelled out in our Partner PRIDE Performance Assessment *Living PRIDE and Delivering Value* document. This is the annual partner performance discussion between partner and office managing partner where the discussion centers around the five attributes of Partner PRIDE: client service, marketing, staff development, succession planning, and good citizenship. For each attribute, there is a paragraph that describes a model BKD partner. The partner will rank themselves 1–5, A "3" meaning, I'm performing at the level expected of the typical partner; a "1" meaning the partner performance is unacceptable; and a "5" meaning an exceptional, rare performance. The managing partner in the office will also evaluate the partner independently and close any gaps during the discussion.

Additionally, during this process, the partner and managing partner review goals established during last year's session and agree on goals for the upcoming year, as well as start to set expectations on compensation increases or decreases for the next year. Every firm can utilize a standard system or prepare a unique system like this one, but regardless of your system, the most important element is the face-to-face discussion.

In this way, unique to BKD, LLP, people rank themselves, and their supervisors give them specific feedback and coaching. Every firm can utilize a standard system or prepare a unique system like this one.

To read more about coaching, training, and mentoring see chapter 7, "Teaching, Coaching, and Mentoring: Multiplying Your Leadership."

Performance Scorecard

A system that I like to use is called the performance (balanced) scorecard (see figure 8-1), which has also been referenced by several of the leaders quoted in this chapter. What makes the scorecard such a useful tool is that it takes different measures important to each individual and gives one overall performance score. The scorecard is divided into the following four broad categories:

- ▲ Financial
- ▲ Internal or oerational
- ▲ Business growth
- ▲ Learning and growth

Within each category, individual and companywide measures can be entered and tracked by entering a minimum level of performance (shown as 0) and a goal level for each measure. Once this is established, interim levels of performance or results are filled in from the base to the goal. The performance of each measure falls into the scorecard (shown as yellow highlighted cells). If the performer exceeds the goal level of performance, additional credit can be earned to reward performing better than the goal level.

The scorecard score is determined by multiplying the multiplier by the weight of each measure (shown in the second to the last column, always adding to 1.00) and then adding all the measure's individual scores together. For example, charge hours for employee X were 983, putting performance into the interim level of 956 (highlighted yellow). The score for that measure is determined by multiplying the multiplier by the weight o(85 x 0.20 = 17). The weight of each measure is determined by the employer. The higher the weight of a measure, the more influence it has on the overall scorecard score, making it more important to the employee. Bill Hubly, founder and managing principal of Corbett, Duncan & Hubly, PC, was an early adopter of the scorecard system.

> We started a balanced scorecard system some years ago, and in the beginning, it really challenged us. We decided we're going to have specific, granular goals on these scorecards that you need to achieve. And we're going to tie the compensation to these goals. And if you're not getting it done, we're going to hold you accountable, and it's going to be more of a forced accountability. And you know what, that's just the way that we need to move the organization. Today, leaders have become more self-accountable. They understand why it's important.

Most systems evolve over time to where people are holding themselves more accountable. Once Bill got the buy-in at the highest level, he started setting some firm objectives. Those firmwide objectives were discussed at partner meetings and firm staff meetings.

Bill goes on

> Then, we took the objective setting down to the department level. If I could go back and do it again, I would probably roll it out at a firm and department level at the same time and get that complete leadership team working on understanding the scorecard and the

Figure 8-1: Performance (Balance) Scorecard

Employee: X

Measures	Level	-10	Minimum 0	50	60	70	80	85	90	95	Goal 100	105	110	Weight	Score
Financial															
1. New Client Revenue	Ind.	0	10,000	12,500	15,000	17,500	20,000	21,250	22,500	23,750	25,000	26,000	27,000	0.20	20
2. Charge Hours	Ind.	0	563	675	788	844	900	956	1,013	1,069	1,125	1,175	1,250	0.20	14
3. Realization	Ind.	0%	50%	55%	60%	65%	70%	75%	80%	84.5%	89%	90%	91%	0.20	22
Operational															
1. People Development	team	0%	50%	60%	65%	70%	75%	80%	85%	90%	95%	96%	98%	0.10	9
2. Days in WIP/AR	ind.	170	140	135	125	100	90	80	70	65	60	55	50	0.10	10
Business Growth															
1. Client Survey	Firm	0%	50%	60%	70%	80%	85%	87.5%	90%	92.5%	95%	96%	98%	0.05	3.5
2. Internal Survey	Ind.	0%	50%	60%	70%	80%	85%	87.5%	90%	92.5%	95%	96%	98%	0.05	4.5
Learning and Growth															
1. Strategic Plan	Ind.	0%	60%	70%	75%	80%	85%	88%	90%	93%	95%	98%	100%	0.10	10

1.00

Score	96

objectives and the terminology at the same time to shrink the learning curve on it. I would start with one or two key objectives in each of those areas because you'd be able to keep people more focused.

Performance Pay

How is the scorecard used in a performance pay system? The scorecard score can be used as a percentage of a total available bonus per employee (bonus = bonus potential × (scorecard score/100)). For example if employee X had the ability to get a $10,000 bonus this year, based on the scorecard, employee X would receive 96 percent of the available bonus, or $9,600.

Bonus = $10,000 × (96/100)

Bonus = $10,000 × .96

Bonus = $9,600

Where does the bonus pool for each employee come from? There is no correct answer for this question; it depends on the firm and what you are willing to set up. Bonus pools can be based on individual employee profitability, group or team profitability, or organization profitability. For partners, the bonus pool can be created using a percentage of firm profitability. How much incentive pay is needed to be effective? Research has shown that approximately 3 percent to 20 percent available incentive pay is needed, depending on the complexity of the system and delay of incentive payouts. This may seem high, but when there is a large possible incentive payout, high annual "I like you" raises are no longer necessary.

Phil Holthouse, founder managing partner of the top-100 multioffice firm Holthouse, Carlin & Van Trigt LLP in Los Angeles, CA, endorses the performance compensation method. "In our view, a lot of that comes back to how compensation and profits are allocated; that is big on accountability. So, it's a core part of our strategy that our system reinforces and rewards highly motivated, productive people."

When firms implement a pay for performance system, several things typically happen. First, employees become interested in how the company is doing and what can be done to improve the organization's success. Second, some people quit. However, these are typically low-performing individuals who you might have wanted to get rid of anyway. Third, high-performing people become more loyal to the company. When individuals are rewarded for their efforts, they are more likely to stay. Finally, the organization becomes more successful. When all employees think like owners and have stakes in whether the company does well, they will find ways to make the organization as successful as possible.

Keeping a Well-Rounded Perspective

As critical as accountability is to a successful firm, it can be used like an iron fist to the firm's detriment, as well. Bill Hermann, former managing partner of Plante & Moran, PLLC, says

Plante Moran isn't a very hierarchical organization. We don't have a lot of rules, and we've resisted a lot of guidelines. While accountability is not a bad word, the real word is self-accountability, in my mind. That's where the real power is. I've heard that term "you get what you measure." I understand that you need to measure. But I also think if you are not careful in how you do it, you may get only what you measure. Accountability loses something when it becomes too hard-wired or it's too numbers driven.

Conclusion

Accountability fits very well inside a firm where there is also a high level of empowerment, as we'll discuss in the next chapter. Accountability is not simply for the underperforming team members. High performers work more effectively when they are held to their own high standards and also when they know that their performance is not producing a result that allows low performers to ride the system. Accountability works best when goals are written, protégés set their own stretch goals, and the leader provides an environment for success, coaching, and resources for the team.

Challenging Personal Growth: Leading the Whole Person

"When the best leader's work is done the people say, 'We did it ourselves.'"

~ LAO-TZU

Although it is true that most of your partners and senior team members are extremely well qualified accountants, are they fully developed as people? Are they the kind of people who can carry and build a conversation with you, your other team members, and your clients? Are they devoid of quirks, poor manners, odd behaviors, and career-limiting communication skills? Some would call this being boardroom ready. A person who is well rounded and well spoken and understands social graces is a person whom clients will seek out for advice and counsel. A person who can only complete a tax return or financial report on historical data will limit himself or herself and your firm.

The challenge that many firms have is bringing in team members from a variety of experiences and family backgrounds. Some are well-rounded people, and some have been limited by their training, innate personalities, and blind spots. Rich Caturano, office managing partner, Boston, of the national firm McGladrey & Pullen, LLP, shares

> I found out that I am an introvert, and when I looked at what my goals were in life, I determined that I'm not going to be successful as an introvert. If you want to be able to accomplish all of these things, how do you deal with that? So, that's probably my blind spot that comes out in me every once in a while. And when it comes out, it means that you are not getting things done that you should get done; you are not picking up the phone; you are not striking up conversations that you should.

One of your roles as a leader is to help your protégés identify and deal with career- and personally-limiting blind spots. You must have the courage to challenge the personal growth of your team members, so they are bringing the whole person to your team.

The best leaders have an intensity about them that can focus everyone's attention on the task or goal at hand. Usually, this intensity or sense of urgency has been developed through many years of personal growth. These leaders are clear about their visions and missions and how these connect to the work at hand.

In this chapter, we'll discuss the leader's role in developing your team members' whole person. Some call this process getting boardroom ready or challenging personal growth. In other words, it's taking the work that we did in chapter 7, "Teaching, Coaching, and Mentoring: Multiplying Your Leadership," and applying it to the individual, beyond his or her professional expertise. We will cover the barriers to challenging team members' personal growth and give you some tips to work through those challenges. Then, we'll wrap up by sharing some ideas to help your entire team grow into people who can communicate well in many business and social settings.

Personal growth begins in childhood as we become civilized. Without nurturing and training, a baby would mature into just another wild animal. Parental guidance provides a framework for early personal growth, such as mind your manners, pick up your room, say thank you and please, and share your toys with your friends. Through these guiding words, parents help their children begin the personal growth necessary to cope in a complicated world and to take responsibility for themselves.

To be effective in life or business, a person must continue this personal growth into adulthood and on into retirement. Some of your team members have been well trained and have grown into well-rounded adults. Others are still using some childlike coping mechanisms to navigate their adult world. Childlike coping mechanisms, such as lying, telling you what you want to hear, avoiding conflict, and using anger to get their way, are frustrating and off-putting to those around them. As a leader in your organization, you have to model personal growth and challenge your team members to continue their own personal growth.

Even after Chris Allegretti, CEO of the regional firm Hill, Barth & King, LLC (HBK) in Boardman, OH, met his goal to become a partner of HBK, he never stopped learning. "I absolutely consider myself a lifelong learner. I grew up the son of a schoolteacher. And I frankly always wanted to be a teacher, but my father led me in a different direction." Allegretti is constantly evaluating the best way to manage his staff and company. "We all need to grow, and if you're not growing, I'm not sure where you're heading."

A Path to a Better Person

Personal growth has nothing to do with becoming a better accountant, though that may be a side benefit. It has everything to do with growing into a better person. Stephen Covey's eight habits would be a good road map here—things like being proactive, beginning with the end in mind, and doing first things first.

Some of the best growth lessons we learn are from our own mistakes. Frank Ross, director of Howard University School of Business Center for Accounting Education in Washington, D.C., challenged his supervisor in front of other people. It was through his own embarrassment and self-awareness that he learned. He says

> One day, I was in the middle of meeting with my client when this senior manager came over and began loudly yelling negative statements to me. In the past, I'd ignored it as much as possible. But this was the day I would let him know how I felt. Once he'd gotten started, I stood up and let him know in no uncertain terms that I had had enough of his bullying and didn't appreciate his speaking to me in that way, especially in front of the client's staff—the same people I was expected to get answers from.
>
> We met in the elevator later that day. He turned the elevator off and let me have it right there, saying I could be fired. The point is, I had lost my temper and could very easily have lost my job. Now that I know myself better and understand office politics better, I would have certainly have talked to him alone, not in front of the whole room. At that instance, though, I didn't focus on what could happen after that.
>
> But I would never stop learning important lessons about myself and how to turn what others perceived as my weaknesses into strengths inside the corporate world. For instance, it took a while, but I eventually learned how to use my quiet demeanor—what some partners thought would be a detriment to my career path—to my advantage.

Ross used this very negative experience and his poor reaction to that experience to take responsibility and grow in a manner that enabled him to function at a high level in some of the largest organizations in the country.

Challenging team members in the area of personal growth takes courage and insight. Many people do not achieve their potential simply because they have not been challenged. In high school, I was able to make good grades without studying much, so I spent four years just cruising and having fun. Ms. Mildred Lindsey, my Latin teacher, was the only one who really challenged me, and she is the teacher whom I remember and appreciate the most today. Ms. Lindsey had the courage to hold my feet to the fire, but she also had insight. She knew that I was more than a C student, and she would not let me settle for an average grade.

Personal Growth, Firm Growth

Personal growth also ties to firm growth. Rick Dreher, CEO of the megaregional firm Wipfli LLP in Green Bay, WS, is all about growth in both areas, and his entire staff knows it.

> As part of my campaign to become managing partner, I challenged the firm this way: if you're not growing, you're dying. And I don't know how else to say it any simpler than that. Everybody in this firm knows, and they accuse me, at times, of, "Well, Rick, you're just all about growth." If you truly want to be a survivor, there is nothing else in my mind but growth.

Rick continues to work with all the partners to ensure that they are helping to shape the firm's culture and focus on growth. " I'd say our partners are on board with that, and there are probably still a few who'll go to their graves never getting on that train, and that's just the way it is. Somehow, those people are confused that the past is somehow a guarantee of the future, and that is just so incorrect."

In business or life, most successful people have had a leader who looked beyond their personal limitations and saw something that could be improved, something that the protégé might not have been able to see. If we define success as progressive accomplishment of personal worthwhile goals, then success becomes a never-ending process. Progressive means that each goal is higher than the last one.

Growing Pains

Your protégés' growth potential is limitless because we live in a world of abundance. Opportunity is everywhere. As a leader, you can help your protégés sort through the many choices they face. We all become a product of those choices, and by making consistently good choices, we will continue to grow and succeed. Debbie Lambert, managing partner of the top-100 multioffice firm Johnson Lambert & Co. LLP in Raleigh, NC, shares, "I was captain of my cheerleading team in high school. My husband calls me the cheerleader because I'm always cheering people on. I love to root, I love to build people to their potential, and I really love to compete in the marketplace."

Some people view success as beating the competition, but that is not a true definition of success. Success is a realization of a personal accomplishment, not besting your opponent in a rivalry. If your potential is limitless, then your realizations must be limitless, also. Discovery is infinite because inside one discovery lives the potential of another. Potential is only limited to your ability for acceptance. A goal is like a target: in order to hit a target, you must know your target, take aim, and then shoot.

Some people just want to grow into better accountants, but they resist the personal habit of being proactive, described by Covey's habit one. Habit one, or being proactive, means that when challenged to make choices in accordance with good principles, protégés may exhibit a hostile or passive-aggressive attitude. Being proactive means that you control your response to events, so they are in alignment with good principles of human dynamics, not your emotions.

"While it may be difficult to confront hard issues, it is more unfair to not confront them," says Kris McMasters, CEO of the national accounting firm CliftonLarsonAllen LLP in Milwaukee, WI. "If we fail to confront the tough issues, they will not go away or get better. They will always get worse."

Each team member's potential for success lies within. We are each the ultimate factor in our own development—no excuses, no recourse. However, part of the job of a leader is to see hidden potential in your protégés and challenge them to more satisfying careers and lives. As a leader, your role is to challenge your staff members to take advantage of the abundance that surrounds them. The reason most people don't achieve success is because they don't have a clearly defined concept of success in the first place. They won't take that first step because they don't know in which direction to step.

"As a leader, you must be willing to have really tough conversations with your people. Sometimes, those are uncomfortable situations," says Bill Hubly, founder and managing principal of Corbett, Duncan & Hubly, PC. "But if you're going to grow as an organization, and the individual is going to grow, and the leader is going to grow, you have to be willing to have these conversations."

I think there are two fundamental ways to provide challenging and difficult conversations in uncomfortable situations. First, you must talk straight while, at the same time, being respectful. Preface your feedback with a phrase like, "Bill, you have a lot of potential, and I am disappointed that you are not achieving your best work here." Such a phrase shows that you recognize that your protégé has untapped potential, and you are willing to help him get better. Another phrase that you might use would be, "Jane, I want to share with you some of my observations, and they may be totally off-base, but it's important that I give you my perceptions; then, I'd like to hear your perceptions on this matter." After showing respect for the other person's capabilities or perceptions, you will be able to give the person direct and challenging feedback and keep the emotions in check. When you become hostile and make broad charges or name call, you will lose your effectiveness in having tough conversations.

Second, I recommend that you do not use the old method of giving someone the so-called "crap sandwich." This method suggests that you give a compliment at the beginning, corrective feedback in the middle, and end with another compliment. Unfortunately, many of these "sandwiches" fail to communicate the tough information. They often fail because too much emphasis is given, by the leader, to the compliments, and cursory attention is given to the correction. Other times, the hearer will disregard the corrective feedback because two-thirds of the message was good, so that may be interpreted that no real change is necessary.

Personal growth comes to those who understand that success is more than money. Personal growth is about becoming the master of your life, rather than the victim. Success is fulfillment and meaningful personal growth. We all have the potential to achieve worthwhile, predetermined goals, but most people end up being pushed and pulled around, never mastering their lives and never receiving the guidance that could put them on the right path.

Steve Mayer, founder, chairman, and CEO of the regional firm Burr, Pilger & Mayer LLP in San Francisco, CA, says

> If you don't grow, you can't attract great young professionals into your firm. We had a situation at a meeting yesterday where a person was saying she wasn't going to do something. I said, "For a long time, I've been meaning to tell you that you are really difficult. You do things that really hurt you, and nobody will call it to your face, but I am now." I got home that night, and she sent me a scathing e-mail about how rude that was. The next morning, I got up, and I e-mailed her back, and I said, "When somebody that I've known for 25 years tells me that I'm doing something wrong, and they've been meaning to tell me for a long time but just never had the right time…" I said I really listened to them. And I said, "I was trying to give you some constructive criticism. I was trying to help you." Interestingly enough, a couple of hours later, I got an e-mail from her, and she said she thought about it and thank you very much; I was probably right. So, that was a touchdown.

As a leader, your role is to help your team members master their lives and make their own choices. You want to challenge them to see their potential and the abundance around them and learn from their weaknesses. Your leadership mission should be to make leaders out of your followers; otherwise, they will be doomed to despair because they are blind to what they have the power to do.

Accountants who play the victim card frequently are not being responsible and seem to be pointing fingers and blaming. Jim DeMartini, managing partner of the top-100 firm Seiler LLP in Redwood City, CA, says

> Problems are not fine wine. They do not get better with age. We've never lost a client over an error being made. In fact, we've had circumstances where clients have become significantly bigger clients today than they were at the time we immediately went to them and handled an issue. It seems like common sense, but you have to be committed to do it. Blaming is unacceptable to me. One of the things I learned a long time ago is when people make a mistake, my strategy is to get with them and say, "What do we need to do for the client?" If you blame people, they'll stop talking to you. All professionals are great at the blame game. Blaming isn't tolerated in our culture.

Leader Profile: Debbie Lambert, founder and CEO of the top-100 multioffice firm Johnson Lambert & Co. LLP in Raleigh, NC

Debbie Lambert's leadership style was molded early in life as a cheerleader and camp counselor. She believes that people need to be encouraged and challenged to reach their best potential in life and business. Her worldview was expanded significantly living with a family in Pretoria, South Africa, as a member of the American Field Service.

Debbie, a founder and managing partner of Johnson Lambert & Co. LLP, has served as chair of the North Carolina Association of Certified Public Accountants. She has served as a member of the board of the AICPA, chair of the Auditing Standards Board of the AICPA, chair of a task force developing small business implementation guidance for the COSO Internal Control Integrated Framework, and a member of the Securities and Exchange Commission Advisory Committee on Smaller Public Companies.

Partner Diane Walker says

> The development of a clear mission, vision, and core values for Johnson Lambert has been a focal point of Debbie's. The way we developed them speaks to Debbie's inclusive leadership style. Our mission, vision, and values were initially drafted during a partner-manager retreat, with input from everyone. Debbie drew comments out of everyone in attendance. When we updated the strategic plan last year, she personally visited each office to present a draft and obtain feedback. Debbie inspires people to follow her leadership. She challenges each one of us to grow personally beyond our accounting abilities. She is passionate for our firm and public accounting. Debbie has brought real transparency to our firm, which contributes to the high level of trust and respect with which she is viewed throughout all levels in the firm.

> Debbie disciplines herself to focus on the moment, whether it's skiing in Utah, chairing a professional board, or reviewing audited financial statements. When you meet with her, you genuinely have her full attention. I think a great example of how she balances her life is her periodic ski trips to Utah during busy season. She wakes up early and holds calls with us on the East Coast before heading off to the ski slopes. She has shown us that if you are disciplined with your time, you can be responsive to your clients and coworkers and still have the opportunity to vacation at a busy time of year.

Debbie graduated cum laude with a bachelor of science degree from Wake Forest University, where she is a member of the board of trustees and has chaired its Finance Committee, Audit and Compliance Committee, Athletic Committee, and Graduate and Professional Schools Committee. Debbie holds leadership positions in numerous professional and service organizations and has been named several times as one of the top 100 most influential people in accounting.

Intentional Success

If you agree that the definition of success is a progressive movement toward one's life goals, then success cannot be realized by accident. Success is a forward movement; it is an expansion process. All of creation is expanding as it moves forward in time. That which is not expanding becomes stagnant and dies, you can only coast one way.

Outstanding firms are created from an extraordinary bond from within. At the core of this bond is a genuine love for your work and people. A good firm will always involve love—the kind of love that is patient and kind, not rude or arrogant, but also the kind of love that will challenge your people to give the best they can give. It is your role as the leader to love your people enough to not play games with them and to challenge them to grow personally.

Bob Hottman, CEO of the top-100 firm Ehrhardt Keefe Steiner & Hottman PC (EKS&H) in Denver, CO, says

> Most of my day is meeting with people. I meet with every one of our partners at least once every other month. I believe you can change a person, but they have to see the benefit of focusing on others. If they don't, you won't change their intent.
>
> I challenge all our partners to get better as individuals, so we can get better as an organization. In order to be successful in our profession, you need to get outside your comfort zone and stretch your personal limits. And that's a risk.

Barriers to Personal Growth

Challenging people to respond to situations from a solid core of values and to not allow their feelings to guide their every move makes you and your team stronger. When you work with your team, your feedback is an essential part of their development. Don't overuse the phrase "great" because everyone can always improve. Instead, use the phrases, "good," "that's good," or "that's getting better" or "come on, you can improve on this." Even high-achievers can be challenged to continue to improve, so I think you should hold your "greats" for that small percentage of really outstanding achievements.

Scott Dietzen, managing partner, Northwest Region, of the national accounting firm CliftonLarsonAllen LLP in Spokane, WA, says, "I can't just rely on inspiration. I always have to be the father who is demanding excellence and accountability, even when it's unpopular or uncomfortable. It's an obvious observation when you step back and think about it, but for me, it was a key learning."

The reason for feedback is to challenge or educate; feedback should change behavior. It takes great skill to challenge people without engendering ill feelings. If you develop animosity or anger in the team member you are challenging, it will be destructive.

Lisa Cines, office managing partner, Rockville, of the megaregional firm Dixon Hughes Goodman LLP, remembers a partner who she encouraged to develop new skills as they were creating a new product line. "She said, 'I'm never speaking publicly; just know that.' We worked together, and she began to slowly develop. Within a few months, she had a 10-minute part of a presentation. Within a few more months, she became a vocal expert. Now, she speaks everywhere."

As leaders, we have to confront the barriers that prevent us from reaching our potential and from challenging our team members to reach theirs. Some are external, some are internal, and some barriers to personal growth can be remarkably personal—what goes on in the head. You must help provide the knowledge, time, and resources that keep your people from getting stuck in ruts and never getting out of them.

Some barriers to personal growth and development include the following:

1. *Mind barriers.* This is the most challenging barrier to personal growth because there can be no positive growth when there is overwhelming victimhood, cynicism, or fear. Such negative emotions can overwhelm our protégés.

"I think that to have a fresh perspective and diversity of experience is an important element of challenging who we are every day. We sometimes need someone else to break our mental blocks to progress," John Wright, managing partner of the top-100 firm Padgett Stratemann & Co. of San Antonio, TX, says. "One of the most significant things that we've experienced in our firm was the willingness to bring in outside leadership. This allows these new people to challenge what we do, how we think, and our culture."

2. *Environmental barriers.* We all are limited by our coworkers and peers. If our peers have their own set of limiting beliefs of how to live successful lives, we too will be strongly influenced. Peer pressure doesn't subside as people mature.

3. *Heritage.* We are all born with certain imprinted characteristics. I think Tiger Woods was born to be a golfer, and with the help of his father, he nurtured that skill to become one of the top players in the game. What would have happened if Woods's father had not seen the potential in him and challenged him to grow in that skill? How many other Tiger Woods are there in the world who were born with that nature but have never picked up a golf club? Many people have been raised under difficult circumstances: death of parents, divorce, mental illness, or abuse, to name just a few. You have people joining your team from a wide variety of family cultures, and they may bring some of those perceptions with them.

4. *Lack of experience or poor experience.* People who do not value personal growth are mostly unmotivated. Poor experiences, including education, will not hone the budding leader to improve himself and grow. One of your roles is to challenge those who lack the education or experience to supplement their shortcomings in these areas.

5. *Bad habits.* With routine accounting work coming at staff all the time, it's easy for them to fall into ruts, keep their heads down, and never look up.

6. *Laziness.* Let's face it, some people are like I was in high school. They only do what they need to get by, and if they have lots of natural talent, they may have the most potential to contribute if they can be motivated. Although I appreciate the professional challenges that public accounting presents each one of us, when I compare our work lives with the work lives of lawyers and doctors, the excuses begin to fade. It is not uncommon for lawyers to bill 2,000–2,500 hours per year while working 3,000 hours or more. The same is true with many physicians who work, on average, 60–80 hours per week.

Barriers will always exist. As a leader, one of your roles is to help your protégés see ways to go around, over, or through the barriers, even their self-imposed ones. You can create an environment to challenge their personal growth. You role is to teach staff members how to prevent barriers to personal growth from happening or recurring in their lives.

In the last few pages of this chapter, I've suggested a few strategies, techniques, and exercises to help you and your protégés overcome many of these barriers.

Dealing With Change

One constant that accounting firm leaders can count on is change—constant change. Change in technology; the rules; firms; competition; people, partners, and staff members; and, yes, the economic climate. How you, the leader, anticipate and respond to the constant and turbulent change that envelops a firm is usually the difference between success and failure.

The past few years have also changed the kind of work available for accounting firms to build their businesses, says Larry Autrey, managing partner of the top-100 firm Whitley Penn LLP in Ft. Worth, TX. "I think we created a group of people who thought that compliance was the answer because that's all we really had time to do. There's a group of people who are now managers, maybe even some young partners, who didn't grow up having to go and hunt for work and didn't have to do consulting."

In chapters 11, "Vision: Reality in the Future"; 14, "Managing Processes for Your Future Firm"; and 15, "Building the Future Firm Continuously," I deal with building and managing the future firm. We can either allow change around us to regularly upset our lives, or we can anticipate or create the change in our lives and businesses. Choosing the former, allowing change to upset our lives, is also choosing to be the victim of circumstances—a malady that great leaders shy away from. Choosing to anticipate or create change in our business, so that we are in sync with, or ahead of, the change cycle, will allow us to master our circumstances.

Leader Profile: **Phil Holthouse, founder and managing partner of the top-100 multioffice firm Holthouse, Carlin & Van Trigt LLP in Los Angeles, CA**

Phil Holthouse, founder and managing partner of Holthouse, Carlin & Van Trigt LLP (HCVT), Los Angeles, CA, learned to manage interpersonal conflict and make tough decisions early in life. Despite knowing that his father was a die-hard Notre Dame fan, Phil chose the University of Southern California School of Business. As penance for his sins, Phil was required to display a Notre Dame coffee cup throughout his college years!

It was during those years at USC that Phil developed one of the most critical skills of a good leader: communication. He was editor of the university business school newspaper.

HCVT partner John Van Trigt says, "When Phil and I first started the firm, we both had the same color hair. My hair's still the same color. His is now white. That may be a penalty for the rigors of leadership."

John explained that Phil led the creation of an open and transparent culture within the partner group, and he doesn't tolerate complaints about partners or partner meetings to others. "Phil is pretty blunt about saying what's on your mind, even if someone disagrees with him—especially if someone disagrees with him," says Van Trigt. Disagreements in their firm are highly encouraged inside the partner meetings, but unity is expected when the partners face their other team members.

About 10 years ago, we were contemplating a roll-up into a larger organization. There were some partners who wanted to do it and some who didn't. We had a split vote at that time. Phil was able to talk to the partners who voted for the merger and refocus them on our long-term future, rather than the short-term gain we might have gotten. At the time, we were around $15 million in revenue; now, we are close to $60 million. I will tell you that there isn't a single partner who voted for that roll-up who has any regrets that we decided not to do it. That's real leadership.

A summa cum laude graduate, Phil holds a master's degree in business taxation and a bachelor's degree in business administration, both from the University of Southern California, and a law degree from Loyola Law School Los Angeles (Order of the Coif). He began his career with Peat Marwick & Mitchell in Los Angeles and worked as a tax manager in Peat Marwick's national tax practice in Washington, D.C., where he monitored tax changes for the firm's affiliate offices.

He cofounded Holthouse Carlin & Van Trigt LLP in 1991 and helped lead the firm to one of the largest 100 firms in the United States. Phil serves as managing partner of HCVT, with 7 offices and 250 employees in Southern California.

Phil served as a part-time faculty member for USC's graduate taxation program for approximately 10 years and is a member of the board of advisors for the Leventhal School of Accounting at USC and the graduate tax program at Loyola Law School. He serves on the boards of Ascent Media Corporation (NASDAQ) and several nonprofit organizations, including the Curtis School; Harvard-Westlake School; and Young Presidents' Organization, Los Angeles chapter.

Overcoming Barriers

I have thought about ways to overcome personal growth barriers during my 30-year career leading large and small groups of accountants, sales and marketing professionals, and technicians. Most technical and business people dislike uncertainty. Uncertainty breeds distrust, fear, loss of confidence, anger, rumors, and all the attributes that complicate and usually impede progress and success in the office or at home. Therefore, the first priority for the leader should be to reduce uncertainty in the workplace and replace the undesirable attributes previously mentioned with facts, sensitivity to employee concerns, and clarity about group goals and objectives.

Here are four rules to follow, especially in times of uncertainty and turbulence:

Rule 1: Believe in the Meaning of Your Work

The best leaders have an intensity about them that rivets everyone's attention on the goal. When this intensity is intelligently applied, you may express disappointment in the performance of one of your key leaders without berating him or her. How will you be able to ask others to control themselves if you, as a leader, cannot control yourself? Emotionalism produces an inconsistent result, and the leader must know the difference between intensity and emotionalism. You need to guide staff members to take pride in their work and assume ownership and accountability for their results.

Rule 2: Communicate Regularly and Honestly With Team Members

Communication takes many forms. In addition to full staff meetings, departmental meetings, and one-on-one and partner meetings, periodic written communication will help stabilize a team or firm. Also, the leader should continuously improve and employ keen listening skills. Employees need to be heard, and their issues should be discussed and resolved. By practicing these various communication skills, a leader can find a pathway to motivate and even inspire the workforce.

Rule 3: Leaders Must Always Be Moving Toward the Larger Goals

Keep your and your team's eyes on the bigger goals. A micromanaged person or team will be demoralized and cynical. Leaders should focus on their goals and make it clear that they are always available when needed to support employees who seek help.

Rule 4: Recognize Your Team Members

Recognizing includes both moral and financial support. Most people like to be recognized for a job well done. Recognition takes many forms, and the successful leader deploys many types of recognition, including financial bonuses and raises and verbal or written recognition that is given in a public or private setting. The key benefit of this rule is that employees will feel that their work is important, appreciated, and valued by their leaders.

Consistently practicing these four rules during good times and bad will help establish a stable team not churned by the emotion of the times. These guidelines work best when the senior leader practices them and requires direct reports to also use them. One of the performance measures of the senior leader's staff should be how well they are able to implement these rules.

For many accountants who believe deeply in the value of their work, they often are not able to express that conviction to others because of their weak communication skills. Ray Strothman, managing partner of the local firm Strothman & Company, PSC, in Louisville, KY, provided a terrific model for his team as he set out to improve his communication skills, so he could better express his passion to others (rule 1) and move toward a larger goal (rule 3) of building his firm into one of the largest in central Kentucky.

> While I had built my skills as an able accountant, I had not learned how to attract new business to our firm as well as I should to really be a leader. I really believe you must be a business developer to lead a small or a large firm. I decided to join Sales and Marketing Executives International (SMEI) because I needed to learn more about how to be a business developer. I felt that by joining SMEI, the skill would flow to me through osmosis—that it would ultimately sink in. Here I was with all these gregarious, free-spirited people, and I was this conservative accountant, and little by little, I started coming out of my shell.
>
> SMEI was very influential in helping me become the business developer and leader I am today. I think that a number of successful people aren't as extroverted earlier on in their careers. Then, they find out that they must learn to be great communicators. It takes the

discipline to commit to personal self-improvement. Today, much of what I do with my team is to challenge them out of their comfort zones by getting involved with things that will improve their whole person. I want our team to not only be great financial advisors, I want our team members to be the kind of people to which others are attracted.

Finding Balance

Unfortunately, a great many people are unhappy in their jobs. They go to work every day out of necessity, not because it is of interest to them or a challenge. Each day, they spend eight hours in misery, with no room for personal growth. Personal success is only a flicker because the fire is never able to ignite. The desire to succeed is a human trait that is there in the heart waiting for the right moment to become a blazing inferno, but the necessary drive to succeed is often squelched by a desire for security and a need to please the family.

As a leader, you can help your people find their jobs—and lives—more meaningful. The challenge for all of us is to find that right balance, so that we succeed in both our personal and professional lives. As a busy professional, you may experience pangs of guilt when you're working late or traveling away from the family. Sometimes, when you are with your friends or family, you may feel the gnawing responsibility of a work project. The only way that most people cope with these competing demands is by drawing clear boundaries. One of my friends makes it a practice of eating dinner with his family at least three nights per week, and he leaves his iPhone in the car and does not check e-mail until early the next morning. These boundaries allow him to be present with his family from 6:00 PM to 9:00 PM. If you or your protégés have difficulty with these conflicts, you might consider what rituals or boundaries might work for you.

Often, the tension that is created from the pull between one's professional and personal lives boils over into hostility. Ted Mason, president and CEO of the top-100 firm Laporte Sehrt Romig Hand in New Orleans, LA, says, "Recently, one of our vice presidents blew up at one of our directors. He really crossed the line. Later, both of them acted coolly toward each other. Probably 15 years ago, I would have just gone to each of their offices and ranted and raved. But by having patience and working through the issues together, we came out with a great relationship among us all." As a leader, you will teach powerful lessons when you can help your team members resolve their friction in a productive manner.

Many messages in the marketplace discourage personal growth, but self-assured people face life on the assumption that they will be successful. There is no maybe or perhaps, only doing. They know that they must be precise in formulating a plan for success by acquiring knowledge, becoming as professional as possible, and being persistent. They realize that there is a price to be paid, and they are willing to pay it. They develop a desire that drives them toward better things. Their family; religion; and financial, social, and physical elements are balanced for continued growth. The formula for this balance is as varied as there are people on your team. I've learned that the leader must understand the personal mission and core values (discussed in chapters 12, "Values: The Character, Actions, and Outcome," and 13,

"Mission: Making a Difference") of each one of his or her protégés and make certain that this mission aligns with the mission of the team that he or she is leading.

Because self-motivation is self-induced, there are no guarantees for sustaining its endurance. No one can work at full capacity every hour of every day. It is more desirable to maintain a balanced, structured approach to the work schedule, with each work period directed toward a final outcome. Through planning and sticking to it, you can minimize nonproductive times that might threaten to undermine your success. The more you are active, the more you want to be active.

Tips for Achieving Personal Growth

Challenging people to grow is not about taking tests or attending seminars; in fact, most of that stuff is a waste of time and money. Personal growth really comes from challenging team members and their beliefs. Stimulating your protégés well and encouraging them to perform at higher levels will take time and patience and a willingness to change.

Bob Bunting, former CEO of the megaregional firm Moss Adams LLP in Seattle, WA, says

> During the course of leading the firm, I have had responsibility for dealing with people who are very eloquent, and yet, they have performance problems. They didn't want to take responsibility for their performance problems.
>
> I changed from a guy who liked people to agree with me to a guy who realized that if people won't disagree with me, nothing was going to happen because they weren't engaged. If there is no real conflict, nobody is helping improve the decision, nobody is really buying into the decision, nobody is committed to the decision because there is nothing going on.

Personal growth is an investment in myself that I take very seriously, and I always have. I spend a lot of time on introspection and understanding why people are the way they are. I've worked very hard to understand my core values and to also understand the values that others use to operate. Doing this consistently has transformed me as a person, making me much more able to comprehend new situations and better equipped to understand and control how I respond to them.

Personal growth is not just about identifying and developing professional skills; it's a broader pursuit of personal excellence. Here are seven tips you can offer to your team members to challenge them to grow personally:

1. *Understand what you value most.* Most people have a sense of the right thing to do in any given circumstance. Whenever that small voice tells you that something is wrong, ask yourself why you feel that way. Keep trying to break each answer down into more and more fundamental pieces—things that you are sure are right and things that you are sure are wrong. If you invest some time into this, you'll find that your beliefs and reactions of right and wrong slowly begin to make more sense to you, and you can explain them much better, as well. More importantly, it becomes much easier to figure out the best ethical and moral decision when something new comes up.

According to Mike Cain, founder and comanaging partner of the top-50 firm Lattimore Black Morgan & Cain, PC (LBMC), in Nashville, TN

> A tricky aspect of managing your firm's growth is figuring out how to manage multiple partners who all bring something different to the table. As professional services firms get larger, you have multiple partners, all of whom are very responsible, very confident in their own abilities, and very interested in the overall direction of the firm.
>
> So, you do have to do much more consensus building and put in much more effort to get people on the same page throughout the organization if you are going to be successful moving forward. That doesn't mean you have to run everything by committee, but you do have to get more buy-in from a broader group of people than a lot of our clients do in their businesses.

2. *Commit to an activity that benefits someone else.* By this, I mean volunteer work. Spend time on any sort of volunteer project, preferably for the benefit of a group that fuels your passion. Perhaps you can spend time helping out at a soup kitchen or building a Habitat for Humanity house if you sympathize with the poor, or maybe, you can start a small volunteer project at a retirement home if you feel passionate about helping the elderly. Many accountants find that committing time to improve our profession really helps you grow personally and professionally.

3. *Travel.* Intentionally travel to experience different peoples and cultures. Although I travel over 150 nights per year on business, I still periodically take a half day or more to visit cultural sites. I've visited most of the U.S. presidential museums and libraries; over 20 state capital museums or archives; and many, many other things to expand my horizons. I've visited automobile factories in Detroit, Munich, and Stuttgart; zoos in San Diego, Detroit, and Belize; and art galleries in New York, Paris, Florence, Cape Town, Amsterdam, Accra, Cologne, London, and many other cities. Get off the beaten path for more than a few days. If you live in a small town, spend a few days in a big city. If you live in a city, go live in the country for a while. Visit other parts of the country you live in, and if you can afford to, visit other countries, as well. Vacationing is fine, but the real value comes from exposing yourself to the life of people who you don't know.

One experience that had a significant impact on the career of Marc Elman, CEO of the local firm PSB Boisjoli in Montreal, Canada, was a project he led for eleventh grade students.

> Two years ago, I was a chaperon for 36 grade 11 students on something called the March of the Living, a two-week trip where you go to Poland to visit concentration camps from World War II, and then, you go to Israel and see what they've built there. It's meant to show the transformations that have taken place amongst the Jewish population from the 1930s until today. It involves a tremendous amount of preparation: you have to learn about the Holocaust, Israel, and about Jewish life. I'm Jewish, and it was an outstanding experience in understanding human nature, leadership of student,s and our heritage. One of my inspirations for going was my older daughter, who had gone the year before.

It involved 2 weekends of preparation plus another 20–25 meetings. I think in terms of introspection and in terms of looking at this world and asking questions of yourself about what you're all about and what other people are all about. I found it a great leadership experience, both in terms of trying to give very impressionable young minds a sense of who they are and a sense of their Jewish heritage.

It showed me both the frailty of humanity, while at the same time, there were so many inspirational stories. We traveled there with survivors; we met people who risked their lives to save other people.

I left the students with a few questions, and one of the questions was, "Take yourself being a Jew at that time and stuck in a camp; how would you behave?" Some Jews survived on cunning and their ability to use other people for their own advantage. I asked, "How would you have behaved if you were a German who was recruited into the army? How would you have behaved if you were just a person living in France who had neighbors that were Jewish or that you knew were in peril?: And I said, "The answers may appear obvious, but when you really think about them, it's not obvious as to what you would've done. Would you have risked your own family for someone else?"

4. *Read challenging books.* A John Grisham novel is fun, but it doesn't really stretch your understanding of how human life works. Read books that challenge your perceptions, such as *Mandela's Way: Fifteen Lessons on Life, Love, and Courage* by Richard Stengel or *The John Wooden Pyramid of Success* by Neville Johnson. I recommend picking up any Pulitzer Prize-winning novel or any of the *New York Times* all-time best nonfiction books. Almost all of those works will force you to reach a little bit, to understand lives and existences different than your own. When you walk away, you'll have a deeper understanding of what it means to be different, and the more you read, the deeper your appreciation for the varieties of human experience will become.

   Lisa Cines is an avid reader. "My day isn't complete unless I've read something, unless I have read a book. I enjoy reading how people have overcome what's been put in front of them or they have managed or led their way through it."

5. *Explore the spiritual side of life.* The vast majority of people on earth incorporate some form of spiritual experience into their lives. I've attended a variety of religious services, and I've found that they have a lot more in common than most people tend to think: they all involve people trying to connect with something greater than themselves. It is this commonality, paired with the huge diversity of the specifics of practice and belief, that really makes clear that most people on earth are trying to take different, parallel paths to the same goal.

6. *Connect with a mastermind group.* Napoleon Hill coined the term "mastermind group" as a small group of like-minded people who meet regularly to support each other's growth. The common denominator is that each member of the group accepts responsibility for supporting, advising, and challenging other members in pursuit of their goals. Hill defined a mastermind to be created through harmony of purpose and effort between two or more people. In his book *The Law of Success in Sixteen Lessons*, Hill said, "Success in this world is always a matter of individual effort, yet you will only be

deceiving yourself if you believe that you can succeed without the co-operation of other people."

Mike Cain says, "No matter what role you play in your firm, you can always learn plenty from other industry professionals. You come in contact with great people throughout this profession. Involvement in our professional associations builds practice in leadership skills that you can bring back and apply in your own organization."

The Private Companies Practice Section of the AICPA has a variety of networking groups that are built for sharing ideas to help build your personal and professional life. With your own mastermind group, you have your own personal group dedicated to supporting you, challenging you, cheering you on, and inspiring you to achieve your goals. The group's interest and attention to your goals provides a subtle yet powerful incentive for accountability. Though your growth is personal and individual, something only you can accomplish, you will benefit from the support, encouragement, and energy of others.

7. *Relentlessly pursue personal growth.* Without personal growth, a team slowly dies. Without personal growth, your people will stagnate and lose their value in the marketplace. Because most employees are likely to change jobs multiple times throughout their careers, it makes sense to develop new skills every year. These skills should be transferable and consistent with the business and technical goals of the firm. Each year, as part of an employee's performance appraisal, a section addressing personal development goals should be jointly discussed and pursued. Most employees will find this exercise motivational and view it as a strong signal that the leaders value and depend on their contributions.

Conclusion

You might try all seven of these personal growth activities and find that only one or two work really well for you. Never use that as an excuse to not bother to grow as a person. No matter what, seek out things that challenge the fundamentals of what you believe, both about yourself and others. You'll either reinforce your deeply held ideas or you'll discover that, perhaps, they weren't as perfect as you believed they were, and both things are incredibly valuable.

Empowerment: The Secret to Exponential Growth

"The chief danger in life is that you may take too many precautions."

~ ALFRED ADLER

Empowerment is a word that has gotten a lot of buzz in recent years. It seems like this word is similar to other buzzwords that are easy to pronounce and hard to implement, often bringing more buzz than change. Ideally, empowering staff members releases the energy, experience, and education of people, so they are more engaged. We want to create an environment where people can do their best and are committed—one where they act more like entrepreneurs. Leaders who empower others share their power in order to accomplish more than anyone could do alone.

Unfortunately, you can't just tell people they have power. Overuse of the word *empowerment* leads to skepticism and confusion. When people hear that they are about to get the right to make significant decisions, they may doubt it. Given the number of times that employees are promised something that never comes through, who can blame them? Consequently, staff members wait for empowerment to be bestowed, and the novice leader wonders why people won't take initiative.

In this chapter, we are going to discuss empowering people and their teams. We will delve into how to benefit from the positives of both micromanaging and abandoning your team members, without getting the negatives. We will discuss various forms of leadership and how each can be effective with giving power to individuals and their teams. This chapter is all about releasing the power from within your staff members to enable your firm to experience exponential growth.

What Is Empowerment Really?

We need to revise the way we view empowerment. It's not something that a leader does for a follower. Instead, empowerment is the process of a leader and protégé working together to assess the risk of the situation and the experience of the person to successfully handle the role. Empowering an individual should allow him to stretch in his comfort zone but not blow up the firm. Partners and leaders must create a work environment that fosters the ability and desire of staff members to act in empowered ways. They must also remove obstacles that limit the ability of staff to act.

Empowering leaders neither micromanage nor abandon their direct reports. Micromanaging fits some accountants' personal style: it's quick; predictable; and, most of all, safe. Accounting is an exacting profession, and micromanaging is intended to assure high levels of excellence. However, micromanaging can be demeaning to team members or result in poor decisions, lack of commitment, indecisiveness, and uncertainty. And of course, it fails to grow and develop the people reporting to you. Some partners find it safe to surround themselves with doers and order-takers.

On the other hand, some leaders abandon their people because they don't take the time to properly supervise them; the leader isn't sure about what to do, or he or she wrongly believes that the person can handle the job without guidance. Abandonment can allow total freedom and even some creativity, but it more often leads to no accountability and anarchy. Some novice leaders bounce from micromanaging to abandonment. I've seen many firms that had a former managing partner who was a micromanager swing to the other side of the spectrum to a no-control situation in which partners and others did their own thing without any accountability.

Terry Harris, managing partner of McKonly & Asbury LLP in Harrisburg, PA, works hard to find the middle road between micromanagement and anarchy.

> I am not a micromanager of the other partners in our firm. Partners are allowed autonomy and freedom to lead their practice areas with my full support. One of the biggest challenges that most partners have is being accountable for individual goals. In our firm, each partner has goals that are developed together with a member of our executive committee, and partners are measured and compensated based on attaining those goals. Key leaders are given a fair amount of leeway in utilization of firm resources.

Terry's firm directly benefited from his empowering the firm's leaders.

> In the late '90s, it was a goal of mine to develop the strongest tax practice in the region. In 2004, we hired a senior manager named Kurt Trimarchi from a national firm. His background was in the tax practice of national firms and included a stint in a local accounting practice. While Kurt was clearly on the partner track in the national firm, he saw the opportunity to build something special at McKonly & Asbury. We shared a vision for building a tax practice that rivaled the local offices of the national accounting firms. He attracted others to our tax practice who complimented his leadership and had strong tax expertise. He took steps to change how the practice functioned within M&A. Today, we have a strong tax practice that rivals the national firms in our region.

Keys to Effective Empowerment

One of the keys to empowering staff members is in knowing what kind of structure to impose and how much. Certain events are somewhat predictable, such as people and teams waste billable time, team members jockey for position and fail to perform, and partners begin to worry whether firm goals are being met. In many firms, groups of staff members are "anointed" as teams, told they are "empowered," and expected to act accordingly. This approach can result in a flurry of interest and excitement about teaming, and some groups may even achieve a measure of success. However, at some point in the life cycle of most teams, unresolved internal issues threaten a team's ability to meet its business objectives.

Empowering people the right way allows a leader to gain all the pluses of both control and abandonment, without the negatives. Empowering requires the leader to weigh two important aspects of his people: confidence in the person's experience, character, and motivation versus the visibility and financial risk of the situation.

Mike Cain, founder and comanaging partner of the top-50 firm Lattimore Black Morgan & Cain, PC (LBMC), in Nashville, TN, explains, "When you deal with empowerment, you choose the amount of authority and accountability based on your experience with that person. If the risk to the firm in the event of failure is major, then you want to be much more careful about the level of authority that you give that person."

A performance (balanced) scorecard (reviewed in detail in chapter 8, "Accountability: Trust but Verify") is a great tool to use for empowering people. In the balanced scorecard process, you discuss a person's goal or desired results, the authority that he or she may have in the pursuit, resources that may be allocated, and how and when accountability will be measured. Knowing what everyone is accountable for creates the standards and measurements for determining progress. Accountability should be measured in terms of quality, quantity, and time.

Sam Coulter, founder and president of the local firm Coulter & Justus, P.C., in Knoxville, TN, says

My biggest challenge in leadership has been to learn to delegate and empower people. One of my former partners at Ernst & Young, Walter Borff, taught me that there are many more ways of getting things done than doing it myself. I was accustomed to the hard work and living by the fruits of my own labor. Walter was careful about to whom he delegated, but I think he was very good at choosing the right people, and then, he also was willing to let someone struggle with it.

I learned that delegation is key to moving up in any leadership role. I have told many of our up-and-coming leaders, "You are robbing these younger people of the opportunity to do this work or learn how to do this work." To me, it is wonderful to see how teaching this concept changes people and helps them move up into larger leadership roles.

Leader Profile: Ted Mason, president and CEO of the top-100 firm Laporte Sehrt Romig Hand in New Orleans, LA

Ted Mason grew up in New Orleans, LA, and always wanted to be a business owner or entrepreneur. He was the first college graduate in his blue-collar family. Coming to work at Laporte Sehrt Romig Hand right out of college, Ted was a driven man, and his enthusiasm to succeed became both a blessing and curse. He moved up the career ladder quickly, but he discouraged people from following him because he was so demanding. After a few years in public accounting, he succumbed to an offer from a large financial institution to become their head of audit services.

From a leadership perspective, Ted's father had a profound impact on his life. His dad taught him that there are ramifications to every decision and that you ultimately are responsible for those decisions. Another mentor was his supervisor at a bank. She taught him to consider the organization holistically when you are making decisions. He learned to temper his action orientation by evaluating each decision in relation to the potential ramifications that were not so obvious, which reinforced his dad's advice.

Ted missed the excitement and diversity of public accounting, so he returned with a focus on becoming an owner.

Deb Lockwood, CEO of RSM McGladrey Alliance, says of Ted, "Ted's actions and tone at the top are the things I find most impactful. He focuses on the important leadership components of running a firm. He focuses on mission, vision, and strategy. He works diligently on key client contacts. He is involved in high-profile proposals. He knows how important growth is, and he is very focused on providing opportunities for others to grow."

Partner Chav Pierce says

> As a leader, Ted is someone you respect, who you strive to emulate. He is someone who will challenge you, help you face those challenges, and hold you accountable for your results. Ted is a person capable of seeing a need, setting a course of action, and empowering the team to be successful. He is a person lifting your hand in victory and giving you a hand up in defeat, and he is aware of the wake he is leaving behind.
>
> Ted is a true lion and a dominant personality. Ted has never been shy in expressing his opinion as to the results he expects. However, over the past 15 years, I have noticed that he has learned to listen more before expressing his opinion and, unlike in the distant past, educate others on the rationale behind his opinion, helping them to see more clearly the possible results, whether they agree or disagree. Ted's conscious efforts to consider the personalities and the way others process information makes him a more effective leader today, and those efforts are admirable.

Ted's strategy for leading others comes from the energy generated by the great ideas, vision, and goals upon which he has been able to gain agreement and create excitement from within the partner group. Chav worked in the firm's tax department until 2000, at which time he was asked to move into business valuation full time. In 2004, Ted offered Chav the chance to operate and grow the business valuation department. Chav relates that empowering meeting

> Ted gave me the following parameters, if I was to take the leap:
> - ▲ I would work in the business valuation and tax departments.
> - ▲ I was expected to grow the business valuation department at 25 percent per year.
> - ▲ I was expected to produce a quality product.
>
> I took the leap. Ted did not micromanage the process; he gave me all the resources that I needed to grow the firm's BV practice. We have successfully grown the business valuation department to 2 full-time people, besides me, and annual revenues increased from approximately $50,000 in 2003 to $400,000, in 2009.

Ted serves as president, CEO, and managing director and is responsible for setting the firm's strategic direction and focus, along with the day-to-day management of the firm. His decisiveness really paid off for the firm in the aftermath of Hurricane Katrina, which destroyed his firm's offices and computers and dispersed his staff throughout the country. He led the owners to pay staff salaries and bonuses and keep all employees in the face of significant uncertainty about the survivability of the firm and many of its clients.

With more than 20 years of experience in auditing, accounting, and taxation, Ted has also been involved with the management of construction contractors and financial institutions for both public and private companies. He has extensive experience with initial public offering issues and Securities and Exchange Commission registrants, as well as the facilitation and development of strategic business plans.

Ted is the former CFO of a $200 million financial institution and holds a BS in accounting from the University of New Orleans and Louisiana State University Graduate School of Banking. In addition to many professional associations, Ted is treasurer of St. Tammany Economic Development Foundation and a board member of St. Tammany Industrial and Economic District.

Existing Leadership Philosophies

The primary leadership philosophies in existence today run the gamut from very directed and controlled to autonomous. Table 10-1 outlines the most predominant leadership philosophies and their common characteristics.

Table 10-1: Leadership Philosophies

Leadership Philosophy	Characteristics
Dictatorial	All decisions are made by the leader. Buy-in is not sought or received well. Work activities are tightly structured and controlled. Interaction of lower-level staff is minimal across functions. People keep their heads down and do their work.
Abandonment	Decisions are made by individuals, often in silos. Partners use their own staff members and processes. Work may be structured and controlled, depending on the individual style of the partner. Lower-level staff may interact across functions if no control issues exist.
Democratic	Decisions are reached by majority vote. Buy-in is considered desirable but not essential—just vote. Responsibility for structuring and controlling work may be assigned to individuals or committees. Individuals interact across functions, as directed.
Empowered	Decisions are reached with input from those affected. Buy-in is considered important. Work activities may be structured and controlled, depending on the experience of the team member and the risk of the assignment. Individuals interact across functions at their own discretion, usually at their own level.
Consensus	Decisions are made by consensus. Buy-in is considered essential, and the vision is tailored to accommodate as many workers' needs and wants as possible. Work is structured and accomplished by cooperative teams. Individuals are encouraged to interact across functions at whatever level is most appropriate.

Mistakes: Both Risky and Rewarding

One of the biggest fears of leaders in accounting firms is that their people will make serious mistakes. A good leader is not afraid of mistakes, so long as those mistakes are made by people attempting to accomplish something. A great leader teaches people to be quick, make decisions, and take action. It is important to distinguish between mistakes of commission and those of omission. Failure to act is one of the biggest plagues in the accounting profession.

As a leader, you must be confident enough to hire people who aren't afraid to speak up. If you are willing to listen, it means little if nobody is willing to talk in a substantive manner.

I saw an interview with one of the Boston Celtics a few years ago. He was telling about the final seconds of a close game when Larry Bird came into the huddle and said, "Give me the ball, and get everybody out of my way."

The coach yelled, "I'm the coach here, and I will call the plays." Then, he said to all the players, "Give the ball to Bird, and get out of his way."

When you begin developing protégés who are empowered, something magical begins to happen: these empowered team members infect their teams. As people gain the freedom and confidence that the empowerment gives them, they subconsciously transmit that freedom and confidence to others. So, as your individual protégés work in teams, your empowering leadership can have an exponential impact throughout work teams, sales teams, practice groups, and the entire firm. The process works from the inside out; in other words, individuals who are empowered model this behavior for others, and you can create an entire culture of empowerment throughout your firm.

Empowering Members of a Team

Although empowerment can work for everyone on an individual level, there are special considerations for team empowerment.

You may need to help develop self-assurance. The first aspect of sharing power is giving team members the ability to act. That means a number of things, including providing the knowledge and resources they will need as well as creating the proper atmosphere. Your team members have to believe that they can make decisions and that they have the backing to do so.

Everyone on a team can be empowered; however, if staff members are not accustomed to exercising authority, you may need to coach them, so they will accept this new level of authority. In some cases, you might find that people resist because they have either lost the belief in their ability to be effective or never developed it in the first place (or they don't want to take responsibility). This will make your leadership role more difficult.

When staff members lack the self-assurance to take on power, something is wrong. Watch some children; even at play, they are daring and willing to create worlds and imagine themselves with tremendous abilities. Coaching team members who lack confidence will be a tedious process of giving them small amounts of responsibility at a time. Later, as they gain experience, you can increase the scope of what you expect them to do.

Even if staff members have self-assurance, the leader will also need poise and confidence. It may not come naturally, and you'll need to create your own process to increase your acceptance of the strategy. You'll need to convince everyone that you mean it when you use the word empowerment. Persuading yourself is like persuading team members of their own worthiness. You hand off some power, see positive results, and then try more. When it comes to winning over others, you must show that you mean it when you talk about empowering people on your team.

Bob Bunting, former CEO of the megaregional firm Moss Adams LLP in Seattle, WA, took on a challenging leadership role when he was made the chairman of the AICPA's Board of Examiners. Bunting says that leading a group of technical experts when you have none of the technical expertise is leadership at its most challenging.

The chairman of the AICPA felt that the board needed a different kind of leader, and he appointed me as the chair. At the first meeting, I was not a very popular guy because I was parachuted from the outside, and they always had people come up from within. And I also knew nothing about psychometrics or exam testing or anything like that. And most of the people on the board were PhDs; I had a bachelor's degree. Most of the technical staff were also PhDs. And so they sent this guy from the outside in there to organize and improve processes he knew nothing about. I had to lead them despite being the least knowledgeable person about what they did. I was the least knowledgeable person about testing methodologies or all the protocols they went through to develop the exam. But I had to get them to accept leadership from me.

I clearly acknowledged their expertise and made it plain that I would fail unless they helped me. But then I contributed by organizing their processes, so they were more productive. What I brought to the table was the ability to organize them and help them become more productive, and what they brought to the table was a huge depth of knowledge about the technical issues related to the CPA exam. That was a great experience in learning how to be a nontechnical leader instead of being a shop foreman.

Principles of Empowerment

Following are the six most important principles for empowering people in a way that results in the work being delegated to the right level in your firm. These principles will help you allocate the right amount of authority and control based on the risk of the project and experience of the worker:

Develop a Rational Shared Vision

Paint as clear a picture of your vision as possible for the outcome of the initiative or project. Let team members know that they are part of something bigger than themselves. Make sure that they know, and have access to, the firm's overall mission, vision, and values and how they can contribute. Share the most important goals and direction for your group. When possible, either make progress on goals measurable and observable, or ascertain that you have shared your picture of a positive outcome with the people responsible for accomplishing the results.

Jim DeMartini, managing partner of the top-100 firmSeiler LLP in Redwood City, CA, says, "What I've learned with accountants is they're not used to being empowered, and they're not used to being held accountable. The trick is to get them to think beyond that and to feel really responsible and accountable for the success of what they're doing."

Provide Training and Information for Good Decisions

Make certain that team members have all the training and information that they need to make well-thought-out decisions. Delegate the important meetings, committee memberships that influence business development and decision making, and projects that people and clients notice. The team member will grow and develop new skills.

Raise the Level of Conflict

Many people avoid conflict. As a result, important issues do not get raised and discussed. It's your job to encourage people to argue about approaches. You are doing your protégés and other team members a serious disservice by not confronting those habits of "going along to get along" that don't bring everyone's best to the project. (In the worst case, not contributing is a passive-aggressive strategy to sabotage results.)

As leader, you are responsible for providing constant information, so that people know how they are doing. You can be the role model to raise the level of conflict. Sometimes, the purpose of feedback is recognition; other times, it is corrective in nature. Your team members deserve your constructive feedback, so they can develop their knowledge and skills. When a problem occurs, ask what is wrong with the procedures and systems that caused failure, not what is wrong with staff members.

Scott Dietzen, managing partner, Northwest Region, of the national accounting firm CliftonLarsonAllen LLP in Spokane, WA, says

> I've gone from more hands-on, very active, lots of touches with people to trying to be much more strategic and to prioritize where my time is spent, so I can spend it with people who bring the most impact. When I'm dealing with difficult challenges or hygiene issues (cleaning up other people's messes), maybe with owners, I set very clear expectations and a clear time frame to deal with those quickly. Whereas before, I was just so uncomfortable dealing with those difficult situations that they would extend for long periods of time. And the consequence of that was confusion in the people around them: "Why is that behavior being tolerated?"

Allocate Proper Resources

The allocation of resources must be clear in terms of money, people, and time. The budget allocation should be very clear regarding the amount to be invested, when the funds will be available, and who controls the money. It should be clear who will be assigned to the team, both inside and outside the firm, and what their experience and training needs to be in order to succeed. The time line for allocations of resources should specify when dollars and people flow to the project, department, or team.

Reward Staff Members for Empowered Behavior

When protégés feel undercompensated, undertitled, undernoticed, underpraised, and underappreciated for the responsibilities they take on, don't expect results from empowerment. The basic needs of staff members must be met for them to give you their discretionary energy, that extra effort that people voluntarily invest in work. You should even give rewards for mistakes. When someone makes a mistake while attempting to accomplish something, that should be applauded. I will tell my team and clients, "Those who make no mistakes aren't doing much." However, mistakes that occur from vacillation, hesitancy, or fear are not acceptable.

Trust People

Trust the intentions of people to do the right things; make the right decisions; and make choices that, although may not be exactly what you would decide, still work.

Gary Shamis, founder and CEO of the top-100 multioffice firm SS&G Financial Services, Inc., in Cleveland, OH, says

> To really grow our business, I have learned to delegate and empower other people. That has been the entire secret of our growth. There have been some losses, but I've had to tolerate those in order to grow. For example, I developed a great client and helped them grow. When I had to delegate their work to someone else, the person I delegated it to didn't respond well and didn't take great care of their needs. The long and the short of it was they ended up finding another accountant because they thought that we were too expensive and not responding to their needs. This experience was gut-wrenching for me, but I had a huge choice to make. Was I going to step back into the client server role and save this client, or was I going to allow one of my partners to learn a tough lesson from this loss?
>
> We were a $12 million firm at the time, and now, we're a $60 million firm. I realized that when I focus on leading our firm, I'm going to take the risk of losing some things. But I'm transferring over client responsibility to allow me to leverage my skills. Things like that are going to happen, and I just have to get over it. It was a really good learning experience for me.
>
> Anyone here will tell you that I'm absolutely famous for giving people all the rope they possibly can handle. If we are all going to grow, we must delegate and empower. My rule is if I've empowered you to do a job, I'm giving it to you, I don't want it back, call me when you need me.

Leader Profile: **Gary Shamis, founder and CEO of the top-100 multioffice firm SS&G Financial Services, Inc., in Cleveland, OH**

Gary Shamis started organizing and building organizations when he was in high school. Not satisfied with the available clubs, Gary formed his own, the Auden Society, for students that didn't fit in the normal fraternities. This was preparation for organizing one of the largest alliances of accounting firms in the world later in life. His father was a CPA, and he got a lot of pressure from his mother to become a professional. Gary says, "As with many Jewish mothers, she wanted me to be a doctor."

Growing up in the harsh Cleveland, OH, winters, Gary selected Tulane University in New Orleans, LA, for the weather, as many young people do. He majored in biology but became intrigued with accounting because it seemed like a logical and fun game for him. As president of his senior class, Gary became more serious about studying and was accepted into medical school. But after a short period, he decided that business and accounting were a better fit for him.

Gary got into The Ohio State University Fisher College of Business and graduated first in his class. All the large international accounting firms recruited him, and he accepted a job with Touche Ross in Atlanta and later went to work with his father-in-law. Then, he joined his dad's firm. In the first year, his dad's firm grossed approximately $225,000 in total revenue. SS&G Financial Services, Inc., has grown under Gary's leadership to be one of the largest 100 accounting firms in the United States.

SS&G partner Michelle Mahle says

> I've known Gary Shamis since I joined the firm 15 years ago. I worked for 2 other public accounting firms prior to joining SS&G: a large national firm and a small local firm, both in the Cleveland area. Though I had the opportunity to work for 2 very different firms, the leadership of each was very similar. In both environments, I was instructed what to do, how to do it, and monitored every step of the way by someone at a level higher than me.
>
> When I started at SS&G, under Gary's leadership, I was assigned to a client, and it was *assumed* that I had the expertise and professionalism to provide quality, timely service. At first, it seemed odd to me that I didn't have someone constantly looking over my shoulder and checking up on me. Then, I found myself motivated by it. Rather than working to achieve the expectations of someone else, I worked to exceed my own expectations. Through this personal experience, I now understand the power in empowerment.
>
> As I reflect on my career at SS&G, I realize that having the latitude to be instinctive, decisive, and act independently afforded me the opportunity to grow, mature, and develop professionally. Unlike others I have worked with and for in the past, I find that Gary doesn't try to model others after himself or attempt to replicate his own strengths. More importantly, he creates opportunities for others to be accountable, acknowledged, and to excel on their own merits and individuality. Gary Shamis has really brought out the best in me.

Partner Mark Goldfarb says

> Gary Shamis came to me one day and said, "Why don't we just start our own association of firms?" We were the first firm to sell stock to employees who were not directors, back in the mid-'90s. Gary and I were featured in an article for *Wall Street Journal*. You know, we were doing testimonial advertising from clients back in the late '80s when nobody was doing it. And we were hiring women and letting them work part time when no one else was doing it. So, our modus operendi has always been to kind of go against the grain and do things—you know, maybe thinking outside the box. And this was a real outside-the-box thought to start our own association.
>
> So, we talked to Lattimore, Black, and a few other firms that we'd gotten to know and seemed kind of entrepreneurial like us. The growth and success of the

(continued)

(continued)

> Leading Edge alliance is indicative of what a good decision it was.
>
> The advantage is that best practices are shared at so many different levels other than the managing partner level. There are special interest groups for marketing, for HR, for IT, for international tax, for state and local tax, for employee benefit plan audits, for I mean so many different things that really allow our professionals to interact with professionals from other (*a*) similar sized firms and (*b*) people with the same industry or technical expertise from other firms. It really allows all of our people to share their best practices with people who are practicing in similar positions in other large firms, not only domestically but internationally. It allows us to be better at what we do and to better serve our clients.

Gary assembled a group of 15 large firms at a meeting in Cleveland, OH, to form a new alliance: the Leading Edge Alliance (LEA). This alliance was made up of large and leading firms from 15 markets around the United States that believed they could compete with the large international firms. LEA did not have geographic exclusivity, but it did focus on the homogeneous leading firms that wanted best practices collaboration for all partners and that wanted to compete for large international clients. LEA is now one of the top-10 international accounting alliances, with total revenues approaching $3 billion.

Gary was named the 2008 Ernst & Young Entrepreneur of the Year (Northeast Ohio) in the financial services category and as one of *Accounting Today's* most influential people in the industry 11 times. He received the Champion Award from the Alzheimer's Association, Cleveland Area Chapter. He continues to be recognized for his industry insight, commitment to service quality, and leadership of the profession.

Working With Teams

Can teams be empowered while at the same time working within the structure and discipline imposed by their firm? Best-practice firms think so, and those that fail at teaming often cite the lack of firm structure as a contributing factor. In this section, I'll use the terms *team* and *firm*. In some cases, a firm is made up of many teams, and in others, the firm is one team.

It's nearly impossible to move an entire firm in any direction. However, most leaders break down their firms into small teams, each commissioned with a purpose that supports the overall mission of the firm. In the past, to be successful, a business needed a group of people with technical or functional skills and another group with key interpersonal skills. Not so anymore. Accounting firms are recognizing that it's important to have people with a mix of talents who can interact effectively. They have also realized that soft skills can take a team a long way in relationship building and staff member and client satisfaction. Effective communication is a primary key to team success.

The following are some tips for building and working with teams:

▲ We have found that a team size of 8–12 is optimal. Why is this important? What impact does the team size have on its results? One thing to remember is that teams meet more to share information than to carry out their work. If all members must be involved in a decision, it will take longer. In a smaller group, information is communicated much more quickly.

▲ It is important for a team to have a common purpose, performance goals, and approach. If they don't, you'll have chaos. Each member of a team has his or her own perception of what the team is about, and each person is different. Without a common purpose, each individual works toward his or her own goal. The team, as a unit, should have a defined mission that is focused on the overall mission of the firm. The team should know why they exist to help accomplish that mission. Each team should have goals and objectives to accomplish the team purpose, and the goals should link directly to the departmental and company objectives.

The team approach includes operating guidelines, rules, and commitments that define how they will communicate, how decisions will be made, when they meet, why they meet, and the meeting format and guidelines. These are working agreements, which help eliminate confusion and foster cooperation.

▲ Get buy-in from leaders, managers, and partners in the early stages and throughout the life cycle of the team as business needs change.

▲ Mutual accountability means that each person takes responsibility for his or her actions within the team. It's important that both team and functional roles and responsibilities are defined within the team. It's also critical that team processes are defined to ensure that each team member can assist in making the others successful. If team members aren't clear on who does what, how can they be responsible and accountable? When mutual accountability is practiced within a team, there is high commitment and trust among the team members; team members take ownership of their work products. Mutual accountability and ownership lead to empowerment and enable higher levels of productivity, quality, and achievement of goals.

In our strategic work with accounting firms, we will almost always form several special teams to carry out the major tasks of the strategic plan. The successful teams all seem to have a pattern of characteristics, as illustrated in table 10-2 and explained in the following sections.

Table 10-2: Comparison of Great Firm and Poor Firm Characteristics

Great firms	Poor firms
Shared mission	Fuzzy mission
Mutual respect and trust	Low trust
Frequent substantive communication	Rare communication
Shared processes	Individual methods
Different talents	Generalists
Adaptability and flexibility	Rigid
Continuous improvement	Improvement when problems occur

Shared Mission

Partners and team members share a common reason for their existence. Their priorities are clearly defined, and they work collectively toward achieving common goals, focused on results. They are committed and accountable for high standards and quality results. Contrast this with a shared-services-type firm where partners work in silos, and each has his or her own vision. The team leader is an active member of the team, and everyone is accountable for the team performance. Team members coach each other and provide ongoing support and encouragement for other members.

Mutual Respect and Trust

Team members are authentic and honest. They request, receive, and give honest feedback. They value other members' opinions and are interested in ideas. They are proud to belong to the team. Contrast this with the firms whose partners won't introduce other partners to their clients either because they don't trust the other partners' skill set, or they may fear that the client will like the other partner better.

Frequent Substantive Communication

Meetings are held regularly in person or on the phone. Team members say what they think and feel; there are no hidden agendas. They have the information that they need to work together and individually, and they participate openly in team discussions. They handle differences in opinion and conflict openly by attacking the problem, not the person. Contrast this with firms whose partners rarely meet and know little about each other's clients.

Shared Processes

Processes, policies, and rules are documented by the team to enable team members to perform their jobs more successfully. Decisions are made based on the conditions to be satisfied, and risks are considered and minimized before implementation. Contrast this with firms where each partner has his or her own book of business, staff, and way of doing things.

Different Talents

Members make full use of the different skills, knowledge, and personal strengths of individual team members. They also seek information, ideas, and opinions from people outside their team. This allows partners to develop deep specialties in important areas. Contrast this with firms whose partners are all generalists.

Adaptability and Flexibility

Members respond quickly and flexibly to changes in the external environment. They follow existing processes but challenge them when appropriate. They value change as an opportunity to improve.

Continuous Improvement

Continuous improvement is built into the team operating guidelines. Members readily admit to, and learn from, mistakes. They take time to think and agree before they act and evaluate. Contrast this with firms that only make improvements in processes after a problem has occurred.

Building Highly Empowered Teams and Firms

So, how do you move a firm from where it is to a highly empowered one? We have discovered in our consulting work that when you build groups or small teams with high empowerment, then you are able to fuse them together as a firm. Guiding teams through their formation creates a strong sense of ownership for team results, staff member empowerment, and accountability. When team members take pride in being a part of a team from the formation and have control over the outcomes, they are more engaged.

A good basic methodology for building empowered teams, as illustrated in table 10-3, is to first define what you want the team to do; then lay out the purpose or mission of the team; and lastly, guide the team through the operational steps to success.

Table 10-3: Methodology for Building Empowered Teams

Team Vision	Select team members
	Define business objectives and expectations (vision)
	Allocate resources
	Understand internal or external client demand
	Acquire approval of CEO, partners, and so on
Team Missioning	Define purpose with clarity
	Define required skills
	Set clear boundaries and operating guidelines
	Define roles for each team member
	Create performance measurements
	Write action steps
Team Operations	Execute action steps
	Monitor performance against objectives
	Actively promote and engage conflict
	Continuously improve processes
	Review and learn from experiences
	Celebrate successes

The Seven Elements of Empowerment for Teams

Fostering teamwork is a top priority for many leaders. The benefits are clear: increased productivity, improved client service, more flexible systems, and staff member empowerment.

But is the vision clear? You can't just hand this methodological framework to your newly created team and tell them to get busy. To effectively implement teams, leaders should guide new teams through the following seven elements of empowerment:

Communication

For a person or team to reach full potential, staff members must be able to say what they think, ask for help, and risk making mistakes. This can only happen in an atmosphere where team members are trustworthy and focus on solutions, not problems. A commitment to regular communication plays a vital role in creating such cohesiveness.

Regular and open communication is equally important to a team's success. To assess work performance, members must provide constant and honest feedback, accept constructive feedback, and address issues head-on. Positive communication affects the energy of a work team. When members talk about what they like, need, or want, it is quite different from wailing about what annoys or frustrates them. The former energizes; the latter demoralizes.

Keith Farlinger, CEO of the national firm BDO Canada LLP in Toronto, Canada, empowers his team to be able to make informed decisions.

I used to go into a meeting with our policy board and say, "Here's what I've done, and here's what I want to go through," thinking that they had the same knowledge that I had. I expected they would debate and ask lots of questions. This caused some confusion. Now, I give them the background information to get them up to the level of understanding with me. I'll do a PowerPoint presentation, so it's there in front of them.

To enhance staff member and team communications, leaders can provide skill training in listening and the use of speaking or writing, as well as consensus building.

Conflict Engagement

No one grows without conflict or other problems, teams included. And of course, it is inevitable that bright, diverse thinkers will experience conflict from time to time. The problem is not that differences exist but in how they are confronted and managed. If team members sweep conflict under the rug, then misperceptions, ill feelings, and misunderstandings will ultimately result. Soon, the conflicts reappear. They take on the form of tension, hidden agendas, and stubborn positions. On the other hand, if leaders help teams work to manage conflict effectively, the team will be able to maintain trust and tap the collective power of the team. Three techniques that help staff members confront conflict are reframing, the "moccasin method," and affirmations.

Reframing is looking at the glass half full instead of half empty. Instead of thinking, "If I address this issue, it'll slow down the meeting," consider this thought: "If we negotiate this difference, trust and creativity will all increase."

Terry Snyder, president of the accounting firm alliance PKF North America in Lawrence, GA, says

> You want people to have the ability to make decisions. As a leader, I have to have confidence they can make those decisions. As I have matured in my leadership, I've improved my ability to allow people to make mistakes and learn. I've also learned that a leader can't

control every decision. They may not make them like I make them, but they'll get more done toward the ultimate goal than if I had made the decision for them.

You must have the willingness to allow mistakes. I have had to coach myself to widen the gate on decision making, knowing that they can make mistakes. Most of the time, we can go back, and they'll learn from them or correct them if they're not appropriate.

The "moccasin method" is a technique used to practice empathy by mentally walking in the shoes of another person. You answer questions such as, "How would I feel if I were that person being criticized in front of the group?" and "What would motivate me to say what that person just said?"

Affirmations are positive statements about something that you want to be true. For example, instead of saying to yourself right before a negotiating session, "I know that I'm going to blow up," force yourself to say, "I am calm, comfortable, and prepared." If team members can learn to shift any negative mental conversations to more positive ones, they will be able to shift obstructive paradigms and manage conflict more effectively.

Contribution

The more individuals feel like part of a team, the more they contribute; the more members contribute, the more they feel like part of the team. To enhance feelings of inclusion, leaders need to keep team members informed, solicit their input, and support an atmosphere of collegiality. If staff members are not offering suggestions at meetings, invite them to do so. If team members miss meetings, let them know that they were missed.

To enhance balanced participation on a work team, leaders should consider three factors that affect the level of individual contribution: inclusion, confidence, and empowerment. When ideas (even wild ideas) are offered, show appreciation for the initiative. Even a crazy idea can be used to stimulate more practical brainstorming.

Confidence in self and team affects the amount of energy that a team member invests in an endeavor. If it appears that the investment of hard work is likely to end in success, staff members are more likely to contribute. If, on the other hand, success seems unlikely, the investment of energy will wane. To breed confidence on a work team, leaders can highlight the talent, experience, and accomplishments represented on the team, as well as keep past team successes visible. You can bolster the confidence of team members by providing feedback, coaching, assessment, and professional development opportunities.

Another way to stimulate contributions on a work team is to enhance staff member empowerment. When workers are involved in decisions, given the right training, and respected for their experience, they feel enabled and invest more effort. It is also important to have team members evaluate how well they support the contribution of others.

Connections

When a work team feels connected to the firm, members discuss team performance in relation to corporate priorities, client feedback, and quality measures. They consider team needs in light of what's good for the whole firm and what will best serve joint objectives. Leaders can encourage such connections by keeping communication lines open. Management priorities, successes, and headaches should flow one way; team needs, successes, and questions should flow in the other direction.

Tom Luken, president of the local firm Kolb+Co in Milwaukee, WS, says

> I think the art of doing this is to surround yourself with good people, empower them, and demonstrate that you have confidence in them. You encourage them and tell them it's okay if they make an error. You refrain from ripping their faces off when an error does occur, and you demonstrate the confidence that they will be able to resolve the error.

> When a work team has developed strong connections among its own members, peer support manifests itself in many ways. Colleagues volunteer to help without being asked, cover for each other in a pinch, congratulate each other publicly, share resources, offer suggestions for improvement, and find ways to celebrate together. Need a few ideas for developing and maintaining such connections? Consider the following:

▲ Allow time before and after meetings for brief socialization.
▲ Schedule team lunches.
▲ Create occasional team projects outside of work.
▲ Circulate member profiles.
▲ Take training together.
▲ Provide feedback to one another on development.

Cooperation

Most challenges in the workplace today require much more than good solo performance. With increasingly complex client needs and accounting firms, success depends upon the degree of interdependence recognized within the team. Leaders can facilitate cooperation by highlighting the impact of individual members on team productivity and clarifying valued team member behaviors.

On a team that works well together, members trust that when a colleague agrees to return a telephone call, read a report, talk to a client, attend a meeting, or change a behavior, the job will be done. There will be follow-through. Team members are keenly aware that as part of a team, everything that they do or don't do affects someone else.

When work team members are truly cooperating, they respect the time of others by turning team priorities into personal priorities; arriving for meetings on time; sharing information promptly; clustering questions for people, communicating succinctly; and asking, "Is this a good time?" before initiating interactions.

Being on a work team is a bit like being part of a family. You can't have your way all of the time, and to add value, you must develop a generous spirit. Leaders can help work teams by addressing these rules of team spirit:

▲ Value the individual.
▲ Develop team trust.
▲ Communicate openly.
▲ Manage differences.
▲ Share successes.
▲ Welcome new members.

Change Initiators

In today's competitive business climate, firms must not only respond to change but actually initiate it. To assist teams in initiating change, leaders should acknowledge any perceived dangers in the change and then help teams see the inherent opportunities. They can provide the security necessary for teams to take risks and the tools for them to innovate. They can also reduce resistance to change by providing vision and information and modeling a positive attitude themselves.

Commitment

Commitment to the purpose and values of a firm provides a clear sense of direction. Team members understand how their work fits into the firm's objectives, and they agree that their team's goals are achievable and aligned with the corporate mission and values. Commitment is the foundation for synergy in groups; individuals are willing to put aside personal needs for the benefit of the work team or company. When there is a meeting of the minds on the big picture, this shared purpose provides a backdrop against which all team decisions can be viewed. Goals are developed with corporate priorities in mind. Team ground rules are set with consideration for both company and individual values. When conflict arises, the team uses alignment with purpose, values, and goals as important criteria for acceptable solutions.

To enhance team commitment, leaders might consider inviting each work team to develop team mission, vision, and value statements that are in alignment with those of the entire organization but reflect the individuality of each team. These statements should be visible and walked every day. Once a shared purpose is agreed upon, each team can develop goals and measures, focus on continuous improvement, and celebrate team success at important milestones. The time spent up front getting all team members on the same track will greatly reduce the number of derailments or emergency rerouting later.

Conclusion

Teams that connect well with other work groups typically think of those groups as internal clients. They treat requests from these colleagues with the same respect shown to external clients. They also ask for feedback on how they can better serve both internal and external clients. They engage in win–win negotiating to resolve differences, and they share resources, such as training materials, DVDs, books, equipment, or even improvement ideas. To build stronger connections with other groups, work teams might consider scheduling monthly cross-departmental meetings, inviting representatives to their own team meeting, lending personnel during flu season, and combining efforts on a corporate or community project.

To compete effectively, leaders must fashion a network of skilled staff members and teams that support each other in the achievement of corporate goals and the delivery of seamless service.

Section 3

Leading Strategy

"Hope is not a strategy."

~ RICK PAGE

Once you've created your own foundation for leadership, and you're working with empowered people and teams, where do you go? To put strategy and its components in context, we need to look at vision, mission, and values. Successful accounting firms formally and strategically plan their future. Firms may create a vision for the next year, but more typically, a firm will look 3–5 years in the future, and some extend their vision to 20 years.

In the three chapters that follow, we will closely evaluate the benefits of vision, mission, and values. These three elements form the basis of the leading strategy level in the pyramid structure of this book.

Mission permeates everything we do with strategy, but it's not the starting point. Values define our firm, and mission touches and is bounded by our values. Mission connects the present and future: our vision. Our objectives should align with our mission and be constantly compared with the mission to ensure that we're staying on track toward our vision and within the bounds of our values. Mission and values exist both today and in the future, whereas the vision is not truly in the present.

Vision: Reality in the Future	Mission: Making a Difference	Values: The Character, Actions, and Outcomes
Chapter 11	Chapter 13	Chapter 12
Section Three: Leading Strategy		

To determine where a firm is going, leaders need to exactly know its present state. Only then can the leadership determine where it wants to go and how it will get there. When documented, this becomes the strategic plan. The following is an overview of these three building blocks that make your firm and strategy unique.

Vision (Chapter 11)

Vision defines the desired or intended future state of an accounting firm in terms of its fundamental objective or strategic direction. Vision is a long-term view, sometimes describing how the organization would like the world in which it operates to be. For example, a partner group might have a vision to double their revenue within five years.

A shared vision provides a starting point for business decisions, firm operations, marketing, technology, and finance. We have found that firms that have no central vision but are

Shared Overhead Firm Versus Shared Vision Firm

	Shared Overhead	**Shared Vision**
Leadership and Governance	Managing partner who manages everything but the other partners or committee	CEO
Planning	Little time for planning	Integrated plans with partners, teams and staff members
Decisions	Partners' interests come first, then the team's	Firm's interest comes first, then the partners'
Management Focus	Book of business	Professionals in key roles
Partner, Shareholder, or LLC Agreements	Protect the individual	Protect the firm
Retirement	Unfunded	Funded; unfunded portion is limited
Leadership Succession	No development	Invests in leader's' development
Technology	Overhead	Strategic asset
Training	Continuing professional education	Evolving mix of technical, professional, business, and communication skills focused on learning, application, and return on investment
Staff Focus	Charge hours and book of business	Goal oriented
Firm's Policies and Processes	Policies that are not enforced and varying processes, depending on partner preferences	Adhered to by everyone

essentially organized to share overhead differ significantly from firms with a vision shared by all stakeholders (leaders, partners, employees, families, clients, and communities). The following table illustrates the differences between a firm that operates as a shared overhead firm and one that operates with a shared vision.

Mission (Chapter 13)

Mission succinctly defines the fundamental purpose of an accounting firm, describing why it exists and what it does to achieve its vision. A mission statement answers the question, What do we do? For example, Clifton Gunderson LLP's mission is "Growth of our people, growth of our clients, all else follows."

Values (Chapter 12)

Values define what the firm stands for, the kind of people that you want to employ in your firm, the actions that you want them to take, and the results that they should get in the marketplace. Many firms will have 3–10 core values, along with a set of behavior principles, that they follow.

Some values that you'll see among accounting firms include a commitment to community service, integrity, teamwork, excellence, great client service, spiritual and physical well-being, having a positive workplace, respect for individuals, and lifelong learning, just to name a few.

Leader Profile: **Richard Caturano, AICPA Chairman of the Board (2012-2013) and Office Managing Partner, Boston, of the national firm McGladrey & Pullen LLP**

Richard (Richie) Caturano grew up in the blue-collar town of Revere, MA. As the eldest child, Rich never had fewer than 3 jobs to support himself and his family. His father pointed out a neighbor CPA who wore a suit to work, went to work at 8:00 AM, and came home at 5:00 PM, so at the age of 12, Rich decided that he wanted to become a CPA.

During his high school years, Rich worked construction jobs and learned the art and science of building things. He applied this skill to his business pursuits, building Caturano and Company to one of the 50 largest firms in the United States. He and his partners recently sold to RSM McGladrey, Inc.

Before the sale, Caturano and Company had become New England's largest regional full-service CPA, consulting, and wealth management firm and one of the top 40 CPA firms in the country. Rich led his firm through a period of 400 percent growth over a 5-year period. In 2008, the firm ranked number 28 on the *Boston Globe's* "Top 100 Places to Work" list and "No. 1 Best Place to Work For" by *Vault Accounting Guide*. The firm was also named one of the best places to work in Massachusetts by the *Boston Business Journal* for a third consecutive year.

(continued)

(continued)

Rich was named by *Accounting Today* as one of the 100 most influential people in accounting for 4 consecutive years and was recognized by *Winning Workplaces* as one of the best bosses nationwide. He is very active in advancing the accounting industry. He recently served as chairman of the AIPCA's Private Companies Practice Section Executive Committee, is now serving on the AICPA's board of directors, and is a past president of the board of directors of the Massachusetts Society of Certified Public Accountants. Throughout his career, Rich has specialized in management consulting and business valuation services for a wide variety of industries. He is a frequent speaker on issues relating to firm leadership.

Strategic planning cannot foretell exactly how the market, economy, competition, and clients will evolve and what issues will surface in the coming days or years. Therefore, strategic innovation and regular adjustment of the strategic plan have to be acceptable for a group of owners to thrive in the turbulent business climate. Even an airplane on a well-charted course from New York to Paris continually adjusts its direction as it flies through the buffeting winds and weather systems.

A successful firm's initiatives are constantly changing because of all the variables occurring in the real world of implementing strategy. Although you may launch your intended strategy through a series of initiatives, you will discover that the environment is constantly changing, and some initiatives work better than others. Initiatives that falter might be abandoned. At the same time, you will discover emergent strategies that will propel you along the way toward your vision more surely. With the right leadership, you will arrive at your destination or vision.

How Vision, Mission, and Values All Fit Into Strategy

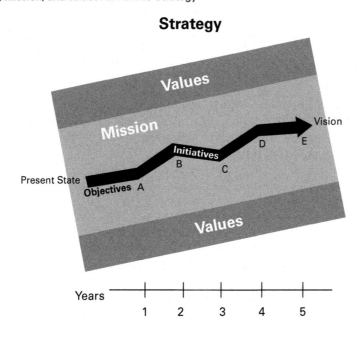

In my experience, a firm without a vision simply floats along aimlessly, vulnerable to the winds of the economy and competition. Employees do not fully engage, clients may be satisfied but not loyal, and leaders and partners don't reach their full potential. With a clear, successfully communicated vision that everyone embraces, leadership and management have a clear focus when making decisions, and employees feel that they are part of something bigger than their individual positions.

Neal Spencer, former CEO of the megaregional firm BKD, LLP, in Springfield, MO, discusses his work on visioning this way:

> In my role, I focus on leading us into the future, helping us seize opportunities and avoid major problems. For me, one of the major distinctions in leadership and management is that I can lead and think strategically, and my chief operating officer and professional practices partner can focus on managing the day-to-day business. Strategy helps us get very specific about the steps we will take toward our vision. It helps us answer what we will do to achieve our vision and be guided by our values.

Which comes first, the mission or vision? That depends. If you have a start-up firm, new niche, or plan to reengineer your current services, then the vision will guide the mission statement and the rest of the strategic plan. If you have an established business where the mission is established, then many times, the mission guides the vision statement and the rest of the strategic plan. Either way, you need to know your fundamental purpose—the mission, your current situation in terms of internal resources and capabilities (strengths and weaknesses), and external conditions (opportunities and threats)—and where you want to go: the vision for the future. It's important that you keep the end or desired result in sight from the start.

Next Steps: Goals and Objectives

Once you have developed your vision, mission, and core values, you can derive the goals and objectives needed to achieve your vision.

Goals

Goals are general statements of what you want to achieve, so they need to be integrated with your vision and mission. Examples of strategic or tactical goals include the following:

- ▲ To improve profitability by 15 percent
- ▲ To increase efficiency by 3 percent
- ▲ To capture a bigger market share in our construction niche
- ▲ To provide better client service and increase our client loyalty scores to 4.6
- ▲ To improve employee training and reduce turnover by 10 percent

A goal should meet the following criteria:

▲ Suitable: Does it fit with the vision and mission?
▲ Acceptable: Does it fit with the values of the firm and employees?
▲ Understandable: Is it stated simply and easy to understand?
▲ Flexible: Can it be adapted and changed as needed?

Make sure that the goals are focused on the important aspects of your firm (types of clients served, geography, financial metrics, and so on). Be careful not to set too many goals because you run the risk of losing focus. Also, design your goals so that they don't contradict and interfere with each other.

Objectives

Objectives are specific, quantifiable, time-sensitive statements of what is going to be achieved and when it will be achieved. They are milestones along the path of achieving your goals. Examples of company objectives are as follows:

▲ Improve utilization from 60 percent to 62 percent and realization from 90 percent to 95 percent.
▲ Gain one new construction client per quarter.
▲ Visit each partner's largest 10 clients once every 6 months when not working on client matters.

Objectives should meet the following criteria:

▲ Measurable: What is the measurement of success?
▲ Commitment: By what date will this be complete? What are the resources dedicated to achieving this objective?
▲ Ownership: Who are the team leader and members of the initiative task force?

The Role of Strategies and Initiatives

Strategies are statements of how you are going to achieve something. In a sense, a strategy is how you will use your mission to achieve your vision. A strategy is a series of actions or initiatives designed to achieve the goal. Goals and objectives provide milestones for measuring the success of the strategy in achieving the vision.

You can use several business analysis techniques in strategic planning, including SWOT analysis (strengths, weaknesses, opportunities, and threats) and PEST analysis (political, economic, social, and technological). They can help you assess the present state of your firm, as well as identify forces that might affect your go-forward strategy.

Initiative or action plans or tactics are statements of specific activities used to achieve an objective. You need to identify specific individuals who have the responsibility for implementing the initiative plans, along with a timeline for completion.

Example Plan

The following is a sample strategy, goal, objective, and action plan for a typical accounting firm. Note that the components of the plan cascade from the vision and mission. Goals are statements of what needs to be done to implement the strategy. Objectives are specific milestones for meeting the goal. Action plans are specific actions for reaching the milestone.

Vision

To be a $25 million revenue firm (or division) with dominance in the construction, real estate, and health care industries.

Mission

To help our clients obtain and use their financial resources more wisely.

Strategy

Have two of our partners become "famous people" within the construction industry niche that we have chosen to dominate.

Goal

Become number 1 or number 2 with every potential "A" client within the general contractor and road builder subniches of the construction niche within five years.

Objective

To propose on at least 10 potential clients in each subniche each year, win at least 4 of the 10 proposals, and maintain 100 percent client loyalty with the present clients that we have.

Action Plan

Form a revenue team around each niche. Identify all the potential "A" clients within our geographic markets. Devise a personal contact plan to interact with each one. Become active in each trade association where these prospects are active. Prepare an annual financial survey of some type in each industry segment, so that we can have annual contact and provide value. Speak at trade shows and industry meetings at least twice per year. Prepare some type of regular correspondence into each niche.

In the chapters that follow, I will explain how many different firms approach vision, mission, and values. We'll discuss the benefits and barriers to all these vital elements, and I'll give you some step-by-step approaches to their development in your team or firm.

Vision: Reality in the Future

"Vision without action is a dream. Action without vision is simply passing the time. Action with vision is making a positive difference."

~JOEL BARKER

A *vision* is a clear picture of how things will look at some point in the future; it should paint the picture of where you are going and how things will look when you arrive. A vision gives a sense of direction to everyone on the team or in the firm. A clear vision helps a firm resolve to stay the course over the long term rather than meandering in different directions in short bursts of activity with little results.

In this chapter, I'll provide some of the benefits of vision and how it can help propel you and your team forward together. You'll read a few examples of well-crafted visions and some of the stories behind how they were developed. You'll learn how to craft a vision, even if you are not visionary. Finally, you'll learn the importance of frequently communicating that vision.

Rick Anderson, CEO of the megaregional firm Moss Adams LLP in Seattle, WA, says

> All our partners have a common vision and mission, so we are working together, and there is little waste of energy. In the business world, the competitiveness of our profession simply doesn't allow for inefficiencies. So, everything you do needs to have synergistic opportunities. We have to make sure that our business objectives and our business offerings are absolutely consistent with what our clients want and need. We can't sell our favorite product or service if that's not what the marketplace wants.

For a vision to be compelling, it must tightly tie your passions to your clients' passions. A vision answers the questions, "Who is important to us?" and "What is important to them?" Even more fundamentally, vision should be the answer to this simple question: "Where are you going?"

Ken Baggett, co-managing partner of the national firm CohnReznick LLP, shares

> Our vision was best communicated with the words 10 cubed, or 10^3. That meant over the next 10 years, we needed to have 10 locations around the country and be the 10th largest firm in the U.S. In a full partner meeting, right after I became MP, we announced this; we were doing $55 million in 4 offices on the eastern seaboard. We are going to have to have at least 100 partners to be able to get there. Today, we are in 10 locations with revenue of $200 million and very much focused on achieving 10 cubed.

Vision: What It Is and Why You Need One

A business vision is critical to providing a clear direction for your firm. Thus, you'll create a vision describing your firm as you'd like to see it, say, three, four, five, or more years from now. Note the emphasis on the future; the vision statement isn't true today. Instead, it describes the organization as you and your planning team would like it to become in the future.

Scott Dietzen, managing partner, Northwest Region, of the national accounting firm CliftonLarsonAllen LLP in Spokane, WA, believes

> The key difference in leadership and management is vision. Vision and the resolve to push the organization forward towards that vision is required for leadership. As a manager, I'm taking somebody else's vision, and I'm required to implement it. But in the leadership position, I have to understand it; I have to embrace it and own it in a way that makes it so clear to everyone why we are doing it, why it's important.

Vision is one of the most misunderstood business concepts because many confuse it with mission. Here's the difference:

Vision. Articulates what you want for your business—what it will look like in the future. A vision is idealistic: how big the company will grow and how it will be perceived by the outside world. A vision does not exist today, only in the future.

Mission. Clarifies your purpose—the value you'll offer, the products or services you'll provide, and the ways in which you want your clients' lives to change. A mission exists today and tomorrow.

Visions are as varied as the companies that create them. Some focus on competition, others center on product and service, and others highlight their community contributions. Some visions articulate an ambitious goal, but others specify market share. Here are some examples of effective vision statements:

▲ "Before this decade is out … [land] a man on the moon and [return] him safely to the Earth."—President John F. Kennedy, 1961

▲ "To become #1 or #2 in every market that we serve and revolutionize this company to have the speed and agility of a small enterprise."—General Electric Co.

▲ "10-10-10. We will be the 10th largest accounting firm in the United States in 10 years with 10 offices."—Ken Baggett

▲ "By 2014, in our three organizations (our accounting firm, our wealth management company, and our technology company) we want to have combined revenue of $100 million; we're about $45 million today. We are a very seasonal firm, and by 2014, we want to be profitable every month."—Scott Dietzen

▲ "In five years, we will be twice as big as we are today. We will have Capin Crouse University, where we will have an educational arm that educates our clients, board governors, CFOs, or bookkeepers. We will have some consulting products like succession planning for colleges and universities."—Bill Haller

▲ "Our vision is to be recognized as the premier CPA services firm in the region providing exceptional accounting, tax, technology, and special services for businesses, successful individuals, nonprofit organizations, and public sector agencies."—Ray Strothman

Henry Ford had a vision of a United States reshaped by affordable automobiles. Successful ventures, from Walt Disney's theme parks and movies to Mark Zukerberg's Facebook to Bill Gates's Microsoft to Oprah Winfrey's inspirational empire, have all been made possible by the combination of vision and strategy and insight and execution.

Mike Cain, founder and comanaging partner of the top-50 firm Lattimore Black Morgan & Cain, PC (LBMC), in Nashville, TN, believes, "You've got to be able to get out of your comfort zone and be willing to take some risk and predict the future, knowing that you may be very well be totally wrong."

Social and religious leaders such as Mahatma Gandhi and Martin Luther King, Jr., had the same combination: an inspiring vision of what society could be and strategies to make their visions reality. Most accounting firms aren't planning to reshape our society, but vision and strategy are required to make your enterprise succeed, as well.

Leader Profile: Ken Baggett, Co-Managing Partner of the national firm CohnReznick LLP

Ken Baggett, CEO of the Reznick Group, believes that the most important component of leadership is integrity, and he comes by his integrity honestly. "I'm a simple guy from south Alabama. My definition of integrity is what you do when you believe your mother is watching you. I believe that integrity is doing the right thing, no matter what the consequences are."

Ken grew up in a small town in south Alabama, played sports throughout school, and graduated from Auburn University in 1977. He worked for a small tax firm for eight months before moving to Atlanta to work for Habif, Arogeti & Wynne, LLP (HAW). Merrill Wynne, the managing partner of HAW, took Ken under his wing and steered him during the formative years of his career. He became a partner at HAW in 1981 and its managing partner in 2002. Ken left HAW to open the Atlanta office of Reznick Group in 2005, where he now serves as the firm's CEO and managing principal.

Reznick Group partner Tom Fassett says

> It's pretty obvious that in any profession or area of endeavor, a leader's true colors come out during times of crisis. This was certainly true of Ken Baggett as a leader and Reznick Group as a firm.

> Being mostly real estate centered, we naturally flourished during the glory years of the past decade when real estate prices were soaring, and pretty much all of our clients were making money hand over fist. When all that suddenly fell apart in late summer 2007, Ken and the firm found themselves facing some immediate, tough decisions. The first was a 10 percent reduction in force that hit every office and every department within the firm. Ken made that difficult decision early on, knowing full well it would adversely affect scores of people during extremely challenging times. Nevertheless, he made the tough call; communicated openly, honestly, and compassionately about how he came to that painful decision; and, in so doing, rallied the rest of us to pull together going forward. Ken did what he had to do with both honesty and dignity, and those are definitely hallmarks of a true leader.

> Another characteristic of a great leader is his or her ability to motivate and bring out the very best in others. A good case in point is my own election to office managing principal of the firm's Los Angeles office. Now L.A. might be a great place to live, but at the beginning of last summer, moving out here lock, stock, and barrel was just about the furthest thing in my wife, Tammi's, and my mind. All four of us, including my daughters, were ideally settled in Charlotte, NC, with a nice home, a nice community, wonderful friends, a great office full of talented colleagues, and a significant client base to service. Life was good, but the firm definitely had its own manpower requirements.

> Ken approached me on several occasions, doing what he does best—articulating the need for solid West Coast leadership; expounding on the firm's future regionalization plans; laying out the market opportunities that exist in southern California across the entire spectrum of industries and sectors; and finally, presenting me with the opportunity to have a free hand in building and shaping the future direction of the LA office. How do you say no to that?

Suffice it to say, we made the move, and I'm glad we did. And true to his word, Ken has backed me all the way—giving me the resources I've needed to make this office grow in both personnel and efficiencies .... I still can't quite believe he talked me into all this, but I guess *that's* the mark of a great leader, too!

Ken says, "Growing up, I always wanted to be in charge, whether as captain of the team or head of the youth group activity. I thought it was important to help others achieve their goals while at the same time influencing the direction of the group."

Ken has steered Reznick Group to its present ranking among the top 20 largest public accounting firms in the United States. Under his leadership, the firm has been consistently ranked among the top accounting firms in the cities where Reznick Group offices are located. Ken is consistently listed as one of the top 100 most influential accountants by *Accounting Today*, as well as one of the top 100 most influential practitioners by *CPA Magazine*. He was also named one of the 5 most admired CPAs by his peers in a survey of the managing partners of the top 200 CPA firms in the country by *INSIDE Public Accounting*. Ken's leadership has also been recognized through the firm's ranking as one of the country's 25 best-managed public accounting firms for 3 consecutive years by *INSIDE Public Accounting*.

He currently serves as the chair of the International Group of Accounting Firms, Limited (IGAF Worldwide), a position that he has held since June 2008. He is president and a board member of the Georgia Affordable Housing Coalition.

Making the Vision Real for Your Staff Members

The accounting firm you lead will proceed toward one of two places: the destination of your choosing or one you didn't intend. The catalyst for determining the *right* direction is vision. Yogi Berra said it best, "If you don't know where you're going, you might not get there." Rather than just a dream or far-reaching, unattainable goal, vision is a realistic picture of what you want your organization to become and the impact that change will produce. It's also a reflection of your values, why your business exists, and what your business will become in the future.

Keith Farlinger, CEO of the national firm BDO Canada LLP in Toronto, Canada, says

When you are helping your firm move towards a common vision, it is a very exciting part as leader of the entire firm. And I think that the youngest leader will get the same buzz by setting a vision for his or her project and helping his team succeed. For people to move towards that vision, you have to keep communicating with them until it sinks in. You need to be relentless, so, you know, part of that is mundane, and it's the same message over and over again, but it's very, very important to do that to keep people aligned. There is lots of hard slogging every day.

BDO Canada LLP and Grant Thornton of Canada began talks a few years ago to combine forces in that country. They developed a vision that together, they could compete for larger engagements against the Big Four accounting firms. Although that merger did not proceed, it did serve as a catalyst for Farlinger and his team to adopt that same vision on their own. Farlinger goes on

> A few years ago, we were in merger discussions with Grant Thornton. We would strengthen ourselves in cities and in specialty services that we are not in. We would have a critical mass of people. The merger didn't go ahead. So, after the merger discussions ended, our leading partners developed a vision, which was enunciated in the new strategic plan: we want to get to a similar place in five years on our own.

BDO Canada LLP has taken that vision and turned it into a working plan, Keith says. "We appointed four people to take what our partners had discussed over the last few months and put our vision and values into words. One of the big parts of that vision is growth. And all the [merger-derived] strategies to become one firm—our governance, our business development culture, our employer of choice—those are all in the [new] strategic plan."

Growing the business is part of everyone's job at BDO Canada LLP, Keith says. "We expect that all our people are involved in business development. Each person can help us decide where your entry point is and what you do on it. But we expect that everyone will play a role on the BDO team." As the firm makes its vision more concrete, it will also begin working to ensure that the entire firm contributes to fulfilling the vision, he says.

In *The 21 Irrefutable Laws of Leadership: Follow Them and People Will Follow You*, John Maxwell writes, "The truth is that almost anyone can steer the ship, but it takes a leader to chart the course. Leaders see the whole trip in their minds before they leave the dock. They have a vision for their destination."

You must connect and align the individual visions of your owners and employees with the vision of your firm. Without this connection, your firm's vision will be simply a pipe dream. Understanding the needs of all your owners, partners, employees, clients, and families will help you design a vision for a future that responds to these needs.

Most employees probably don't think much about it, but if a vision is to be attained, everyone in the organization must share it. Leaders can talk about mission statements, but unless they convince subordinates to share the vision and equip them with the purpose to achieve it, the effort will not be enough. The captain can't get the ship to port alone; he or she needs a crew motivated by purpose and the ultimate goal of reaching the destination. Every single detail of how to get there might not be available, but the captain puts goals in place for the crew and knows above all else that they will reach their destination together.

John Wright, managing partner of the top-100 firm Padgett Stratemann & Co. of San Antonio, TX, says, "You know, as managing partner, you're ultimately leading leaders, so that they can lead their teams. There are some different dynamics in that. You give them a fair amount of responsibility, but you're still charged with leading the vision and getting them to understand the vision and communicating that and then holding them accountable."

A vision should satisfy not only the corporate needs but be in alignment with the needs of the owners, employees, and clients in varying degrees. People need to feel that they make a difference in the lives of others. Sharing new ideas and coaching or mentoring other professionals is an excellent part of developing this vision.

Our Vision Shapes Our Future

Many people gain a sense of who they are from the opinions, perceptions, and paradigms of the people around them. They allow circumstance, conditioning, and other factors to mold and form who they are and what they achieve. The most effective people, however, shape their own futures. Instead of letting other people or circumstances determine their destinies, they mentally plan and then physically create their own positive results. What they have in their minds shapes their futures. The most effective leaders will follow this example for the lives of their accounting firms, as well.

The First Vision

Every accomplished vision begins as a mental vision: a thought, plan, perception, or motive. Although the physical vision does not exist, in reality, today, it develops in a person's or team's collective mind.

One of the most important steps in developing a vision is this first mental thought, idea, or dream of the strategic plan, design, and layout for who we want to be and what we want to do as individuals and organizations. I like to call a vision reality in the future.

Bob Bunting, former CEO of the megaregional firm Moss Adams LLP in Seattle, WA, says, "Managing partners must have a vision and a plan for their company. If a new leader doesn't have some kind of road map, then problems become overwhelming. But if he has a road map, then these problems kind of fall in order."

Consider some of the following examples:

▲ If you have a clear picture of what you want to accomplish in an upcoming meeting, you can establish the agenda for the meeting, enabling the attendees to focus on and meet the intended goals and objectives.

▲ If you want to have a loyal team and best place to work, you can create a vision of what that looks like to you and your partners then set about creating the picture that is in your mind.

▲ In the movie *National Lampoon's Vacation*, Clark Griswold had a vision of taking the family to Wally World. He then set about the tasks of servicing the family car and moving out of Chicago toward his destination. His vision was Wally World. His mission was to bring his family together and have a good time. I love Clark because he didn't let anything deter him from attaining his vision; when he got to Wally World, it was closed and he opened it up. Clark combined vision with action—my kind of guy.

The Value of a Vision

There are many benefits of crafting a vision for your firm. A vision does the following:

▲ Encourages you to think deeply about your business
▲ Expands your perspective
▲ Clarifies what is really important to you
▲ Provides direction

 A Leader's Perspective

Rich Caturano on the Andersen breakup

Primarily due to the famous Enron scandal in 2001, the highly regarded Big Five accounting firm Arthur Andersen disbanded. Around the United States and the world, clients were left scrambling for an accounting firm, Andersen partners and staffers were looking for homes, and Andersen competitors were lining up to feast on the spoils. In every city, the story was different. Rich Caturano, managing director of RSM McGladrey, Inc., in Boston, MA, tells how his firm handled the Andersen breakup and found a home for several of the Boston-area partners, propelling his firm to even greater success.

In May 2002, the Boston office of Andersen was about to migrate over to KPMG. Eighty percent of the partners were going to KPMG, 10 percent were going to Deloitte, and 10 percent were going to E&Y, and the staff members were following them.

We were in the middle of a merger with another small firm, Harte, Carucci & Driscoll, PC (HCD), at the same time. KPMG decided that they would be inheriting successor liability on Enron if they brought in too many people from Andersen, so they reneged on the deal to bring in the Andersen people. We became aware of the fact that, suddenly, there were 25 or 30 partners looking for a new firm. The clients were already transitioned to KPMG, Deloitte, and E&Y.

There was no recourse for the Andersen partners to get their clients back. Many of the clients were public companies that had already filed the change of auditor registration forms with the SEC. They were not about to renege on that, so here were 25 guys and ladies without a firm. We interviewed all of the 25 and met with Dave Clarkson, who was their HR director, and George Massaro, who was their managing partner.

We made an offer to 8 partners. We asked those partners to select the best managers, staff, and administrative people to come with them: another 37 people. Those partners were all making more money than we were. We were competing with several other national firms, so to bring all 45 on it was $4.5 million of additional payroll coming into a $14 million firm!

I did a graphic illustration of what the plan was, and I showed that plan to our partners and the partners from HCD and Andersen. While everybody had questions, they all concluded it would be amazing if we could execute against that plan. And I said, "I'm telling you, it's going to happen," and they all believed in it. We borrowed $4.5 million from the bank to make payroll because they had NO clients. I mean, they literally showed up for work on Monday morning without one client. Everyone agreed we'll go out and get some business. We had a vision, we had a plan, and all the partners bought into it.

We now had the challenge of a merger of people from a large firm, a small firm, and a midsize firm all coming together. One of the first steps was to get everyone together at a full-day meeting of the entire firm (firm day). At the firm day, we shared the graphic illustration of the plan. We had break-out groups where the participants could challenge and ask questions about the plan. We did a Brady Bunch video, which was an animation of the Brady Bunch opening from the TV show with our own lyrics and pictures of all the people from the three firms who were coming together. The message was we've got three families coming together. We are all going to live as one family. We are going to have one culture. We are going to sit at the same dining room table and have dinner together. We are one firm, with a clear vision of how we are going to be successful.

Our existing partners deferred all profit distributions. We ended up making less money for a while. Partners who came in from Andersen also made less money than they did at Andersen, although some made more money than we did. But we believed in the vision. The partner compensation challenge was just one of hundreds of challenges that we had to overcome. A big part of the strategy was that while we weren't directly bringing on any Andersen clients, we all had a huge network, and the world was about to change. One of the Big Five had just been eliminated, and it was clear that the other four would not have the capacity to handle all of the work. That was all clearly illustrated on the strategy graphic. In addition, we were about to enter an era of a billion dollars of new business because of Sarbanes-Oxley.

Soon after the Andersen partners came on board, we hosted a party at our offices for all the Boston Andersen partner alumni. We said, "You guys haven't seen each other for four months, and you have been through this traumatic experience; let's get everybody in and have a party." Our office was packed with Andersen people.

CFOs at all the big companies here in Boston were there. I spoke

> We have 8 of your partners here; we have a total of 45 people who came from your former firm, and they need your help. I want to put a mental picture in your mind of that Verizon TV ad where the guy is on his cell phone with 7,000 people behind him.
>
> The punch line of the TV ad is that it's the power of the network, and WE are banking on the power of YOUR network. Your expartners standing right next to me are holding their cell phones, and they are banking on the thousands of people who are standing behind them—all of YOU who were their colleagues and who have trust and confidence in them. We need your help; we need to build a business here.

There was silence in the room. They got it.

The next day, the referrals started coming in like you wouldn't believe, and a lot of them were coming in from E&Y and Deloitte partners. Can you help us with tax provision work? Can you help us with a valuation project, and can you do the

(continued)

(continued)

SOX work? The calls just started coming in.

The growth rate just went off the charts: 30 percent, 40 percent growth. We quickly grew from $14 million to $60 million organically without merging any more firms. Most of it just came from the power of the network. We have very few former Andersen clients, but we have a lot of ex-Andersen contacts who are now clients. We grew to be larger than Grant and BDO combined in Boston.

It's one thing to have the vision; a lot of people have the vision, but they never go for it because they think that the challenges are too great. A brilliant accountant can always come up with dozens of potential problems with any new move. A strong leader needs to go beyond this. I look at challenges more as opportunities. Vision clarifies what your services look like, how clients might respond to you, and the financial aspects for your clients and yourselves.

First, you must understand the present state before launching off on your tasks at hand. Before making commitments on behalf of your team, you must have a thorough understanding of the present situation.

Next, a good combination of optimism and clear facts are necessary to move forward toward a vision. When I first launched my business in 1991, I experienced a series of disappointments, but I knew that there was a strong market for what I was pursuing, and I had extraordinary optimism that I could not fail.

Some people are born with great vision; others have to work hard to develop it. For example, in our Leadership and Rainmaker Academies, each participant prepares a plan at the end of each class. This plan must be executed before the very next class. Preparing a four-month plan then executing that plan builds planning muscle. In appendix E, "RAIN-MAKER ACADEMY Revenue Action Plan/Results Report," you will find an Excel version of this plan. Planning muscle builds vision. When a person has successfully executed five four-month plans, then he or she is ready to prepare a one-year plan.

Steve Mayer, founder, chairman, and CEO of the regional firm Burr, Pilger & Mayer LLP in San Francisco, CA, shares his vision of "ringing the Bay."

["Ringing the Bay"] meant that we wanted offices located all around the San Francisco Bay. Our first office was San Francisco, second was Palo Alto, third was Walnut Creek, fourth was San Jose, and then Santa Rosa. Those offices ringed the Bay and it was a very deliberate strategy of not having little satellite offices; they're all full-service offices. And the idea was to have an office that was close geographically to where people live, so they didn't have long commutes, because I firmly believe that people ought to live and work in a community, and their kids will go to school with our clients' kids, and they would be on the soccer field together or the PTA or whatever organization. The only way to do that in the San Francisco Bay area was to locate in each of those different areas. And so, we found similar CPA firms with similar cultural values in each of those locations, and then, I approached them about mergers. So, that was the "ringing the Bay" strategy.

Building Your Vision

Having been personally responsible for a company's vision for many years, I believe that it covers more than what most people think. I believe that a vision must consider every aspect of the business. This includes everything from high-level, broad elements, such as the organization chart, right down to details such as service and delivery. Management expert Peter Drucker said that business has three main functions: marketing, innovation, and production. It seems to me that Drucker is missing vision.

Once you have a vision, you can bounce all major business decisions against it. For leaders who want strong forward movement, vision statements will be more specific. This helps ensure consistency across departmental goals and helps eliminate other major factors that can split a business into fractional pieces, such as two departments going after different objectives and effectively dividing your resources across these objectives or even markets.

As I help CEOs begin the vision-building process, I ask the following questions all along the way:

▲ Does your vision describe a future that is more attractive than the present?
▲ Will your vision challenge your owners and employees?
▲ Will it motivate talent to join your firm?
▲ Can it serve as the basis to formulate strategy that can be acted on?
▲ Will it serve as a framework to keep decision making in context?

There are usually five major business areas in firms (accounting and tax operations, finance, marketing, IT, and HR), with two parts to each (the strategic and tactical levels). The vision is everything needed to make the firm work across all these functions. Remember that you will produce a series of these snapshots over time for planning and growth purposes because the firm must evolve slowly, not make big leaps. I would recommend business snapshots for today, one year out, two years out, three years out, and even five years out. The further out your vision, the less detail you will need to have because many things will change over time.

Of course, the key financial performance indicators should include each month or quarter in great detail for the first year. With each additional year, the vision will contain less detail, and the current probability of being right diminishes greatly.

Get a Mental Start

Our consulting group helps our clients develop or revise visions for their firms. We usually do this by organizing a team that defines a vision for the organization. This work involves gaining an understanding of the firm; validating the business's core values; clarifying expectations of leadership, employees, and clients; and evaluating those expectations in light of the company's market position. I believe in creating a vision in your mind before committing it to paper. Of course, you may jot down thoughts, ideas, and words to begin organizing your vision, but don't be in too big a rush to commit final words on paper.

If your organization lacks a vision, it's not too late to create one. Here are four steps toward articulating a successful vision:

▲ *Think big.* Creating a business vision allows you to think big about your firm. Let go of your objections and insecurities, and listen to your employees' ideas. Think optimistically and enthusiastically about the dream for your future state.

▲ *Clarify your firm's core purpose or mission.* Why are you in business? Dig deep to reach the value that your firm provides to clients and others. How are your clients better off after doing business with you? What specific problems, challenges, or pains do you resolve for them?

▲ *Identify your business's core values.* Core values are the four or five principles that guide your operations. Examples include results, integrity, lifelong learning, responsibility, and client service.

▲ *Collaborate with your leadership and management team.* Draft a few possible visions and get feedback on them. Brainstorm a few vision statements with key employees and other invested parties. Narrow down your choice, and you've got a vision.

Developing a Vision Statement

When you are committed to the visioning process, and you have worked on the mental creation, it is time to begin crafting the right words to convey your message. Shoot for one or two paragraphs for the finished product, but length is less important than content. It's what the vision statement says that counts and the positive effect that it has on people's enthusiasm and performance.

Ted Mason, president and CEO of the top-100 firm Laporte Sehrt Romig Hand in New Orleans, LA, says, "We had a goal, we had a target, and we started working a plan. We worked on our culture. We have seen the benefits of what is done in terms of creating enterprise value. It has provided a ton of opportunities for our younger people to advance and get to places to which they wanted to grow."

Things to Keep in Mind as You Begin

The vision statement includes a vivid picture of the accounting firm as it effectively carries out its operations. The process for developing a vision statement should be culture specific. The approaches for creating a successful vision vary: participants may use methods ranging from highly analytical and rational to highly creative and divergent, such as focused discussions, divergent experiences around daydreams, or sharing stories. Visit with the participants to learn how they might like to arrive at the description of their organizational vision. The statement should be a compelling description of the state and function of the organization once it implements the strategic plan.

Leader Profile: Chris Allegretti, CEO of the regional firm Hill, Barth & King, LLC (HBK) in Boardman, OH

After graduating from Edinboro University, Chris Allegretti began his career at a small local accounting firm before joining Hill, Barth, & King, LLC (HBK). Thanks to strong role models, he moved up the rankings quickly, becoming partner in nine years. But Chris's rise to the top wasn't a cakewalk. He learned early in his career to establish goals for himself and to pay close attention to practice development.

HBK principal Phil Wilson says of Chris

> Chris's passion for leading is clientcentric, believing that attracting and retaining great people will lead to attracting great clients. Chris's focus on clients is exemplified by establishing the firm's Gold Client Service Program, which emphasizes cross-servicing, not selling. This deepening of the relationship is beneficial to both parties.
>
> Early on, Chris ushered in an era of transparency at HBK, with regular open discussion meetings with all professionals, publishing financial information internally, and sharing details such as criteria for admission to principal. Chris's style allows him to view challenges as opportunities—strategically placing those with specific talents where they can provide the most value for the firm.
>
> Chris has driven a culture change at HBK. Everyone is cognizant of the need to bring value to the client through application of firm resources. Teamwork is essential to achieving this goal. He expects client-service personnel to proactively address client issues and bring solutions to the point of solving a problem even before the client has recognized that they have a challenge. By doing so, we create opportunity.

HBK principal Keith Veres says

> His ability to see and share better versions of each professional and office team has allowed our firm to break out of the mold of traditional thinking and be at the forefront of industry changes. The accounting profession has its fair share of entrepreneurs, and Chris looks for, and encourages, HBK's entrepreneurs to contribute at their highest level. I have been with HBK for 20 years, and I appreciate the opportunity that Chris has been providing for me to redefine how I can best contribute to the firm.

Chris is a community and professional leader through his involvement with BDO Seidman Alliance and on the board of Edinboro University. He spearheaded his firm's entrée into financial services with HBK Sorce Financial, which has become one of the largest 10 CPA firms with assets under management.

Bake In the Buy-In

The vision statement could be something inspiring on a grand scale, or it might be something as simple as a quarterly goal. Regardless of its scale, as a leader, you must have a vision and inspire those around you to achieve it. Here are five tips:

▲ *Communicate with clarity.* Specifics are not necessary, but clearly communicating your vision to others is crucial. Communicate your intentions through group meetings, one-on-one meetings, telecasts, newsletters, and other modes of communication, so that everyone within your firm knows what course is being charted. Create a destination that is challenging yet realistic and a time line for achieving it.

Chris Allegretti, CEO of the regional firm Hill, Barth & King, LLC (HBK) in Boardman, OH, shares, "I really operate in three different ways: I either try to build consensus around an issue; I try and sell the idea because I think it needs to be sold; or frankly, there're times where you just tell people, 'I appreciate the input, but this is what I need you to do.'"

▲ *Involve everyone.* Resist the urge to design a grand vision without aligning all your owners' and employees' needs with the overall vision. Although you may have a good understanding of your vision, allow others within your organization to give feedback, help shape the process, and fully develop it. Ask of everyone, "Is this a vision that is good for you, or is this vision only good for others in our firm?" Make your vision their vision, and get real with your listening skills.

▲ *Create meaning beyond more money.* Many accounting firm partners are well paid in relation to their community peers, and it is often very difficult to motive them to work differently for a few more bucks. Andy Stanley writes in his book *Visioneering: God's Blueprint for Developing and Maintaining Personal Vision,* "Vision gives significance to the otherwise meaningless details of our lives." Stanley goes on to explain how the job of filling bags with dirt is an exercise in mundaneness, but when you are filling bags with dirt to save your home from a flood, it has exceptional purpose. Including the higher purpose in your vision will make more people give their hearts, along with their heads, to the service of the vision.

▲ *Personalize your vision.* Too many corporate visions have been created by executive teams on retreat, only to die upon the team's return to the real world where no one else wants to adopt the well-meaning vision. Incorporate personal goals for each person within your firm that contribute to the cause and are in line with your overall vision. Not only will this make each person feel like he or she contributed to capturing the vision, but it will also increase commitment and progress.

▲ *Keeping the vision alive.* There will always be unforeseen events that cause distractions and setbacks. To maintain forward momentum, regularly remind team members and yourself of the vision. Encourage your staff members to regularly ask themselves whether what they are doing is moving toward or away from their destination. Reward and recognize positive steps taken in the direction of the vision.
Tony Argiz, founder, CEO, and managing partner of the megaregional firm Morrison, Brown, Argiz & Farra, LLP, in Miami, FL, says, "You must live that vision on a day-to-day basis in everything that you do, so people can see that leadership."

One thing that I have discovered is that some accounting firms have vision in their DNA. Many leaders recognize that the best talent is attracted to firms with a compelling vision. The staff members work there for reasons far more important than just earning a paycheck. I consider profit as the equivalent of the food that we eat and the air that we breathe; they are not the reason we're alive, but without them, there is no life. Like Abraham Maslow's hierarchy of needs, Frederick Herzberg's research showed long ago that a lack of money can cause dissatisfaction, but once an acceptable level is reached, people are only motivated by things like challenge, autonomy, and opportunities to be creative—just the things that a shared vision provides!

Communicating Your Vision

Developing a vision takes time and effort. Don't waste that investment by keeping your vision a secret. Tell the world, and get people excited about it! GE's Jack Welch, one of the business world's greatest visionaries, had a vision to make his company "the world's most competitive enterprise." For Welch, true leadership comes from a clear vision and the ability to spark others to perform extraordinarily.

In the case of one of our clients, the CEO and his leadership team communicated the new vision to launch the company's strategic planning process. A manager said, "Now that our vision is clear, our strategic plan will be focused and make sense." By communicating your vision, you ignite people's passion for their work. When people feel invested in a larger purpose, their individual roles become more meaningful.

One of a CEO's most important roles is to communicate the vision to management and the employees and, yet, be open enough to the possibly superior experience of others in a specific area to modify it as they learn more. We can debate how much of this vision that investors and customers need to know because this will vary greatly from time to time and by industry and competitive environment, but the employees need to understand how the vision affects their jobs. At a minimum, they need to know at least enough to make day-to-day decisions that are consistent with that vision.

Don't Limit Your Vision

A vision is the design of everything needed for the business to work, combined with the experience to know that it *can* work that way in the real world. So, a vision is a very complex model that you can run in your head, taking into account all the major business disciplines and thousands of real-world practical factors that are only learned through long experience. I think this is a pretty good working and practical definition of a vision, and there is no doubt that having one can greatly increase your chances of success.

HBK partner Barry Holes says

> I believe Chris Allegretti has been a very talented leader of our firm for almost seven years. He did not have a predecessor to learn from since this was a new position for our firm. His first step after being elected CEO was to ask the Executive Committee if he could hire a coach who could help him learn the ropes, understand issues that arise, and provide feedback and insights that were relevant in our industry.

Chris scheduled meetings with his coach, Bob Bunting, and always showed up with an agenda of topics. He discussed many situations with his coach and tried to absorb the experiences and knowledge from Bob's many years of leading Moss Adams LLP, a large, innovative, regional accounting firm in the northwestern United States.

After utilizing the coach for the first couple years, Chris then continued to broaden his horizons by interacting with many other CEOs of large accounting firms by participating in various groups and round tables.

Barry continues, "A very important trait for a successful leader is understanding that you don't have all the answers. Chris is very adept at taking pieces of knowledge and using it to enhance HBK."

Chris learned to build a cohesive vision for his partner group by interacting with many other leaders. He did not limit his vision to his own or that of his partners. Allegretti challenged himself to find a bigger vision by opening himself up to other great leaders. Holes concludes, "Over the last few years, a testament to Chris's leadership skills is how now he gets calls from other CEOs to discuss issues with him."

The work that I do with CEOs and executive groups has made me realize that it is difficult for them to stretch their thinking toward the future because they're very grounded, realistic people. They are drawn toward missions, which describe what an organization does now, rather than visions, which describe why an organization engages in these activities. Visions must describe the desired long-term future of the organization—a future that typically is not quite achievable but not so fantastic to seem like a ridiculous pipe dream.

The vision-development process is a balancing act. It requires imagination, a mental capacity for synthesis, and a trust in intuition. Visions need to challenge people and evoke a feeling that draws people toward wanting to be a part of something quite special. When a vision is framed as something quite achievable within a set amount of years, then it falls into the terrain of a strategic plan.

Personally, I get motivated by challenging visions that reach out to the future and serve as a beacon for firmwide direction. Strategic plans don't turn me on; they don't turn most people on, but they are necessary. By the way, we are now also quite clear that strategic plans have a much higher probability of failure if there is no overarching vision informing them.

Phil Holthouse, founder and managing partner of the top-100 multioffice firm Holthouse, Carlin & Van Trigt LLP in Los Angeles, CA, says

> We don't set goals and say we'd like to be a $200 million firm in the next 10 years or something like that. But we feel like the growth is critical in terms of attracting and retaining motivated professionals. On the technical side of our work, as much as people will talk about gray areas and interpretation, I think the rules are clear, and the problems tend to be more discrete. In leadership roles, the general principles that you work on are much broader, and the rules are not as helpful.

Common Stumbling Blocks

I mentioned the need for alignment and synergy, imagination, and a trust in one's intuition. When an executive needs to be in control, fears mistakes, is uncomfortable with ambiguity, and tends to judge rather than facilitate the creation of ideas, then the result will probably be a vision constrained by a short time horizon.

Typically, accounting firms produce visions that are not far-reaching enough, not big enough. Often, a vision is so generic that people cannot latch onto it; they can't feel it in their hearts and guts. Even when there's a good vision, it's guaranteed to fail miserably if senior partners don't walk the talk.

What is the source of these problems? Some key prerequisites often don't exist as leaders begin the process. Without them present, any vision that gets built will have severe limitations and no impact on the bottom line.

First, the group involved in this process has to acknowledge that emotion is involved. Vision depends on the ability to feel. It requires *passion*, a deep visceral commitment that signals to others what they stand for. I'll admit, this can be scary as hell because when it comes down to it, figuring out what you stand for requires that you clarify who you are. Although vision building isn't group therapy or as touchy-feely as this may sound, it does require that each individual involved in the process look inside and talk about what is really important to him or her.

Carl George, former CEO of the national firm Clifton Gunderson LLP in Peoria, IL, shares

> I think many leaders make the mistake—they think they're leaders; they're just managers, and they don't touch the people; they don't touch their feelings. A leader is caring and inspires his followers to dream. Today, the leader of even a $5 million firm needs to have a lot of vision and a lot of attributes to take their people to the next level or their clients to the next level. Otherwise, they are merger candidates because they don't have the leadership to go to the next level. If you don't get to the next level, you lose your best players.

Second, the group must accept that the process is, by nature, imprecise, frustrating, and tedious. Done well, it's a creative and often chaotic process that, at the start, seems to defy linear thinking. It requires synthesis and imagination, and it often involves confusion. Put all these emotions and cognitive processes together and one realizes quickly that this is not the kind of stuff that many executives have much fun with. In fact, many just run away from a process like this when they realize that it isn't all rational, linear decision making.

A third stumbling block is reserved for entrepreneurs. Yes, many, if not most, entrepreneurs can be quite visionary by nature, and that's what makes them so successful. But we see some baggage that can come along with the entrepreneurial CEO that can be a stumbling block to a successful, vision-driven organization.

Entrepreneurs have a tendency to create structures and work environments that they can personally dominate. Often, decision making is too top-down and contradicts what we found in the firms that did guide their growth through vision. And entrepreneurs often delegate impulsively. Certainly, not all entrepreneurs bring these traits into their firms, but they should be on guard that these organizational manifestations don't happen. If they do, the vision will backfire.

Ten years ago Larry Autrey, managing partner of the top-100 firm Whitley Penn LLP in Ft. Worth, TX, argued that accounting firms didn't need a vision; they just needed to show up and do good work to grow their business. Today, he understands the point of focusing on the future of his business.

What I think we have learned is that 10 years ago, each partner had a similar expectation. I expected each partner to generate the same amount of new business each year, do the same amount of work, and manage the same number of people. What I have learned is that with our group of partners, if somebody is really good at generating business, they probably ought to generate more business than the guy who is not. If somebody is really good at the technical, they ought to do more of that.

For many, many years I would say, "We are an accounting firm; how much vision do you need you know?" We show up; we serve clients; and if we do it really well, we grow. We have to grow in order to have good people, and good people will help us grow.

What I realized over the years is that some people need a little more detail of the vision than that, and so, we end up spending more time now than I would personally prefer talking about the vision of the firm.

Unfortunately, it is impractical to expect every partner and service-line leader to understand the entire vision. As a matter of fact, it is virtually impossible because it is likely that they do not understand the other service lines, either. However, a good CEO makes sure that each service-line leader has a complete understanding of his or her responsibility for a portion of the vision and how it is phased in properly over time with the other departments.

Each day, a CEO will use the vision to measure progress and decisions about the future. Each day, the COO, CMO, and all service-line leaders should be making decisions consistent with their portion of the vision. If you have someone measuring his or her results and decisions against a vision at a former firm or in a former role or just a favorite way of doing things, then you have a personnel problem that should be confronted.

Strategies for Success

Getting people to hold the same vision requires some straightforward strategies. *First and foremost is communication.* Vision statements are not nearly as important as the way leaders talk to people about the visions in their own way using their own language.

We've found that stories are profoundly powerful: stories of the firm's history as it illustrates part of the vision, stories of organizational heroes who exemplify values embedded in the vision, and vivid stories about what the future can look like. I believe in preaching to the converted—preachers do it all the time! Strengthening the commitment, intellectual performance, and morale of those already on your side is essential.

Benchmarks along the way are vital. If your firm is going to move toward the vision, you must set benchmarks along the way to indicate progress. People who are challenged and motivated by the vision stay and thrive; those who cannot buy into it ultimately leave.

Noel Tichy and Ram Charan, both well-known academics, consultants, and authors, have studied a number of huge organizations that continue to lumber along the growth path despite their size. They assert that, "[t]he greatest source of risk in a business is failure to understand the needs of the client or end user. If people don't look from the outside in, external change will overtake them, no matter how much energy they lavish on their business …. Reach into your customers' thoughts, see their needs and work backward. The rest is execution."

Conclusion

Strategy must begin with a vision; otherwise, you and your team will meander through business being blown about by the winds of outside forces. A vision gives you purpose and gives your team something to rally around. As you pull together in harmony toward a common vision, the synergy that will occur will propel you forward more rapidly and surely than most any other business principle. Once you have clearly in mind where you want to go, then you can begin to craft your purpose (mission), your values, and the milestones (objectives) along the way.

12

Values: The Character, Actions, and Outcomes

"Open your arms to change, but don't let go of your values."

~ DALI LAMA

As I've said before in this book, you can manage processes and projects, but you cannot manage people; you must lead people. Leading people is much more than telling or forcing people to do what you want. A prison guard can do that. A good leader creates belief in the mission and values of the firm and will attract people who share those values. When people in a firm share the same values, they behave in acceptable ways without a heavy hand of management. Having a set of shared values is a strong predictor of getting a team to work together successfully.

Values are difficult to understand and espouse. Each person brings his or her own life experience to the discussion of values. For example, one person may have grown up in a family where everyone was very direct and spoke the brutal truth, but another person grew up in a "polite" family environment filled with varying degrees of white lies. Some people view values as standards not to be broken, and others view values as aspirational.

Then, of course, there is the case of the "corporately correct lip service" values where everyone espouses one thing but does another. For example, I see many firms that espouse integrity as a core value then regularly run late on serving each other and their clients. I meet with firms whose partners espouse teamwork but are reluctant to introduce another partner to their clients. These firms often have strategic planning meetings and agree on sets of core values that are nice for public consumption, but they don't use them to govern their lives. The challenge is to bring a variety of life experiences and views together around a set of values that partners and team members will identify with; be inspired by; and most of all, live by.

In this chapter, I'll explore the purpose of core values and how they help us govern the behaviors of a team or an entire firm. We'll discuss whether core values are standards or aspirations and whether, under either circumstance, they are realistic. Lastly, we'll delve into the dimensions of values: how to find your own and how to sustain them over time.

A good leader will set the tone for a team with the values that he or she actually demonstrates. Values determine how owners and employees will act, and how people truly act creates a culture. If you, your owners, and employees are open, direct, accountable, and responsible, then you will create a culture of high performance and trust. On the other hand, if owners play passive-aggressive games, gossip, backstab, and don't share credit for success, your culture will be one of low performance and mistrust. Have you ever heard employees complain, "It's not what they did; it's how they did it that hurt the most"? Your values, often called codes of conduct or operating principles in a business context, must be lived and enforced.

Usually, a firm expresses a set of shared values, and then, it establishes some working rules or principles based on those values. In our firm, we have a set of values and principles of service. The values are those things that we are always striving to do, realizing that we may never be perfect. The principles are those behaviors that we expect from everyone on our team. Together, the values and principles give us a code to live by and a language to explain how things should work.

When it comes to good leadership principles, Marc Elman, CEO of the local firm PSB Boisjoli in Montreal, Canada, says that his firm goes by the Golden Rule: do unto others as you would have done to yourself.

Bill Hermann, former managing partner of Plante & Moran, PLLC, says

The core values are pretty simple: we care about one another, and do unto others as you would have done unto you. The value part of that is an understanding that we're in this as a group. One of the principles—teamwork—means that we're going to do everything we can for the individual but not to the detriment of the team. It takes a while for folks to understand that. If this is something that's good for you as an individual,1 but it screws up the team, it's probably not going to work.

Although the Golden Rule has been a basic value in our culture for 2,000 years, one author, Tony Alessandra, proposed a refinement that he calls the Platinum Rule. Interestingly, most people understand the distinction immediately, and Gordon Krater, managing partner of the megaregional firm Plante & Moran, PLLC, in Southfield, MI, has come up with it spontaneously without renaming it. He says, "The Golden Rule is how we function. The Golden Rule is typically defined as do unto others as you would have them do unto you. We have defined it as do unto others as they would want to be done unto them. That is, recognizing their differences, and I think diversity has sort of brought a little bit of that."

The partners at Plante & Moran, PLLC, value placing a client's interest ahead of their own. Maximizing individual opportunities within the context of the team is another crucial value for this firm. One of the key reasons that Plante & Moran, PLLC, has been selected for many years as one of the top 100 best places to work in the United States is its value of preserving and enhancing the spirits of its team members. Krater continues

There are certain business decisions that might have been good business decisions but sure wouldn't have done anything for our culture and spirit. And so, we decided not to do them.

We have 225 partners, and from time to time, we must deal with a violation of our core values. I will sit down and talk to that person. Quite frankly, mostly, it's a misinterpretation, or sometimes, it's a little bit of stubbornness. But over time, usually, the person realizes, "I shouldn't have done that."

With all these difficulties in understanding, why should we try to state our core values? We'll look into this in the next section.

The Purpose of Core Values

Core values have two dimensions: regulation and inspiration. Although our firm's values must regulate our behavior, they should also inspire us to a higher level of moral and ethical conduct. Values for resolving ethical questions line up along these two dimensions. For example, if moral standards are rules of the game that we must follow (regulation), moral ideals are the goals of playing the game well and winning (inspiration). Moral ideals portray character traits, acts, and achievements we should aspire to. For accountants, these ideals are implicit in laws, regulations, policies, and customs. We also find these ideals in the examples set by our moral heroes and mentors. And we find them in our core values. Although moral standards are usually expressed in rules, moral ideals are often expressed in stories of extraordinary virtue, acts, or accomplishments. Moral standards demand compliance, and we hold violators accountable. Moral ideals, however, inspire striving, and we admire those who thrive on their ideals.

In any particular case, the line between standard and ideal may be blurred. Indeed, the ideal in some circumstances may be the standard in others. In a values discussion, the nice to have at one time and place may be the bare minimum at another.

Core Values as Standards or Aspirations

We must view core values as both standards and aspirations. Of course, the words used to express a firm's core values, such as integrity, balanced life, teamwork, and so on, cannot capture all the obligations and aspirations that the core values contain for people. They do, however, provide a basis for discussion when core-value issues need to be discussed and resolved in a firm.

Don't confuse standard values and aspirational ideals. Both are necessary. Without standards, it is not possible to maintain order, and without aspirations, it is not possible to grow.

 Many firms confuse the two and make compliance with standards optional or try to make achieving ideals compulsory. This leads to frustration all around.

Leader Profile: **Bill Hermann, former managing partner of the megaregional firm Plante & Moran, PLLC, in Southfield, MI**

When Bill Hermann attended Catholic grade and high schools, he enjoyed himself and got by on the least amount of studying possible. Bill's father gave him three choices when he ventured off to college: (1) maintain a 3.0 average, and his family would pay; (2) quit school and work, or (3) figure out a way to pay for school himself.

Jesuit discipline didn't take hold for him until the end of his freshman year in college. Falling below the required 3.0 average, Bill selected the third option and began the long road toward self-reliance and personal leadership. People who know Bill today find his youthful escapades hard to believe because he seems to be one of the most articulate, well-educated men in our profession. He was voted by his peers as one of the five most respected and admired CEOs in the United States.

Plante & Moran, PLLC, partner Bruce Shapiro says

> One thing that has always stood out for me, even when I was pretty young, is that Bill was equally focused on my career as he was his own, probably more mine.
>
> So, he would always give you more of the credit than you deserved in the client's eyes and certainly less of the blame.
>
> He really built me up with clients. He knew the clients well enough to anticipate how the meetings would go, and he'd make sure that I had enough of an assignment in the meeting to kind of show my stuff or to show our stuff because we would have talked about the solutions. He'd give me the things to talk about that the client wanted to hear about. You know, opportunities we had for them, whether it was credit that might be available or different tax plans, or how we were going to get them out of trouble on some personnel issue.

I knew he was looking out for my well-being. We laugh and joke around here about prepartner syndrome. I honestly don't think I ever had it because he worried so much about me becoming a partner, I didn't see why I should spend any time on it!

You always knew how he felt, whether he thought you did well or whether you came up a little short. You didn't have to read between the lines, which I always appreciated. If he took you to task, he was doing it for your own good.

Most of my really high moments were with client interactions that we were involved in together, face to face with the client. We'd be well prepared for the meetings. He always made sure you rode together. So, we'd talk about how we saw the meeting going and what our roles were, and then, we'd debrief on the way home, which was always educational. So, that windshield time was pretty valuable.

Plante & Moran PLLC's current managing partner Gordon Krater says

Bill Hermann is one of the most effective, yet humble leaders I've ever been around. He led our firm's growth for 8 wonderful years, in all of which we were selected by *Fortune* magazine as one of the top 100 places to work in America. Bill could have been reelected as managing partner of our firm, but he chose to not stand for reelection to allow another leader to emerge. He now works closely with me and helps mentor others in our firm. That's the kind of selfless leader that Bill Hermann is; he is for the team first and himself last.

Core Values Are Worthless Unless They Govern

There are many ways to describe values. Espoused core values are those with which people agree. For example, everyone believes in integrity, but unless your behavior demonstrates integrity, espousing this value is of little consequence. The problem is that often, these values are nice, and people say them, but they don't govern their lives. I can say that I value honesty, but if I get an extra $1 back in change at the checkout counter, only I will ever know how much I truly value honesty by how I handle this situation. I can come across to everyone as honest, but in the moment, when no one is looking, only I can really know for sure.

Governing values are those that can be witnessed by people with whom you live and work. We express these as principles of communication. These are the "true" values that you share and the ones by which you make decisions and take actions.

Terry Harris, managing partner of McKonly & Asbury LLP in Harrisburg, PA, gives an example

Responsive service is probably the number one core value here. We want to be able to differentiate ourselves from competitors by our responsiveness. I was at an annual board meeting about a month and a half ago with this client. We were presenting the financial statements of a very respected $300 million dollar, family-owned company. The CFO was singing our praises to the board, and he said, "Just to give you an idea. Last week, my cell phone in my pocket accidentally dialed, and I opened it, and it was ringing Kurt Trimarchi, who's my tax partner at McKonly & Asbury. I immediately stopped it and put it back in my pocket. Five minutes later Kurt was calling me back to see what I needed." He was saying to the board it's an example of how responsive we are. That is central to our whole organization.

Building governing values goes far beyond creating a list of words or phrases that look and sound nice. Governing values emerge when we put our stated values to the test in live situations. We might include integrity and respect in our list of stated values, but how do we apply these values when we learn something negative about one of our coowners or workers? You must actually *use* the values to make choices. Observing yourself and your team members in real situations will reveal your true governing values.

Bob Hottman, founder and CEO of the top-100 firm Ehrhardt Keefe Steiner & Hottman PC (EKS&H) in Denver, CO, says

> The single most important thing that I have to do as a leader of our firm is make sure people understand our values and live those values. They'll make mistakes, but breaking core values is a mistake that we don't take lightly. We will not give very many chances to break core values again.
>
> I sit down with every new employee, and I go through our core values. I go through our mission. I go through our vision. I talk about our culture. I talk about the things that are important to us from a firm perspective, and I let them know that we can tolerate mistakes, but we do not tolerate core-value mistakes.
>
> Our first core value is integrity, which is nothing more than doing the right thing. We'll support people 100 percent for doing the right thing. The next core value is direct, honest, and open communication, and we call that DHOC.

What we truly value as leaders will guide how we work together and will affect the results that we achieve. Our core values have a direct effect on our outcomes because those values guide our decisions and actions. If we are not committed to the values that we espouse, then we will always experience unintended consequences.

Aristotle said, "We are what we repeatedly do." He was talking about character or the habits that we have formed from the values we live, rather than the values that we simply agree with. Finding what you repeatedly do is often illusory, so how does a person or firm discover those values?

Finding Your Values

While developing your core values, you must ask yourself some questions. Are our values too simple or forceful? Are they so simple, so general, that they can mean anything to anyone? If so, will they turn out to be only this year's "framed whatever"? On the other hand, are they so demanding that they are unrealistic? Will the values lead to ignoring them, or will they lead to hypocrisy?

How are values defined? What do they look like? They might be written down; more likely, though, they are already part of the genetic code of your organization. They are the norms—the way we do things around here. Often, there was no conscious determination of your core values. They just developed and then evolved randomly, depending on changes in leadership. By looking at your values explicitly, you will have a more coherent and integrated set of values that don't contradict each other. You will know what you stand for.

Here is a partial list of values that you might consider. Check 10 of them that seem to match your own behavior. Write down any others that you believe describe the way you act.

Integrity	Happiness	Acceptance	Risk Tolerance	Risk Aversion
Wisdom	Power	Joy	Passion	Fun
Peace	Justice	Wealth	Decisiveness	Respect
Recognition	Friendship	Career	Excellence	Teamwork
Spirituality	Innovation	Alignment	Open-Mindedness	Achievement
Compassion	Honesty	Authenticity	Fairness	Health
Optimism	Caring	Status	Enthusiasm	Love
Results	Success	Fame	Motivation	Pride
Comfort	Balance	Truth	Family	Influence

If you are having difficulty identifying your values, think about how you would describe your character, how you behave, and what you are like. These are all indicators of your core values. Once you've selected your top 15, rate them from 1 to 15, with each of the items on your list to narrow it down. What items do you disagree with? Which ones are inconsistent? Those are not as likely to be core values for you. Once you have a list of 10–15, begin the process of elimination. Eliminate half of the ones that you've checked or written down. One week later, reduce the list again by half. What remains will be your core values. However, the ones that you always live up to, the ones that you are consistent at, and the ones that others consistently describe you to have or be like are quite likely your strongest values.

Leader Profile: Thomas P. Luken, president of the local firm Kolb+Co in Milwaukee, WI

Thomas P. Luken, president of Kolb+Co, has been in public practice since 1979. He joined the firm in 1984 and launched Kolb+Co's tax practice, leading that practice until he was elected president in 2000. Tom leads the firm's strategic direction and oversees client services for the firm's eight divisions and four industry niche groups. A Notre Dame graduate, he is very active in the Milwaukee community as a former board member of St. Michael's Hospital Community Foundation, Covenant Healthcare System Council on Philanthropy, and Westmoor Country Club.

IGAF Worldwide President Kevin Mead says

Within IGAF Worldwide, there is actually a rule called "the Tom Luken rule." This was first developed a number of years ago when IGAF Worldwide was looking at a potential merger. The merger in question would have likely been beneficial for IGAF Worldwide, but for Tom, it was the worst-case scenario, with his strongest competitor being a part of the other association. Within a board meeting, Tom said, "Look, this is a great thing for IGAF Worldwide, and I am voting for it. I will,

(continued)

(continued)

however, then quit, as it is really bad for my firm."

As events unfolded, the merger in question did not occur, but the attitude and ability to show others how they should conduct themselves as a board member was an outstanding example.

Kolb+Co partner Mark Miller shares

Tom has leadership abilities in many areas, especially in developing and executing a leading strategy.

Luken came to Kolb+Co to establish and lead a tax practice. At that time, the firm had about 20 employees, 2 shareholders, and no tax department. Under Luken's direction and leadership, the tax department grew and developed the reputation as the top tax department in the city. It now has 5 shareholders and 28 professional staff.

During Tom's tenure as managing partner, he initiated firmwide semiannual updates. At these updates, firm financial information is disseminated, divisions provide progress reports, the HR department reviews benefits and results from employee surveys, and the marketing department summarizes the practice activities and success rates. These meetings have been instrumental in getting employees to feel part of the firm and its growth and success. Tom has been the driving force behind the firm's five-year business plans. These plans have been very successful for our firm.

Shareholder Steven Spector says

I am our insurance specialist and spent 22 years as an agent for Northwestern Mutual. I joined Kolb in June 2005. At our first meeting , I was extremely impressed with how Tom viewed the CPA firm and their Kolb Financial Adviser, LLC (KFA) service. Tom's belief that our clients value comprehensive, coordinated services was very evident. He indicated that we will never grow KFA without hiring a true specialist that can work closely with our clients and our CPAs.

During these last five years, our practice has become a national one. We have developed outstanding referral alliance relationships; our shareholders, managers, and supervisors all ask the clients they work (as well as new prospects) if they would value an independent, unbiased review of their insurance programs. Through Tom's leadership and his guidance with our CPAs, we act as a team, which has made clients feel very comfortable and trusting when dealing with insurance planning. His vision was that we could grow substantially if we could leverage me (being one person).

Kolb+Co shareholder Keith Kamperschroer says

Tom has been in a leadership position as an officer with IGAF. In this association, Tom has helped our firm and others with cross-referrals of work, both nationally and internationally. Through his substantial efforts and meetings, he has involved many members of our firm to be involved in the organization. We know through Tom's work he is also doing his part to have high-quality accounting standards, both for this country and the world.

In the area of truthfulness, especially within the recent tough economic times, Tom has put in place strong receivable policies and has been forthright with clients relating to no extension of credit and stop work orders, if necessary, to help maintain our firm's cash flow and help our firm during difficult times. He has come across both with clients and employees also as sincerely caring for them. By example, he has instilled these values in others.

So, how many values should we write down and use to govern? Some firms use 5–10 values. Most organizations can make do with 3.

The Elements of Core Values

Core values can be boiled down to three fundamental elements:

1. The *character* of the persons in your firm
2. The daily *behaviors* of the people or their *actions*
3. The *results* or outcomes from the actions of the team members.[1]

In our firm, FiveStar[3], LLC, we use these elements to state our core values:

▲ Integrity—The character of our team members
▲ Exceptional Five-Star service—The daily behaviors of our team members
▲ Excellence and return on investment for our clients—The outcomes we obtain

We state our core values as ideals to which we aspire. Although we will have some patience with a newer person on our team who does not do what he or she says, we must see improvement, or we will make a disciplinary decision, up to and including separation. Our tolerance for low integrity is much less for a long-term team member or one of our leaders.

We add to our core values a set of principles of service and communication: the observable behaviors that give life to the core values.

Our Principles of Service and Communication

Go Deep

I will go deep in connecting with team members and clients (especially new ones) to build strong and everlasting relationships. I will be loyal to others, absent or present, by being respectful and nonjudgmental. This principle gives life to the value of Five-Star service by building personal and institutional relationships with our team members and clients.

---

[1] Ethics strategies are often placed in three groups. In the book *Critique of Applied Ethics: Reflections and Recommendations*, Abraham Edel, Elizabeth Flower, and Finbarr W. O'Connor describe three families of concepts used to formulate ethical issues. They are virtues and vices and the moral atmosphere, the moral law—the straight and narrow path, and the good—ends and means. In his book *How Good People Make Tough Choices: Resolving the Dilemmas of Ethical Living*, Rushworth M. Kidder describes three principles for resolving ethical dilemmas. They are care-based thinking, rule-based thinking, and ends-based thinking.

Be Responsible

I will be responsible in solving all problems, whether mine or others'. I will take ownership and recover, even when in doubt. I will recover, not only for my errors, but also for the errors of our team members and clients. This principle supports our value of getting results for our clients.

Understand First

I will seek to understand first by listening, asking, and restating all orders, whether I am the giver or receiver. Without understanding, we could not live out the value of integrity because the expectations of our client would rarely be met.

Deliver Excellence

I will strive to deliver excellence in everything by doing my best and always building my competence to be better. I am good enough to get better. Delivering the best we can deliver on every project enables us to live out the results and return on investment value that we espouse.

Never Assume

I will never assume that my team members or clients are satisfied. I will be vulnerable and accountable for my promises. I will get over my fear of criticism, so I can improve. Without being vulnerable and accountable, we could not deliver our value of excellence.

Make Their Day

I will make the day brighter for everyone. I will choose an attitude of gladness and service and give the unique gifts that only I can give. I will strive to make a difference in the lives of everyone with whom I work. Each person on our team has certain strengths, and when we work as a team, these strengths enable us to live all our values.

Invest in Myself

I will invest in myself by taking responsibility for growing my capacity to earn, learn, and love.

Bill Hubly, founder and managing principal of the local firm Corbett, Duncan & Hubly, PC, in Itasca, IL, has a similar model

We have three core values at the firm right now, and those core values are

▲ integrity. The premise here is that you don't get a second chance. If you breach integrity, you will be let go from the organization. Also, integrity encompasses keeping promises and individual responsibility and accountability.

▲ continuous improvement. If you're not continuously getting better, you're probably dying. If you're not growing, you're dying. If you're not improving, you're stagnating, and we can't be tolerant of that. It's about growth.

▲ respect. That's how we treat one another within our firm and how we function in teams and how we respect our clients, our industry, and one another.

In our set of three core values, like those at Corbett, Duncan & Hubly, PC, integrity is about the team member. Five-Star Service is about what the team member does on a daily basis and is ruled by our principles. Excellence and return on investment are about the outcomes that we get for ourselves and our clients. In this way, our core values can completely describe any dilemma that we may encounter.

The first element describes the character of the person who acts, and in our case, we want people to do what they say they will do because that means they will possess integrity. Whenever I interview a potential candidate to work in our firm, I usually ask the person to do some small thing. If that person says that he or she will, then I wait and observe to see if that person follows through. If he or she doesn't, then we go no further, and we make no offer to join us. But I must realize that even if the person does follow through, the testing is not over.

Trusting someone else has a lot to do with the other person's intentions. Intentions matter because you want to understand whether a person's motive for truthfully reporting is a sense of duty or a fear of punishment if caught lying. Today's Western philosophy has its origins in these questions. Socrates practiced his belief that the unexamined life is not worth living by asking deep questions about justice, courage, and other virtues.[2] Aristotle believed that moral virtues are habits acquired through practice by finding the mean between extremes.

Are Strong Values Realistic?

Some leaders of accounting firms develop a written set of core values, only to change them frequently or ignore them as standards for working together. Staff members will sometimes not pay attention to espoused core values because they know that the values will not be enforced, or they may be changed. They could be a fad. Businesses of all kinds have bought into the notion of core values. Management tools change, however, and core values may sooner or later go out of style. If the core values du jour become tired, will the firm's current core values last? Will another leading partner name new core values?

Among accountants or other professionals, a more relevant question about a firm's stated values is whether they are so unrealistic that they are not meaningful. If we take values literally (integrity, service, and excellent results), they seem impossible to attain. Integrity seems easy; just do what you say you'll do. But if we take human nature into account, no one can be 100 percent successful with integrity or honesty. We have good and bad days. No one can follow all the service principles all the time, and no person or firm can provide excellent outcomes all the time. Although we do achieve excellent results in most cases, I hate to admit that there are cases when we have failed to help our clients get the best outcomes. If it seems inevitable that people, including firm leaders, will fall short of these impossibly high principles, is it not just as inevitable that cynicism and hypocrisy will result? Stating that you

---

[2]   In the *Apology*, Plato asks Socrates to explain why the unexamined life is not worthy of a human. The *Laches* is about courage, and *The Republic* is about justice in the individual and state.

will hold individuals accountable for violations of unrealistic values can only increase the cynicism with which the values are held.

This is why I've emphasized that a big part of values is their forward-looking, challenging aspect. They should give you something to strive for, to push your firm to grow. Values that are routinely attained are almost meaningless. Of course, no one is perfect, and values won't make you perfect. However, without standards and goals, there is no progress. To paraphrase the old saying, if you shoot for the moon and fall short, you can still be among the stars.

Leading by Example

To operate under shared values, the leader must be willing to advertise those values and be held accountable to them. In some firms, the leading partners espouse respect for the individual but allow 800-pound gorilla partners to violate this value. When this happens, the so-called value becomes a laughingstock and can infect the entire firm, with horrible consequences. Most firms have at least an implicit value to help their people when they are in need, but sometimes, they don't live up to it.

> John Wright, managing partner of the top-100 firm Padgett Stratemann & Co. of San Antonio, TX, shares a telling story
>
> I had kind of a critical point in my life where my youngest son who was then 18 months old got real sick and had been in the hospital throughout the end of March. As you know, the end of March is a pretty important time. The doctors didn't know what was wrong. He was running a 105.3 degree temperature fever, and so, I was at the hospital on a daily basis. That week changed my life.
>
> I had moved to a small Andersen office in San Antonio and had several March 31 deadlines. One could have been the most difficult engagement I'd ever worked on. When he heard about my sick son, the manager of that engagement basically said you take care of what you've got to take care of. I have this under control.
>
> But another senior manager I worked for got really upset that I wasn't there. We had a conference call, and my end was from my son's hospital room. This senior manager was screaming at one of my associates about me not being on the job. While he wasn't really screaming directly at me, he was complaining that nobody was there to help him. The most difficult thing to understand was that this really was a false crisis; the work was complete, and the report wasn't due for another six weeks. There was no real urgency, except that the partner and senior manager decided it was urgent.
>
> In a small office, that negative leadership style really cast a big shadow, and it was not my value system. I had never had that kind of run-in with anyone at other Andersen offices. I knew this was totally against the firm's culture and values, but I believed that there was little I could do, except I called my buddy over at Padgett and said, "I'm lost in the hospital, but as soon as we get this done, I'd like to come and visit." I did, and I moved firms ASAP. And so, the worst week of my life turned out to be the greatest blessing of my life.

Core Values Help Frame Our Behavior

Your core values create a comprehensive framework for observable behaviors in your business. Some leaders attempt to reduce the importance of actions and outcomes and over-promote aspects of character. However, a narcissistic focus on character will invite some to excuse themselves from moral rules. They might reason, "I am a person of integrity, and so, by definition, I am right, and rules others need to distinguish right and wrong don't apply to me."

Some leaders devalue character and consequences by insisting that there is moral worth only in doing the right thing. Similarly, some results-focused leaders see little value in character or moral acts, except to the extent that they produce results. Usually, the person who claims this approach is the high-performing partner with the big book of business. By focusing exclusively on performance and outcomes, you undervalue character.

Well-considered core values can give you balance among people, their actions, and the outcomes, albeit never a perfect balance. The framework of integrity, Five-Star Service, and excellence with return on investment allows the leader and team members to keep the entire structure of values in balance.

Sustaining Core Values

Good values get passed down from one generation of leadership to the next. They become part of the selection, reward, and promotion mechanisms of the firm. It's no surprise that successful firms with strong values do a lot of promoting from within. And those who prosper do so because there is a natural fit among their abilities, their values, and the type of behavior that brings success in that particular organization. They do not prosper merely by being sycophants. Great firms that make it beyond the first few generations can point back to people like Neal Clifton, Frank Moran, and Don Seiler, who had strong core beliefs that they instilled in their followers.

An intriguing question is, Why have the values of sustainable, continually growing accounting firms remained stable and relevant over the years? Perhaps it is due to the visionary genius of the founders. They no doubt had their own notions of what it took to be successful in their particular fields, and their own personal values and belief systems reflected those notions. This, in turn, helped shape their own basic blueprints for the kinds of people and behavior that fit the nature of the business that they wanted to create.

The values established by founders of firms remaining sustainable over the long term have a common theme: they are not constraining (for example, efficiency). On the contrary, they are empowering (for example, innovation). Although long-held values continue to serve as guides to "the way we do things around here," the early struggles actually created a climate for collective learning that acted as a catalyst for each individual's continual development. In these organizations, it became possible for the original values to be revisited and reinterpreted in ways that remained not only true to the spirit of the founders but also relevant to the modern world. The core values did not change, and one value—continual learning—seems to be consistent across the great firms. The clarity of values stands out in these firms. These values serve, in effect, as permission statements, allowing people to act on their own for the good of the company.

Jay Nisberg is one of the top and most successful consultants to accounting firms in the United States and Europe. Of the active consultants, he has the longest tenure: over 40 years. He has spoken to hundreds of thousands of accountants and consulted with over 1,000 firms during his storied career. Jay holds a PhD in psychology and is affectionately known by his friends as Dr. Jay.

Jay has been instrumental in the merger or acquisition of some of the largest firms in the United States. He was a founder of the original Horizon Group; The Advisory Board Company; and the Professionals Alliance Group, a money management firm in association with Oppenheimer.

Jay describes a client who has a unique set of values that give him great leeway in both regulation and aspiration. These values basically depend on the adult actions of the partners. Jay tells

> There's a particular firm that I'm thinking of that is a multioffice firm that has in excess of 100 partners. And the managing partner of this particular firm really has 3 fundamental leadership principles. The first principle is that he expects everybody in the firm to do what they're supposed to do when they're supposed to do it. Now, that's a pretty broad-based principle, if you will. People are always debating, "Well, what does that mean?" And when you go back to this particular managing partner, and you have a dialogue with him, and say, "Hey, you know, what do you mean when you say everyone should just do what they're supposed to do?"
>
> He says, "You know, at our point in life, you know, when you make partner in a CPA firm, one would think one knows what they should do. We have all these job descriptions for partners, job descriptions for functional areas, and job descriptions for technical expertise.
>
> Why do people who've been practicing in the accounting world for 15, 18, sometimes 20 years need a definition of what they're supposed to be doing?"

It's because they still want to operate like an employee instead of an owner. Jay goes on

> Once you become an equity partner in an accounting firm, you own a business. You have to turn the switch from employee mentality to owner mentality. And if you can't do that, then you can't subscribe to the first fundamental premise or principle of leadership that this managing partner subscribes to, which is doing what you're supposed to do when you're supposed to do it. Many would call that integrity.
>
> Now, what are those things? Well, there are really basically three things partners need to be doing, one of which is taking care of clients. The second, very obviously, is bring in new business. The third is take care of staff members.
>
> The second leadership principle is also pretty simple: if you act like a jerk, you're out. Some people in firms just don't know how to behave any other way than being either disrespectful to people or enamored with their own stature in life or caught up with their own academic credentials or their guruism, if you will, and they become that 800-pound proverbial gorilla that we've talked about for years.

This particular concept, you know, that this partner espoused—if you act like a jerk, you're out— is one of his fundamental premises by how, anytime he leads. When somebody acts like a jerk, there's actually a book that was once written with that title. He has a stack of these books. And when somebody's behaving like a jerk, he places one of these books on their desk. And when they come in in the morning, and they see a copy of this book, they're on a short leash. It's supposed to be a clue. And the clue basically is, "Hey, look it, you know. I'm getting too much noise in the system about you acting like a jerk. You can't do this."

Lastly, Jay explains leadership principle number three

You cannot expose the firm to technical, interpersonal, or managerial risks. I didn't say no risks. It's just don't expose the firm to risks that may put the firm in a bad place. Those aren't business risks where you might invest money in a service or venture or product. These are risks that might be technical, psychological, or related to human capital. For example, if you're going to abuse staff or employees here, you probably don't fit into that leadership principle. The last thing our firm wants is a sexual harassment suit, a wrongful termination suit, what have you.

Sometimes, people have a tendency to modify, bend, or cajole the principles of public accounting to the point where they do things that probably are not within the industry standards of how to behave. "Sometimes, they're so simple that they're so profound," concludes Jay. That's the way it is with values as both standards and aspirations—sometimes they are so simple, they are profound.

Conclusion

My hope is that you will invest some time and energy in finding your core values. They will help you decide on things you will and won't do, the kind of people you will hire, the kinds of clients you'll accept, and the way you live out your mission. In chapter 11, "Vision: Reality in the Future," we discussed a compelling vision, and in chapter 13, "Mission: Making a Difference," we'll get into mission. The values of this chapter tie mission with vision and set the behavioral boundaries that will govern our quest.

Mission: Making a Difference

"It's easy to make a buck. It's a lot tougher to make a difference."

~TOM BROKAW

13

As you put your values into practice, working toward your vision, you'll need a clear mission (what you are about) guiding your firm every day. As a reminder, vision and mission are related, but they don't express the same idea. Here's the difference:

Vision. Articulates what you want for your business—what it will look like in the future. A vision is idealistic: how big the company will grow and how it will be perceived by the outside world. A vision does not exist today, only in the future.

Mission. Clarifies your purpose—the value you'll offer, the services you'll provide, and the ways in which you want your clients' lives to change. A mission exists today and tomorrow.

Missions come in various forms; some are written statements, but others may not be written. The statement itself and its form are not important. The key is for the mission to capture the passion of the firm to serve others. Missions must state your defining purpose for obtaining and serving your clients and communities. Sometimes, the mission will include serving your employees and their families, as well. That purpose is timeless.

In this chapter, we'll discuss the benefits that a mission brings your accounting firm. I'll share with you many examples of well-crafted missions to which you may compare your mission. Included in this chapter will be various worksheets to guide you through the missioning process. Finally, I'll point out some pitfalls with missions and then how to build your personal mission.

"Our mission is probably similar to a lot of other firms," says Rich Caturano, managing director of RSM McGladrey, Inc., in Boston, MA, "We want to provide opportunities for our people, we want to deliver outstanding client service, and we want to make money. The goal is to be the best firm that we can, the best firm in New England. If you really want to be the best, you can't stand still. The challenges in today's marketplace are going to require us to change."

Don't be a leader who majors in minor things! That won't take your team very far. "Our mission is to serve and protect," David Deeter, founder of the top-100 firm Frazier & Deeter, LLC, in Atlanta, GA, says.

> We serve the clients' compliance needs and help them attain their financial goals. And we help protect their financial assets from outside forces, like taxation, government incursion, and competition.
>
> We've started a couple of sister companies. We have the largest wealth advisory firm in the Southeast, as far as I know. Signature FD has $1.1 billion of assets under management. We also have insurance and mortgage divisions. We are now starting a commercial insurance company. We've tried to become more of a full-service firm to our clients.

Without a mission, leaders tend to be hesitant and indecisive, and they focus on lower-priority strategies. Hesitancy and indecisiveness are not characteristics of good leaders. To develop a solid mission, an owner group must understand its real stakeholders. Naturally, the owners have a capital stake in the firm, but employees and their families also share a stake. Clients have a stake in the success of your firm, and the community has a stake in your firm.

A large percentage of companies have mission statements. Mission statements are designed to provide direction and thrust to a firm, an enduring statement of purpose. A mission statement acts as an invisible hand that guides the people in the firm. When you ask accountants in well-led firms what it is like to be part of a great accounting firm, what is most striking is the emphasis on the meaningfulness of their experience: people talk about being connected to something larger than themselves. It becomes clear that their experience as part of a great firm stands out as a singular period of life lived to the fullest.

Many leaders also define their personal missions. A personal mission is a bit different from a company mission, but the fundamental principles are the same. Writing a personal mission statement offers the opportunity to establish what's important to you. A key to developing a mission is to connect with your own unique purpose and the profound satisfaction that comes from fulfilling it. When you have your own personal mission clearly in place, then you can better determine the kind of accounting firm with which you should best be aligned.

Leader Profile: Carl George, former CEO of the national firm Clifton Gunderson LLP in Peoria, IL

From the age of 10, Carl George worked in the A&W Root Beer franchise restaurant that his father owned. Carl did everything from making the hot dogs to car hopping. As he learned to manage the A&W store, he paid his way through college and graduate school, where he obtained his master's degree. This experience in his young life gave him tremendous skills in working with people, reading their intentions, and supplying their needs.

A Ball State University graduate, Carl was always good in math. The combination of learning to deal with the public and his math skills helped him grow into one of the finest leaders in the public accounting business. In his 16 years as CEO of Clifton Gunderson LLP, Carl helped grow the firm from annual revenues of approximately $50 million to over $250 million. In addition to leading the phenomenal growth of Clifton Gunderson LLP, Carl was one of the driving forces behind the creation and development of the 360 Degrees of Financial Literacy initiative sponsored by the AICPA.

Current Clifton Gunderson LLP CEO Kris McMasters says of Carl

> He's not a leader who works over your shoulder all the time. He is willing to invest in a vision and invest in you, because he believes in you, and let you run with it. Carl led our strategic plan. That plan was very important to CG; it focused us on targeting larger opportunities and managing our operations in larger regions.
>
> When we were developing the strategy, Carl continued to emphasize the importance of keeping our mission simple, concise, and easily understood. We had a mission prior to this strategic plan that was similar to many CPAs': a thoughtful mission but one that was fairly lengthy and not something that was easily remembered. He came up with the mission that we continue to use today: Growth of our people, and growth of our clients. All else follows. That mission perfectly describes our focus as a firm; all our partners and staff know it and understand the importance of it. It was, and continues to be, the center of our strategy.

Chief operating officer David Bailey says

> One of Carl's best leadership attributes is his ability to connect with people. I observed many times in merger and acquisition meetings how quickly complete strangers would open up to Carl and trust him with their concerns and issues and, eventually, their futures. He has the gift of making people feel at ease, and as you

(continued)

(continued)

know, you can sense it when a person is genuinely interested in helping you.

Carl's ability to connect with people has not only been a valuable asset in the merger and acquisition arena but also invaluable to him in his CEO role. Partners and staff alike trust Carl because they feel the connection and know he is always putting the best interests of the firm first.

Another key example of Carl's leadership that I personally observed was his own succession plan as CEO of Clifton Gunderson. Carl put a very well-thought-out, formal process and time line in place that led to ensuring the firm selected the best candidate, Kris McMasters, to be his successor. As a result of the formal process and time line, the best candidate was selected, and the partners were very much represented in the process. Kris McMasters worked closely with Carl as the CEO-elect for the year before she actually took over the CEO reigns on June 1, 2009. Because of the formal process and time line that Carl laid out, the actual transition was very smooth and trouble free.

Carl was named one of the top 100 most influential people in accounting by *Accounting Today*, and he was chairman of the National CPA Financial Literacy Commission for five years. He was the 2007 recipient of the AICPA's Special Recognition Award for his work on the 360 Degrees of Financial Literacy initiative. Carl speaks throughout the country on the need for enhanced financial literacy for all ages and serves as a speaker or moderator at many practice management conferences.

The Benefits of a Mission

Notice that I am using the word *mission*, not *mission statement*. I think that too often, people and firms get so hung up on the wording that they fail to capture their true purpose in life or business. Developing a mission is a very challenging process, if done well. Owners of accounting firms must make a serious commitment to the process, but the benefits are well worth the effort.

The benefits of a well-thought-out mission include the following:

- ▲ *Missions build culture.* The culture of a firm emanates from the owners' purpose and their mission. The effort to modify firm culture can be daunting, but the acceptance of a firm mission can ease the task and help overcome resistance to these changes.
- ▲ *Missions build unity and balance.* A well-crafted and understood mission can rally the entire firm around a core set of values and reasons for being. Focusing on the most important purposes of a firm brings clarity to expectations.
- ▲ *Missions keep you focused.* A shared mission is the simplest way to keep everyone in the firm focused on what you need to do now. Without that day-to-day mission, people can drift away from your long-term vision without realizing it.
- ▲ *Missions help allocate resources.* No firm has all the resources it could use, whether financial, environmental, or human. Resource allocation decisions are among the hardest, but linking those decisions to a firm's mission makes them more reasoned and defensible.

▲ *Missions help stimulate ideas into action.* Undertaking the strategic planning steps of goal setting, developing objectives, and defining measures are impossible without the critical step of defining the purpose or mission. This applies to the firm as a whole, as well as to service specialties, industry niches, and individuals.

One of the guiding principles of defining your firm's mission is to allow the mission to percolate up from all your stakeholders. The more they are involved, the more they will be committed to executing your mission or purpose regularly. Of course, we must connect what matters to our clients and passion to serve.

Examples of Missions

The following are some examples of excellent missions from various businesses, including some accounting firms.

Our core purpose is to be a caring, professional firm deeply committed to our clients' success.

— Plante & Moran, PLLC

Deliver outstanding service to our clients.
Provide fulfilling careers and professional satisfaction for our people.
Achieve financial success and constantly grow.

—Caturano and Company

The Ritz-Carlton is a place where the genuine care and comfort of our guests is our highest mission. We pledge to provide the finest personal service and facilities for our guests who will always enjoy a warm, relaxed, yet refined ambience. The Ritz-Carlton experience enlivens the senses, instills well-being, and fulfills even the unexpressed wishes and needs of our guests.

—Ritz-Carlton

The mission of BKD, LLP, is to always strive for excellence in providing services to clients, create rewarding career opportunities and maintain sound professional, business and financial standards.

—BKD, LLP

To provide economy and quality minded travelers with a premier, moderate priced lodging facility which is consistently perceived as clean, comfortable, well-maintained, and attractive, staffed by friendly, attentive and efficient people.

—Courtyard by Marriott

Growth of our people and growth of our clients. All else follows.

—Clifton Gunderson LLP

Our mission is to transform the lives of accountants. We do that by helping them become better financial communicators.

—FiveStar³, LLC

Great missions capture a purpose that people care about beyond their own self-interests. They transcend time and provide a strong sense of direction for everyone involved in your business.

Clarifying *Your* Mission

As you get started, remember that a mission describes the overall purpose of the firm. If your firm already has a vision statement or writes a vision statement before developing the mission statement, use the vision statement as you begin writing the mission. Read the vision statement; then, ask yourself, "Why does this vision, this future image of our firm, exist? What is its purpose?" The purpose is often the same as the mission.

Just as we discussed about vision statements in chapter 11, "Vision: Reality in the Future," the process that your firm will use to create its mission should reflect the firm's culture. Your process may be highly analytical and rational or highly creative and divergent. Make sure that the process feels right to all participants based on your firm's personality and values.

The mission should be a concise statement of business strategy developed from the customers' perspective. It should fit with the vision for the business. The mission should answer three questions:

▲ What do we do?
▲ How do we do it?
▲ For whom do we do it?

What Do We Do?

This question should not be answered in terms of what is physically delivered to clients but by the real or psychological needs that are fulfilled when clients buy your products or services. Clients make purchase decisions for many reasons, including financial, economical, convenience, logistical, and emotional factors. Or to put it another way, think of the *benefits* you provide clients, not the features. For example, although we might physically deliver an audit report, the client's need may be for financing. We might deliver a tax return, but the client wants the convenience and assurance of having a professional provide this service.

How Do We Do It?

Most accounting firms do their actual work in similar ways, but there are important differences in how firms are organized. The most prevalent one that I've already mentioned is as individual "empires," where each partner handles a wide variety of clients, which is in contrast to firms that are organized into true expert specialty areas, such as construction practices, hospital practices, and so on. Similar issues to note would be how new accountants are trained as they advance and how new work is obtained.

For Whom Do We Do It?

The answer to this question will help you focus your marketing efforts. Though many small business owners would like to believe otherwise, not everyone is a potential client because clients will almost always have both demographic and geographic limitations. When starting out, it is generally a good idea to define the demographic characteristics (age, income, and so on) of clients who are likely to engage you, and then, define your geographic service area. In the age of the Internet, we still find that over 90 percent of an accounting firm's clients originate within a geographic area close to its office. However, as those clients relocate to other parts of the world, they tend to keep their accounting firm if the service is good. Although that phenomenon may change in the future, the original personal relationship seems to be a major factor for clients. As you grow, you can add new client groups and expand your geographic focus. The best way to begin this is to segment the largest 20 percent of your client base as the demographic that you are most well-suited to serve.

More Than One Mission? Maybe So

Most businesses have multiple client groups that engage you for different reasons. If this is the case for your firm, you can write one mission statement for each client group. For example, a construction niche group might have a mission that reads as follows:

> The mission of the construction specialty group of Smith & Smith CPAs is to give our clients the tools they need to acquire below-market financing, competitive surety bonding, and the ability to estimate and complete projects on time and on budget.

As a final thought, remember that your vision and mission are meant to help guide the business, not lock you into a particular direction. As your company grows, and the competitive environment changes, your mission may require change to include additional or different fulfilled needs, delivery systems, or customer groups. With this in mind, revisit your vision and mission periodically to determine whether changes are needed.

Leader Profile: Ray Strothman, managing partner of the local firm Strothman & Company, PSC, in Louisville, KY

Ray Strothman grew up in a German Catholic neighborhood in Louisville, KY. The nuns and teachers at St. Xavier High School provided him a crucial framework of discipline that has served him well. Ray joined Ernst & Young after graduating from Bellarmine University. He helped found Strothman & Company, PSC, in 1983, now the largest local firm in Louisville.

Strothman & Company, PSC, partner Melissa Fraser says

> Success in public accounting is 100 percent built on solid relationships, and Ray is the king of building and keeping them. Ray treats everyone he meets with genuine interest and respect. When we go to restaurants or walk in the city, it will generally take three times as long as it should because he will stop to chat with people

(continued)

(continued)

who he has gotten to know throughout the years. Ray has never been a collector of business cards. He has always just been genuinely interested in the livelihood of others.

Ray will spend an hour or two interviewing young intern hopefuls even when he has piles of work to do. He genuinely takes an interest in their futures and always puts people first. Ray is a creative thinker, and he teaches our team members how to think more out of the box. It is really fun to watch him do a second review of a tax return. He usually finds something most people wouldn't think of. He takes the time to teach our team how he found this tax savings or tax angle by walking us through his thought process. This teaches all of us to look for opportunities for the client to take advantage of various tax incentives.

Ray empowers the people with whom he works. He will allow me to lead myself into a hole if I don't ask him for help, but if I ask him, he is always there for me. He gives me the freedom to succeed or to fail, and I appreciate that because sometimes, you just have to learn from experience. I have learned to appreciate his enormous amount of wisdom through this and have learned the value of being less and more interdependent with him.

James Flynn, president of CPA Associates International says

From 2007–09, I had the privilege of working very closely with Ray Strothman when he served as North America chairman of our international association of CPA and chartered accounting firms. Ray is a strategic thinker, and during his tenure, our North America region developed a new strategic plan, including for the first time a vision statement, set of core values, and annual strategic theme that provides increased focus and direction for the region. Our new vision statement, mission statement, and core values impressed many people, and they were adopted by our entire international organization. Ray's very optimistic personality had a very positive influence on me personally and our entire association.

Ray has served on numerous boards of professional and community organizations and his alma mater.

Six Steps to Developing a Mission Statement

Exercises 13-1 through 13-6 encompass the six key exercises to developing a mission statement. Work through these exercises with your key partners, team members, and stakeholders to develop a comprehensive mission that clarifies the key what, how, and whom questions previously mentioned. Arriving at a mission statement that all stakeholders can support may require several iterations. The hardest part is usually developing a brief but descriptive statement that is unique to you, rather than a long corporate-sounding one that could apply to any firm.

Exercise 13-1: Client Statement

The client statement is the "who" of your firm; it identifies the target market and basic strategies that you will employ to reach that market. In one sentence, articulate for whom your firm is intended, using the following questions as a guideline:

Who have you identified as the target market of your firm (for example, publicly listed companies, small and midsized businesses, individuals, medical doctors, just to name a few)?

_____

_____

What activities and subsectors are they engaged in (for example, nonprofit schools, construction companies, high-net-worth individuals, bankrupt individuals and businesses)?

_____

_____

Where are they located (for example, within 50 miles of your office, regionally within 500 miles of your office, nationally, or internationally)?

_____

_____

How will you reach them (for example advertising and public relations, word of mouth, direct sales calls)?

_____

_____

_____

Exercise 13-2: Problem Statement

The problem statement is the "why" of your service line. It defines the problem that you are seeking to address. In a few lines, summarize the problem, using the following questions as a guideline:

What is the predominant need that you identified among your target population (for example investment capital formation, government grants, tax savings redeployed into capital, convenience of compliance, confidence in provider, prestige of provider)?

_____

_____

What are the constraints that the target populations face in maximizing profit in their businesses (for example adequate capital, skilled workforce, leadership, competition)?

_____

_____

If you have identified several problems, be pragmatic about which ones you can realistically tackle.

Exercise 13-3: Statement of Purpose

The statement of purpose describes "what" your firm seeks to accomplish. It answers the question, What will be the ultimate result of your work? The statement of purpose uses infinitive verbs such as *to eliminate*, *to increase*, *to improve*, and *to prevent*, indicating a change in status related to the problems that your firm is seeking to alleviate.

In defining purpose, focus on results rather than methods. Consider questions like "How is the situation going to be different because of the services of our firm?" and "What is going to change for the target clients?" For example, the purpose of a quarterly client meeting schedule would not be "to provide quality accounting services to entrepreneurs" but to "improve the financial well-being of our client entrepreneurs."

It is crucial that your statement of purpose be focused on filling a *need* in the marketplace, not your financial profits.

In one or two sentences, using infinitive verbs, describe the desired result of your firm and the problem or condition that you aim to change.

_____

_____

_____

Exercise 13-4: Business Statement

The business statement describes "how" your firm will achieve its purpose by depicting the activities that you will undertake. Most purpose statements yield several potential strategies, each one constituting a different business or service line. For example, if your statement of purpose is "to improve the financial well-being of client entrepreneurs," your business statement could be "provide regular advice around forward-thinking strategies, business training, and improved technology," among other options. Writing a business statement clarifies the means to accomplishing your purpose.

If the word *and* appears in either your statement of purpose or business statement, ask yourself if you are equally committed to both ideas connected by the word *and*. If not, acknowledge that one idea is more important by prioritizing your ideas while writing your mission statement.

Write a business statement for each statement of purpose.

_____

_____

_____

Exercise 13-5: Value Statement

The value statement communicates the "who" of your firm by embodying the beliefs and principles of your service lines from chapter 11, "Vision: Reality in the Future." Values guide team members, management, and leadership in performing their duties. Often, the values of a firm, such as commitment to lifelong learning, integrity, innovation, and excellence, are important elements in a staff member's decision to work with a firm. Ideally, the personal values of stakeholders are aligned with the values of the service lines of the firm.

Through a participatory process of developing a written value statement, staff and leadership have an opportunity to delineate the values that they want the firm to encompass and to realign them, if necessary. In addition, such a statement holds stakeholders accountable in their everyday work lives.

In a few lines, write a value statement for your firm.

_____
_____
_____

_____

Exercise 13-6: Writing a Mission Statement

Synthesize the work completed in exercises 13-1 through 13-5 into a comprehensive statement. Remember, a mission statement should be brief, consisting of just a few lines or sentences.

Problems to Keep in Mind

There are many reasons that missioning projects fail to work very well. Often, the mission is purely aspirational, and there is little or no commitment or follow-through. Some missions are not reinforced by the business owners, and their employees do not buy in to the mission. Sometimes, the employees can't even quote the mission. Some missions don't make sense, or they are not clear. One firm said, "Our mission is created by our people, and the best way to have a vision is to create one." Laughable, yes. Many firms say something like, "Our mission is to provide quality services to our clients." Although this sounds positive, this is an example of a poorly thought-out mission; it says nothing about how the firm is going to make its clients' lives better. Also, the sentiment is so generic that it could be written about many companies.

Here are some final considerations on preparing your mission:

1. When wording your mission statement, consider the firm's products, services, markets, values, and concern for public image and maybe even the priorities of activities for survival.
2. Once you have a mission statement, consider any changes that may be needed in the wording during a strategic planning process. Ensure that the mission statement makes priorities clear for leaders and team members, showing how services should be delivered.
3. When refining the statement, a useful exercise is to add or delete a word from the mission to see how this changes the scope of the mission statement and to assess whether its wording is concise.
4. Ensure that the mission statement includes sufficient description to clearly separate your firm from others.

Successful mission statements can vary widely depending on the firm, but most will have a few characteristics in common, including the following:

▲ *Simple.* Your mission statement should be simple. This doesn't mean that creating the statement is easy; it may require several drafts. But it does mean the statement should be concise. Use just enough words to capture the essence; most mission statements are too long. People want to add additional information and qualifications to the statement. Usually, these statements just confuse the reader and cloud the real meaning of your statement. Each successive draft of your statement should simplify and clarify the mission.

Carl George, former CEO of the national firm Clifton Gunderson LLP in Peoria, IL, says

We had a mission statement that was very typical of all CPA firms: quality service, client-oriented, value-added profit—all those terms in the mission statement—forward-looking, all good stuff. Back in the early 2000s we were in a retreat and I asked a question. I asked, "If you guys had to come up with two goals for CG, what would they be?" They said people and clients. So, we started playing around with it, and we came up with a mission: if you take care of your people, and you take care of your clients, everything else will fall into place.

We continued to work on it and developed another iteration: growth of our people, growth of our clients; all else follows. We wanted to have a mission that everybody remembers.

▲ *Easy to remember.* Your statements of vision and mission should be single thoughts that can easily be carried in the mind. To test the effectiveness of a mission statement in a business, ask its leaders, managers, and employees to tell you their vision and mission of the business. If they cannot instantaneously tell you both, the mission statement is of little use. The vision and mission guide the everyday activities of every person involved in the business. To be effective, your statements need to be short and simple, capturing the essence of what you want to accomplish.

▲ *Fluid process.* People agonize over writing mission statements. Granted, it is usually not an easy process. Don't cast your statements in stone when you're done; you should instead plan to update and modify them as your firm grows and changes. Once you've written your mission, use the statement for a period of time, and then, revisit it a few months or one year later. It is often easier to sharpen the statement at that time.

▲ *Unique businesses.* It is usually more important to write mission statements for unique or nontraditional businesses when the purpose of the business is not generally known. For example, if your firm only works with clients in one industry, you'll want to emphasize this feature. Or if your firm contains a large percentage of highly unique service, such as state and local tax or international consulting, this may be an opportunity to make this clear in your mission. Mission statements are important for these businesses, so that everyone involved in the business understands what the business will accomplish and how it will be done. In essence, this means keeping everyone on the same page.

Another Way to Craft a Mission Statement: The Q&A Model

There are many ways to develop mission statements. Consider the following framework as an alternative to the one mentioned previously. In the Q&A model, focus on getting answers to the following three vital questions and then building those answers into the mission statement:

1. What is our most significant client type? Who do we serve? Who makes our business worthwhile? Which part of the market is our target?
2. What is our contribution to the market? What value do we add to the customer's life and work? How are the members of our target market better because of us?
3. How do we rise above the competition in making that contribution? What distinguishes our product or service from our competitors? *What should* distinguish us? What is our unique niche?

As these questions are evaluated, a mission statement will start to evolve.

Developing a Personal Mission Statement

As part of the firm's work, you may want to encourage individuals to create their own mission statements and encourage them to tie these to the firm's statement. Share exercise 13-7 with your staff to assist them.

Exercise 13-7: Personal Mission Statement

The following steps will help you develop a personal mission statement.

Step 1: *Identify past successes.* Spend some time identifying four or five examples when you have had personal success in recent years. These successes could be at work, in your community, at home, and so on. Write them down. Try to identify whether there is a common theme or themes to these examples. Write these down.

Step 2: *Identify core values.* Develop a list of attributes that you believe identify who you are and your priorities. The list can be as long as you need. Once your list is complete, see if you can narrow your values to the five or six most important. Finally, see if you can choose the one value that is most central to you.

Step 3: *Identify contributions.* Make a list of the ways that you could make a difference. In an ideal situation, how could you contribute best to your

- ▲ family?
- ▲ firm?
- ▲ friends?
- ▲ community?

Step 4: *Identify goals.* Spend some time thinking about your priorities in life and the goals you have for yourself.

Make a list of your personal goals, perhaps in the short term (up to three years) and long term (beyond three years).

Step 5: *Write your mission statement.* Based on the first four steps and a better understanding of yourself, begin writing your personal mission statement.

Sample Personal Mission Statement Development

Here's the thought process that one person followed through the five steps shown in exercise 13-7 to develop a mission statement.

Past Successes

- ▲ Developed new service features for tax and financial planning.
- ▲ Part of a team that developed a new positioning statement for tax planning.
- ▲ Helped Rotary Club with a fund-raiser that was very successful.
- ▲ **Themes:** Successes all relate to creative problem solving and execution of a solution.

Core Values

- ▲ Hard working
- ▲ Creativity
- ▲ Problem solving
- ▲ Positive
- ▲ Honest
- ▲ Spiritual
- ▲ **Most important value:** Creativity

Identify Contributions

- ▲ **My family:** To be a leader in terms of personal outlook, compassion for others, and maintaining an ethical code; to be a good mother and loving wife; to leave the world a better place for my children and their children.
- ▲ **My firm:** To lead by example and demonstrate how innovative and problem-solving products can be successful in terms of both solving a problem and profitability and revenue generation for the firm.
- ▲ **My friends:** To always have a hand held out for my friends for them to know that they can always come to me with any problem.
- ▲ **My community:** To use my talents to give back to my community.

Identify Goals

- ▲ **Short term:** To continue my career with a progressive accounting firm that allows me to use my skills, talent, and values to achieve success.
- ▲ **Long term:** To develop other outlets for my talents and a longer-term plan for diversifying my life and achieving both professional and personal success.

Mission Statement

To live life completely, honestly, and compassionately, with a healthy dose of realism mixed with the imagination and dreams that all things are possible if one sets his or her mind to finding an answer.

Other Examples of Accounting Firm Mission Statements

Ehrhardt Keefe Steiner & Hottman PC (EKS&H) Mission

EKS&H is driven by a passion for its culture, people and clients to help business owners and executives reach their goals by delivering proactive, innovative and comprehensive solutions. We as a firm are committed to the success of our clients and guarantee their satisfaction by providing:

▲ Services that exceed their expectations.

▲ Timely service.

▲ Service at the highest quality standard.

▲ A team of experts who assist them by providing creative counsel.

▲ Personalized services and products built on business relationships.

▲ A networking base in the business community that serves their needs.

We are dedicated to creating a corporate culture where each business advisor in our firm is committed to:

▲ A spirit of fun and cooperation.

▲ The firm as a team member.

▲ Developing a sense of ownership in the firm and the profession.

▲ Quality and integrity within the firm and the profession.

▲ Helping the firm's clients succeed.

▲ Developing professionally and individually.

▲ Open and honest communication.

▲ Firm growth and profitability.

▲ An awareness and sensitivity to the individual and firm needs.

Frazier & Deeter, LLC Mission

To help our clients and people achieve success and realize their potential

CapinCrouse LLP Mission

CapinCrouse is dedicated to helping our clients operate with financial integrity so that they can dedicate themselves to fulfilling their mission.

SS&G Financial Services, Inc. Mission

SS&G provides professional services of the highest quality and value that enable our clients to thrive. We promote a collaborative culture for our employees, are committed to the communities in which we operate and continue to cultivate the entrepreneurial spirit that is the foundation of our organization.

Final Thoughts

A personal mission statement is, of course, personal, but if you want to truly see whether you have been honest in developing your personal mission statement, I suggest sharing the results of this process with one or more people who are close to you. Ask for their feedback.

Your firm may want to undertake a comissioning process to align its corporate mission with those of the partners and team members. In comissioning, each service line, department, team, and person writes his or her mission and ties it into the firm's mission. Leaders and employees talk about what is important to them and the value that they bring to their roles in the firm.

Finally, remember that neither a firm's nor an individual's mission statement should be blasted into stone. Set aside some time annually to review your firm's mission statement and your own career, goals, and mission statement, and make adjustments, as necessary.

Creating the statements previously described may seem like a lot of busy work, but if done properly, mission statements (and the goals and objectives that follow from them) can save money and time and increase the odds that your business venture will succeed. Creating these statements will help you focus on the important aspects of your business. They will force you to focus on where you are going and how and when you will get there. Think of these statements as living documents that are changed as the needs of the business change. Too often, these statements are treated as iconic relics to be stored away in a safe place. If you don't use them, you have wasted your time.

Conclusion

Missions come in all types: long and short, complex and simple. You will set yourself apart from your competitors and attract the best staff members and clients when you know what you are about: your purpose. When you can explain it to all your stakeholders, you, as a leader. will raise your game to the "big leagues."

Once you've done the solid strategic planning of setting forth your vision, values, and mission, you have done the leader's job of doing the right thing. Now, you can turn to the next topic of building management systems that will do things right. These topics are discussed in section IV, "Leading Systems," and chapters 14, "Managing Processes for Your Future Firm," and 15, "Building the Future Firm Continuously." Having both leadership and management in harmony is the ideal combination for the progressive future accounting firm.

Section 4

Leading Systems

The systems necessary to operate as a sole CPA are radically different than those needed to manage a multimillion dollar, multioffice, multipartner business. The same is true for the incremental steps along the way. One of the reasons that I wanted to interview so many founders of firms was to get them to describe for me the incremental systems that they used and the continuous changes that were employed along their growth path. Many of these leaders led their firms from start-up to being a part of the elite top 100 firms in the United States.

Section four, comprising chapters 14–15, is all about management systems and processes and their continuing changes as your firm evolves into your future. One of the biggest mistakes we witness in stagnated CPA firms is that they are still using the same processes that they used 5, 10, or 20 years ago. For example, it is common for us to encounter partners in firms that handle 300–700 clients: 280–650 small individual tax clients and 20–50 significant individual or corporate clients. In many of these firms, the managing partner carries a large book of business, and he or she is constantly challenging the other partners to do more.

Managing Processes for Your Future Firm	Building the Future Firm Continuously
Chapter 14	Chapter 15
Section Four: Leading Systems	

A visionary leader's role cannot be carried out without someone, or a group, ensuring that the processes being used in the business fit the leader, team, and leader's strategy. Too often, the antiquated processes hold the team hostage to doing things the old way and to not move forward.

Much has been written and said about managing an accounting firm. Management of an accounting practice conferences have been occurring on international, national, and state levels for more than 30 years. Jay Nisberg spoke at one of the very first in the United States and has been a leading authority on managing a firm. His book, along with coauthors Gary Shamis and Marsha Leest, *How to Manage Your Accounting Practice: Taking Your Firm from Chaos to Consensus*, is an excellent resource on this vital subject. David Maister's *Managing the Professional Service Firm* has been the management bible on this topic for over 15 years. This section is not designed to cover all the topics that are already covered very well in these other forums, but I will put management in context with leadership to illustrate the high value that great management offers the accounting firm.

Napoleon quipped, "An army marches on its stomach." No matter how great a leader may be, without processes, supplies, and management, the best defined vision will fail. Leaders must rely on good managers to understand and carry out the vision of the firm within the values adopted by the organization. Managers and leaders need efficient, repeatable processes to ensure success. If you don't have a system to provide structure, each decision becomes a "new" issue. By having a systematic approach to how you do things, you can more quickly learn from experience and implement your initiatives more successfully and easily. Most importantly, the processes must support the leader, team, and strategy. The people and strategy must not be slaves to the processes.

During the first 13 chapters of this book, we covered the leadership aspects of doing the right things. Management systems will help the leader actually accomplish his or her vision by doing things right. When leaders and managers work together, potential business harmony and synergy can be realized. Without such harmony, owners will constantly grapple with organizational friction that will impede growth.

Leader Profile: **Lisa Cines, Office Managing Partner, Rockville, of the megaregional firm Dixon Hughes Goodman LLP**

Lisa Cines became a leader because she enjoys helping other people develop. As a senior in high school, she became a teacher's assistant in a school for children with discipline problems. Lisa was struck by how much progress she could make by working with each child on a personal level. Lisa's mother was a teacher, so teaching has been in her DNA. During her years at the University of Maryland, she worked at a small accounting firm and really enjoyed seeing the inside of business.

Lisa describes the operations of her firm like an orchestra playing beautiful music, each team member playing his or her role in concert with the others. She says

> I always reflect on the last few weeks of busy season, when we deliver 3,000 tax returns, is just the orchestra playing because it's all flowing. The accountants are doing what they are supposed to be doing, the reviewers are doing what they

are supposed to be doing, the preparers are doing what they are supposed to be doing, and it's just flowing. And that's what allows for the growth in that the infra-structure is in place and everything is capable of doing it.

Aronson partner Hope Lane says of Lisa

I've worked with Lisa for a long time, and she's been my mentor and has helped me to be a better leader and to understand what leading meant. Over the years, there were things that she said that didn't always make sense to me at the time.

Recently I said, "Lisa, I finally understand what you meant when you told me, 'I can't let the gap between the strongest and the weakest change.'

I now lead a group of consultants, and I am mentoring an emerging leader. We're very innovative and take a lot of initiative. What I'm hearing from this protégé that I'm mentoring is, "Why do we always have to be the ones doing this? Why isn't anyone else doing these events?"

And so, that was telling to me that I had let the gap get too big. What was hap-pening was that by letting the stronger get stronger, I was getting resentment from them that I had not forced the weaker ones to get stronger at the same pace.

At the same time, I saw evidence in the weaker ones that they were complacent. What I had breached was letting the gap get bigger instead of working to keep it the same. I was feeding into the stronger, and I needed to work hard on the weaker. And that was when I finally understood what she was talking about and why that was so important.

When I first joined the firm, the partners would do these industry speaking events. I remember standing at the back of the room and saying to Lisa, "You'll never get me up there," pointing to the partner that was talking.

She said, "You just wait."

Now, the group that I lead did 25 speaking engagements in 2010, and I do my share.

I was very hesitant about taking on this new leading consulting role because I had built another whole practice. I had personally built the technical expertise upon which I built a practice area, and it was running smoothly. And then, I was asked to turn that over to somebody else who I was mentoring and to take over leading a broader consulting practice area, which had no definition behind it, and no one knew what it should be. They just knew we needed it. So, there were no rules.

I kept letting the fact that there was no rulebook—and I didn't have the techni-cal expertise—stand in my way. I was okay with building technical knowledge and then building a practice on top of that. Lisa was my biggest mentor through this, and she showed me how to be a leader without being the technical expert. I didn't know what that looked like. I didn't know how I could possibly do that. How can I go from building it on what I knew but I couldn't understand what I didn't necessarily know and what I might need to find in identifying others. Now, having learned to lead, I tell people, "I am more knowledgeable and less expert every single day." But I have a team of technical experts.

It was in that experience that she taught me that I could live in a state of con-stant uncomfortableness.

Lisa now serves as Aronson's officer in charge of business and corporate devel-opment. She served as the firm's managing officer for nine years, and under Lisa's

(continued)

(continued)

leadership, the firm was named to *INSIDE Public Accounting's* top 25 best-of-the-best list for the years 2002–09.

Before moving into firm management, she served as a partner in Aronson LLC's Government & Technology Services Group, specializing in accounting, tax, and consulting services, with a special emphasis on implementing high-level business plans and strategies.

Because of her reputation within the profession, Lisa is frequently asked to make presentations to various groups of accounting professionals, and she is an active participant in many industry organizations and community groups. Lisa was a member of the board of directors of the AICPA from 2006–09, after having previously served on the AICPA Council. Her efforts have been recognized by several media and industry outlets, and in 2005, she was named one of the *Washington Business Journal's* 25 women who mean business.

Lisa is a member of the AICPA Board of Examiners and serves on the boards of several civic and business organizations.

The best leaders recognize that managing is a different role than serving clients with accounting, tax, or consulting services. Management is a specific skill that requires training, experience, and dedication. One of the most difficult issues that confronts growing firms is expecting excellent management from part timers. After my son, at age 10, suffered a knee injury playing football, he told me that when he grew up, he wanted to be a quarterback and part-time bone doctor. I still chuckle at that childish remark, and yet, that is the challenge for many CPAs: they want to spend most of their time serving clients and also be part-time managers, which is very difficult.

Jim DeMartini, managing partner of the top-100 firm Seiler LLP in Redwood City, CA, explains, "One of the best decisions we made was off loading most of our management responsibilities to a chief operating officer who is a professional manager." Many small firms take a step toward hiring a firm administrator, which will ease the growth pangs for a while.

As you can determine, I believe that good management is a subset of good leadership. Without management, a leader will fail every time, but management may not be the leader's strength. In chapters 14–15, we will discuss the role of the manager; some of the metrics of running an accounting firm; and most importantly, a challenge to continuous improvement in all the processes and procedures. The most important point I want to make is that management, processes, and procedures are the tools of great leaders, not the other way around. I believe that many accounting firms are overmanaged and underled, which can be disastrous for a firm. You could fall into the trap of doing the wrong things in the right way, leading you to be very efficient in a poorly conceived direction.

Managing Processes for Your Future Firm

"Quality is not an act, it is a habit."

~ARISTOTLE

As pointed out in earlier chapters, the distinction between leaders and managers is that leaders set the vision for what the firm does, and managers get the work done through team members. Of course, leaders do some managing, and most managers are building their firms toward the future. However, when leaders get caught up in managing, they tend to ignore setting the direction for the firm, and it becomes detached from its vision and mission. Similarly, when managers only do work or micromanage others, they tend to ignore training and developing others, and their scope of work influence is limited to what they do themselves. Jim DeMartini, managing partner of the top-100 firm Seiler LLP in Redwood City, CA, says, "I think that accounting firms give way too much training to professional accountants on management. I believe that firms should employ full-time managers who have that skill set."

> This chapter will cover the importance of good management to leadership. Leaders can have good self and staff leadership but still fail without good management. Leaders can have a compelling vision and mission but still not move forward without good management. In this chapter, I'll touch on the key processes and metrics necessary for managing an accounting firm. Many books and seminars are devoted to the management of accounting firm. What I am attempting to do in this chapter is place management in its proper context with leading—managing follows strategy.

Setting up Business Processes

Leaders can only do their jobs well when good managers ensure that processes and projects are carried out within the policies and values of the organization. Great managers make great leaders possible. Without great managers, leaders lose focus and momentum. Without great managers, leaders and their firms will be constantly frustrated in growing their talented people and serving the needs of their clients. Bill Haller, managing partner of the national firm CapinCrouse LLP in Indianapolis, IN, says

> I can't really carry out my strategy unless I have these executives deployed doing practice development, coaching, running systems, and building infrastructures for the firm. I meet with our process owners quarterly to see how they are doing against their blueprints. We are very much a goal-oriented firm that breaks down the business plan and parcels it out to all the players.

According to Charly Weinstein, CEO of the megaregional firm EisnerAmper LLP in New York City, NY

> We have great managers in all aspects of the firm, so I don't have to spend a lot of time on the metrics of the business. I watch it and make sure it's okay. If something sticks out, I try to jump right on it quickly. But we have good people in place who do the traditional management things. I can focus on our direction, leading our up-and-coming leaders and making good investments in people.

Jim DeMartini adds

> When we introduced the COO here, there was plenty of friction around the idea that partners would be asked to cede their administrative responsibilities. It took a lot of cajoling

and, frankly, a little bit of table slamming every once in a while to kind of get everybody to the point where they now realize that it's probably the best thing we ever did, and the end result is great for them. They are actually the ultimate beneficiaries of this because they don't burn time doing things that were not highest and best use. And the actual processes and the results are far superior to what existed before. Bottom line: the clients end up getting overall better service.

A business process is a way of systematizing and then ensuring that all the routines in your firm flow well and reliably; it defines steps to take, inputs to respond to, and the appropriate actions to take for any given decision.

Many of the world's biggest corporate failures can be traced to poor management of their processes. MCI WorldCom's former leader had a powerful vision for the consolidation of telecommunications in the 1980s and 1990s. He was a bright, energetic, compelling leader, but his company failed. One of the major reasons was a failure to integrate its acquisitions under a common management structure. It was reported that at its peak, MCI was using approximately 50 different billing and collections systems that did not work together. If you were a customer of MCI, you may have been billed several times for the same service, or you may not have been billed at all. As a result, cash flow eroded, and the firm's top leaders and managers began to fabricate their reported numbers. They ended up bankrupting MCI and serving time in prison—a sad ending to a rising star of a company.

Very few accounting firms will ever end up like MCI, but I wonder how many suffer from a lack of key business processes. How many multiple-partner firms have different processes to support each partner? How many multiple-office firms have different processes, software, hardware, employee policies, accounting, auditing, or tax processes for each office?

We see it all the time in our consulting practice: firms that plateau in their growth. The owners have enjoyed some growth but are frustrated in moving the firm to the next level. They seem to hit a ceiling of complexity. Their management is designed for the firm of the past rather than the firm of the future. The processes that were useful to the old firm will not sustain the new multimillion dollar firm.

 As a firm progresses through various stages of growth, managers must always be building processes that will be useful to the next-level firm.

Most of the issues that we encounter are with processes that were useful in start-up mode. As a firm grows, the owners must be willing to adopt policies and procedures that support a business, rather than a sole practitioner. As a firm grows, the biggest frustration to growing is the unwillingness of partners to give up their personal preferences, so the work can be done faster and better in a more uniform manner.

Leader Profile: Sam Coulter, founder and president of the local firm Coulter & Justus, P.C., in Knoxville, TN

Sam Coulter, founder and president of Coulter & Justus, P.C., in Knoxville, TN, learned his leadership style from farming. Sam grew up on the family farm, and he believes that leadership is about growing people. His firm has been selected by *INISDE Public Accounting* newsletter as one of their best of the best in the United States. Sam and cofounding partner Ron Justus became partners of Ernst & Young (E&Y) then purchased their Knoxville office in the mid-1990s.

Coulter & Justus, P.C., partner Mike Parton says

> Sam Coulter is a great example of a leader who approaches issues with calm and careful consideration. Even in the midst of an emotional issue or discussion, he has the ability to remain patient while others are not, to keep the discussion focused while others get carried away, and to present opportunities for solutions that are practical and consider all parties involved.

This patience came from Sam's farming experience. "Too many people act more like a mechanic and try to fix people," Sam says.

> This turns people away from a potential leader because people do not want to be fixed. However, people do want to grow and thrive and prosper. So, it is my job to create a fertile environment where people can be challenged and grow. And sometimes, I do have to spread a little fertilizer or prune a vine to encourage growth, but leadership requires patience.

"Sam has always had the ability to be calm in the midst of a storm," says Ron Justus. "He does not get excited and lose his temper or get overly exuberant. This is particularly beneficial when things get heated up, as they sometimes do over partner issues."

Sam began his public accounting career in 1969 after receiving his BS in business administration from the University of Tennessee, Knoxville. His experience in public accounting includes serving clients in manufacturing, retail, wholesale, and health care. He also provided extensive services to public companies, including assisting them in the registration process. As a partner with E&Y, he served on the Southeast Region Technical Committee and the National Retail Committee. He also served as a member of a special national task force to recommend changes in accounting for income taxes.

Sam has held numerous leadership positions in the community, including treasurer of the Knoxville Salvation Army and president of the Knoxville Rotary Club.

Just like Sam Coulter, founder and president of the local firm Coulter & Justus, P.C., in Knoxville, TN, describes in his farming background, managing can sometimes feel mundane and repetitive. Every month, managers repeat some of the same processes: collecting the bills, paying the invoices, hiring new staff members, scheduling engagements, giving performance reviews, and on and on. In Jim Collins's book, *Good to Great: Why Some Companies Make the Leap…and Others Don't*, the level 5 leaders possessed a dogged determination to get things done. This was their way of leading the managers who actually built and operated the day-to-day processes, key performance indicators (KPIs), and projects. And just like on Sam's farm, every day, there is management work to be done. In the book *Faster Cheaper Better: The 9 Levers for Transforming How Work Gets Done*, coauthor Michael Hammer says

> Even the most mundane work can be given meaning and value for those who perform it if they understand how it benefits, even in the simplest of ways, the lives of others …. A late classical Jewish text contains a paean to the spiritual value of work: "Precious is work, for of all the creatures that God created in the world, He granted work only to humankind."

Advantages to Structured Procedures

There are many benefits of regularly updating and standardizing business processes for the firm of the future, rather than the firm of the past. Some are described in the following sections.

More Consistent Results

Implementing standard processes makes the outcome of your work more predictable. Think about it: if you follow the same steps every time you're faced with a routine problem, then your outcomes will also become routine. The firms that allow partners to perform work using their own preferred systems dramatically limit their potential growth. Clients want consistency from your firm, and team members respond much better when there is one system for doing all work.

Bill Gates said

> Virtually every company will be going out and empowering their workers with a certain set of tools, and the big difference in how much value is received from that will be how much the company steps back and really thinks through their business processes … thinking through how their business can change, how their project management, their customer feedback, their planning cycles can be quite different than they ever were before.

A few years ago, a 10-partner firm we consulted with was processing 7,000 individual tax returns. The partners were still doing those returns in the same manner they did them when the firm had been founded 25 years earlier. Each partner met with the client, assigned the work to a preparer, consulted with the preparer, acted as a go-between with the client, reviewed and signed the return, and either met with or discussed the return with the client over the phone.

To improve procedures, in a nutshell, this firm redesigned its processing of tax returns toward the firm of the future, away from the way it had done it 25 years ago. In the new firm, processes like those used by volume outsourcers were adopted. Tax managers and preparers met with clients, and managers reviewed and signed over 6,500 returns. The client turnaround improved by several weeks, profits went way up, and busy-season stress was dramatically reduced.

Measurable Outcomes

When you have a standard process producing predictable results, then you can effectively quantify and measure the quality of the results that you produce; when you don't follow a process, and the results are unpredictable, then the task of measuring the quality of your output is virtually impossible. In the client situation previously mentioned, the firm had 10 different processes because each partner was the one who determined his or her own process.

Because the partners did the intake, review, and signing, there was no measurable quality standard—there were 10. Once the new process was in place, it allowed the tax compliance partner to ensure that the same quality existed for each preparer and manager.

Training for Team Members Improves

Having a standard business process significantly reduces the complexity of training other associates simply because you already have a tested, proven process that produces quality results when followed. Again, referring to the previous client example, before the firm changed, the managers and preparers had to learn how each partner wanted his or her work done. Once the new systems were put into place, there became only one way. This is the whole philosophy behind the profitability of companies like H&R Block, Southwest Airlines, and Walmart: predictable, repeatable processes.

John Wright, managing partner of the top-100 firm Padgett Stratemann & Co. of San Antonio, TX, says

> Business development is everybody's responsibility, especially our leaders. The primary responsibilities I have are recognizing in the marketplace where services need to be delivered, recognizing the skill sets we have in our firm to deliver those services, identifying the gaps in those, and leading the charge to fill those gaps to build the team to be able to deliver. Then, we focus on having the systems in place for executing consistent client service.

Benefits of Creating the Process

The act of defining a business process is in itself extremely helpful because it allows you to uncover the flaws in your current systems. Breaking your processes down to their components helps you look at them with fresh eyes. You can refine your business methods without incurring the cost and lengthy duration of trial and error.

Establish Standards, Policies, and Procedures

Your firm likely needs standards for things as simple as entering time into the billing system and for more complicated issues, such as tax processing, audit file retention, and virtual operations. Write down as many policies and procedures as you can, and train each person in the firm. Appendixes A, "Affinity Diagram"; B, "Four Whys"; and C, "Flowchart," have examples of affinity diagrams and flowcharts that will help you document your processes. Flowcharting is a great way to document your procedures in the form of a picture, and of course, a picture can be worth a thousand words. Managers can then hold employees responsible for meeting the clear standards.

Kris McMasters, CEO of the national firm Clifton Gunderson LLP in Peoria, IL, says, "I have three people who work for me directly. My job is to set the vision for them, to set their goals and their expectations to keep them on track, and provide that vision to our board. I spend a lot of time communicating both with our employees and communicating with our partners."

Improve the Consistency of the Client Experience

All standards, policies, and procedures must consider both the external client and the internal one (employees). Client loyalty—their willingness to engage you for more services when needed and to refer you when they have the opportunity—will depend on both extraordinary bedside manner and the proactivity and responsiveness you have in turning around their engagement on time and on budget. Good processes and procedures increase the chances of accuracy and quality.

A few years ago, one of our consultants went to work with a major investment firm. Because he was an attorney, his role was to meet with clients of the firm who had a net worth of over $10 million and provide estate planning for them. He was assigned a 7-state territory, which covered approximately 20 offices of the firm. He was to meet with the large clients, entertain them, and sell them the investment services and products of this firm.

Before he could get reimbursed for his travel and entertainment expenses, he had to submit his expense report. The firm did not provide him an expense advance, but that wasn't the big issue. The big problem came in the manner he was reimbursed. Before he could recover his money, he had to file an expense report and include a copy of the canceled check showing that he had already paid the expense before the firm would pay for his entertainment. The consequence of this process totally subverted the strategy to entertain clients of the firm.

Standardizing Work-Flow Management

The idea of controlling the flow of business processes and other work dates back to the construction of the pyramids, but it was not until the 1980s that the modern concept of work-flow management for service firms began to come into vogue.

How a firm will assess the work flow and convert that flow to an automated process will differ with each firm, but there are three basic rules:

1. *Adapt the process to the firm's existing work flow.* Nothing is more disruptive to a firm than a sudden change in the way processes are handled. When you implement a new process, be sensitive to the existing work flow, even if it is manual. Adapt the process to the firm, rather than the other way around. The process of altering how work flows through the office is generally called *business process engineering*.
2. *Don't sacrifice human interactions.* One of the most enduring criticisms of work-flow automation, from the efficiency studies of the 1920s to today's sophisticated digital systems, is that they disrupt long-standing human relationships. Administrative staff who used to handle tasks are displaced by technology. Partners communicate by e-mail, rather than in person. Clients

are sent to a portal, rather than paid a personal visit. Work-flow management does not require the end of these critical, personal relationships, and it should not interfere with them. When technology disrupts human interactions, take care that alternate means of human contact, such as client meetings, staff meetings, personal lunches, and team-building events, are used to keep the interactions vital.

3. *Save time, not money.* The two are, in fact, closely related, but if the focus on assessing work flow is simply to cut costs and corners, then the result will likely be poorer service to clients. The goal should be to reduce waste and the time needed to turn tasks around, two goals that clients and accountants can agree upon.

Once the firm understands how work currently flows from the client to the staff and back to the client, it is time to address the software and hardware of work-flow management. As CEO of the regional firm Hill, Barth & King, LLC (HBK), in Boardman, OH, Chris Allegretti devotes a lot of effort to figuring out the best way to service the firm's clients. "I spend a lot of time reassigning clients. We pay particular attention to 'A' clients because of the 80/20 rule that about 80 percent of our revenue comes from about 20 percent of our clients. And we want to make sure that those 20 percent of our clients are getting our best effort."

Process Should Follow Strategy

Really, there is no reason *not* to incorporate processes into your business activities; they make it easier to train new employees, help you uncover errors in your current routines, help make activity outcomes more predictable, and enable you to effectively measure the quality of your output.

An important point is that companies should be as concerned about how a business achieves its financial results as they are about whether it meets its financial targets. Value drivers help companies understand the reasons for their current performance and how their future performance will likely develop. To understand value drivers, managers must have performance measurement systems designed to capture information on all aspects of the business, not just the financial results. A performance measurement system comprised of multiple measures allows managers to better monitor employees' actions and guide firm behavior.

Leader Profile: Dan Schreiber, managing partner of the local firm JGD & Associates LLP in San Diego, CA

Dan Schreiber grew up in Green Bay, WI, and played many different sports. He was captain of most of the sports teams and believes that his leadership skill is mostly a God-given talent.

Dan says

One of the guys who really helped me when I first got into public accounting was Wally Steinhoff. He was the managing partner of the first firm where I had an internship. I was always impressed by his ability and style and how he tried to always engage everybody, challenge everyone, and throw out the vision of where they wanted the firm to go at that particular time.

He was always out there saying, "This is where we're going to be." It was part of every meeting that I was ever a part of with that firm. It was amazing, and I've always remembered how important it is to continue to cast the vision of where we want to go.

In order to achieve this vision, we learned to create standard systems, processes, and policies. Without these standards, everyone just operated on his own.

JGD & Associates LLP has been selected as one of the best-of-the-best accounting firms in the United States by *INSIDE Public Accounting* newsletter. "In our firm, although I am a managing partner, in a lot of ways, it tends to be more of an administrator role from time to time, where I'm just trying to gather agreement on key issues," Dan says.

JGD & Associates LLP partner David Brzezniak says

Dan certainly remains calm during stressful situations. I think that's really important. He very seldom displays any anger or loses control of his emotions. He is a steady, calming influence despite being surrounded by differing opinions, which can be really difficult when we'll have meetings or situations where everyone thinks we should do something different. He's very steady and very adept at trying to get everybody to go in the right direction—only in one direction. And he's not afraid to try different approaches in order to strive for improvement.

As we were buying out the firm from the founders a few years ago, Dan was very good at analyzing the financial impact and helped us understand what the risks were. And I think that was probably his greatest contribution: to help stick to a disciplined plan to attack the problem and to try to resolve it and move forward.

JGD & Associates LLP partners have guided their firm to become one of the best managed in the United States by their intense attention to operating to strong metrics and key performance indicators.

In an accounting firm, poor processes directly affect the efficiency of operations and the ability of team members to serve clients. They can distract accountants and staff from doing their jobs and cause mistakes. Unnecessary mistakes delay jobs and create significant cost overruns. Cost overruns, delays, and mistakes all decrease the profitability of the firm.

Manage to a Written Strategic Plan

Too often, firms manage to a budget or last year's numbers, rather than a strategic plan. At one level, owners should view their roles as investment managers, investing dollars in production, marketing, training, technology, and innovation and seeing a return from those investments. Managing to a strategy requires identifying the firm's objectives and its expected returns on initiatives, assignments, and due dates. Then, managers must be held accountable for investing those dollars wisely.

In some of our consulting, we help firms develop a strategic vision of where they want to go in 3–5 years and prepare a series of action steps for each year. We then help the firm break down the yearly actions into manageable 90–120-day chunks that are assigned to team leaders on their performance scorecards. All performance scorecards, which are fully described in chapter 8, "Accountability: Trust but Verify," use certain generic measures. These generic measures tend to be core outcome measures that reflect the common goals of many strategies, as well as similar structures across segments of the firm. This combines the strategic vision of the firm and accountability on a steady basis.

Ray Strothman, managing partner of the local firm Strothman & Company, PSC, in Louisville, KY, tells

> We grew to a point about nine years ago that I hired a chief operating officer [COO]. The COO was to help with the administrative running of the firm. The first person I hired was an accountant/controller type, and she did an excellent job. She got everything organized, and it worked really well; then, she decided to leave after about five years. One of my partners, Mellissa Frasier, is now our COO, and she does an exceptional job of recruiting, retaining, and accountability.

Management for the Future

In an accounting firm, manager roles should be designed for the firm of the future, rather than the firm of the past. In other words, manager roles in the $1 million firm should be designed for the $3 million firm. One of the first pure manager roles that most firms find very useful is the professional firm administrator. We see many firms at the $1 million revenue level that can grow very well into the $3 million level with a well-qualified person to handle accounting, billing, collections, payroll, supervision of the administrative staff, coordinating human resources functions, and many other functions. Firms that split these functions among the partners on a part-time basis get low-grade results that stymie growth and reduce the attention on client service.

Once an accounting firm is looking to grow beyond $8 million, a full-time COO can be very useful. At some point, a marketing manager, a CFO, industry service-line managers, an audit department manager, tax department managers, and client accounting managers are appropriate. They key decision is, Will we need this manager when we double our revenues? If so, then we need the person now. Always be looking forward, not back.

Lisa Cines, office managing partner, Rockville, of the megaregional firm Dixon Hughes Goodman LLP, adds

> I have three senior leaders; there's a CFO, there is a senior HR professional, and there is a gentleman who has a unique split in both IT and marketing. We have coined the phrase Aronson 2.0, and it means every area of the firm should be doing what is necessary to prepare to double our size. And that's what those three people are responsible for within their departments.

The Balanced Scorecard Framework

The performance (balanced) scorecard discussed in chapter 8 is designed to translate the firm's strategy and mission into measures that managers can use to manage the organization. The scorecards contain both generic and unique measures that are tailored to the firm's competitive strategy. The following generic measures show up in most firms' scorecards:

▲ Staff delegation, leverage, and training
▲ Customer satisfaction and loyalty
▲ New client development
▲ Profitability

These measures typically fall under four hierarchical perspectives: learning and growth, internal business processes, customer, and financial. When building strategy maps, we can see the clear cause–and–effect relationships between different perspectives. For example, a well-trained staff will improve customer satisfaction, which leads to increased retention and profits.

Based on its strategic direction, every firm will have some unique measures that are included on the scorecard:

▲ Share of industry market
▲ Percentage of realization of standard revenue
▲ Utilization of staff
▲ Gaining additional skill
▲ Penetrating and developing a new market

Ensuring meaningful accountability on these measures or the ones that your firm uses requires management, and there is a crisis of undermanagement in most accounting firms. In his book *It's Okay to Be the Boss: The Step-by-Step Guide to Becoming the Manager Your Employees Need*, Bruce Tulgan explains how many leaders and managers struggle with the entire concept of management. Many professional accountants are not trained and do not want to be involved in management; they just want to serve their clients. Management is a completely different skill set from the profession of accounting. Your firm's managers need to become experts in management, not just accounting.

Debbie Lambert, managing partner of the top-100 multioffice firm Johnson Lambert & Co. LLP in Raleigh, NC, says

> I find that many accountants really prefer specified processes. In leadership, there is no checklist, and you must make decisions in real time. Our firm's technical committee is led by two partners. These people not only set the quality standards of our practice, but they also deal with things like our client communications. They deal with the infrastructure that supports how we're doing our audits and with questions that arise in our work or from our

clients. If a question comes up in the field that's relevant to everybody else (since we audit 350 insurance companies), then it's this group's role to make sure we have a good answer.

We have several functions that report to the CFO for administrative purposes. In addition to our controller, our marketing and HR directors report to the CFO.

Before you are trained in it, management may seem like one of those mysterious talents that you are or aren't born with. You'll hear people say, "Oh, he's good with people," or "His staff would walk on water for him." And you hear the opposite kind of remark, as well, such as, "My boss is such a jerk." These vague kinds of remarks can make it sound like managing people is an inherent skill or deficit, but you can learn to manage people and use systems that make your expectations clear to them.

When you're using the balanced (performance) scorecard system, you will select particular measurements that matter to your firm about individual and collective performance. These KPI are valuable tools in the hands of managers using a scorecard system to manage projects and processes.

Selecting the Right KPIs

The ideal KPI would be easily standardized; viewed as valuable by all leaders, owners, and managers; and readily computable, meaning firms already have the data at hand or could easily get it. For the accounting industry, the most relevant and telling KPIs would provide insight into daily and weekly operations, sales, utilization of staff, and client service. By examining these KPIs, users can easily get a comprehensive view of the firm across a wide range of business operations. Viewed alone, each of these indicators could be misleading about the future of the firm. Hugh Parker, executive partner of the regional firm Horne LLP in Jackson, MS, says, "Processes and systems need to have flags that jump up if there is a problem."

KPIs such as revenue per client, revenue per owner, revenue per employee, realization per client and per owner, and utilization of each staff member help management make informed decisions that can lead to higher cash flow and earnings. Because management relies on these measures to guide business decisions, the information tends to be reliable and verifiable within an organization.

Most data that ultimately shows up in a KPI is information that firm owners already have or should have at their fingertips. But how many KPIs are too many, and how many are too few? Firms are not going to use 100 different indexes. Instead, a few carefully selected KPIs could create the indicators that stakeholders need to get a good sense of future performance.

Gary Shamis, Jay Nisberg, and Marsha Leest, in their book *How to Manage Your Accounting Practice: Taking our Firm from Chaos to Consensus*, say "Accounting firms can't charge the same fee to every client or for the same type of engagement." They discuss various ways to calculate profit and productivity using utilization, realization, and margin rates. In addition to those three, I believe that two other KPIs are needed as a baseline to create a comprehensive set of performance indicators for accounting firms. Adding my two to Shamis's, Nisberg's, and Leest's three, I like to use the acronym LUBRM, which stands for leverage, utilization, billing rate, realization, and margin. Each of these is described subsequently:

1. *Leverage.* The total number of nonowner employees divided by the number of owners. This index recognizes the owner's ability to attract and retain talent to whom work can be delegated. The higher the leverage, the more revenue each owner can manage. The average midsized firm may have a 5:1 or 7:1 ratio, yet you will find many of the best-managed firms are able to achieve greater than 10:1 ratios.

2. *Utilization KPIs.* Compare a firm's billable hours to total worked hours. Utilization KPIs can indicate an excess or shortage of capacity, an inappropriate percentage of time being spent on administrative activities by fee earners, or work that is being inappropriately leveraged within the firm.

3. *Billing rate.* Usually a blended rate for all billed hours divided into the total revenue. This can be calculated for various engagements and various months or seasons of the year.

4. *Realization KPIs.* Measure write-downs (produced billable fees not billed), net fees (gross fees less write-downs), realization percentage (net fees divided by gross fees), net fees per partner, and net fees per full-time employee (net fees divided by total full-time employees). If a firm's write-offs are too large, you may be discounting work in order to win it. If write-offs are too low, it is usually an indication that the market will bear a higher fee for your services.

5. *Margin KPIs.* Measure profitability and efficiency of operations. "Cash is king," says Tony Argiz, founder, CEO, and managing partner of the megaregional firm Morrison, Brown, Argiz & Farra, LLP, in Miami, FL. "We don't pay much attention to accrual accounting in our firm, and that is why we have some of the lowest WIP and AR in the profession." Keeping a close eye on the efficiency and effectiveness of billing and collection activities is critical.

Standardizing KPIs

According to Kelly Platt, editor of *INSIDE Public Accounting*

> Unfortunately, not all accounting firms use the same internal KPIs to measure performance. Moreover, the right KPI for one firm may not be appropriate for another (due to size, niche, or market) or as easy to generate. Even those companies that use similar measures may not be using the same underlying definitions that allow for comparisons in the marketplace. We have selected standard measures that will not unduly burden the firms. This allows us to report these numbers in comparison to others, so they get real value from our annual benchmarking service.

We have found the *INSIDE Public Accounting* annual benchmarking survey to be one of the most valuable tools we use to help firms set the right KPIs and measure themselves against the industry standard. If you are not benchmarking yourself, make it a point today to reach out to *INSIDE Public Accounting*, and join their survey team next year.

Bill Haller operates his firm from a remote office using a series of KPIs. He says, "Every month, I get a report by office by person of all the returned client surveys, the scores for each office. Every client that returns one with a three (out of a possible five) is sent to every partner in that office." Bill's firm believes that its most important KPI is client loyalty, so it monitors client loyalty at the granular level. Client loyalty is a predictor of future revenue.

By designing your own predictive KPIs, you can begin to guide your firm by looking forward, rather than in the rearview mirror. The use of KPIs can help an accounting firm's leaders identify, investigate, and manage emerging trends in key business activities in a timely fashion. Most likely, firm administrators are already tracking some key metrics; however, these metrics might not be the most meaningful for your firm or might not be analyzed sufficiently to interpret trends and identify root causes.

Remember to design KPIs that are easy to gather, report, and understand. The goal is not to do fancy statistical analyses but to have quick, accurate ways to track your firm's progress in real time. Generally, KPIs for accounting firms measure productivity of the fee earners, value delivered to the client, producer efficiency, and the profitability and efficiency of firm infrastructure. When choosing KPIs, managers must ask, What are the key drivers of our practice, and how can we best track and manage them?

It is important for firms to understand how well their current structures can support a financial return that allows the firms to reward their people and invest in continuing practice development. These metrics include salaries and benefits/net fees, other operating expenses/net fees, days in accounts receivable (average AAR/(net fee/365), days in unbilled work in progress (WIP) (average unbilled WIP/(net fees/365), collection percentage (fees collected/fees billed), average unbilled WIP/gross fees, and a listing of incurred but unpaid expenses.

Rich Caturano, managing director of RSM McGladrey, Inc., in Boston, MA, says

> We have whittled our accounts receivable down to 45 days of sales. In our old firm, we never thought we could do it. But, we've learned you build an advance, and you get the client to pay you in advance before you start the work. We thought we could never get away with that with our clients. Well, you know what? It wasn't easy, but 8 years later, 70 percent of our clients are billed that way now.

Once a firm has established its KPIs, it can track and analyze trends. Benchmarks and interrelationships can be established and used to set goals. Then, administrators and managing partners can read between the lines to assess difficult-to-measure activities like leadership development and client satisfaction. This gives you a chance to correct behaviors or activities that are counterproductive to your firm's strategic and financial goals. Don't try to track all possible KPIs; you will get hopelessly bogged down in detail. Pick the four or five that you find most useful.

Business Process Management Overview

Many of the accounting firm leaders I interviewed for this book took exception to management expert Peter Drucker's view that businesses only have three main functions. In addition to Drucker's marketing, production, and innovation, some of them added firm governance and finance. As you look into each area that requires management, you will also find many subareas that will need their own brands of management. For example, almost every firm has a manager of assurance and accounting, as well as a manager for tax.

Business process management (BPM) is a management approach focused on aligning all aspects of an accounting firm with the wants and needs of its clients. It is a holistic management approach that promotes business effectiveness and efficiency while striving for innovation, flexibility, and integration with technology.

BPM attempts to continuously improve processes. It could therefore be described as a process optimization process. It is argued that BPM enables organizations to be more efficient, effective, and capable of change than a functionally focused, traditional hierarchical management approach.

A business process is a collection of related, structured activities that produce a service or product that meets the needs of a client. These processes are critical to any organization because they generate revenue and often represent a significant proportion of costs. As a managerial approach, BPM considers processes to be strategic assets of an organization that must be understood, managed, and improved to deliver value-added products and services to clients.

BPM Activities

BPM activities can be grouped into five categories: design, modeling, execution, measuring, and optimization. Each of these is described subsequently.

Design

Process design encompasses both the identification of existing processes and the design of "to-be" processes. Areas of focus include representation of the process flow, the actors within it, alerts and notifications, escalations, standard operating procedures, service level agreements, and task hand-over mechanisms. In their book, *Faster Cheaper Better: The 9 Levers for Transforming How Work Gets Done*, Michael Hammer and Lisa Hershman say

> Most managers have a worm's eye view of the world. They need a bird's eye view, an understanding of what your company really does and the role they play in achieving its goals, or better yet, its results. Once you understand what your organization does, you can begin to design better ways to do it, ways that break you out of the old trap of "we've always done it this way."

Redesigning your processes for the future is a critical role of the managers.

Good design reduces the number of problems over the lifetime of the process. Regardless of whether existing processes are considered, the aim of this step is to ensure that a correct and efficient theoretical design is prepared.

Modeling

Modeling takes the theoretical design and introduces combinations of variables (for example, changes in rent or materials costs, which determine how the process might operate under different circumstances). It also involves running "what-if" analyses on the processes, such as the following:

▲ What if I have 75 percent of resources to do the same task?

▲ What if I want to do the same job for 80 percent of the current cost?

Execution

One of the ways to automate processes is to develop or purchase an application that executes the required steps of the process; however, in practice, these applications rarely execute all the steps of the process accurately or completely. Another approach is to use a combination of software and human intervention; this approach is more complex, making the documentation process difficult.

Measuring

Measuring encompasses the tracking of individual processes, so that managers can easily evaluate information on the work. For instance, measuring can determine the state of a client engagement (for example, engagement letter signed, staff scheduled, awaiting review, invoice paid), so that you can identify and correct problems and improve the process.

The degree of measuring depends on what information the business wants to evaluate and analyze and how the business wants it to be monitored: in real time, near real time, or ad hoc. Select your measurements carefully. "The right measurement metric not only focuses process redesign correctly but also shapes behavior to an extraordinary degree," according to Hammer and Hershman.

Business intelligence mining is a collection of methods and tools related to process monitoring. The aim of mining is to analyze current, actual processes vis-à-vis the standard. Mining also allows you to analyze your time and billing systems, tax software, accounting software, and client relationship management systems to identify opportunities for cross-serving.

Optimization

Once you have process performing information from your modeling or monitoring phases, you can optimize the process. In optimization, you identify the potential or actual bottlenecks and opportunities for cost savings or additional client needs. For example, clients with deductions for retirement plans or dividend income may be candidates for wealth management services or financial or estate planning services.

As CEO of the megaregional firm Wipfli LLP in Green Bay, WI, Rick Dreher has recently expanded his business into other countries, and the firm has invested in technology to improve its business process.

> We've [built] a Web-based interface that sits on the top of QuickBooks, so a small business owner won't need a bookkeeper, in theory; they won't need an HR person; and they shouldn't need a CIO inside their organization.
>
> Wipfli small businesspeople in the U.S. will become more advisers and reviewers of work, and we're moving toward doing a lot of that work in a factory concept. What we're trying to do is get repetition. To actually feel like one firm, we had to prove that work could move between the computer screens and the phone lines. We had to prove that we were

truly in this cloud environment where the clients are up in the cloud, and it doesn't matter what office of Wipfli you're in, including the two in India.

We can all basically access the cloud, work on the cloud, put it back in the cloud, and the next person can work on it, as long as we're [using] common processes.

Issues to Look Out For

Although the steps in developing processes can be viewed as a cycle, economic or time constraints will likely limit process development to only a few iterations. This is especially the case when an organization uses the approach for short- to medium-term objectives, rather than trying to transform the organizational culture. True iterations are only possible through the collaborative efforts of process participants, but many organizations start a BPM project simply to optimize an area that has been identified for improvement.

Accounting firms simply do not manage themselves, and those that have a full-time managing partner (without a book of business) tend to grow much faster than those that have a part-time leader and part-time practitioner at the helm. As Ray Strothman says

> A few years ago, [we took] all the management responsibilities for the day-to-day operating of the firm out of the hands of the partners and hired a professional chief operating officer who reports directly to me. That allows me to spend time thinking about the business, focusing on where we're going, and she keeps the trains running on time.

Too often, managing partners get saddled with managing everything *but* the partners. They view their role as an administrative duty, rather than a strategic one. Many managing partners also manage a book of business to retain security and status. Michael Gerber, author of *The E-Myth*, says, "Most entrepreneurs are technicians who had an entrepreneurial seizure." This statement definitely applies to professional service firms. The technicians prefer to work *in* the business rather than *on* the business. If you're going to lead a large and growing firm, you'll need to have someone working *on* business processes, rather than everyone simply working *in* the business.

Conclusion

Managing processes and projects are vital ingredients to a well-led team, office, or firm. In order for managers to do their jobs well, they must understand the strategic direction of the group. Most importantly, managers must not become too attached to the processes of today but be continuously striving to build the future firm. In the next chapter, I'll review the necessity to build that future firm by continuously improving the processes and methods to support the strategies of the leaders.

Building the Future Firm Continuously

"Be uncomfortable being comfortable, discontent being content."

~ COACH JOHN WOODEN

Nothing stands still. In his book, *The World is Flat: A Brief History of the Twenty-first Century*, Thomas Friedman describes many of the rapid changes taking place today. The business world, competition, technology, communications methods, and our communities are constantly changing. You can build the perfect accounting firm for today, and soon, it will be behind.

 Therefore, you must not be content on building your firm to operate well today; your continuous improvement efforts should be devoted to building your firm for tomorrow.

One of the major assignments of leaders and managers is to implement processes that will carry the firm into the future, rather than simply positioning you for today.

Gary Shamis, founder and CEO of the top-100 multioffice firm SS&G Financial Services, Inc., in Cleveland, OH, talks about his firm's and partners' attitude toward continuous change and improvement

> You could go around this country and ask people, "Who are the best CPA firms?" We'll probably get our fair share of people saying that SS&G is one of the best firms in the country. On the other hand, if you spent time with our partner group, you would never find a more dissatisfied group with what we have now on a daily basis. It's never good enough, and there is not a piece of this organization that has not been reengineered 10 times over to try and improve what's there—every single thing—and so, it's just a continuing process.
>
> After I read Thomas Friedman's book *The World Is Flat*, I was actually convinced that we needed to be doing more offshore work. So, we ended up spending three years working with our tax software provider to reengineer our 1040 process. We basically moved all of the clerical functions of the 1040 preparation to India. You've got to be good in tax to be successful in practice development, and we needed to move the clerical roles out of our offices, so our partners could focus on giving great tax advice.

In this chapter, I'll review the ongoing process that the best managers adopt in order to keep the systems, processes, and procedures not only up-to-date but ahead of date. Great managers ensure that their systems and processes are subservient to strategy and people, and for that reason, those systems can never be static. Leaders are influencing their team members on a journey. Anytime there is movement toward a goal, friction will occur. Therefore, managers must always be adapting the systems to reduce the potential problems caused by friction. We will discuss a variety of methods being used to improve processes, such as business process improvement, Lean Six Sigma, and Six Sigma.

This chapter, like many others in the book, just touches the surface of the concepts surrounding continuous improvement of business processes. In appendix D, "Eight Continuous Process Improvement Phases," I've reviewed some of the events that are important as you proceed through any change process. In appendix F, "Business Process Improvement Resources," I've listed a number of resources, books, and websites to which you can refer to become more knowledgeable in this subject. In addition, you may want to consult a firm called Lean CPA, LLC, a division of Rea & Associates, Inc., in Ohio, that specializes in Lean Six Sigma for accounting firms.

Commit to Continuous Improvement

A huge part of managing any business is a commitment to regularly improving the internal management of operations. Because an accounting firm is such a high-margin business, it makes sense that the most successful leaders of firms focus their attention on business growth. After all, an incremental dollar of revenue can create an incremental 80 percent or more of margin in the short run and as much as 40 percent in the long run. However, high-margin businesses cannot ignore their operations, either; they can always improve the level of work handled by partners and client cycle time on projects (the turnaround time on client matters). Some firms look to "lean" improvement or Six Sigma processes to regularly evaluate and upgrade their work, as we'll discuss later in this chapter.

Chris Allegretti, CEO of the regional firm Hill, Barth & King, LLC (HBK), in Boardman, OH, is building his firm of the future by consolidating offices. After the economic recession that began in late 2007, HBK went from 17 offices down to 10.

> You can do a lot of things in small offices, but it's very hard to have someone with deep skill sets who's a great auditor, someone who's a great tax practitioner, or someone with specific industry knowledge. In a merged environment, we get a little more efficient. It allows us to get our people concentrated in certain areas, so they can develop their skill sets to service our clients better.

Two key reasons that firms focus on improving their management of operations are as follows:

1. Reducing wasted efforts inside all processes, so that the firm is more productive
2. Compacting steps in each process, so that client work can be performed more effectively and turned around more efficiently

In Gary Shamis's firm, outsourcing low-level tax operations to someone else allows his tax partners to focus on being business advisors. Rick Dreher, CEO of the megaregional firm Wipfli LLP in Green Bay, WS, is leading the same kind of change for all his experienced service providers. The same concepts will apply to changes taking place from an outside regulatory body, as well as from an internal process improvement program. Rick Anderson, CEO of the megaregional firm Moss Adams LLP in Seattle, WA, and Bob Bunting, former CEO of the megaregional firm Moss Adams LLP, are leading the preparation for International Financial Reporting Standards. Mark Twain said, "Continuous improvement is better than delayed perfection." I have heard leading CPA firm consultant Gary Boomer say many times, "We are looking for progress, not perfection."

Firms have undergone massive changes in the last 10 years, and the expectation is that the next 10 years will not be any slower. Massive changes in the regulatory environment (for example, the Sarbanes-Oxley Act of 2002); shifts from all paper to less paper and, in some cases, paperless; new practice management systems, availability of talent; and the dramatic changes in worldwide competition are all driving continued change. The rapid changes taking place in the accounting, tax, and financial services industries and professions over the next 5 years are numerous and cannot be covered here. It is the role of your strategic planning to understand the environment and forces of coming changes to which you must adapt your future firm processes. The AICPA's Horizons 2025 Project is one resource to look to when researching the many possibilities to consider.

A leader must set realistic goals, but once they are achieved, you must not become satisfied. Achievement will continue at the same or a greater level only if you do not permit the infection of success to take hold of you. Success breeds satisfaction, and satisfaction breeds failure. The symptom of that infection is called complacency. Contentment with past accomplishments or acceptance of the status quo can derail a firm quietly and surely.

Leader Profile: Larry G. Autrey, managing partner of the top-100 firm Whitley Penn LLP in Fort Worth, TX

Larry Autrey's parents instilled a strong work ethic in him. During his high-school years, Larry worked 40 hours per week at the family's service station and an additional 30–40 hours per week stocking shelves at the grocery store. He was driven to obtain a college education and knew he'd have to pay for most of it himself. While he worked his way through Texas Tech University, his grades weren't straight As, and as a result, his professors guided him away from the Big 8 accounting firms. He interviewed with them anyway and received offers from 6 of them, a testament to his well-rounded young life.

Larry learned that by applying himself diligently, he could be successful in life. So, he made a commitment to himself to never give up and always persist. Such a lesson in leadership would serve him well because he has led his firm from approximately $3 million in annual revenue to being an elite member of the largest 100 firms in the United States. His firm has also been named by *INSIDE Public Accounting* as one of the 25 best-managed firms in the country.

Partner Mark Topel says

> The first part of leading a CPA firm is to set the vision. The most difficult part is to get everyone to follow your lead and to pull the rope in the same direction. Larry takes the time to visit with every one of our 25 partners often. While these conversations may be brief, Larry has the ability to gauge a person's temperature and find out what is going on in his or her life, both personal and professional. He consistently develops a genuine one-to-one relationship with each of us.
>
> As Larry is preparing to wrap up a meeting, he has a knack of saying the right thing at the right time. Whether he gives words of comfort that are needed because of a health issue of someone near and dear to us or if a swift kick to the butt is needed to remind us to go out and have a face-to-face meeting with that difficult client or situation, he will encourage or challenge in the right proportion.

Partner Alan White says of Larry

> Some years ago, we were hearing through the grapevine that our employees (and even some of our partners) felt disassociated from the management of the firm. They didn't feel that they were getting enough feedback and communication about

the management decisions being made and the direction that the firm was taking. Larry led the charge to address this concern. He commissioned an independent survey of the entire firm to help determine how we were doing in the eyes of the entire team and to help us identify areas of weakness that we could work on as a management team. Sure enough, the survey said that lack of communication was a major issue.

Larry set about to rectify that issue with a number of directives. He began sending out the agenda for the monthly Management Committee meeting to all of the partners a day or two in advance of our meetings. He also directed that the minutes from those meetings be sent out to the partners as soon as practical after each meeting. He set up a monthly meeting in each office where he would give a general management update to all of the employees who showed up, and he would answer any questions that they had.

Subsequently, the concerns and comments have gone away, and everyone feels more knowledgeable about the direction of the firm.

For his first five years in public accounting, Larry worked six days per week every week, not just in tax season. On Saturdays, he would catch up on reading, reviewing, and planning. On many of those Saturdays, he would have lunch at the Ft. Worth Club, and he became acquainted with the older businessmen who were also at the club on Saturday. As he developed those relationships, they became the backbone of his practice development skills. Although he was a young professional, he was not intimidated by older businessmen, and he embraced a way to develop relationships and grow his budding career.

Critical Success Factors for Change and Growth

In an environment where continuous change is necessary, these five factors are essential to the success of building your future firm:

▲ *Strong leader and manager alignment.* Both leaders and managers must communicate a shared purpose and sense of urgency for any changes that are being made for the future. Leaders who wait for systems and processes to break down will be the laggards in our industry. Whereas the leaders who can engage their managers to build the next generation firm before it breaks are those leaders who will take their firms far. Top leadership and manager support must be highly visible early in the process and reinforced throughout. When the leaders and managers are aligned, the friction caused by changes will be reduced.

▲ *Measurable goals.* Goals for any change initiative must be in line with the firm's strategy, and they must be measurable. Both leaders and managers must agree upon and clearly define the criteria for measuring progress toward the goals and overall vision.

▲ *Actionable business case.* Strategic benefits and returns on investment must be clearly communicated throughout the implementation team and all others who may support the progress. Firmwide and individual performance measures must be aligned to the objectives of the strategic plan.

▲ *Clearly defined roles.* Key leaders, managers, team members, and stakeholders must be identified early in the plan. Roles, responsibilities, and a time line need to be clearly defined. In many firms, the leaders and team members of any planned change will need training and experience. After all, you are building a business that you've never led before. One great way to gain this training and experience is to interact with leaders in larger firms who've gone through similar changes and can advise you of the opportunities and pitfalls. Approximately 30 alliances of CPA firms will help you do this. In addition, most state CPA societies and the AICPA provide various in-person and online forums for interacting with other like-minded firms.

▲ *A well-designed execution plan.* Managing change must be an integral part of the program. The execution strategy must be well defined and clear to all stakeholders. Program milestones must be designed to deliver program goals and objectives. Affected individuals need to be trained and ready for their new assignments.

New ideas from those under your leadership are essential for achieving and maintaining a competitive edge. Welcome those people strong enough to speak up and offer alternatives, but beware of those who do it in a manner that crosses the line. Look for people who can engage in a robust exchange of ideas without causing disruption. Bob Bunting shares

> I changed from a guy who liked people to agree with me to a guy who realized that if people won't disagree with me, nothing was going to happen because they weren't engaged. If there is no real conflict, nobody is helping improve the decision, nobody is really buying into the decision, nobody is committed to the decision because there is nothing going on.

For effective and efficient process improvement to be developed, every manager will need input from the people doing the work. They will always know where the bottlenecks are. All the leaders I spoke with discussed their commitment to continuous process improvement, and several felt that there would be an increasing emphasis on reduction in cost and cycle times as the world continues to become more competitive.

There is no progress without change, but not all change is progress. Although we want to continuously improve our processes, change must be well thought out. Don't carelessly discard processes that have stood the test of time. When you change a process in a large organization, you must start with communication and training and then hold people accountable. If you do not follow these steps when making changes, you will be very frustrated in how sloppily the changes are implemented.

Building a System to Manage Change and Improve Processes

Successful accounting firms don't just accept change; they understand it and plan for it. They design and manage processes that will improve their outcomes and client service. To do this, some accounting firms are now using concepts from the manufacturing business, such as Six Sigma, Lean processes, and Kaizen. These concepts are defined as follows:

▲ Six Sigma works to improve quality. High-quality, efficient processes allow you to deliver services in a proactive manner, rather than a reactive one.

▲ Lean processes focus on efficient operations, cutting out unnecessary steps.

▲ Kaizen is a principle that focuses on continuous, small improvements.

Six Sigma

Six Sigma is a management technique that aims to develop and deliver near perfect products and services. It has been claimed that Six Sigma is only useful for problems that are hard to find but easy to fix versus a more radical reengineering approach whose advocates focus on problems that are easy to find but hard to fix. As mentioned previously, Lean CPA, LLC, a division of Rea & Associates, Inc., a CPA firm in Ohio, specializes in helping CPA managers with gaining knowledge and certification in these concepts.

The term *Six Sigma* refers to statistical constructs that measure how far a given process deviates from perfection and then systematically determine how to improve them. Its focus on process quality evolved out of the quality movement that began in the 1980s. It is now used for a much wider range of process improvement activities, and organizations like Accenture, IBM, GE, Bank of America, and DuPont have proven that Six Sigma can be used in service industries as easily as it can be used in manufacturing.

The principles of quality applied in implementing Six Sigma are almost always defined in terms of the firm's vision and strategy. Processes are designed from the perspective of the client and enabled by a commitment to thinking in terms of processes across the organization. Metrics such as utilization, leverage, reliability, price, on-time delivery, client loyalty scores, and accuracy provide the targets. The client focus creates market knowledge that can illuminate the need for process change in areas where the company can add value or implement improvements that clients themselves value most.

Six Sigma uses a concept called DMAIC, an acronym for define, measure, analyze, improve, and control, as described in the following:

▲ Define the project: your not-for-profit audit process, 1040 tax process, or strategic planning process. Determine the team members and their roles, especially the team leader.

▲ Measure how the process currently flows to identify potential areas of waste.

▲ Analyze each step regarding its potential for value adding or its lack of value.

▲ Improve the process and identify the potential for gains.

▲ Control the outcomes. All these steps can be perfectly executed, but you will gain nothing unless you take this step. You control the outcome by documenting the new procedures, training everyone in the new process, and then requiring that everyone operate in a consistent manner.

Tom Luken, president of the local firm Kolb+Co in Milwaukee, WS, has used these techniques before and is planning a complete review this year to continue improvement. He says, "When we went to document management, we flowcharted our entire tax flow, tax return process, flowcharted the D&A process, to help us understand that process and then improve it and integrate it with our new document management process."

Lean Processes

The origins of Lean date back well before the 20th century, long before it was called Lean. The word *Lean* came from an MIT student while researching the differences between some Japanese and North American car makers. The key thought processes within Lean are identifying waste or nonvalue-added activities from the clients' perspective and then determining how to eliminate them the right way.

Determining value is at the heart of Lean. *Value* is defined as an item or feature for which a client is willing to pay. The Lean framework is used as a tool to focus resources and energy on producing the value-added features while identifying and eliminating nonvalue-added activities. For example, clients of accounting firms often tell us that they'd be willing to pay more for things like clearer invoices and simply meeting deadlines.

One of the most effective ways to improve processes is to flowchart them. Using a visual display can help you identify the value-adding and nonvalue-adding steps in any process and will provide you a common language when improving those steps.

Lisa Cines, former managing partner of the top-100 firm Aronson LLC in Rockville, MD, says

> We evaluate how we keep people in their seats. Every time they get up from their seats, inefficiency is created. A simple example is when we went to online billing, but we still distributed paper. So, we made an announcement that six months from now, no paper. It was a huge transformation for the billing process, which has also increased our collection rate significantly.
>
> We've made terrific strides in collecting work-in-process [WIP] and accounts receivable [AR]. We were not in a good place, and we were late collecting and losing money being the client's banker. Each partner had standards, but we needed firm standards. We have now broken down WIP and AR into their own separate DSO buckets, and we have set standards for each of those buckets. We have probably brought it down maybe 30 days in total. Our target is 45 days total in WIP and AR.

In appendixes A–D, you'll find a variety of simple tools, such as affinity diagrams and flowcharts to help you internally design and carry out some aspects of formal Six Sigma and Lean improvements.

Many items of waste and inefficiency in processes are small when viewed alone and can be easily overlooked. Almost every step of any process will have some element of waste. We must identify every element of waste and then look at their total impact. Eliminating minor elements of waste can add up to huge improvements in efficiency. Lean concepts utilize a variety of metrics to measure results: value-adding and nonvalue-adding steps, cycle time, lead time, and voice of the clients. Cycle time and lead time measure the total time that a project is in process. Cycle time is the more important because it is the total time from the start of a project to the delivery of the report, whether written or oral. Lead time is that time it takes you to get started on a project. Then finally, we must ensure that the client's voice is heard, and our delivery meets their expectations.

Kaizen

Kaizen, a Japanese concept, is often translated in the West as ongoing, continuous improvement. Some authors explain Japan's competitive success in the world marketplace as the result of the implementation of the Kaizen concept in Japanese corporations. In contrast to the usual emphasis on revolutionary, innovative change on an occasional basis, Kaizen looks for uninterrupted, ongoing incremental change. In other words, there is always room for improvement and continuously trying to become better.

In practice, Kaizen can be implemented in corporations by improving every aspect of a business process in a step-by-step approach while gradually developing employee skills through training and increased involvement. Principles of Kaizen implementation are as follows:

▲ People really are the most important company asset.
▲ Processes must evolve by gradual improvement, rather than radical changes.
▲ Those improvements must be based on a quantitative evaluation.

The following principles will help you to successfully implement continuous improvements:

1. *Performance Driven.* All process changes must be based on client needs and measurement. Measurement techniques such as balanced (performance) scorecards or blueprints indicate whether you are acting consistently with your strategic goals, which should be based on client needs and traceable to key performance indicators.

    This principle in no way says what the right measurement indicators should be. Every accounting firm is different and has its own strategy for identifying which goals are achievable. Nonetheless, it is vital that each firm chooses wisely; the old adage "You get what you measure," is universal to all businesses.

    Bill Hubly, founder and managing principal of the local firm Corbett, Duncan & Hubly, PC, in Itasca, IL, says

    > We used to get our billing out by the 25th day of the following month, and we've moved that process down to the 10th of the following month. And we're working to get that reduced. That was really driven 2 or 3 years ago on the scorecard. Whoever was doing billing, they had a goal. You need to get your billing done by the 10th of the month, and if you're not getting that done, then you're not going to be awarded those points, and it's going to affect your compensation.

2. *Client focused.* Will the improvement initiative solve or improve an identified client issue? Why would your client care about the change? To analyze the gap between your current

processes and the client's needs in the future, consider two key factors. First, you should have a strong grasp of your client's needs. Second, you should understand the state of your current relationship and have a vision of what you want these relationships to be in the future. Gaps between these two states will drive your change efforts. The future state view will also provide a set of evaluation criteria for change from the current reality, which then will be translated into balanced scorecard key performance indicators (KPIs) (see chapter 8, "Accountability: Trust but Verify," for a thorough discussion of the scorecard and KPIs).

To use the improved billing practices previously mentioned as an example, clients experience three distinct pricing emotions: price resistance, price anxiety, and payment resistance. Dramatic studies with our clients have demonstrated that when you speed up the billing process, clients are more willing to pay your higher rates. When you discuss the estimated bill up front and agree on a retainer and progress billing arrangement, you are dealing with both price resistance and anxiety. When you obtain progress bills, so that your final bill is a small portion of the total, you are effectively dealing with their payment resistance. And when you employ a change-order system, you overcome those convenient memories and have clients who happily pay your fees. All these changes are adding value to your work without doing more work, just changing your processes.

Debbie Lambert, managing partner of the top-100 multioffice firm Johnson Lambert & Co. LLP in Raleigh, NC, says

> We serve over 350 insurance companies, and our audit template is a mission critical system for us. We have audit templates for insurance, employee benefit plans, and nonprofits. The way we build those templates and implement them is critical to our practice. We are continuously improving our systems. We have an e-mail box where we can send comments throughout the year. So, if a particular form is too difficult for the benefit it provides, we can recommend a more effective method. So, if people don't like the way something works, they just send in recommendations right there. It's amazing how much we get.
>
> We have lots of input in process improvement. We have two tiers: one is the technical, and the other is the efficiency. We put them into different groups to look at it because we obviously want a top-quality audit. And we need to be cost effective as we do these things. So, if you have a form that feels like it's taking too long for the benefit, let's look at that form, let's see what we could do differently to streamline it, and so comply with the standards to give the quality and the efficiency.

3. *Traceable to client expectation.* If you cannot trace an improvement to a specific client expectation or need, then the initiative needs to be questioned. In some cases, firms have undertaken business process changes just to suit the personal preferences of one or more partners without regard to their impact on client expectations. The challenge is to build an initiative that is traceable to client expectations and balance that with the firm's operational objectives. Conflicting business and political drivers can devastate a sound decision-making process. Change initiatives wasting thousands of hours and dollars can be found in almost all accounting firms of any size and complexity. Typically, the

root cause is poor decision making or poor interpretation of the firm's needs and client expectations.

4. *Aligned across departments and business lines.* This principle deals with the importance of cross-functional collaboration and integration. Management structures that are overly rigid are too slow to respond and will eventually become obsolete and nonresponsive to client demands. The most friction in firms occurs from one department to another over things like getting the tax department to review the provision in the field or getting the partners to get the bills out on time.

5. *Integrated with firmwide strategic-plan goals.* Some initiatives are often used simply as ways of creating a document or developing the communication strategy for implementing a technology system. We must recognize that during initiatives such as implementing an enterprise resource, a client relationship management system, or paperless workflow, we are not just affecting technology, data, or processes. We are also striving to identify champions and transform people into enthusiastic supporters and participants who will enable change initiatives.

   During transition, the staff must feel that an appropriate level of trustworthy communication is happening. The main take-away is that staff affected by change should feel a sense of contribution as a result of their participation and should be positioned as the beneficiaries of the new process.

6. *Conducted with a well-managed time-line approach.* On the surface, the project management discipline might appear to be simply managing time, deadlines, due dates, and resources. If the discipline is not aligned with the firm's culture, it will be a struggle to meet all objectives and agreed-upon stakeholder expectations.

Leader Profile: Mike Cain, founder and comanaging partner of the top-50 firm Lattimore Black Morgan & Cain, PC, in Nashville, TN

The comanaging partner at top-50 firm Lattimore Black Morgan & Cain, PC (LBMC), Mike Cain is a strong believer in leading by example. Although he strives to communicate solutions and gather input from the people around him, Mike also believes that a leader should never ask anyone to do something that he or she is not willing to do.

Mike grew up working in a grocery store, where he learned great customer focus and integrity. He believes that these qualities are fundamental ingredients of good leadership in an accounting firm today, just as they were 26 years ago when he helped found his very successful firm.

Mike comes by his hardworking nature honestly, growing up in a working-class family. The value of dedicated work was a huge part of Mike's development, and he became heavily involved in Future Business Leaders of America (FBLA) during high school. He was selected president of the FBLA group and, ultimately, Mr. FBLA in the state of Kentucky.

After a stint at the international Big 8 accounting firm Peat Marwick Mitchell & Co. (now KPMG), Cain joined other associates from Peat Marwick Mitchell & Co. and

(continued)

(continued)

> founded LBMC, in 1984 with 11 people. Today, he is comanaging partner (along with David Morgan) of LBMC, one of the 50 largest accounting firms in the United States, headquartered in Nashville, TN.
>
> Mike is past chairman of the Tennessee Society of CPAs and Leading Edge Alliance and continues to be very active with the AICPA and various other organizations.
>
> Karen Kehl-Rose, executive director of Leading Edge Alliance says
>
>> Mike has been a strong leader in Leading Edge Alliance, by his example. Mike is great at solving problems and creating a clear solution. He can communicate the solution and get consensus from others who will follow his leadership.
>>
>> If I were in the middle of the perfect storm, it would be Mike that I would want at the wheel. Mike is extremely patient and in control of himself. He is never one to rush to judgment. Mike bases his decision on objective information, even in situations where your first impulse would be an emotional reaction. Mike will ask the questions but also listens and hears the responses. He is not self-serving or ego-driven. Mike does not seek to shine a spotlight on himself. His deeds and actions speak for him.
>
> Mike's comanaging partner David Morgan says
>
>> He is a great thinker, both strategic and tactical. His thinking is always grounded in our mission and core values, which he and I wrote. I can honestly say that in the 35 years that we have worked together, I have never seen him make a business decision that was not grounded in our core values. Mike is one of the most organized persons I know. He doesn't function well in clutter, and when that occasionally happens, as it does to us all, he simply takes a step back and gets things organized before he proceeds. He has always been willing to delegate client responsibilities, management responsibilities, and most anything else to people whom he has seen demonstrate the ability to handle more responsibility. People just naturally like Mike Cain, and they want to work with him and be around him. He is a very positive person.

Flowcharts for Seeing and Improving Processes

Whether you use one of the manufacturing-based methods or work outside of those parameters, a flowchart is a useful tool for process improvement (see appendix C, "Flowchart," for full details on flowcharting). When I worked at PricewaterhouseCoopers LLP, we charted the work flow of large departments of accounting personnel to help assess internal control and eliminate bottlenecks. A flowchart is a picture of a process; it illustrates the details of a process, including the following:

▲ The individual steps
▲ The sequence of steps
▲ The relationship between steps

In a standard flowchart, the steps are arranged one after another until the end. This is the most common approach, and it works well with very simple processes. In a functional flowchart, the steps are arranged by sequence and step owner. This flowchart is useful when many groups are involved in a process. It provides a good overview of what is happening, who is doing it, and the complexity of the process.

Make the chart only as detailed as it needs to be. Inexperienced flowcharters often get into too much detail. The chart quickly becomes huge, confusing, and unmanageable. Each decision point makes the chart much more complex. Before putting a decision point into the flow, ask yourself whether a decision is normally made at this point. Often, you are dealing with a rare exception that can be dealt with later after you've created the whole chart.

When you first begin building your chart, try to get all the way through to the end before going back and dealing with exceptions and decisions. In other words, if you put a decision step into your flow, follow the "Yes" path until you get to the end.

Create separate flowcharts if the process is too large and complex. Flowcharts often represent a series of steps that are also processes. For example, you could say that the process for preparing a client tax return is as follows:

1. Meet with the client.
2. Send client engagement letter and organizer instructions.
3. Receive client input.
4. Log information into the system.
5. Assign to the preparer.
6. Review the return.
7. Sign the return.
8. Deliver the return to the collating department.
9. Send the invoice.
10. Mail the tax return.
11. Review the return with the client.
12. Obtain client loyalty feedback.
13. Collect fees.

Any of these steps could easily be broken down into another group of steps. If you have a need to break a step into that kind of detail, create a separate flowchart. In continuous improvement language, there is the concept of a value-added step. To meet the definition, the step must meet all three of the following criteria:

1. Physically changes the work passing through the process to make it more valuable to the client
2. Is a step for which the client is willing to pay
3. Assumes things get done right the first time

Examples include entering financial data into a tax program, a review of the output, a review of significant transactions for proper classification, and a review for ideas to improve the tax position of the filer during the next tax cycle. Maximizing value-added steps increases the client's value perception of the service, thus improving process effectiveness.

If a step does not meet all the value-added criteria, then it is nonvalue added. Generally

▲ the client is unwilling to pay for it.
▲ the step does not change the output in a way that makes it more valuable.

Examples include waiting, storing, moving files, checking, recording, approvals, testing, reviewing, copying, filing, reworking, tracking work, and so on. Minimizing or eliminating nonvalue-added steps cuts the waste in the process, thus improving process efficiency.

While you are considering improving processes to build the future firm, here are some questions that you'll want to consider with your partners or change team:

1. Are there any low value-added outcomes?
2. Are there other outcomes that we should produce?
3. Are there too many hand-offs? Are hand-offs appropriate?
4. Do any bottlenecks or inefficiencies exist?
5. Do all steps add value?
6. Which steps add the most value?
7. Which steps have the highest error rate?
8. Where is work done, and why is it done there?
9. When is it done, and why is it done then?
10. How is it done, and why is it done that way?
11. Who does it, and why is it that person doing it?
12. How many departments are involved in the process?
13. What measurement systems are currently in place?

To improve your process, eliminate bottlenecks and nonvalue-added steps, and transfer value-added steps earlier or later in the process to even the workload.

What sets Lean or Six Sigma apart from its individual components is the recognition that you cannot do just quality or just speed; you need a balanced process that can help an organization focus on improving service quality, as defined by the client, within a set time limit.

The Benefits of Continuous Improvement

Accounting has the stereotype of being a staid, unchanging profession. Leaders in our profession have learned to embrace change, specifically working to improve their firms on a continuous basis. Nonetheless, some accountants are not comfortable with change.

Rick Dreher is striving for forward movement toward the future firm, "The biggest thing that I've tried to change is still probably the biggest challenge that I see going forward, and that is the level of communication that we had inside our firm previously," he says. Rick focuses on keeping his fellow partners at Wipfli LLP in the know, sharing insights with both partners and the entire staff through regular blog posts.

When things get tough, Rick is always willing to step up, and he says leadership from the top is critical to share the vision, especially during tough times. "The going is tough many times, and you've got a choice at that point," he says. "You can look for someone else to solve the problem, or you can solve it yourself. I like to listen to a lot of my partners who are close to the issue, ask for their opinions on solutions, and then work collaboratively to solve the tough issue at hand. If we get stuck on an issue, and there is no clear answer, I will make the final call."

We must recognize that in any given time, our stakeholders will have a set of requirements that are in flux and can be influenced by environmental, competitive, and market demands. If we accept the fact that change is constant, we should also recognize that using iterative processes in the overall change process is critical to the success of our initiatives.

Steve Mayer, founder, chairman, and CEO of the regional firm Burr, Pilger & Mayer LLP in San Francisco, CA, says

> I believe that the business has to reinvent itself every so often with new products and ser-
> vices. But I firmly believe that you have to have sales and marketing getting your clients,
> you have to produce the product, and you have to know how to count the beans. If you're
> constantly throwing innovation into the mix, and you can keep coming up with new ideas
> and new concepts, it works. So, that's how I think we have done it with our firm. We have
> reinvented it a number of times, and we're constantly adding new things, so we can lead
> into that future firm.

Conclusion

From reading this chapter, I hope you are motivated to build your firm of the future continuously and that you'll strive for progress every day. You should have an overview of several tools (for example, flowcharts) and concepts (Kaizen, Lean Six Sigma, Six Sigma, and so on) that will help you with the continuous improvement process. In conclusion, a leader can only coast in one direction. If you are not improving, you are moving backward as the world is moving forward at an accelerated rate of change.

Section 5

Leading Synergy

A number of years ago, I toured an automobile assembly plant in Detroit and was stunned at the choreography of the systems and how well they seemed to work. As a black chassis came down the line, black doors arrived from feeder lines. Everything seemed like a symphony of manufacturing. The same is true as I've visited some of the world's best brands: Southwest Airlines, British Airways, a Disney theme park, or a Ritz-Carlton Hotel. I can feel the smoothness that has gone into aligning the many systems to support the people and their strategy. As this smoothness occurs, and friction is removed, businesses achieve a synergy that Terry Snyder, president of the accounting firm alliance PKF North America in Lawrence, GA, calls magic.

Synergy comes from a Greek word that means cooperative or joint work, but in business, it means that you produce an effect greater than the sum of what individuals can produce. As author Stephen Covey puts it, you achieve synergy when the whole is greater than the sum of the parts. Author John Maxwell calls it momentum.

In chapter 16, "Synergy and Alignment: One Plus One Equals Three," we will go in depth into synergy and alignment, so that the teamwork that takes place is like a symphony, with everyone playing his or her part to achieve the vision and mission within the values of the firm. We'll discuss preparing your firm for crisis and how to make sense when bad things interrupt the flow. When accounting firms achieve this synergy, leaders are developed, and succession planning (see chapter 17, "Sustaining Leadership: The Ultimate Succession Plan") becomes almost a no-brainer. Building the enduring firm is the goal of synergy and succession.

Accounting firms are complex communities and systems of people working together and with clients, with many different elements that must be aligned to produce synergy. Some firms do not attempt to achieve synergy because it is too difficult. They settle for operating in smaller silos. Some of the primary elements of leading synergy include the following:

▲ Leaders who understand themselves
▲ A well-defined vision, mission, values, and strategy
▲ Leaders who understand the team members
▲ Well-defined work processes
▲ Systems and technology that support the people and their strategies

Alignment and synergy are never fully achieved. After everything is in place, leaders and managers continually tune the systems to run more smoothly. Another way to look at alignment is the absence of misalignment, which is usually easier to detect. Misalignment occurs when one part of the system interferes with or inhibits other parts. For example, suppose an accounting firm changes into niche teams but fails to consider the office layout and compensation system. The office walls that separate team members prohibit communication, and the company continues to reward individual performance instead of team performance.

Strategic Alignment

From the 30,000-foot level, the strategy of the accounting firm must be consistent with its leadership and team members; business environment; and vision, mission, and values. A strategy is important because it guides the operations of the entire firm. All the objectives in a firm's strategy can't be pursued with the same level of priority. By clearly agreeing on shared values, a firm can obtain a better alignment between financial and other objectives, such as client satisfaction and loyalty.

Objectives Alignment

Once a firm aligns its objectives with a strategic vision, it must specify and align goals at different levels and for different groups. Although leaders often acknowledge the importance of aligning goals, they often underrate the difficult work needed to make it happen. Teams of accountants produce their outputs through work processes that cut across accounting, auditing, tax, consulting, and administration. Goals for core processes must contribute to the firm's goals while they satisfy customer expectations and ensure that work is effective and efficient.

Internal Alignment

All internal elements of a synergistic team—structure, subsystems, processes, and practices—must be aligned with the firm's objectives. For example, in order to create a high level of client loyalty, the internal teamwork must be aligned, so there is little friction felt by the external client. The reward systems of the firm should reward staff members for their contributions to goals of the entire firm. All client and internal work processes should be aligned with one another. For example, performance scorecard, measurement, and information systems should support each other and provide employees with feedback to track progress toward their personal and team objectives.

Creating synergy requires the leader to consider the entire ecosystem of the firm: how each department interrelates, how teams are formed, how teams are led, and how people and systems work together. The ecosystem includes the leader and his or her attributes, members of the team and their capabilities, strategy, and management systems. To obtain true synergy, you must align the various parts of your firm's ecosystem to remove potential friction.

Keith Farlinger, CEO of the national firm BDO Canada LLP in Toronto, Canada, says

> It is very difficult to get a firm of 340 partners and 100 offices in alignment. So, I spend a lot of time making sure that alignment happens. I received a call yesterday that presented the opportunity to send someone to Australia for a period of time to work in credit unions and International Financial Reporting Standards. This would be a real benefit for our firm. It's also a real perk for the staff. The office we approached didn't want to participate because their staff members were working on some very important projects at that time. It wasn't in the best interest of that office to send someone. So, I had to phone the managing partner to remind him that I understand the situation, but the firm is more important than one particular office, and this is very beneficial to the firm.

Many leaders have difficulty working as a member of a team. Keith clearly remembers when he began to develop those skills

> When I became managing partner of Toronto, I was fairly young—40ish—and felt that I had to do everything myself. If there was a problem, I had to fix it, and if there was a new strategy, I had to make sure it was carried out. I was killing myself, literally, and one of my sage partners took me aside and said, "Keith, I don't know whether you recognize it, but there's a whole bunch of us around who can help you on everything that you do, and so, don't think BDO is all about Keith. BDO is about all of us, so let us help you." It was like a revelation, and it's something that I really believe in.

Firms succeed best when they become more than the sum of their people. That is one of the tests of any great leader. No group will consistently progress unless the leader is able to create a synergy that will propel the organization forward more than the followers think is possible.

Leader Profile: James G. B. DeMartini, III, managing partner of the top-100 firm Seiler LLP in Redwood City, CA

James DeMartini is the managing partner of Seiler LLP, a top 100 accounting firm with offices in Silicon Valley and San Francisco. Jim is the second leader of Seiler LLP, which has been chosen by *INSIDE Public Accounting* as one of the best-of-the-best accounting firms in the United States for a number of years. Jim and his partners have achieved this recognition, in large part, due to the synergy that they have achieved within their firm. The firm specializes in providing services to high-net-

(continued)

(continued)

worth individuals and families, as well as closely held businesses.

Seiler LLP partner Brian Dinsmore says

When Jim succeeded our founder as managing partner, Seiler had been around for more than 40 years and was highly successful. Anyone stepping into this role was going to face many challenges. Jim's leadership style, however, allowed for a successful transition. Jim leads by example, and his style is both challenging and supportive. He gets involved as necessary with the day-to-day issues, yet he's constantly looking ahead to the future and how to position the firm accordingly.

Leadership skills are learned early when you grow up as the oldest of six children. Jim was raised in the San Francisco Bay area and played a number of sports; he was chosen as captain or cocaptain of several teams. Raising three sons himself, he has coached baseball for over 20 years. Coaching teenagers in competitive sports taught him the important skills of considering the entire ecosystem of a team, including the players and their families.

Tax partner Lynn McGovern shares

Shortly after I joined Seiler in 2001, Jim told me that many tax professionals believe they have met the client's expectations when they deliver an accurate tax return. He then encouraged me to set my client service goals beyond the expected and to strive to provide creative tax planning ideas and valuable advice to our ultrahigh-net-worth clients. In this way, he reflected, you will eventually become their most trusted and key adviser.

As I have grown with the firm, I have been fortunate to observe Jim in action, as he masterfully navigates difficult client situations, all the while keeping in mind one of his mottos: "Remember, the client is always right." Jim has instilled in me the goal of developing his same uncanny ability to blend the technical with the practical to arrive at effective, efficient solutions to a myriad of client issues ranging from creative tax structures to family governance issues. I strive to pass on to the individuals who will one day be partners in the firm this same desire for becoming the client's most trusted and key adviser and to instill in them his motto.

Partner Kenneth Everett tells

Jim recognized early on that changing the culture of a firm to meet the demands of the 21st century could be most difficult, but he also understood that leadership is not always about taking the path of least resistance. For example, he knew that relying on a few rainmakers for the continued growth of the Firm was unsustainable, yet because of the success of a few partners, business development was not a priority. He had to change this mindset, build accountability, and ingrain a culture of client-centered business development focus across the firm. He didn't expect this to happen overnight but, instead, did so in stages. He worked with team members to develop key niche marketing groups and then brought in a coach. He encouraged mentoring and networking. Jim personally followed our progress; he still does. I'd say that we've reached the point where there isn't a professional in the firm who doesn't recognize the importance of business development and how it relates to both the firm's and their professional success.

Jim was instrumental in starting a noncompetitive winter baseball league in the San Francisco Bay Area modeled after Major League Baseball's instructional winter leagues and a similar program that originated in Florida. He, along with other leaders, created an unwavering commitment to maintain the noncompetitive nature of this league, and it was so popular with the players, parents, and coaches that a league of 90 teams located in 16 cities with 1,600 players (ages 9–14) became self-policing and was managed by a handful of volunteers without the need for the usual, and often ineffective, board of directors and committees that are typical of youth sports. A crucial lesson learned was the importance of establishing and nurturing an unwavering commitment to the culture of an organization.

Currently, Jim is a member of the board of directors of the Skoll Foundation and the Stupski Foundation. Jim told me that he is passionate about working with large private foundations with living donors, and he feels that it is very important to give back to his community. As mentioned, Jim was a founder of the Sports Association for Youth, a noncompetitive baseball league that currently benefits more than 1,000 Bay Area youths annually. Jim successfully transitioned the management of this league to three individuals who have continued to foster the unique culture of the league.

During 1999–2004 Jim served on the board of directors of Mid-Peninsula Bank. He attended the University of California at Los Angeles, holds a bachelor of science degree in accounting from Golden Gate University, where he also studied advanced taxation. Jim is a gifted financial communicator and is regularly sought out by large groups.

Synergy is not necessarily a frictionless environment; think of it more as a smooth-sailing boat. The exhilaration you get when sailing a boat is an amazing thing—the wind in the sails; the strong waves across the bow; the rudder holding the boat firm in the cross-currents; and you, the sailor, steering, adjusting, and tacking to sail anywhere you want to go.

Bill Haller, managing partner of the national firm CapinCrouse LLP in Indianapolis, IN, says

> I make sure when I go to bed at night, there is no controversy that I am aware of in Capin-Crouse. If there is, I want to put myself in the middle of it and resolve it tonight. One guy that I hadn't seen in years told me, "I never forgot what you taught me. You always equipped us to go into a room without you and deal with our issues with someone else, so that we kept our bags empty." I think that's really important for the synergy of the firm if you are the protector of the culture. You make sure people know it's meaningful and it's important that we don't go to bed at night with unfinished anger.

We don't like a calm sea; nothing happens in a calm sea. When there is no wind, your sailboat won't sail. The fact is that when movement occurs, there will be friction. As you advance toward your vision, the great leaders anticipate and welcome the problems that crop up. Leaders who fail to anticipate the problems get derailed and lose the opportunity for synergy or, as Bill might say, "smooth sailing in a windy sea."

Synergy and Alignment: One Plus One Equals Three

*"Great players are willing to give up their own personal achievement
for the achievement of the group."*

~ KAREEM ABDUL-JABBAR

Accounting firms are made up of many talented professionals who must work independently yet together. Even when partners agree on values, mission, and vision, it can be difficult for leadership to keep everyone moving in the same direction. How can leaders build momentum within their firms? How can the firm leverage a reputation for vision and growth to attract the best and most talented people? How can leaders create an environment that attracts the most desirable clients? How can leaders, managers, processes, and team members be so aligned with the vision, mission, and values of the firm that the whole is larger than the sum of its parts?

Terry Snyder, president of the accounting firm alliance PKF North America in Lawrence, GA, says, "We've all walked into a client, a vendor, or a customer, and there's a certain harmony, a certain rhythm that exists. You know you're someplace that's successful. Our goal here at PKF is to create that rhythm, that harmony, so when somebody walks in, they experience that magic."

In this chapter, we'll discuss a variety of ways to achieve synergy within your firm. First of all, I'll warn you that forward motion will create friction. The great leaders anticipate friction long before the friction or problems occur. We'll discuss how leaders adapt and learn from crisis in their organizations, and we'll discuss the phases of teamwork and how they contribute to synergy and alignment. I'll introduce you to two leaders who have achieved excellent alignment in their firms: Terry Harris and John Wright, managing partner of Padgett Stratemann & Co. of San Antonio, TX. As you'll see, I believe that synergy is only possible when we have a well-led team striving for a compelling vision, with management that is continuously building the future firm—all the concepts of the previous 15 chapters rising to a crescendo of harmony.

Leader Profile: Terry Harris, managing partner of McKonly & Asbury LLP in Harrisburg, PA

Terry Harris, managing partner of McKonly & Asbury LLP, grew up on a farm with 4 brothers and learned the value of hard work early. His father was stricken with polio at age 18, but he was a very entrepreneurial and driven man. Terry's father purchased a gas station to give his sons business experience. Terry says, "My father was not in the gas station business, but he bought the business when his boys were teenagers, and we all worked there part time to earn money for college. It was my first real work in a service business, and it taught me how to deal with customers."

Terry recalls the time that the gas pump failed to shut off automatically while he was filling a customer's tank.

Gas began spewing all over the car and the ground as I was cleaning the windshield. Of course, I rushed to turn off the nozzle, but the damage was done, and I had an irate customer on my hands. I handled it the best I could: gave him a free car wash to clean the car. Another customer who witnessed the whole thing later related to my father that I had handled the situation well with the customer. I learned that the customer always comes first, and it isn't so much that a mistake is made but how you handle a mistake when it does happen. I also learned to appreciate the "little guys" in life who take care of things like checking your oil or washing your car. And I learned that there are people who will try to scam you. I was scammed one time and learned a valuable (and relatively inexpensive) lesson about not trusting everyonAs a young man, Terry was involved in leadership activities with his church youth group, church council, and as a coach of the diving team. He became a partner at McKonly & Asbury LLP at age 27 and has risen to lead one of the best firms for which to work in the United States.

Kevin Meade, president of IGAF Worldwide, says

Terry Harris clearly understands horticulture. He was one of the first people I knew to apply the principals of pruning to an accounting practice, with great effect. A part of the practice within his firm had served the organization well and was instrumental in the early success of the firm. Additionally, the people within that area were well integrated into the firm on a personal and professional level. Having said that, Terry recognized that there were aspects that were actually holding the firm back from moving to the next level.

He approached the problem like a skilled gardener. Areas that were no longer going to support vigorous growth of the firm or that detracted from the focus on specific goals and objectives were "pruned," so that resources could be more clearly devoted to the agreed-upon direction for the firm. The ability to do this well is so elemental and often missing that it reflects leadership on multiple levels and in multiple areas.

According to Scott Heintzelman, a partner at McKonley & Asbury LLP

Terry was a bit skeptical of our jump into social media and blogging. I started my blog two and a half years ago, before it was popular, cool, or known. I remember Terry sitting in my office as I explained what, why, and how much time I needed to do this correctly. He looked at me and said, "I am not sure I understand how blogging and social media help us, but I trust you and will support this endeavor."

Well two and a half years later, our firm has six blogs, and my blog is considered an industry leader, and it creates and strengthens many key relationships for our firm. No doubt he understands how it benefits our firm now, but back then, he had the vision to let something he knew nothing about develop. That trust and vision to empower others is huge in Terry and part of the reason we are a special organization!

Building a Shared Purpose

To turn a mission and vision into a truly shared purpose that inspires synergy among all members of the firm, a leader must consider the following questions:

1. Do I have the right people reporting to me and other leaders?
2. How can I make sure that my direct reports have accurate and timely information?
3. Who needs additional nurturing, training, motivating, supervising, or challenging?
4. How should processes be designed to support the people and strategy?
5. Is the reward system aligned to motivate people to excel in their roles?

Bob Bunting, former CEO of the megaregional firm Moss Adams LLP in Seattle, WA, says

Your leadership style has to change as you get bigger, and if you don't change, you will stall out. I worked in an environment at IFAC with a board of 23 members plus another 46 or so people who sat in the meetings and had the right of the floor. There were a lot of bright, opinionated, supremely confident people in those meetings. Getting 70 or so people to go in one direction in the course of a two-day board meeting is really fun and interesting because they also come from different cultures, and many speak English as a second language. And it's fascinating work. It's probably the most interesting work I have ever done.

Bob adds that he would identify the "opinion maker" subset of the group and preview the more controversial and difficult decisions with that subset prior to the real meeting to get their input. "They are the most powerful people in the room, and sometimes, you need to do that just to keep key decisions on the tracks. It's helpful to have that conversation in advance."

Often, a leader may want to tinker with the ecosystem of the team or firm without regard to the potential unintended consequences. To make changes in the teaming or ecosystems, you must spend time understanding each element and how they work together, or you will always get surprises. Whenever possible, a leader should beta test significant changes in the systems in a low-risk environment.

Accounting firms have traditionally appointed a great audit partner or tax professional to lead a section of the firm, without significant training in the discipline. Terry Snyder, president of PKF North America in Lawrence, GA, says

We see firms that get an HR professional involved. Maybe that's a contract or a full-time person. They also get a marketing and an accounting department established with people with relevant experience.

What happens when you do this is you put your partners and staff back into the channels where they can deliver what we hired them to deliver. We're not telling accounting and tax professionals to ignore them; we're just saying that we're not going to have them working on recruiting or marketing every day. We're going to have other professionals performing those duties, so you're always working at your highest level. That's when I've seen firms make the biggest progress.

If the firm is large enough, you will have a chief leader and a chief manager. This decreases the amount of chargeable time the leaders have because the leading partner's biggest client is his firm and his partners.

Leader Profile: John Wright, managing partner of the top-100 firm Padgett Stratemann & Co. in San Antonio, TX

John Wright grew up on a multigenerational farm in western Kansas. It was there that he learned the discipline necessary to accomplish great things. On the farm, there were always jobs that needed tending. John and his brother grew up entrusted with $100,000 pieces of equipment. He learned from his mistakes and learned that how you deal with a mistake is more important than the error itself. Once, he broke an irrigation riser, causing water to spew wildly into the air. Although this accident scared John, his father very calmly assured him that everything would be okay. He told him to turn off the water valve, and he would be out to help in half an hour. This calmness under pressure was a crucial lesson for John's future leadership roles.

Padgett Stratemann & Co. former managing partner Ray Berend says

> Our firm is a relationship-driven firm. That starts with John at the top. During the period of economic downturn, bad news arrives for most firms. I know John has experienced bankruptcy of clients, a litigation claim, and partner underperformance. Remaining calm in the face of a storm is key to the success of his leadership of our firm. While panic and frustration will set in with most people, John leaves everyone with the impression he is calm.

John's extensive background includes audit and financial statement assurance services for privately held and family business enterprises. In the past, he has also led financial and operational benchmarking and audit engagements for owner-managed companies with revenues ranging from $10 million to $700 million, as well as worked with business owners on various forms of key employee retention, business succession planning, and ownership transition.

He has presented numerous continuing education seminars and been an expert speaker on business issues for leading industry trade associations, including technical matters, fraud detection and prevention, business succession and transition, and operational issues.

John joined Arthur Andersen in the Houston office right out of college then later transferred to San Antonio, where he lives today. He moved to San Antonio with Andersen and became familiar with Padgett Stratemann & Co., a small, obscure firm compared with the international reach of Andersen. Now, Padgett Stratemann & Co. has grown to become one of the 100 largest firms in the United States.

Leadership in Tough Times

Anyone who has studied business knows that accounting firms will progress through good and bad cycles, very profitable and very lean years, periods of high demand and of a scarcity of new client opportunities, and all kinds of unexpected crises. Tough times really test the leader and his or her team's preparedness for surprises. Although it is definitely easier to get followers' attention when the going gets tough, the great leaders invest in teamwork and preparedness for the certain rough patch that will always come along. It's not a matter of if tough times will cycle through; it's a matter of when. Although there can be enormous synergy when the business cycle is in the upswing, the ultimate test of teamwork and the ability to achieve more with less comes during the down cycle.

Many of the leaders I met with in writing this book grappled with the concept of *when* great leaders do their best work. Some said, "Great leaders do their best work during tough times," but others contended the opposite: that the great leaders do their best work in good times, so their teams are prepared for the difficult times.

Because most accounting firms haven't dealt with really tough years for a number of decades, Larry Autrey, managing partner of the top-100 firm Whitley Penn LLP in Fort Worth, TX, thinks that the recent economic struggles have been defining for many organizations. "I think I'm a much better leader in good times than I am in bad. But I also would tell you that I don't think I saw any bad times until the last 2 years. I think there are a lot of us from

45–65 who have not seen bad times until just recently. We've got a challenge now that we hadn't seen before."

Phil Holthouse, founder and managing partner of the top-100 multioffice firm Holthouse, Carlin & Van Trigt LLP in Los Angeles, CA, adds, "I think leaders have more influence during bad times. You tend not to give credit for people who managed to avoid the debacles. You give more credit to the people who recover from them."

On the other side of the question is Steve Mayer, founder, chairman, and CEO of the regional firm Burr, Pilger & Mayer LLP in San Francisco, CA. "You can do your best work as a leader in the good economic times because you lay a solid foundation. It doesn't get recognized until the bad times. One of the most difficult tasks is to keep your key partners from becoming complacent during the great times."

Whether you consider the annual high-pressure season in tax work or a genuine, unprecedented crisis, the preparation of leadership during the easy or good times will determine many of the outcomes during the tough times. During George W. Bush's term of office as president, the United States was hit by two national catastrophes: the September 11 attacks and Hurricane Katrina. Opinions on his government's crisis response to these two tragedies, from the timing of the responses to the adequacy of the responses, varied greatly.

The immediate White House response to the September 11 attacks was widely seen as effective. Bush's first congressional speech after September 11 was a major success and secured him strong bipartisan support. His personal approval ratings shot up in the wake of the September 11 crisis.

In contrast, the response to Hurricane Katrina was roundly criticized. Bush bore the brunt of unprecedented public condemnation for the bungled disaster response in New Orleans. His presidency never fully recovered from Hurricane Katrina. A congressional committee that examined the decisions leading up to and during the crisis labeled the Hurricane Katrina tragedy as a failure of initiative.

If presidential leadership is largely about "teaching reality," then Bush passed with flying colors in the weeks following September 11. His performance projected a dignified authenticity and launched him as a heroic, charismatic leader. In contrast, he struggled, and was publicly criticized for struggling, during the aftermath of Hurricane Katrina. Hurricane Katrina will go down in history as a failure of leadership in a time of crisis, not just by Bush but at all levels of government involved in the tragedy.

These contrasting cases have much deeper meaning for the essence of true leadership. After September 11, the leadership shown by Governor George Pataki, Mayor Rudi Giuliani, and the first responders rested on groundwork laid after the first bombing of the World Trade Center in 1991. During the good times, Giuliani did many things that were unpopular and severely criticized. He cleaned up parts of New York against the outcries of citizen groups. The police and fire departments went through countless hours of disaster-response training. That New Yorkers responded so effectively to their own tragedy allowed the federal government to do its job of providing help and support, which by law is the federal government's job anyway. The local systems in place in New York made President Bush's response more effective.

The response to Hurricane Katrina was totally different. Although it was the first major test of the new Homeland Security Department, it was also the bungling of the local and state first responders. While the police and firemen rushed into the burning buildings in New York, some of the police were the first to abandon New Orleans. If it hadn't been so tragic, it was almost comical to watch Governor Kathleen Blanco and Mayor Ray Nagin sit on the sidelines and complain that the feds hadn't rescued the city.

The popular press applauded Bush for his response to September 11, whereas they had derided Giuliani a few years before for his insistence on preparation. Then, after Hurricane Katrina, Bush was the fall guy, and most of the state and local officials were given passes.

During crisis, leadership abilities are put to the test. If leaders are seen to have passed the test, their power and authority will increase commensurately. If, however, they are seen to have failed, their political capital will shrink quickly.

How can leaders prepare for, and perform under, the intense personal and political pressures generated by crises? We cannot assume that crises are simply bad news for leaders, with crisis management focused purely on damage limitation. A crisis may also provide leaders with unique opportunities to discard old ways of doing things and kick-start new ones, reform their businesses, and reshape the future in ways that would not have been possible without the tough times.

Crisis: Realities and Constructions

All crises create tough conditions for those who are expected to lead the response. These crisis leaders have to make quick yet far-reaching decisions while often lacking essential information. Accounting firms may face external disasters like the World Trade Center attacks, Hurricane Katrina, office fires, earthquakes, or flooding. Some firms will face internal disasters like a partner's negligence; a partner's legal troubles; audit or tax failures; or in the case of Arthur Andersen, an overreaching federal government and a stampede to judgment.

There are three ingredients in a crisis: uncertainty, urgency, and threat. In a crisis, there is usually a high degree of uncertainty. What is happening? How did it happen? What's next? How bad will it be? More important, uncertainty clouds the search for solutions. What can we do? What happens if we select this option? How will people respond? Ted Mason, president and CEO of the top-100 firm Laporte Sehrt Romig Hand in New Orleans, LA, tells, "Hurricane Katrina hit on Monday, and none of us anticipated anything like what hit us. We learned very quickly that no matter how good your disaster recovery plan is, it can't anticipate every situation."

While many become complacent during good times, crises induce a sense of urgency. From 2002–08, everywhere I spoke, I talked about the crisis of success in our profession. I talked about the complacency, arrogance, and greed that sets in during periods of great success, which the accounting profession was enjoying during those years. Many accounting firm leaders thought that my speech was humorous and didn't lose any sleep over my comments. But when the financial crisis began to take hold in 2009, accounting firm leaders began to feel the holes in training and business development that had been neglected during the good times. The crisis had made these issues urgent.

Crises occur when core values or vital systems of a business come under threat. Think of widely shared values such as security, health, integrity, and fairness, which become shaky or even meaningless as a result of looming damage or other forms of adversity. A crisis could be litigation, a natural disaster, intense new competition, senior partner defections, or a loss of a major client.

The psychological impact of a threat is related to cultural expectations, which vary widely within a firm depending upon existing levels of preparedness and prior experience. Although the sudden demise of Arthur Andersen caused the long-term unemployment, loss of finances, or incarceration of relatively few people, it nevertheless evoked widespread fear among public accountants worldwide.

A crisis is but a label denoting the negative impact of an event. When different leaders are confronted with one and the same set of events, such as a hurricane, potential litigation, massive changes in competition, and so on, they may adopt fundamentally different postures. You can distinguish among the following:

1. Leadership denial that the events in question represent anything more than unfortunate incidents. This stance is likely to produce a downplaying of the idea that the events have any serious repercussions.
2. Leadership acceptance of events as critical threats to the firm and its people. This posture is likely to diffuse criticism from other partners.
3. Leadership recognition of a critical opportunity to expose deficiencies in the status quo. Adopting such a position is likely to lead to blame being leveled at advocates of the status quo and attacks on dysfunctional policies in the firm to marshal support for change and reform.

In business studies, scholars have produced a substantial body of work on corporate crisis preparedness and response (for example, the Tylenol product failure; the Bhopal chemical disaster; the grounding of the Exxon Valdez; and more recently, the demise of Enron and Arthur Andersen, the BP oil well incident in the Gulf of Mexico, and Walmart's astute response to Hurricane Katrina).

In the case of Walmart, the executives and employees contributed $20 million and 1,500 truckloads of merchandise to the victims of Hurricane Katrina. In addition, all Walmart employees who were displaced during and after the storm were guaranteed their jobs with full pay. Their CEO, Lee Scott, said that he wanted the company to respond to the disaster in a manner that matched its size. He did not want the response to be measured but to be huge, like the company. Scott was deemed a hero in the press. In chapter 5, "Preparation: Ready for Seizing Opportunity," you read about Ted Mason, who led his firm in a very similar manner.

These cases are told and retold to prepare corporate leaders for reputation damage, market shifts, frauds, and other contingencies threatening their firms. In this field, crises are viewed as major opportunities to improve market perception and market share, help a firm's reputation, and dramatize commitment to corporate citizenship.

During unexpected events, there are many challenges for senior leaders of accounting firms to iron out: understanding, decision making and coordinating, terminating, accounting, and learning. These are executive tasks.

Understanding

The attack on the World Trade Center took the United States by complete surprise on September 11, 2001. In the hours and days that followed, officials at all levels of government scrambled to understand what exactly had happened, why, and how. They worried what would be next and what could be done to prevent it. In hindsight, it is clear what happened that day, but for those who lived through it, September 11 was the day when nothing made sense.

Most times, a crisis comes as a surprise. During that awful day, I was in the high-rise office of an accounting firm in Denver, fully expecting the next wave to hit us. Everyone I talked with that day was expecting the next wave to hit them, even in Des Moines, Nashville, and Amarillo. Crises, especially in the very early stages, produce vague, ambivalent, and often conflicting signals, which leaders must interpret and recognize as a crisis.

For example, is a sudden departure of a key partner an isolated incident, or is it the beginning of a series of defections? Is the cause of the departures something systemic within the firm or idiosyncratic to one partner? Leaders must make sense of events as they unfold. Leaders need to determine the likely level of threat, who or what will be affected, and how the crisis is likely to develop, without overreacting in a way that can deepen the crisis. Signals come from many sources: some loud, some soft, some accurate, some rumor and speculation, and some bearing no relation to reality. How can leaders judge which is which? How can they extract coherent and credible signals from the noise of crisis?

Decision Making and Coordinating

After Hurricane Katrina broke the levees and flooded New Orleans, the response to this natural disaster just seemed to fall apart. Survivors spent days in their homes, the Louisiana Superdome, and the Ernest N. Morial Convention Center without food, water, or ice. A wide variety of organizations—national and international, public and private—gathered to help, but logistical chains did not reach some of the survivors for weeks.

In chapter 5, I recounted that Ted Mason and his partners gathered all the information they could during the time that Hurricane Katrina was bearing down on New Orleans. Ted and his partners clearly decided who was in charge and what they were going to do. With their preparation, Laporte Sehrt Romig Hand partners did not forget their long-standing commitments to their employees and clients, an area in which other firms blinked.

An effective response to a large-scale event requires coordination among leaders and their departments. After all, each decision must be implemented by a set of organizations within a firm and, sometimes, those from the outside. Only when these organizations work together is there a chance that effective implementation will happen. True synergistic efforts produce the highest levels of cooperation.

Terminating

Although tenacity is a strong leadership quality, knowing when to terminate an initiative is another quality of great judgment. My father used to say to me, "Troy, when the horse is dead, get off," because he observed that I tend to believe so strongly in my own ideas that I will persist beyond reason. This tendency showed up in my early audit days at Price Waterhouse when I would go over budget because I wanted to get it so perfectly right that no one could question my work. Former PricewaterhouseCoopers partner Olaf Falkenhagen taught me to evaluate the risk in audit situations and back off in the lower-risk areas. He would accept over auditing in higher risk areas. What I learned was that as I did a better job of assessing risk and backing off my perfectionist tendencies in the low-risk areas, I gained some confidence to terminate my work in the higher-risk areas, as well. A leader's role in the launch of an initiative is to give the initiative time to blossom but to know when to pull the plug and terminate.

Accounting

The best leaders find a way to review not only the failures but the wins. An after-action review is a process by which the military has looked at all events, whether very successful or very painful. Neal Spencer, CEO of the megaregional firm BKP, LLP, in Springfield, MO, says, "I use the term autopsy. Using an autopsy without a blame when we have issues with the way things have gone. Let's let the dust settle, and let's autopsy the sucker and see what we did wrong, so we can learn the next time. Not to see what we did wrong to blame somebody."

Learning

Only weeks after Hurricane Katrina destroyed coastal areas in Louisiana and Mississippi, Hurricane Rita entered the Gulf of Mexico. When the projected trajectory of Hurricane Rita included Houston (the fourth largest city in the United States), the Texas authorities quickly ordered an evacuation. The lessons of Hurricane Katrina had been learned! Unfortunately, in the chaotic evacuation, more than 100 people died. Then, Hurricane Rita changed course and never reached Houston.

A crisis or disaster holds huge potential for lessons to be learned to improve contingency planning and training to enhance resilience in the event of similar episodes in the future. In an ideal world, we might expect everyone to carefully study these lessons and apply them to reform organizational practices, policies, and laws. In reality, there are many barriers to lesson drawing.

Organizations tend not to be good learners, certainly not in the aftermath of crises and disasters. One crucial barrier is the lack of authoritative and widely accepted explanations for the causes of crisis or disaster. Worst-case thinking is rarely high on agendas.

The best way to achieve great synergy and alignment is for people to cooperate in teams, so that everyone does his or her job effectively. People on teams must know that their fellow team members will also do their jobs. It's the bond of trust that team members share that allows each member to focus on his or her job to the best of his or her ability while other team members execute their roles. Teamwork enables firms to maintain synergy and alignment during business up-cycles and crisis. Let's turn now to a discussion of basic teamwork.

Teamwork

A leader must accomplish the very difficult task of getting team members to believe in "we" more than "me." In business, we must share knowledge, experience, information, contacts, and ideas. Many leaders take for granted that their team members know how their efforts help the firm—this is most often not the case.

Coach John Wooden used the 10 hands concept to teach his team that everyone contributed to every basket, not just the scorer. It took both hands from all 5 players to score a basket. In other words, the 4 players who didn't score directly helped with each basket, whether they inbounded the ball, passed to the scorer, or simply blocked out an opposing player.

That is the same in an accounting firm. It takes two hands from every employee to serve a client, so we must ask ourselves the following questions:

▲ What is the impact of a negligible producer, or a ball-hogging glory-seeker, on everyone else on the team?
▲ Why is this person on our team if his contribution is minimal or distracting?
▲ Is there anything I can do to enhance this person's contribution?
▲ Can we move her to another position where she can contribute?
▲ Should we trade this person to another firm?

Rick Dreher, CEO of the megaregional firm Wipfli LLP in Green Bay, WS, has worked hard to get his firm aligned around a team-oriented culture.

> I want to get into a cloud environment, and I want to tear down silos. If I start measuring things at the individual level, you think I'm going to get people to work in a team environment? I equate business and running an accounting firm to a sports team, and the key word there is *team*. In a team, we all have roles, and we all have contributions to make. We're trying to align people to their passions and their strengths. You know, if we only have 11 offensive linemen on our football team, we don't have any great quarterbacks or running backs or wide receivers.

David Maister, speaking at the Winning Is Everything Conference in January 2008, said there are two types of individuals: those who are team players and those who are loners. He admitted that he was a poor team player and, therefore, was best being a loner. He recommended that to build your firm, you must recruit and retain those people who understand and internalize the concept that the best people are those who will make the best team, not those who have individual talents but can't support the team. Often, the most talented individuals will not be a good fit for your group.

All roles on a team offer the opportunity for individual greatness. This idea will be understood and accepted only if the leader reinforces it on a consistent basis. Everyone must believe that his or her contributions count and affect the success of the entire firm.

As a leader, you can create an environment that rewards hard work and improvement as you unleash the unseen talents of those you lead. Team members who feel they can better themselves by doing a great job and helping the team will work at the highest level.

Leading Teams for Synergy

Aligning all the parts of an organization is like aligning your car. When one of the four wheels is out of alignment, the entire vehicle veers one way or the other. Synergy creates a technically elegant system where all the parts work together, so that the team is greater than the individual players, and they help you achieve the firm vision.

Keith Farlinger, CEO of the national firm BDO Canada LLP in Toronto, Canada, says

> Working to give this large firm, with offices of varying sizes and locations, a single unifying vision takes lots of patience and time. I am a big believer, as I travel to the Owen Sound and Cornwall offices and then go to the Toronto offices, that we are the same firm. It's an absolute cop-out that we have to have different values and visions in different offices in the firm. So, we are really focused this year on rolling out a vision and values and expectations that are consistent right across the firm. Frankly, we've got a ways to go, but that's our rallying cry as we go forward over the next few years.

Creating synergy in a constantly changing world is a huge challenge. Change requires a leader to use imagination, rather than just experience, to successfully handle new challenges. So long as you measure your intended choices against solid principles, your results can be more predictable and positive. Leaders must develop the capacity to cope with dramatic changes and shifts in order to build long-term strength.

The best companies in the world create synergy around their teams. They create a set of standards and then train like crazy to equip all team members to deliver behaviors that meet the prescribed standards. Teamwork is a value that many accounting firms espouse, but you can always improve your team.

Jim Metzler, vice president of the AICPA, says

> I've seen it for years and years: in firms that generally get somewhere between $3 million and $6 million dollars of revenue, they tend to hit the wall. They're no longer a small firm, and they want to be a bigger firm. Yet, understanding what it takes to grow both from a business standpoint and a leadership standpoint is very difficult. At some point, they must gel as a team to break through to that other side. They realize that a serious firm is about a business, not about individuals.

Team Development

Leaders understand that a team is not static; it will progress through developmental phases. Leaders must anticipate those phases and allow team members to mature through them. If you shortcut a phase, the team's effectiveness may be at risk. Great leaders know how to form teams and coach them through the following phases of team development:

- ▲ Forming
- ▲ Storming
- ▲ Norming
- ▲ Performing

In each phase, a good leader can adjust his or her leadership style to fit the team that he or she has at the time. In large, multidisciplinary accounting firms, there may be many teams, all at different stages of development.

The forming—storming—norming—performing model of team development (see figure 16-1) was first proposed by Bruce Tuckman in 1965, who maintained that these phases are all necessary and inevitable in order for the team to grow, face up to challenges, tackle problems, find solutions, plan work, and deliver results. This model has become the basis for subsequent models of team dynamics and a management theory frequently used to describe the behavior of existing teams.

In each one of these phases, the skilled leader takes a different leadership approach to create alignment and synergy. In the forming phase of team development, team members are chosen and assigned their roles and responsibilities, so the leader will take a more directive approach. During storming, team members are searching for their voices and boundaries, so the leader must be a teacher and coach. Once the team begins to fall into the norming phase, the leader allows the team members to accept more of the responsibility by helping them through any friction and coaching them toward harmony. Once the team matures into its performing mode, the leader steps back into an empowering role. Each of these phases is described in more detail in the following sections.

Forming

Team forming happens first. The leader may select the members and begin assigning them roles based upon their experience and desires. The team learns about the opportunities and some of the barriers that they may face. During this phase, many team members are very focused on themselves but may act like they are team players.

Too many teams are formed without making sure that members have skills to fit their roles and that not everyone on the team has the same skills. Just like a good basketball team has five specific roles, work teams also have roles. For example, a team full of "idea people" tends to be very creative but has difficulty following through. On the other hand, if all the people are implementers, they may struggle with coming up with ideas. So, in the forming stage, various

Figure 16-1: Stages of Team Development

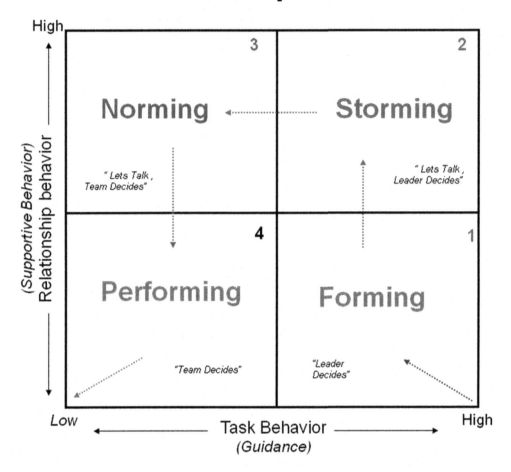

Stages of Team Development

team roles like creator, refiner, advancer, and implementor may be assigned, and mature team players begin to model appropriate team-oriented behavior.

Creators are tasked with idea generation. A refiner's main role is to refine the ideas, so they are workable or marketable. Advancers will usually sell or communicate the ideas to the rest of the team, firm, or clients. Implementers actually love executing well-crafted ideas. Leaders tend to be quite directive during this phase. The members get to know each other, make new friends, and see how they can create synergy together. Processes and policies are sometimes ignored, and certain members may test the leader. Leaders must be prepared to answer lots of questions about the team's mission and objectives and how they fit within the firm's mission and objectives.

Carl George, former managing partner of Clifton Gunderson LLP, says

> I figured out very quickly that an office is a microcosm of a larger practice, and my job is
> to help grow this thing by developing relationships. I think that's a key for our people today
> that any professional business is just as much about people and relationships as it is about law
> or accounting. When we do a merger, the financial model is the financial model, take it or
> leave it. The brain surgery is meshing their culture in with ours. So, we do the psychological
> profiling before we close a transaction.

As Carl suggests, in the early formation of a new team, the leader will be a bit more directive and sometimes say, "Take it or leave it." This is the best time to eliminate team members who are going to be disruptive because as the rest of the team begins to gel, the friction will grow. A great leader will be relationship oriented but will strongly demonstrate passion for the goals of the team, letting everyone know that the team comes first and the members come second.

Storming

A team enters the storming stage when different people and their ideas compete for leadership. Team members address issues such as the team's goals and how they fit with the vision of the future firm, the problems that they should tackle, how they may function together and individually, the role that each person plays, and how they fit with other members' roles. Some team members will open up to each other; they may confront each other's ideas and perspectives. In some teams, storming can be resolved quickly and smoothly, but other teams become bogged down in conflict. Immature team members and rugged individualists may want to demonstrate how much they know. And a few team members may engage in analysis paralysis or focus on minutiae to avoid moving forward.

The storming phase can be contentious and painful to those who avoid conflict at all costs. In this stage, leaders should show tolerance for differences. Without patience, teams can fail, never achieve synergistic functioning, or even be destructive to the firm. The great leader will allow the storming to take place in a controlled environment. Sometimes, getting the team offsite to go through this phase is effective. If your team members begin storming in front of nonmembers, the ensuing confusion can be overwhelming.

Leaders of teams and firms during this phase still need to be directive in their guidance of decision making and professional behavior. During storming, decisions don't come easily. Although clarity increases, uncertainties persist, and power struggles blow up. The primary focus for a great leader during this phase is coaching each member to play his or her role effectively and in context with others on the team or in the firm.

Norming

When the team enters the norming stage, players adjust their behavior to dramatically reduce the friction of working together. Members arrive at this stage by agreeing on shared values, professional behavior, processes, codes of behavior or communication, working tools, and even lists of dos and don'ts. Trust begins to develop as members see each other demonstrate integrity, intent, and results. The leader must watch for too much comfort in this phase because some people may lose their creativity if the norming behaviors become too polite, valuing artificial harmony over effectiveness.

Leaders of firms and teams during this phase tend to adjust their styles to be more participative than in the stages of forming and storming. Members take more responsibility as their roles and responsibilities become clearer. More of the decisions are now made by team members or subgroups.

In a norming team, leaders work to facilitate the team's and firm's efforts in each initiative. By creating success experiences, they help the team bond further. During this phase, it is crucial to get both strong individual effort and team motivation.

Bob Hottman, CEO of the top-100 firm Ehrhardt Keefe Steiner & Hottman PC (EKS&H) in Denver, CO, focuses on this phase in his firm's business development efforts. "In our firm, we've developed business for a lot of reasons. One is for fun, but number two is that we need to provide opportunity for our people. We want to have great people, and we have a very simple business philosophy. You get great people to take care of great clients, which enables you to get more great people to take care of more great clients."

Performing

Many firms and teams will reach the performing stage in which they are able to function as a unit. Now, we achieve real alignment and synergy. If a team or firm gets stuck in storming or even norming, real synergy cannot occur. During the performing phase, members rely on each other and become truly interdependent. When synergy occurs, one plus one now begins to equal three or even more, and these results motivate the team members to excel. A great leader will encourage some conflict and dissent to keep the team improving.

Leaders of performing teams will delegate and empower the team members to make most of the decisions. Bill Haller, managing partner of the national firm CapinCrouse LLP in Indianapolis, IN, has long since dealt with many questions about how work gets done, how the team relates, and how his team performs.

> Once a business is mature, leadership cannot be so domineering. In a business in crisis or in infrastructure building, consensus leadership is not very effective. Once an organization is mature, consensus leadership is probably best, unless you want revolution. Our recruiter is a work-at-home mom who is nowhere near the offices and, yet, recruits all the talent in the firm. I am the managing partner, and I live remotely 500 miles from the nearest office. Some of the issues other firms are [dealing with], asking if they should do that, we've already accepted, like flex schedules and remote work, so some of the basic things that cause turnover we don't have.

During the performing phase, synergistic leaders oversee, delegate, and empower.

Conclusion

Well-designed processes and teams should help people work smoothly, should minimize nonvalue-adding activities, and should provide some flexibility, so people can adjust to unexpected demands and contingencies. The structure of the firm or team should ensure the proper reporting relationships, that team members have their best responsibilities, and that people who fit best on a team should be working together. Leaders must use care in determining who is hired or placed on teams (putting the right people on the bus), overseeing how they are trained, and then providing opportunities for team members to learn and develop themselves. When this doesn't happen, things may never be optimal. For instance, Terry Snyder says

> "One of my roles was as a regional managing partner in a firm, and I just couldn't solve why there wasn't harmony. It was frustrating because the people didn't trust each other there. I've worked in the opposite situation. I first started my profession at Andersen, and to this day, some of those people who were my partners are still some of the people who I have the most confidence in and the most trust in. It was never about how much money we made. It was about how well we worked together and how we were building the practice. When you find that, it is so important."

Leaders must ensure that people have good information in a timely manner to make proper decisions. Leaders should be careful to place the people in decision-making roles who have the best expertise for that role. Finally, leaders must ensure that financial, positional, and opportunity rewards are properly aligned to the strategy and vision of the firm. Rewards must be designed to encourage teamwork and individual effort at the same time.

Sustaining Leadership:
The Ultimate Succession Plan

"It's important to figure out the short- and long-term view of succession. The person who could run the firm tomorrow might not fit the pattern you need 10 years from now."

~TONY ARGIZ

When most accountants think about succession planning, the CEO's or managing partner's role immediately comes to mind. However, when done appropriately, the succession plan should include key positions beyond those of upper leadership. Yet, many firms have not done a great job in building the bench strength of leaders at all levels. Then, when faced with a vacancy at the top, there is little selection to turn to for help. When firms neglect building tomorrow's leaders for many years, those firms get sold for a small price. Not only do the owners lose capital, but the employees and clients get bounced around and lose.

In this chapter, I'll provide some guidance on building an ongoing succession process that leads to an enduring accounting firm: one that remains independent or one that merges on its own terms. Sustainability and succession are natural by-products in the well-led firms. Succession is not accomplished well as a spreadsheet exercise, which is the way some consultants approach the subject. In this chapter, I'll profile two leaders who've been very proactive in succession: (1) Kris McMasters, CEO of the national accounting firm CliftonLarsonAllen LLP in Milwaukee, WI, who led the succession planning team at Clifton Gunderson LLP, only to learn that she was the ultimate choice of her partners, and (2) David Deeter, founding partner of the top-100 firm Frazier & Deeter, LLC, in Atlanta, GA, who led the succession of his firm to a new highly respected CEO and leader.

We will cover the training and experience that succeeding leaders should have, along with a process for identifying and growing your next generation of leaders. Sustainability is the result of a firm that has achieved synergy and alignment through all the other aspects of the matters we've discussed in chapters 1–16. The main thing I want to help you avoid is the dilemma that one of our clients encountered a few years ago when out of 30 partners, there was only one who could succeed the managing partner. I will challenge you to build bench strength in all aspects of leadership in this chapter.

Consultant Jay Nisberg says

> Why do we think all this merger mania is taking place right now? It's probably because leadership takes them to a plateau. Now what? Developing a sound succession planning program is essential to a firm's success, regardless of size. Although many larger accounting firms may have some succession planning processes in place, small firms are often guilty of overlooking the subject entirely.

It is easy to understand how a lack of attention to succession planning can happen. The task of cultivating the next generation of leaders is often an *additional* duty, rather than a primary performance indicator. If you don't do it this year, nothing happens—until you reach a tipping point when it's too late!

Ken Baggett, co-managing partner of the national firm CohnReznick LLP, believes in creating young leaders. "I'm a real big believer in pushing leadership down to as far as you can to as young as you can because exposure early will create much greater long term success." This is how he forms the firm's future partners, which ensures lasting success. Every year, each staff member fills out a report card that assesses what the firm is doing well, where it can improve, and what the firm's goals should be.

I've had a number of firms approach us about opportunities to merge in. One particular firm was north of $50 million, so it's definitely good size firm. And I said, "What's your biggest problem?"

They said "We don't have any future leaders."

I thought to myself, "Well, I know your problem; you did not give partners the opportunity to fail." If you're going to wait for the opportunity for them to succeed, you will be waiting forever. You have to be prepared. As we were meeting with this firm, I brought 2 of our leaders: one was 41 and the other 45. They participated in the meeting and had great questions.

Later, the managing partner asked me, "How many did you say you have?:

I said, "I've got a bunch."

And he said, "That's our dream."

In our firm, I want to know why people in their 30s *aren't* going into leadership roles.

This type of leadership development requires much time and effort and the focused attention of the top leader. In larger firms, the task of developing this type of program is sometimes assigned to the HR department. However, HR team members are not always trained for the issues surrounding extensive succession planning and leader development. HR managers may be able to coordinate basic duties and ensure that development efforts are not merely tossed aside in lieu of more pressing issues, but a responsibility of this magnitude should not be placed solely on the HR department. This is a vital CEO role, as Ken Baggett explains. In all firms, the responsibility of assuring an adequate bench of leader and manager candidates should be job one of senior leadership.

Bill Hermann, former managing partner of the megaregional firm Plante & Moran, PLLC, in Southfield, MI, was a very successful managing and leading partner, but he chose to step down at the end of his second term in order to help build and mentor the next generation of leadership. Although Hermann remains an active partner in the firm today, he devotes his time to coaching and mentoring other leaders in the firm. In his role as CEO, his executive duties often interfered with the mentoring needed for the firm's future leaders. Gordon Krater, managing partner of the megaregional firm Plante & Moran, PLLC, says, "Bill Hermann was a very good managing partner. So, for him to step away when he still had one term he could have served was really walking his talk. I mean, the proof was in his actions. He had identified a number of us who he had trained, given us experiences, and given us feedback to grow."

Succession planning is defined as any process that is designed to ensure a continued pool of qualified candidates, thereby providing provisions to continue effective organizational performance. The issue of building layers of qualified leadership candidates has not been given the focused attention or dedicated resources required to prepare firms for long-term success. Traditionally, the replacement method was used to fill vacancies in leadership. Emphasis was placed only on replacement as an answer to vacancies created by a tragedy, such as death, or a decision to leave for another position. This has been a very passive way to handle the crucial leadership challenge of succession.

The replacement method has been utilized for decades, with a relative degree of success, because

1. typical career paths were rigidly determined (two years to senior, three years to supervisor, and so on), and few employees deviated from the normal routes.
2. technical changes were not as rapid and were more easily anticipated.
3. HR departments of large firms employed staff members who were dedicated to people development.
4. there were fewer mergers, and firms were more stable.

Despite some level of past success, the accounting environment is rapidly changing, and new alternatives to staffing contingencies and leadership development must be considered.

Developing authentic succession planning programs is increasingly important. Many firms have a spreadsheet and have identified successors, but they fail to invest time and money in the up-and-coming leaders, so they'll be prepared to lead when the time comes. Authentic plans must have a budget for training, experience, and mastery. Although the traditional replacement method and succession planning procedures overlap, there are some major differences between the two. In times of unexpected situations, there is a true need to sustain firm control quickly. This need has been demonstrated by untimely illnesses and unfortunate accidents, such as a CEO's heart attack, stroke, or death. This type of loss creates a need for replacement processes as an aspect of risk management leadership.

Succession planning is different from replacement planning because it focuses on forecasting firmwide needs. It is not based upon reactions to unforeseen events. It is based upon proactively securing the human resources needed to ensure the continuity and prosperity of the firm. Talent is observed and cultivated from within the firm. Each individual is groomed for his or her future role through calculated development activities. This is why succession planning has been compared to a relay race. In fact, some refer to the process as relay planning. Each individual in the race is equally qualified and prepared to carry the baton to the finish line. Succession planning deals with passing on responsibility, rather than merely filling a vacancy.

Leader Profile: Kristine McMasters, CEO of the national accounting firm CliftonLarsonAllen LLP in Milwaukee, WI

Kristine McMasters, CEO of CliftonLarsonAllen, graduated from high school in Catlin, IL, where she was first in her class and president of the student council. She brought a humble, high-achieving brand of drive to her many roles at CliftonLarsonAllen, where she has invested her entire professional career. Kris worked her way up through the ranks to the CEO's leadership role with her dedication to growing herself and her teammates. She was one of the first participants in CliftonLarsonAllen's leadership development program. This program was one of the first in the accounting industry under the leadership of then managing partner Curt Mingle.

Her responsibilities as CEO include overall firm leadership, strategic planning, and the overall growth and vision for the firm. Kris became the firm's fourth CEO and first and only female CEO in the history of the accounting profession among the top 25 firms.

You can see through her achievements at CliftonLarsonAllen that Kris is committed and passionate about people and growing strong leaders. She has received numerous awards and recognition for leadership and has been honored by *Accounting Today* as one of the top 100 most influential people in accounting.

Kris was instrumental in introducing the firm to a new human resource structure (Priority One) that enabled the firm to hire the right people, develop their talents, and create an exciting and flexible work environment. She also introduced the firm to WIN@CG: Women's Initiative Now—an initiative that promotes a culture that grows women leaders.

CliftonLarsonAllen partner Steve DeBruyn says

> Kris's leadership can best be defined by her approach to the update of our firm's strategic plan. She has been diligent in studying the economic and business landscape of our country and then using that information, along with input from many of our partners and other leaders throughout the firm, to craft our plan while remaining true to our mission and values as a firm.
>
> As Kris's responsibilities began to increase within the firm, she clearly recognized the need to delegate some of her work to other partners. One area that she delegated to me was our peer review practice. She empowered me by expressing her confidence in my experience and ability and making herself available for guidance as I grew into the job of performing some very large and complex peer review assignments. Her goal was not only to serve the client, but she was also developing future leaders for the firm.
>
> The biggest aspect of Kris McMaster's leadership style is the way she creates synergy among everyone. Not only was she diligent in the development of our new strategic plan, but she has also developed an unwavering commitment to that plan. She communicates regularly and with confidence with every person who has responsibility for the plan, provides support where needed, and she makes sure that everyone has the relevant training to succeed. You can count on Kris to move forward, without exception, once a decision has been made. This really keeps us all on the same page and working with the same vision.

Kris has been a member at large of the AICPA Council. She was named 2008 innovator of the year by *Public Accounting Report*, is a past member of the Financial Accounting Standards Advisory Council and Professional Practice Executive Committee of the Center for Audit Quality, and has been awarded many other professional and community awards.

Developing Your Leaders From Within

Over the last few years, most accounting firms have become intensely aware of the need to develop leadership talent from within their firms. A recent study by the AICPA's Private Companies Practice Section (PCPS) ranked the top 10 issues of highest concern for owners of these firms. Succession planning was listed as the third highest concern for firms with 21 or more professionals.

When thinking about succession of the leading partner, you will want to think both short and long term. Think short term in the event of an illness or accident of the present leader. What would you do tomorrow if your leader could not function? A person who fills this role might be more dominating and directive. In chapter 16, "Synergy and Alignment: One Plus One Equals Three," I discussed the various roles of team development. If something were to happen to your leader today, you are right back to the first phase of leading a team, and in that role, a directive leader may be very effective. After the September 11 attacks, Mayor Rudy Guiliani of New York was a very effective leader because he took charge and communicated. After Hurricane Katrina, Mayor Ray Nagin of New Orleans was a consensus builder, and he came off looking like a buffoon.

Tony Argiz, founder, CEO, and managing partner of the megaregional firm Morrison, Brown, Argiz & Farra, LLP, in Miami, FL, says, "As a leader, I think it's important on a day-to-day basis to figure out the short- and long-term view of succession. What happens if something occurs tomorrow? That same person who you think could run the firm tomorrow in case of an accident might not necessarily fit the pattern that you need at the firm 10 or 11 years from now."

That long-term leader may be a younger person in your firm who is still in development but can operate a team over the long haul through the storming and norming phases to get to the performing phase. A very directive leader may get you from the reforming phase to the performing phase very quickly, but in the long term, such a leader will cause turnover of other leaders and drastic changes that hurt the firm. A disaster plan that appoints a leader for two years in the event of an emergency is helpful, so long as you hold a selection or election within approximately two years after the emergency to make certain that you have the right leader for the firm.

Approaches to Succession Planning

A variety of approaches can be utilized to successfully implement a succession planning program for an accounting firm. The approach of choice depends on the size and overall strategic plan of the firm. Some of the most common approaches are the following:

1. *Top-down approach.* Led by the CEO and other senior firm leaders.
2. *Bottom-up approach.* A comprehensive, firmwide leadership development program starting at the beginning of an accountant's career.
3. *Futuring approach.* Scanning the business environment for coming changes, matching talent with expected labor needs.
4. *Targeting approach.* Focused on solving specific problems for a particular time.

These approaches are described in more detail in the following sections.

Top Down

Usually, the first approach to succession planning, particularly for a smaller firm, should be a top-down approach. The top leader of the firm, along with any other owners, wants to develop a short-term and long-term succession development plan. The short-term plan should lay out the firm's philosophy on the top role of the firm. Is the role one that rotates periodically, or is it a role that demands a different skill set and is more permanent?

Bob Hottman, CEO of the top-100 firm Ehrhardt Keefe Steiner & Hottman PC (EKS&H) in Denver, CO, says, "Our CEO is not a transitional role that you're going to have for 2 to 3 to 5 to 7 or 10 years even. It is a career shift to being our leader, and your client is now the firm. As a result of that, you'll give up your existing external client relationships and focus all your attention on the firm."

Many smaller firms perceive a great deal of risk in this decision. There is a risk that the CEO may not be the best leader. There are risks to the elected leader that his fellow owners may toss him aside, and he'll be without the safety net of a client base. However, there will be very little growth without taking some risk.

Senior leader engagement is vital in the succession planning process. Many CEOs will not view their positions as permanent. They will recognize that the long-term success of the firm depends not only on their accomplishments but also on those of their successor. Current leaders must emphasize the need to develop future talent at all levels of the firm. The current executive should be involved in the development of the succession program, so that it meets the firm's mission and vision.

In Jim Collins's book, *Good to Great: Why Some Companies Make the Leap…and Others Don't*, he discusses a level 5 leader. He found that the leaders who are the most effective are those who possess a dogged determination to win, along with a unique humility. One of the most interesting aspects of his study was that none of the level 5 leaders were the rock star leaders who write the books and give the seminars, but their companies achieved extraordinary results both during the term of their leadership and for 15 years after they left. In other words, these level 5 leaders developed a sustainable form of leadership. Bill Hubly, founder and managing principal of the local firm Corbett, Duncan & Hubly, PC, in Itasca, IL, says. "Being a level 5 leader means that you're willing, at some point, to say the firm's in better hands with someone else at the helm. The same is true with our practice areas. I think a practice leader has 10 years or so to serve. We've got to identify successors now. We're not going to wait until they have 2 years to go and say, 'Who is the next person?'"

Although initial efforts to develop a succession planning program target upper-level leaders and partners, you also need to phase into other levels within the firm. In fact, some experts believe that bottom-up succession planning is far more effective than top-down methods. The bottom-up method does not put top-level partners as the first priority; the focus is on the identification of all key positions, not just those in the upper levels.

Practically speaking, because most succession planning programs are based on the top-down method, it is believed that the bottom-up approach is good for the firm that has identified the next top leader.

Bottom Up

The retention rate in accounting firms is sometimes low because of the changing expectations of the young professional. Given several years of training and experience on technical subjects only, the young accountant gets bored, loses engagement, and looks for greener pastures. Introducing leadership development earlier in their career is a way to keep bright people growing and learning.

Some accounting firms are not placing enough emphasis on cultivating the next generation of leaders that will be required to sustain competitive advantage and business continuity. The accounting environment has historically promoted employees into leadership roles without thoroughly evaluating the leadership capabilities of these individuals. Many have been promoted based upon their longevity with the firm or technical prowess, rather than leadership skills. Possessing a technical skill oftentimes has been the basic reason for promotion; however, technical skill rarely will translate into leadership ability.

Succession planning and leadership development at all levels isn't just something that's good for the firm—it's a necessity for people who want to advance. Rick Anderson, CEO of the multiregional firm Moss Adams LLP in Seattle, WA, says

> In all aspects of our business, leadership succession and development is crucial. It takes place when the senior trains a staff member to take her role. It takes place when the senior manager, who is responsible for many engagements at once, can train another to succeed him. It occurs at the office and industry niche level. And it happens at my level. It is just an incredibly important role. Before you can take on the next role, you have to train somebody to take on the role that you want to exit. If you want to do something different tomorrow, you have to have trained somebody to do what you did today.
>
> At our firm level, our executive committee has a process where every year, the COO and myself do a report to the executive committee on all major leadership roles in the firm, such as office managing partner, industry group leaders, and key administrative office positions. We identify people who would be logical candidates for positions and whether they are ready today, or are they likely to be ready in a couple of years.
>
> If a firm and its leaders deal with all of these things, they're going to be pretty successful.

Often, talented individuals drown in their new roles largely due to the lack of leadership training. Conversely, many internally qualified employees are overlooked for promotional opportunities because top leaders can be unaware of the firmwide talent. Externally recruited leaders are often hired to fill the leadership vacancies. This sometimes causes aspiring leadership candidates to become disgruntled and eventually leave the firm. We have had a number of clients whose senior manager group broke off and formed their own firm because these talented people did not have opportunity at their mother firm.

Bob Hottman adds

> For many of our leadership roles, we put people into all sorts of positions to see how they handle themselves. To see how they react. See if they overreact, underreact. See how they handle people. See how they handle stress. See how they calm down and are steady. We think an important aspect of being a leader is not being hot and cold but being able to be steady and making decisions. Making decisions for the long haul, not for the short haul.

Demands on the recruitment and retention of skilled accounting professionals are increasing, and more emphasis is being placed on leadership development and succession planning. As the war for top talent continues to intensify, accounting firms are being forced to evaluate ways to scan the environment for the next generation of leaders and to develop succession planning programs that ensure the continuity of long-term success.

Futuring

Firm initiatives for the development of future leaders should outline talent recruitment (David Deeter calls this a strategic strike), retention, leadership development, and succession planning programs to increase firmwide performance and accountability. Although finding and retaining the next tier of qualified accounting leaders is a critical key to success, the efforts are futile if the development of these leaders is ignored, and they are inadequately prepared for their new roles. Neglecting the resolution of skill gaps can disrupt the leadership transition for even the most aspiring leadership candidate.

Gary Shamis, founder and CEO of the top-100 multioffice firm SS&G Financial Services, Inc., in Cleveland, OH, says

> We've developed some succession tools internally for all levels of leadership. I basically studied all our offices, how many partners are in each office, their ages, how many years they were from retirement, and so on. Then, we studied the group just below the partners and tried to figure out how many people really had the opportunity to move forward. It was very interesting because what I found was that in three of the four offices, we're in pretty good shape. But in one office, we really need to build some bench strength.

To avoid a shortage of bench strength, it is imperative that accounting leaders appropriately survey their talent roster and plan for continuity in their leadership. Scanning the environment for the next generation of leaders is prudent for any firm, and developing an effective succession program is a key to corporate longevity. However, with the current war for the best talent, it is more than just practical for accounting firms—it is an issue of survival.

Terry Snyder, president of the accounting firm alliance PKF North America in Lawrence, GA, says, "We're going to lose good people, so we've always got to be recruiting. We've always got to be filling up the channels, and we've always got to have capable leadership people in place, so that when something comes up we've got the people to fill those voids."

Scott Dietzen, managing partner, Northwest Region, of the national accounting firm CliftonLarsonAllen LLP in Spokane, WA, shares

> For example, our director of tax is Chris Hesse. He is a very, very valuable and talented individual, and we could just see this big void if something happened to Chris. So, 2 years ago, I asked him to put in his scorecard that he would work with the COOs, and they would select 8–10 people. Once a month, Chris would hold a video conference with a set agenda of how we would begin to develop tax expertise in this group. We would start with people in the 2–5 year experience range. And so, for the last 2 years, every month they have a call about current events and tax and how they do certain projects. They also lead meetings and

come up with agenda items and think about tax processes and tax software. So, we have a
pool of people who have an extensive tax knowledge, knowing that they'll benefit our firm,
but maybe, 1 or 2 people will rise up to the level of being a director.

The AICPA's PCPS has developed an extensive array of resources in its Human Capital
Center to help CPA firms of all sizes address this critical issue.

Targeting Approach

Selecting the appropriate individuals for leadership positions is paramount to a firm's success. Erroneously placing the wrong person in a leadership role can result in problems that
create turnover in team members and poor client service. These problems can range from
lack of employee morale to financial losses. The demand for qualified and skilled leaders far
outweighs the supply.

Other industries outside of accounting are intensifying their efforts to attract new leaders. This creates a mobile workforce that can find multiple positions in multiple industries.
This mobile workforce makes it even more challenging to retain the talented individuals
in accounting leadership roles. However, despite the challenge, the effort must be made in
order for accounting firms to succeed in this consumer-driven market. By combining sound
succession planning procedures and effective leadership development activities, accounting
firms can create a long-term process that will provide them with boundless leadership talent. This strategic initiative is necessary to diminish the ill effects of a shrinking workforce.

Charly Weinstein, CEO of the megaregional firm EisnerAmper LLP in New York City,
NY, has devoted himself to developing the next leadership team. He shares, "Since I became
CEO, we've transitioned all of our major division's leadership. So, we have that next core of
leaders identified, and hopefully, the young leaders behind them are beginning to develop, as
well, because it's a continuous process."

A leader trains, challenges, empowers, and holds people accountable, and each person is
different. Charly says

> What I do is assign projects or difficult issues to our partners who are moving up the lead-
> ership ranks to see how they perform. I am particularly interested in how they are getting
> things done through other people. I'm there if they need me for guidance. But I stay out
> of the way and let people make mistakes or succeed. I want to know how they are leading
> and learning. This is the ticket for the next step up the leadership ladder.

The business environment in accounting firms is more unstable today because of changes
in hierarchical frameworks and the increase in competitive forces. Accounting leaders must
think more strategically in terms of their talent roster. A firm's abilities to master the abundant upcoming labor challenges may make the difference between overall firm success and
failure.

Krista McMasters shares

> Entrepreneurs who start accounting firms get to a $5–$10 million plateau and have dif-
> ficulty breaking through to the next level. At that point, it's a different ball game. You have

to add a lot of resources. You're going to be competing in a different way than you were before. You're going to have to lead the people who are involved in that size of the firm. You can't always lead from a consensus-building way. You have to lead with influence, persuasion, trust, and vision. We see firms that we've acquired that have gotten to a point where it's going to be tough for them to take it to the next level.

Therefore, in order to attract a next-generation leader to your firm, it may be necessary to reach outside your firm, as Bob Bunting, former CEO of the megaregional firm Moss Adams LLP in Seattle, WA, did (with his recruitment of 23 leaders) or David Deeter does (with his strategic strike approach). Sometimes, though, the quest for a savior causes firms to overlook talented individuals already within the firm. These talented individuals often have successfully maneuvered through years of firm politics and culture. With the appropriate training, cultivating leaders from within a firm can provide the most effective leadership candidates. This training should encompass both an efficient succession plan and subsequent leadership development activities. Accounting firms should attempt to use internal employees who are knowledgeable in their particular fields. This utilizes the leadership candidates who have practical application skills and provides a sense of connectivity with employees across the firm.

Leader Profile: David Deeter, founding partner of the top-100 firm Frazier & Deeter, LLC, in Atlanta, GA

David Deeter, a founding partner of Frazier & Deeter, LLC, is a deeply principled man. He and cofounder Jim Frazier have taken their first-generation firm to one of the top 100 firms in the United States with no mergers. Dave grew up in suburban Atlanta and earned his MBA at Georgia State University while paying his way through college working nights.

Dave met Jim Frazier at the Atlanta office of Main Hurdman (later KPMG). At age 25, he followed Jim into forming their firm in the downtown area of Atlanta, GA. Frazier & Deeter, LLC, has been selected several times by *INSIDE Public Accounting* newsletter as one of the top 25 firms in the United States in its best-of-the-best survey. Dave has played a major role in facilitating the growth of his firm. From 2001–09, during his term as managing partner, the firm experienced an average growth of 20 percent annually and became a top 100 firm in the United States. In a recent survey conducted by *INSIDE Public Accounting*, Dave was recognized by his peers as one of the most admired managing partners in U.S. accounting firms.

Roger Lusby, Dave's partner says

> David's greatest strength is his boldness. He is not afraid to ask for business. He remembers people and refers or matches them up with others. He very much enjoys making phone calls; this is how he stays in contact with clients and friends. These traits also allowed him to dream about growing our firm into a top 100 CPA firm in the U.S.

Frazier & Deeter, LLC, managing partner Seth McDaniel says

> In my opinion, one of David's biggest insights was to bring key people in from the outside. David frequently referred to these folks as "famous people," or "strategic strikes," who have been where we are going. He brought those people into the

(continued)

(continued)

> organization and used them to springboard the firm ahead of the competition. This was a critical strategy that allowed us to take advantage of many opportunities that our competitors could not.
>
> A perfect example of this was David's attracting Wayne Reid. Wayne had been a partner at Arthur Andersen for over 30 years and at Deloitte for 2 years after the fall of Andersen. Wayne was an international and corporate tax expert. He lent immediate credibility to those areas of tax for the firm.
>
> Dave loves working with company owners and executives, and he has been involved in numerous corporate and partnership firms. These activities include working closely with clients and their attorneys to obtain the most strategic capital structure. In addition to holding leadership roles in both national and regional accounting firms, Dave has been a leader in the growth of his church and serves as an Atlanta-area football official.

Succession Planning Versus the Traditional Replacement Method

The traditional method of learning one's technical specialty and then somehow becoming a senior, manager, or partner is not a reliable method for producing leaders. Most firms need a more deliberate way to improve the leadership skills of seniors, supervisors, managers, and owners. A formal leadership development program can be implemented in large or small firms alike. Although an investment is required, a development program is a wise use of resources for a number of reasons: well-led firms tend to attract the best professionals, produce loyal team members, incur less unwanted turnover, build loyal customers, and yield impressive financial returns. Current leaders must weigh the small annual investment against the enormous costs associated with less skilled professionals, higher turnover, and the low firm sales price that results when retiring founders haven't built succession of leadership at all levels.

Some of the changes that make the traditional and passive replacement method obsolete for today's firms include the following:

▲ Skilled accountants have many choices.

▲ Technology and competition are changing faster than ever before.

▲ Senior leaders are meeting increased demands. This makes it difficult to dedicate the time and effort required to develop the next level of leaders.

▲ Employee loyalty is a relic of the past.

Long-term business success depends on competitively retaining intellectual capital across the firm: the foundation of effective succession planning programs. Even though studies indicate that leaders cultivated and promoted internally produce significantly better performance than their externally recruited counterparts, little emphasis has been placed on leadership grooming. Making this issue even more significant are the research projects that indicate firms that place a heavy emphasis on leadership development experience considerably higher financial returns than firms that do not.

Potential Labor Crisis

Unfortunately, accounting firms continue to overestimate their potential skilled workforce. This is a dangerous business strategy in lieu of the changes in the workforce. Past decades provided sufficient labor pools without fail, but the workforce of today is much more limited, and the aging partner group is poised to create even larger labor shortages. The number of retiring partners will drastically increase in the next few years, causing a further labor crisis in upper leadership.

Challenges of Implementation

Although succession planning is vital for long-term firm success, most firms do not know where to begin in terms of implementing a program. In chapter 7, "Teaching, Coaching, and Mentoring: Multiplying Your Leadership," I laid out several approaches to leadership development, so that the process of selecting new leaders becomes easier. Issues surrounding successful leadership development are abundant. There are problems associated with transitioning from the passive replacement method to a new, more active succession process. Furthermore, controversy often emerges about whether leaders are born with the required skills or if the skills can be attained.

As the accounting environment continues to change, sensible accounting firms will look beyond their current tier of leadership. A healthy supply of accounting leaders will be required. Successful firms will create succession planning systems that will continuously provide qualified leadership candidates. Considering the replacement of key personnel only as a means to prepare for an unexpected death, for example, will simply not be sufficient. There are other reasons for replacing leaders than just an untimely demise. Some leaders leave because they are ready to retire, pursue different career opportunities, or are politically dismissed. Developing a full understanding of all these issues is paramount in effectively implementing a succession program.

Let me be very clear about the argument that leadership can't be taught but must be "born." That's wrong! Decades of research and practice show that leadership *can* be taught. We've trained hundreds of leaders in accounting firms ourselves, and many quotes throughout this book give examples of leadership lessons learned. The reason that leadership isn't often taught is because few firms set up effective mentorship and training programs to do so.

Leadership training should be implemented, and potential leadership candidates must be shown how common weaknesses on the business side affect the client-care side. It is important to clarify the correlation between the two sides. In a service-oriented industry such as accounting, many employees and leaders are driven primarily by the client-service side.

You can demonstrate that great client service leads to business success. Leadership candidates must be held accountable for both overall business results and the quality of client service.

Virtually every accounting firm will feel the need to build bench strength and widen its pool of qualified leadership candidates. Regardless of size or market dominance, most firms are headed into a talent war. The victors of the war for top talent will emerge with proactive strategies to address the following areas:

▲ A focus on future leadership needs and available career opportunities
▲ Integration of HR departments with senior leaders
▲ Sound retention policies of potential leadership candidates
▲ Flexible work environments designed to maintain aging workers with high potential
▲ Increased awareness of succession planning and leadership development programs

Addressing these issues will provide solid groundwork for developing practical succession planning and leadership development procedures. Attention should be placed on capturing the intellectual capital existent in the firm and developing diverse groups of leadership candidates. Firms continue to be driven to cultivate individuals with specialized skills and solid leadership competencies. Early identification and development of these high-potential employees is vital to business success in all accounting firms.

Some people seem to be born with natural leadership talents. Of course, they may have been trained by their experiences at earlier ages. Left undeveloped, natural leaders will never reach their potential, and those with lesser natural talents can develop into very good leaders if they really want to succeed. Everyone I interviewed for this book agreed that leadership skills can be learned. However, simply learning incidentally on the job is too haphazard a way to ensure the development of great leadership.

Bob Hottman shares his experiences, "Over the last 10 years, I think I've grown a thousand times in my leadership skills. It is such a never-ending process to learn about leadership that you never know everything that's out there. I've learned that treating people fairly is always critical in everything that you do."

Why Succession Plans Fail

Des Dearlove and Stuart Crainer, authors of the *Financial Times Handbook of Management*, suggest that most bungled successions can be traced to five failings:

1. Many incumbents are simply reluctant to give up power, hanging on too long. This can also be manifested in trying to foist like-minded successors on their firms.
2. When choosing new leaders, people often choose a safe replacement, rather than someone who will challenge the status quo, question the directors' roles, and so on.
3. Some candidates have such a force of personality that the selection group often fails to define, or adhere to, an objective set of selection criteria.

4. Many selection groups rely too much on seniority. They don't look beyond the most visible senior management candidates and, therefore, fail to identify strong potentials from the next generation of executives.

5. Finally, short-term concerns, such as clients or owners, are allowed to dictate the succession timetable. In combination with the many other nonobjective forces, such as egos, corporate politics, and greed, you have a recipe for trouble.

Your Leadership Development Program

An effective leadership development program requires six basic steps that should be led by one of the responsible owners. Each step answers a basic question for the firm and participants:

1. What does it take to be a good leader at each level in our firm?
2. How do I stack up as a leader right now?
3. What training, actions, and results should I take to become a better leader?
4. How can my service line or niche group be part of the process?
5. Is there a clear leadership succession plan for a variety of positions in the firm?
6. How can I join the leadership development program?

Overall Approach

An effective leadership development program requires careful selection of high-potential participants, proper funding, and dedicated leadership. Firms can utilize the resources of their alliance, the AICPA, or others, whereas some very large firms may develop their own University for Leaders along the lines of best-practice programs like those at GE, Federal Express, EisnerAmper LLP, and Clifton Gunderson LLP.

In addition to skills training, certain symbolic aspects of leadership need attention. People must be visibly rewarded through recognition and compensation for behaving in accord with published leadership competencies. The partners must not tolerate poor leaders. Dramatic acts demonstrate real versus espoused values around leadership. So, poor leadership students should be removed from any development program quickly, and senior partners who do not operate within the core values of the firm must change their ways or leave the firm.

Jim DeMartini, managing partner of Seiler LLP in Redwood City, CA, says

> We have a very deliberate succession plan that we started working on 3 years ago. We've looked at every partner who is going to retire in the next decade. Not unlike a lot of accounting firms, we have a lot of partners here in their mid-50s. We are taking a hard look at who's on the bench to fill those roles, and where do we need to bring in talent from outside our organization. This includes a very thorough analysis of the specific skill sets we need to add.

Next, give future leaders challenging opportunities during the program and early in their careers. The GE program admits 100 new people each year into its Entry-Level Leadership Program (ELLP). These people should have enough responsibility to make an impact and enough leeway to make mistakes. The wise leadership team tries to accelerate its mistakes, thereby increasing its learning. Mistakes must be tolerated, provided that they are in service to the firm. Young leaders receive targeted training and development based on individual needs, such as provided by GE's ELLP.

At Plante & Moran, PLLC, more mature leaders receive broadening experiences and educational opportunities through an advanced leadership development program. Bill Hermann says, "We identified a pool of people and knew we had to get them exposure to different situations. They needed to be exposed to certain partners and have the right kinds of experiences." Finally, the firm should reward the developers and mentors of the next generation of leaders.

Beyond this general approach, a leadership development program involves the six major steps described in the next few sections.

Define the Leadership Competencies for Each Level

What does it take to be a good leader in our accounting firm? Defining the leadership competencies that correlate with effectiveness tells us what leadership skills should be built into a leadership development program. Most firms should begin by using generic leadership competencies found in other programs, such as the Market Facing Leadership Academy or the AICPA Human Capital Center. Once operating under generic terms for a period, you may want to tailor the program to fit the uniqueness of your firm. Don't wait to start until you have everything exactly right. If you invest a great deal of time building the perfect set of competencies, you may tend to bog down and miss years of effective leader development time. The competency set should vary by level: senior, supervisor, manager, or owner.

When selecting people, you want to find a good match between immediate and future role demands and the applicant's personality. GE's Jack Welch used his four "E" method, and you should attempt to get something this simple. The four "Es" that Jack used were as follows:

1. Do they have the energy to play in a global environment?
2. Do they energize others? It doesn't do you much good to be a whirling dervish if you don't end up exciting other people.
3. Do they have edge? Do they have the ability to say yes or no, not maybe? Do they make the calls?
4. The fourth "E" is execute. Do they deliver?

Admittedly, developing your list is easier said than done. The following list of traits is what I would use as a starting point for selection criteria.

1. *Desire.* Wants to lead, wants to get things done through other people, wants to have an impact. If the candidate doesn't want to do these things, you are wasting your time trying to fix someone.

2. *Purposeful.* Wants to achieve something.
3. *Confident.* Believes that he or she can make a difference.
4. *Centered.* Has sufficient impulse control; stays focused under pressure.
5. *Energy.* Has physical stamina to work long hours.
6. *Intelligence.* Possesses at least average or slightly above average general intelligence.

Bob Bunting says

> We are actively engaged in succession planning all the time. Part of the planning that takes place at the departmental levels is literally looking at succession in each department. So, it's not just who is running that department today, but who are the folks in line who can step up and lead that department in the future. Who is the next person in line who can be there to run the health care area. So, we are trying to build a concept of continuous succession everywhere, so there is a smooth transition at any point in time. When you start talking about the overall firm, what we have done is something that we have talked a little bit before. We have consciously created leadership opportunities for a lot of people.
>
> We have leaders in each of the offices, we have leaders in each of our industry segments, we have leaders in each of our service lines, we have leaders in each of our shared services area, and we are working with all of those people all the time to develop them and, frankly, to see who steps up.

Assess Potential Candidates

Next, you'll want to assess the potential candidates. The use of an objective tool such as a standardized test, 360 degree survey, or formal interview might be useful in assessing the best people to join the program. Usually, you would like to have more candidates than you have positions in the program. This will help create a backlog of aspiring candidates for next year. A crucial but often overlooked step is to promptly notify each of the applicants whether they have been accepted or declined.

Measure Leadership Styles

Now we have a gap—what do we want between what do we have. Ask yourself, What training, actions, and results must I achieve in order to become a better leader? Articulate and write down valid and reliable ways of measuring current leadership styles tied to the competency criteria. Using a 360-degree leadership survey and performance appraisals are good sources of data. These data provide information to assist everyone in creating action plans and expected outcomes.

Utilizing the material in this book, students can first evaluate themselves and where they stack up relative to self-knowledge, trustworthiness, preparation, critical thinking, and self-discipline. From there, each person can begin developing a leadership action plan.

Refer to Your Developmental Process

Provide developmental activities by asking, How can my service line or industry niche group be part of the developmental process? As much as possible, leadership development should occur on the job, not away from the job. Leaders get things done through others; leadership is essentially a transaction between a leader and followers. It makes sense to create developmental programs that attend to the transactional context within which the leader resides. Team-based leadership development reflects modern thinking about leadership. This model downplays the ancient understanding of leadership as dominance of one over many. We step away from teaching leaders how to make decisions by themselves and move them toward developing the capacity of people to maintain themselves within a social setting and achieve group goals.

Ken Baggett says

> We have a leadership camp, which I actually borrowed from Bob Bunting in Moss Adams. When I took over as CEO, I stipulated term limits for everyone. We needed term limits as managing partner, term limits on the operating committee, and term limits as an office managing partner because I felt that if you did not have a defined term in office, there is no goal line.
>
> I selected my "fab five"—five people who I felt have the ability to become managing partner. I have started spending a little extra time with those five. I have taken them to client conferences, industry conferences, and so on because they need to be exposed outside the four walls of Reznick. They need to experience what other firms are doing.

Group-based development is a practical, experiential method of learning. By working on issues within groups, it is practical and immediately applied within the leader's setting. For instance, he or she does not deal with difficult people in the abstract but with a specific difficult member of his or her current team.

The following are some examples of the many methods for teaching the classes and following through with the development plans:

1. Participating in leadership development projects with goals related to the participant's specific skill needs
2. Engaging in case analyses with other participants
3. Job rotation through other departments or on staff exchange programs
4. Receiving special assignments that require high levels of interpersonal interaction
5. Shadowing senior leaders

Build the Next Generation of Leaders

Are there clear leadership succession plans for a variety of positions in the firm? In a sense, leader development and succession planning are synonymous. The leader development program should fit within the firm's strategic goals. The succession plan ensures that an adequate supply of capable leaders is available to carry out strategic intent in the firm for the next 10 years. The succession planning process has several steps designed to develop leadership talent. These steps involve the following:

1. Assessment of program applicants' leadership potential and skills
2. Appraisal of leadership behavior from formal appraisal systems and surveys that answer the question, in the aggregate, How well led is this firm

3. Determination of future management and leadership needs through forecasting and strategic planning

4. Definition of leadership requirements in the near future expressed in qualitative terms for various levels in the firm

5. Creation of a measurement system for summarizing progress and overall leadership readiness

6. Act to meet the immediate needs for leaders

Prepare a Nomination and Application Process for the Program

What is the process for joining the leadership program?

We have found it helpful for the owner group to actively select a group of people who they believe will be successful in the program. Either through a formal or informal nomination process, potential candidates should be encouraged to apply for the program. A formal process would publish a list, or a letter would be sent to the candidates. An informal process might simply have owners mention to selected people, "I think you should take advantage of our leader development program because you are what we are looking for in future leaders."

Carl George, former managing partner of the national firm Clifton Gunderson LLP, says, "I think leadership is rare, and I think it's about people. Leadership is about taking people from point A to point B. So, I don't think there's a difference in leading an accounting firm or any other group; it's the same."

As most of our interviews concluded, leadership skills are more developed and learned than they are natural. They're developed both by training and experience. Carl went on to share

> Curt Mingle believed that we were going to have a shortage of leadership in the profession, not just CG but the profession. He believed that we should be a leader in developing leaders. We decided that it needed to be multifaceted. It wasn't just going to be book learning. We needed some on-the-job training. We got people involved in a group called MFR (Managing for Results), and today, we have people involved in Rainmaker. We made sure that they went to MAP (Management of Accounting Practices) conferences.

At Clifton Gunderson LLP, the leaders always had projects to work on. Carl tells, "I remember one of the projects was the case for part-time partners. Back then, in fact, it was written up in the *Journal of Accountancy*. Back then, to be a part-time partner, you were kind of a weirdo. We were thinking, 'Wait a minute, it's a talent; if we can get half the talent, it's better than none of that talent.'"

At Clifton Gunderson LLP, the leadership training was not only on-the-job training; the developing leaders also had to attend a board meeting. It was a two-year program, and the participants met two or three times per year. They wouldn't go to restaurants; they'd be in a room eating pizza and listening to tapes and have many activities and homework at night.

Carl continues, "We had an industrial psychologist, Dr. Ron Winkler, who developed a profile questionnaire and so on. There were three of us: Curt; myself; and another management team member, Joe Lhotka. We all had different perspectives on leadership, and we didn't leave out the historical part, either. We thought it was important to remember the legacy."

Next, it would be good to advertise the program with e-mails, posters, or memos or in staff meetings. The advertising should answer some of the basic questions that applicants need to know, such as the following:

▲ Expectations of the program should be spelled out. How many days of class, how much time between classes performing extra work, additional hours needed, readings required, and so on should all be spelled out.

▲ Qualifications for the program, such as length of service, roles in the firm, educational requirements for entering, and so on, must be clear.

▲ The outcomes of the program should be clear in terms of leadership opportunities in the firm.

▲ Any follow-up commitments that participants must make to stay with the firm or pay any of the costs or any other follow up that may be expected, if any.

Developing leaders requires considerable effort and expense. Measuring overall success allows you to make the program more effective and efficient. You must evaluate the program, and to do this, you must have clear goals. Once clear goals have been articulated, you evaluate the program at five levels: reaction (level 1), knowledge and skill transfer (level 2), on-site behavioral change (level 3), business impact (level 4), and monetary return on investment (level 5).

Evaluation begins at the very beginning of the program design, not at the end. Generally, each succeeding level of evaluation increases rigor and cost. It is financially prudent, therefore, to consider the program's success criteria. For example, if success is primarily measured by satisfied participants who assert their intention to apply what they have learned, a level 1 evaluation suffices. Conversely, if the program must pay its way to stay alive, you should determine return on investment by tabulating and subtracting program costs from bottom-line indicators, such as revenue enhancement or cost savings.

Terry Snyder says

> I have a very good friend. Mike Hebert was the coach of the University of Illinois women's volleyball team and is one of the leading women's volleyball coaches in the U.S. A few years ago, he had done an amazing job of recruiting but was having a really bad year. And I said, "So, Mike, what's wrong?"
>
> He said, "Terry, this team's a victim of the kind of people like me. We now train these people. These women play volleyball year round, and they've got great abilities. But what we haven't learned to measure and haven't learned to develop is that internal piece yet."
>
> He cited a young lady. When he was recruiting her, he observed her walking down the hallway, and people were around her, looking at her with respect. He could see it in their eyes. When she played volleyball here at U of I, and it came time for that final point, he said, "People turned and looked at her for that thing."

He said, "I can train them to have great volleyball skills, but I can't train that part of it."

He said that has to be part of them, and I've always remembered that.

Selecting Partner Leaders

Promoting from manager to partner is a huge leap for most people. It means that the person is going from an employee to a business owner. The biggest mistake that partners make is not preparing managers (employees) for the step up in their leadership role. The role of a business owner changes significantly in the following ways:

1. The owner's income is at risk depending on the profits of the business, whereas the salary of employees is set and has very little risk.
2. The owners are expected to maintain client loyalty, whereas employees are expected to maintain client satisfaction.
3. The owners are expected to attract significant new business, whereas employees participate in some business development activities.
4. The owners are expected to recruit, develop, and retain staff members through mentoring and coaching, whereas employees are expected to do so in a more limited manner.
5. The owners are expected to produce a profit from the work of the employees, whereas the employee is to meet budgets for billable hours and so on.
6. The owners become business leaders, whereas employees can remain in management roles.

Although in the past, accounting firms have promoted people to partner without requiring them to act like owners, that rarely is the case anymore. As a partner group, you must regularly assess your expectations of your fellow owners and ensure that there is a process in place for aspiring managers to grow into owners and leaders.

Phil Holthouse, founder and managing partner of the top-100 multioffice firm Holthouse, Carlin & Van Trigt LLP in Los Angeles, CA, says

> We have about eight criteria for the admission of a new partner: someone who we trust, someone who's not going to get the firm in trouble. Those are usually the first two. Then, after that, it becomes either being able to manage a client practice effectively and profitably or contribute in some other significant way to the firm. Those are our core principles that we work with.

Rename Your Next CEO as the Leading Partner

Naturally, you can tell from reading this book that I'd like to name the CEO the leading partner of the firm, rather than the managing partner. There are major differences in leading and managing. A leading partner is going to take the firm somewhere, whereas a managing partner may be content to maintain the status quo. In some firms, the CEO or managing partner is really a coordinating partner. Dan Schreiber, managing partner of the local firm JGD & Associates LLP in San Diego, CA, shares

> Leading and managing is what I like to call the "too many cooks in the kitchen" syndrome. You know, everybody wants to be involved, and it can be very challenging to keep all the owners happy. In our firm, although I am a managing partner, in a lot of ways, it tends to be more of an administrator role. I tend to manage everything but the other partners. With the partners, I'm just trying to gather agreement on key issues. Whereas with most of the clients we work on, there's a formal structure where there is a CEO and a formal chain of command.

Usually, the coordinating partner's role is to coordinate all the administrative tasks that the other partners don't want to do. And of course, in many firms, the managing partner or coordinating partner does not lead the other partners.

Depending upon the size of your firm and the depth of your talent, selecting the next leading partner might be a difficult task. Many, many partners just want to serve their clients and leave the leading and managing to others. Some firms have concluded that the accounting partners should focus all their attention on serving clients, so these firms hire professional managers to take care of recruiting, HR, technology, and so on.

Choosing the Lead Partner

A number of firms have term limits, and some have mandatory retirement ages. Each firm seems to be different in these regards.

Jim Metzler, vice president of the AICPA, says,

> So many firms have managing partners for life, and some of those conflict items are things I spoke about before. I believe term limits are the only way to go; the term has to be long enough, but no more partner for life. That's old school stuff. Let me put it this way: not term limits in years. The leading partner can rerun for election, but you have to do a good job. Not a rotation but, rather, an election is what I'm trying to say.

Carl George shares, "With my successor, we developed a process. I told the board I wanted to step down at the age of 62, which is what I did in 2009. So, when I was at 59, we developed a very intricate succession planning process." Carl and his partners talked with other firms, and they found that several baby boomer CEOs have been retiring: Bob Bunting; Darold Rath of Eide Bailly LLP; and Bill Hermann, for example. They decided to prepare a dual-purpose plan. One is a disaster plan, and the second is a process that is a more formal long-term solution.

Once Carl had his plan written, he communicated with all the firm's partners. After all the partners knew of the plan, he set about identifying potential candidates, including anybody who wanted to volunteer. Using an industrial psychologist, Carl set forth a series of the attributes of the next CEO and how those might be different than in the past. The psychologist held 2-hour meetings with everybody in the firm who was in a leadership position, including board members. In addition to those one-on-one meetings, he developed a questionnaire that he sent out to another 25–50 partners to complete.

Carl says, "He initially developed this attribute model, which is an incredible piece of work. It was well worth the money to develop this attribute model based on what the partners think." After all this synthesis, the team derived five primary dimensions for the new CEO: leadership, culture, vision and strategy, business execution, and people.

Carl shares, "The process began with a large number, and we narrowed it down to 10. Then, we narrowed it to 5 and then down to 3 or 4. All the ones we considered are all still here. It's a little different because they are partners, and they have significant responsibilities. I have seen other firms where ones who weren't chosen CEO left the firm, and I think that is a travesty."

Finally, through the process, Krista McMasters was chosen as the next CEO of the firm. CliftonLarsonAllen LLP is the largest firm in the history of the profession to have a female CEO. Carl concluded, "An overwhelming sentiment of the partners said, 'Great choice; proud of the firm for doing it.' All kinds of accolades for Kris, the task force, and the board for choosing her."

When selecting a leading partner, a firm would be wise to use the chapters in this book as a guide. Is this person one who has experience with your firm, clients, and market? Does this person fulfill the personal expectations of self-knowledge (see chapter 2, "Self-Knowledge: The Inner Accelerator); trustworthiness (see chapter 3, "Trust: The Leadership Imperative"); devoting time to critical thinking (see chapter 4, "Critical Thinking: Creating Your Future"); investing time in preparation (chapter 5, "Preparation: Ready for Seizing Opportunity"); and self-discipline (see chapter 6, "Self-Discipline: Be the Master, Not the Victim")? These would be the key qualities that I would look for. Think about the level 5 leader discussed in Jim Collins's book *Good to Great: Why Some Companies Make the Leap…and Others Don't*. Does the person bring a nonanxious presence to the leadership role, with strong determination and humility?

How does your leading partner candidate relate to the other partners? Is he or she a coach or mentor (see chapter 7) or let others find their own way? Is he or she willing to hold people accountable in a manner that gets results (see chapter 8, "Accountability: Trust but Verify")? Is this candidate willing to challenge the people to grow (see chapter 9, "Challenging Personal Growth: Leading the Whole Person") or a conflict avoider? Is he or she willing to delegate or empower others to lead their portions of the firm (see chapter 10, "Empowerment: The Secret to Exponential Growth") or a micromanager?

Krista McMasters says

> For our CEO succession plan, we put together a detailed plan for the selection process of our next CEO. I was very involved in that because of my responsibility in charge of Priority-One. Honestly, it didn't occur to me that the next CEO would be me. That was not even in my thought process. The key thing we wanted was to make sure that we had input from many key people throughout the firm.

If you select a leading partner with the personal qualifications previously described, who also has a strong vision of where the firm should be going, you have a superstar. If the person has all these personal qualities but doesn't have the vision, a facilitator or the other partners can help with crafting a vision. Getting behind a person who has a vision but is not trustworthy, however, will not work.

A terrific way to gauge your candidates is to put them in a variety of positions of leadership, both large and small, and evaluate the preceding attributes. Sam Coulter, founder and president of the local firm Coulter & Justus, P.C., in Knoxville, TN, says

> Ron Justus and I are permanent members of our executive committee. To build leadership, we've had everyone rotate through it. Different partners served two-year rotating terms, and every year, we have a new member. The idea was to let everybody have an opportunity to see what the management committee does. A lot of problems come before us that are not black and white. This gives us the opportunity to have conversations around tough issues and build our leaders for the future.

More of Choosing a Leader

When it was time for Clarence Asbury, founder of McKonly & Asbury LLP in Harrisburg, PA, to consider retirement, he implemented a similar process to Clifton Gunderson LLP's, albeit on a much smaller scale. Terry Harris, managing partner of McKonly & Asbury LLP, says

> I understood how important measured growth was to the success of our growing practice. It was also about this time that Clarence Asbury and I began to have discussions about leadership succession. In the years that followed, until I became comanaging partner with Clarence in 2003, I began a process of self-discovery to explore whether I could, in fact, become the future managing partner of McKonly & Asbury. During this period, I used the services of a professional coach to help me understand my leadership style and how my style interacted with other partners in the firm. I also sought the affirmation of others inside and outside the firm of my leadership abilities.

Identifying a successor is the legacy of a managing partner. Clarence and Terry were partners for over 20 years. Terry shares

> One thing that I remember as a young accountant with the firm in my early 20s, was being asked by Clarence if I would like to lead a new niche area of our firm focused on the affordable housing industry. I was not a very good leader then. Through that experience, I learned to develop a leadership style that empowered others and focused not on process but on outcomes to have success.

The affordable housing niche grew to become one of the largest practice areas, and today, this niche differentiates the firm from others.

Clarence began the process of succession approximately seven years prior to his planned retirement. At that time, approximately two-thirds of McKonley & Asbury LLP's client base was served by Clarence and Terry. Together, they established a transition date for Clarence's retirement and, over the next seven years, worked toward that date. One of the main aspects of the succession plan was the transition of Clarence's and Terry's clients to other leaders in the firm. Terry shares

> Two years prior to Clarence's two-year transition into retirement, I became a comanaging partner with Clarence, and we collectively shifted client service responsibilities to other partners while maintaining relationships with our key accounts. We retained 95 percent of

our clients through this significant transition, to the credit of both Clarence and other leaders in the firm who assumed enhanced roles serving these clients.

Even though it was over one decade away, Terry immediately began to think about his successor. Terry says, "I listened closely to other leaders in our firm, worked with outside consultants, and utilized 360 evaluations for our partner group. Through this input, it became clear who would be the best person to be my successor and lead our firm into the future. It was not only my choice but the feedback from the remaining partners that provided clarity." Because that identification had been done almost seven years before Terry planned transition, it gives everyone time to work on firm leadership matters, gaining input and support for the direction of the firm and investing the time, so that Terry's successor is experienced in the leadership necessary to sustain the firm.

This is a great process for many firms to follow; however, other firms have a selection of choices for leading partner. Several years ago, when Jack Welch was CEO of GE, he made it known that there were three top candidates to take over his role as CEO. He created a selection process and literally pitted each one of the candidates against each other. Jack created a leadership legacy at GE with his famous leadership training school, writings on leadership, and emphasis on leadership development. However, when Jeffrey Immelt was finally selected as Jack's successor, the other two candidates left. To me, this final act of Jack Welch undermined his many years of leadership development. When he left the company, three-fourths of the leadership team was gone, including Jack. I've often wondered how that lost leadership talent has affected the operating results of GE this last decade.

Jim DeMartini, managing partner of the top-100 firm Seiler LLP in Redwood City, CA, says, "I'm not a huge Jack Welch fan in terms of some of his leadership ideas. I think it is a mistake to create war in your firm to pick your successor. I mean, the collateral damage there goes well beyond the two people who leave."

The best process is to adhere to a civil manner in order to retain your leadership talent at the top of your firm, so that your long-term success and synergy can be continued. Rick Anderson shares, "When I was selected as chief executive officer, the process took about six months. The really neat thing that happened is that all the people who were being considered are still with the firm today, leading key areas of Moss Adams."

Neal Spencer, former CEO of the megaregional firm BKD, LLP, in Springfield, MO, echoes Rick's theme at BKD, LLP

> The last time we elected a chief executive officer was four years ago. We asked partners for their input on who the next CEO should be, and about 15–20 names surfaced around the firm. The management committee narrowed the list to 5 individuals. Within 90 days, that list was whittled to 2, and then, it took 4 months for me to be selected as the CEO.
>
> What is so special to me is all the other major candidates are still at BKD today. They all hold very important positions. The firm didn't pit us against each other, and I think we actually grew closer, even though we were vying for the top leadership position. I would not have wanted the candidates to leave because they didn't get the job. I think the beauty of BKD is our success in the way we approach running our firm. None of these five candidates, in my mind, could have left BKD and have the same success that they are enjoying

today. So, maybe that's the beauty of BKD. We were able to retain these people because, regardless of the positions they hold, they recognize that BKD is a special organization, and the role they have still carries a lot of influence.

Can a Leader Serve Clients?

One of the major decisions you must make in the selection of a leading partner is the time commitment. As Michael Gerber's book *The E-Myth* asks, Is your leader working *in* the firm or *on* it? On the one hand, leading the firm requires a different skill set from functioning as a line partner in an accounting firm. To do it well, the leader must give up a significant portion, or perhaps all, of his or her clients. Bob Hottman says, "I have one client, and it is my firm: EKS&H." To me, for a firm that is rising above the $5 million per year revenue level with 40 or more employees, a full-time leading partner like Bob is the right call.

For a firm with revenue below $5 million per year, it makes sense for the leading partner to allocate a portion of his or her year to leading the firm. The more aggressively the firm wants to grow, the more time should be allocated to leading. Then, you have the question of giving up clients, and such a leading partner could have the following concerns:

▲ If I fail at leading, what will be my lifeline back into the firm, or will I have to leave?
▲ What will happen to my income if I'm not able to pull it off?

Quite frankly, you can't keep one foot on the dock and one foot on the boat to lead a firm through the choppy waters of an economy. The leading partner needs to have confidence that he or she can lead, along with a prudent compensation bridge if things change.

Conclusion

Finally, you have traveled a leadership road map with me that will guide you to build and improve people at all levels of your firm. I hope that you take away the priority that I've placed on the five roles of a leader: self, staff, strategy, systems, and synergy. As a process thinker, I've tried to help you build a logical method to lead and build leaders within an organization. My wish is that you will be able to use these concepts to be the master of your destiny, rather than the victim of circumstances, and that you will commit to raising the lid on your own leadership and that of your entire team.

Appendix A:

Affinity Diagram

In chapter 15, "Building the Future Firm Continuously," you are introduced to a number of valuable tools to help improve the processes and systems of your firm. In that chapter, I refer to this appendix describing affinity diagrams. Affinity diagrams are great tools for managers to use to attain an overview one process and display a picture of the many aspects of the system. You might use an affinity diagram to plan the installation of new software or change the way that taxes are processed or new employees are on-boarded.

An affinity diagram is used to organize large sets of items (more than 20) into smaller sets of related items.

Guidelines

1. The rules of brainstorming are followed, but each idea is written (in seven words or less using a verb and noun) on a self-adhesive Post-it note.
2. After all the ideas have been generated and entered on the Post-its, post all the Post-its on a wall or board. Discuss the Post-its to check if there are any questions about what any of the Post-its say or mean.
3. Team members now silently move the Post-its around, grouping Post-its that are related or similar (have affinity) together.
4. If disagreement exists when grouping, make copies of the contested Post-it and place it in more than one group.
5. When the grouping has stopped, discuss each grouping to determine what it is that relates to all the Post-its. Write a header Post-it for each group that captures the theme and concept of the Post-its.
6. If any single idea Post-its do not fit well with any header, have the team decide if they should be kept.

An affinity diagram is especially useful when

- ▲ chaos exists.
- ▲ the team is drowning in a large volume of ideas.
- ▲ breakthrough thinking is required.
- ▲ broad issues or themes must be identified.

Building an affinity diagram is a creative, rather than logical, process that encourages participation because everyone's ideas find their way into the exercise.

Sample Affinity Diagram

What Are the Issues Involved in Missing Promised Delivery Dates?

Most Frequent	Most Damaging	Easy To Fix	Inexpensive	Difficult	Costly
Newest employees not oriented.	Directors treat staff poorly.	Minor errors.	Too slow getting replacement paperwork.	Computer system too slow, use handwritten forms.	Review notes unreadable.
Production bonus system encourages too much speed, not enough accuracy.	Staff room over-crowded.	Measure true cost of errors.	Sometimes substitute staff when night staff unavailable.	Time lag in billing changes on computer.	Practice management system does not work.
High turnover among adminstrative staff.	No place to eat lunch.	How many small clients lost and didn't know about?	When big clients push, switch staff and go.	Allow changes to bills.	Client statements easily damaged, requiring replacement.
High turnover among staff accountants.	Review notes are not explained.	Historical trends of errors.		Client orders still initially handwritten.	
Lack of training for staff.		How many are paperwork errors?		New 11-digit code too long.	
		Need classification by types of errors.		Data entry complexity.	
		Certain staff handle particular clients.			

Appendix B:

Four Whys

The four whys tool is helpful to identify root causes of recurring problems, so they may be addressed and the problem finally eliminated. Often, the tendency exists to address the symptoms of the problem or apply a "bandage" solution, only to find that the problem still exists. Applying the four whys tool to a problem ensures the desired long-term results.

Steps to Four Whys

1. Select a recurring problem.
2. Ask, "Why did the problem occur?"
3. Take the answers identified in step 2 and ask, "Why did they occur?"
4. Continue delving into the problem by asking why until you've identified multiple root causes to the originally identified problem.
5. Brainstorm and implement solutions to a subset of the root causes. Select the root causes that

   a. most likely contribute to the problem.
   b. most often contribute to the problem.
   c. are within your span of control to correct.

6. Monitor the situation to determine whether the problem has subsided and to what extent.

Examples of Four Whys

Problem: Work is repeatedly completed over budget.
Why? (root causes in bold)

Employees are doing more work than they should. Why?
Processes are inefficient.

Employees do not understand the scope of the engagements. Why?
Engagement letters are vaguely worded.
Engagement budgets are not set.
Engagements are rotated among employees.
Engagements are rarely discussed with employees at the outset.

Employees do not see the engagement letters. Why?
Engagement letters are not kept with the work.

Clients are not completing their work. Why? Clients do not understand our expectations. Why?

Engagement letters are vaguely worded.

Employees have not clarified expectations when the situation occurs. Why?
Employees are not allowed to call clients.
Partners have asked employees to complete work and get it out the door.

Clients do not know how to properly complete their work. Why?
Clients do not have trained staff members. Why?
Clients cannot afford a full time-staff member.
Information is not provided to clients.

Clients do not have time to complete their work. Why?
Clients do not have staff members to complete the work. Why?
Clients cannot afford full time-staff members.
The deadlines for information do not work well with the clients' peak business periods.

Clients do not want to complete the work. Why?
Clients have better things to do with their time.

Clients have no interest in the work they are being asked to perform. Why?
Clients feel that the work is "accountants work."

Clients are submitting work in a sloppy form. Why?
Clients do not know how to organize the work. Why?
Clients have not been provided a list, format, or instructions for compiling work.
Clients are not organized, by nature.

Employees are taking too long to complete the work. Why?
Employees are not adequately trained in the accounting principles or on the computer system. Why?
Training is not provided to new employees.
Employees are not mentored.

Staffing selections have been poor. Why?
Limited pool of candidates. Why?
Benefits and wages are substandard.
Low unemployment rate.
Lack of structured interview and reference-checking process.

From the bold list, the most likely root causes are selected and solutions brainstormed and implemented.

It is apparent that this approach is more likely to yield lasting results than the typical solution for remedying engagements that are completed with many hours over budget—applying pressure to everyone to be more efficient.

Appendix C:

Flowchart

In chapter 15, "Building the Future Firm Continuously," I recommend various tools to help display a process or systems graphically. One of the most helpful is the flowchart. It provides a picture with many details and should be used to illustrate an existing process and how you might want it to be altered for the future.

Definitions

Flowchart. A picture of a process. It illustrates the following details of a process:

▲ The individual steps
▲ The sequence of steps
▲ The relationship between steps

Standard flowchart. Steps arranged one after another until the end. This is the most common flowchart. It works well with very simple processes. See the sample that follows this section.

Functional flowchart. Steps arranged by sequence and step owner. This flowchart is useful when many groups are involved in a process. It provides a good overview of what is happening, who is doing it, and the complexity of the process. See the sample that follows this section.

Flowcharting Steps

Decide on the process to be flowcharted.
Decide where the process begins and ends.
Brainstorm a list of all the steps within the process.
Arrange the steps in the proper order.
Connect the steps with arrows.

Helpful Tips

Flowcharting can be more difficult than is necessary. As you are building your skills in this area, it will help to keep the following tips in mind:

1. Always make sure that you have agreement on the beginning input and ending output of the process. Decide this first, and put those points up on the flipchart. Often, problems are discovered immediately because nobody is clear about the process boundaries.

2. Use the conventional flowcharting symbols. These include ovals for inputs and outputs, rectangles for an action step, diamonds for decisions, "Ds" for delays, and circles as connectors. Using standard symbols will help others more easily understand your flowchart.

3. Use Post-it notes for creating the chart. As you build your flowcharts, you will miss steps or decide that steps should be reordered. If you write them on the page, you have to do a lot of erasing as you make changes. Using Post-it notes allows you to easily make changes as you discuss your flowchart in your group.

4. Make the chart only as detailed as it needs to be. Inexperienced flow charters often make the mistake of getting into too much detail. The chart quickly becomes huge, confusing, and unmanageable. The trick is to keep it simple. Each decision point makes the chart much more complex. Before putting a decision point into the flow, ask yourself whether a decision is normally made at this point. Often, you are dealing with a rare exception. These can be dealt with later after you've created the whole chart.

5. When you first begin building your chart, try to get all the way through to the end before going back and dealing with exceptions and decisions. In other words, if you put a decision step into your flow, follow the "Yes" path until you get to the end.

6. Create separate flowcharts if the process is too large and complex. Flowcharts almost always represent a series of steps that, in themselves, are also processes. For example, you could say the process for getting ready in the morning is to (1) get out of bed, (2) shower, (3) brush your teeth and hair, (4) get dressed, and (5) eat breakfast. Step 2 could easily be broken down into another 10 steps. If you have a need to break a step into that kind of detail, create a separate flowchart.

Flowchart Symbols

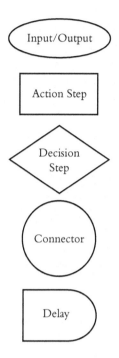

Flowchart Types

Standard Flowchart—Buying a Car

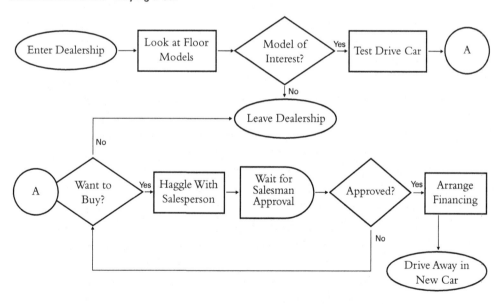

Functional Flowchart - Buying a Car

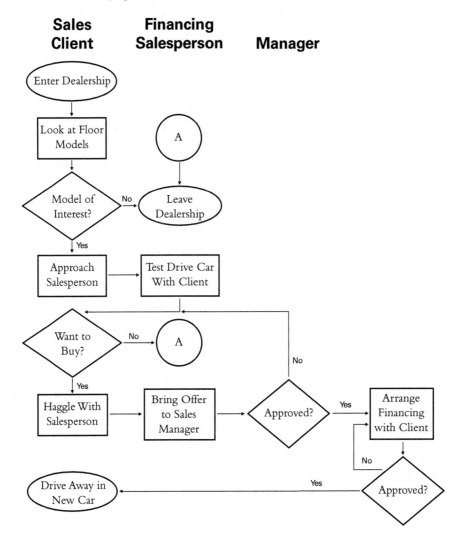

Appendix D:

Eight Continuous Process Improvement Phases

In chapter 15, "Building the Future Firm Continuously," I discuss many methods of improvement in the systems of your firms. The following table lists the eight continuous process improvement (CPI) phases and discusses their benefits and effects on any change program.

Table 1: CPI phases and their benefits to a successful change program

CPI Phases	Benefits	Effect on the Change Program
Define Business Drivers	Identifies business drivers and reason(s) for change early in the program.	Identifies program champions and develops the foundation for organizational buy-in.
Design and Align Strategies	Aligns change program goals with the organization's business strategy.	Ensures early alignment of the CPI initiative with the existing organizational strategy and capabilities.
Develop Vision	Identifies the key business drivers, organizational goals, and performance measures.	Reduces the risk of initiating change programs without clearly defined performance measures.
Current State Understanding	Provides a clear picture of the existing processes and identifies potential areas for improvement.	Identifies the root causes and reasons behind process bottlenecks early and the key features of future state processes.
Future State Design	Defines a clear future picture of the renewed processes and identifies the required organizational assets needed to enable continuous improvement.	Confirms the business case and develops the foundation for developing the implementation road map.
Road Map Development	Defines in detail the future state implementation road map, such as critical milestones and early wins.	Reduces program management risks and identifies the required steps to accomplish key milestones.
Execution	Delivers the early and ongoing benefits of the change program.	Delivers business objectives and secures organizational buy-in.
Continuing Improvement	Initiates the required processes to improve, monitor, and control the new and renewed processes on a continuous basis.	Institutionalizes the steps and procedures needed to continuously improve renewed processes.

Appendix E:[1]

RAINMAKER ACADEMY Revenue Action Plan/ Results Report

PARTICIPANT'S NAME _____

MARKETING PERIOD _____

PERSONAL OBJECTIVES/RESULTS	$ Goal	$ Sold
New Revenue from CLIENTS (Top 21 and Farm Club)	–	$ –
New Revenue from PROSPECTS (Top 21 and Farm Club)	–	$ –
New Revenue from REFERRALS (Top 21 and Farm Club)	–	$ –
Review Marketing Plan with "Managing Partner"		
Teach Material to Firm Team		

Must Complete Goals/Actuals for Activity Report

TOP 21

A prospect should be listed in the Top 21 from whom you will make a sales call and have a good probability (better than 50%) of making a sale within the next reporting period.

Top 7 CLIENTS

Company	Contact	Next Call Date	Marketing Objective	$ Est. Fee	% Prob	$ Adj. Est	$ Sold	Referred by
						$ —		
						$ —		
						$ —		
						$ —		
						$ —		
						$ —		
						$ —	$ —	
				$ —				

Top 7 PROSPECTIVE CLIENTS

Company	Contact	Next Call Date	Marketing Objective	$ Est. Fee	% Prob	$ Adj. Est	$ Sold	Referred by
						$ —		
						$ —		
						$ —		
						$ —		
						$ —		
						$ —		
						$ —	$ —	
				$ —				

Top 7 REFERRAL SOURCES

Company	Contact	Next Call Date	Marketing Objective	$ Est. Fee	% Prob	$ Adj. Est	$ Sold	Referred by
						$ —		
						$ —		
						$ —		
						$ —		
						$ —		
						$ —		
						$ —		
				$ —		$ —	$ —	

FARM CLUB

A prospect should be listed in the Farm Club if they don't fit in the Top 21, you will make a sales call on them within the next 12 months, and believe you have a 20% or better chance of making a sale.

Farm Club CLIENTS

Company	Contact	Next Call Date	Marketing Objective	$ Est. Fee	% Prob	$ Adj. Est	$ Sold	Referred by
						$	–	
						$	–	
						$	–	
						$	–	
						$	–	
						$	–	
			$	–		$	$ –	

Farm Club PROSPECTIVE CLIENTS

Company	Contact	Next Call Date	Marketing Objective	$ Est. Fee	% Prob	$ Adj. Est	$ Sold	Referred by
						$	–	
						$	–	
						$	–	
						$	–	
						$	–	
						$	–	
			$	–		$	$ –	

Farm Club REFERRAL SOURCES

Company	Contact	Next Call Date	Marketing Objective	$ Est. Fee	% Prob	$ Adj. Est	$ Sold	Referred by
						$	–	
						$	–	
						$	–	
						$	–	
						$	–	
						$	–	
						$	–	
				–		$	$	$

MARKETING ACTIVITIES TO SUPPORT TARGET SELLING

Planned Marketing Activities

Advertising/Press Releases	Media	Possible Business	Follow up Step	Est. Date	Act. Date

Write Articles/Presentations	Media/Group	Possible Business	Follow up Step	Est. Date	Act. Date

Newsletter Programs/Direct Mail Campaigns	Target Audience	Possible Business	Follow up Step	Est. Date	Act. Date

Active Organizations	# Clients/Prospects Involved	Possible Business	Follow up Step	Est. Date	Act. Date

Additional Personal Contacts Made

(Over and Above Those Listed in the Plan Above)	Date	Type of Contact	Comments	Follow up Step

Appendix F:

Business Process Improvement Resources

Chapter 15, "Building the Firm Continuously," discusses building the future firm, and many resources are available for further study on this subject, some of which are as follows:

Dustin Hostetler, Lean CPA, LLC, a division of Rea & Associates, Inc.
This firm specializes in providing continuous improvement services to CPA firms and, to my knowledge, is the only one of its kind.

www.asq.org
The official website for the American Society for Quality.

www.6sigmastudy.com
Articles, presentations, news, events, and training opportunities about Six Sigma studies.

www.productivitypress.com
An array of Lean Six Sigma publications, many translated from Japanese, including the *Lean Insider* blog.

The Lean Six Sigma Pocket Toolbook: A Quick Reference Guide to 100 Tools for Improving Quality and Speed. Michael L. George, John Maxey, David Rowlands, and Michael George. New York: McGraw-Hill, 2005.

The Six Sigma Handbook: The Complete Guide for Green Belts, Black Belts, and Managers at All Levels (revised and expanded edition). Thomas Pyzdek. New York: McGraw-Hill, 2003.

The Complete Idiot's Guide to Lean Six Sigma. Breakthrough Management Group with Neil DeCarlo, New York: Alpha Books, 2007.

Printed in the United States
By Bookmasters